ALSO BY JOHN L. PLASTER

The Ultimate Sniper

THE SECRET WARS OF
AMERICA'S COMMANDOS
IN VIETNAM

JOHN L. PLASTER

SIMON & SCHUSTER

SIMON & SCHUSTER
Rockefeller Center
1230 Avenue of the Americas
New York, NY 10020

SIMON & SCHUSTER and colophon are registered trademarks
of Simon & Schuster Inc.

Designed by Karolina Harris
Maps by Jeffrey L. Ward

Manufactured in the United States of America

1 3 5 7 9 10 8 6 4 2

Library of Congress Cataloging-in-Publication Data
Plaster, John L.
Sog: the secret wars of America's commandos in Vietnam / John L. Plaster.
p. cm.
Includes index.
1. Vietnamese conflict, 1961–1975—Commando operations—United States.
I. Title
DS558.92.P55   1997
959.704'342—dc20   96-34557 CIP
ISBN 0–684–81105–7

ACKNOWLEDGMENTS

A book of this scope and detail would have been impossible to produce without the generous assistance of many people. While I thank all who helped, this project was assisted especially by:

Lieutenant Steve Sherman, USA
Mr. Jack Kull
Sergeant Major Jan "Dutch" Wieranga, USA (ret.)
Sergeant Major Gene Adcock, USA (ret.)
CW2 Stanley Steenbock, USA
CW2 Richard Madore, USA
Dr. John Brand
Mr. Paul Cornish, Imperial War Museum (London)
Mr. Z. Frank Hanner, Curator, National Infantry Museum
Mr. Jim Phillips
Sergeant Bryon Loucks, USA
Sergeant Major Bobby Burke, USA (ret.)
Mr. Tim Eldridge, U.S. Forest Service
Mrs. Jeanette Worthley
Messrs. Roger Kennedy and Charles Farrow, photographers

Almost every SOG veteran I contacted consented to be interviewed. Many put me up in their homes, loaned me irreplaceable photographs and trusted me with information that could be declassified only when I submitted the manuscript to the Defense Department. They are listed alphabetically, with either their rank in SOG or upon retirement:

Brigadier General Harry Aderholt, USAF (ret.)
Sergeant Major John Allen, USA (ret.)
Staff Sergeant Tony Andersen, USA
Mr. Conrad "Ben" Baker, Dept. of Defense (ret.)
Lieutenant Colonel Dean Ballmes, USAF (ret.)
Sergeant Major James D. Bath, USA (ret.)
Master Sergeant Rick Bayer, USA (ret.)
Brigadier General Donald G. Blackburn, USA (ret.)
Sergeant Michael Buckland, USA
Staff Sergeant Frank Burkhart, USA
Commander W. T. "Red" Cannon, USN (ret.)
Sergeant Major Jon Cavaiani, USA (ret.)
Colonel Steve Cavanaugh, USA (ret.)
Colonel J. H. "Scotty" Crerar, USA (ret.)
Staff Sergeant William Curry, USA
Sergeant Charlie Dodge, USA
Sergeant Major Norman Doney, USA (ret.)
Master Chief Petty Officer Barry Enoch, USN (ret.)
Colonel James Fleming, USAF
Staff Sergeant Ancil "Sonny" Franks, USA
Sergeant Bob Garcia, USA
Staff Sergeant Robert Graham, USA
Major Don Green, USA (ret.)
Sergeant Major Billy Greenwood, USA (ret.)
Sergeant Major Richard Gross, USA (ret.)
Staff Sergeant Ray Harris, USA
Staff Sergeant Oliver Hartwig, USA
Sergeant Major Sammy Hernandez, USA (ret.)
Sergeant Tony Herrell, USA
Sergeant Major James Hetrick, USA (ret.)
Colonel Robert Howard, USA (ret.)
Sergeant Major Rex Jaco, USA (ret.)
Lieutenant Colonel Frank Jaks, USA (ret.)
Colonel Don James, USAF (ret.)
Sergeant Major David Kahaahaa, USA (ret.)
Staff Sergeant Steve Keever, USA (ret.)
Sergeant Mark Kinsler, USA

Sergeant Major Ronald Knight, USA (ret.)
Colonel Edward Lesesne, USA (ret.)
Sergeant Major Dale Libby, USA (ret.)
Staff Sergeant Ben Lyons, USA (ret.)
Captain Larry Manes, USA (ret.)
Lieutenant General Leroy Manor, USAF (ret.)
Staff Sergeant Jeff Mauceri, USA
Sergeant Major Kenneth McMullin, USA (ret.)
Major Dick Meadows, USA (ret.)
Staff Sergeant John Meyer, USA
Sergeant Major Luke Nance, Jr., USA (ret.)
Sergeant First Class Cliff Newman, USA (ret.)
Colonel Charles Norton, USA (ret.)
Master Sergeant Lloyd O'Daniels, USA (ret.)
Colonel Bill O'Rourke, USA (ret.)
Staff Sergeant John Padgett, USA
Colonel Bill Page, USAF (ret.)
Sergeant Major Robert Parks, USA (ret.)
Colonel Roger Pezzelle, USA (ret.)
Colonel Bob Pinard, USAF (ret.)
Colonel Bobby Pinkerton, USA (ret.)
Sergeant Larry Predmore, USA
Master Sergeant Eulis Presley, USA (ret.)
Colonel Jim Rabdau, USA (ret.)
Colonel Don Radike, USAF (ret.)
Colonel Galen "Mike" Radke, USA (ret.)
Secretary of the Army Stanley R. Resor
Colonel Robert Rheault, USA (ret.)
Lieutenant Commander Don Richardson, USN (ret.)
Colonel Martin "Bill" Rose, USAF (ret.)
Sergeant Major Newman Ruff, USA (ret.)
Master Sergeant Richard Ryan, USA (ret.)
Colonel Ed Rybat, USA (ret.)
Master Sergeant Harvey Saal, USA (ret.)
Colonel John Sadler, USA (ret.)
Captain Hammond Salley, USA
Specialist Five Craig Schmidt, USA

Sergeant Major James Scurry, USA (ret.)
Major General Richard Secord, USAF (ret.)
Major General John K. Singlaub, USA (ret.)
Sergeant Major Lowell W. Stevens, USA (ret.)
Staff Sergeant Bryan Stockdale, USA
Major James Storter, USA (ret.)
Sergeant Major John Trantanella, USA (ret.)
Sergeant Major Joe Walker, USA (ret.)
Sergeant Major Billy Waugh, USA (ret.)
Sergeant Major Larry White, USA (ret.)
Staff Sergeant Ted Wicorek, USA
Mr. Charles Wilklow, Jr.
Mr. Randy Wilklow
Lieutenant Colonel Edward Wolcoff, USA (ret.)
Sergeant Major Fred Zabitosky, USA (ret.)

Although I alone take responsibility for the book's accuracy and content, I thank my editor at Simon & Schuster, Bob Bender, whose insights and advice decisively helped to shape and refine it.

This book is dedicated to all of SOG's secret warriors,

and especially

to the SOG men captured but never released.

CONTENTS

SOG'S THEATER OF OPERATIONS

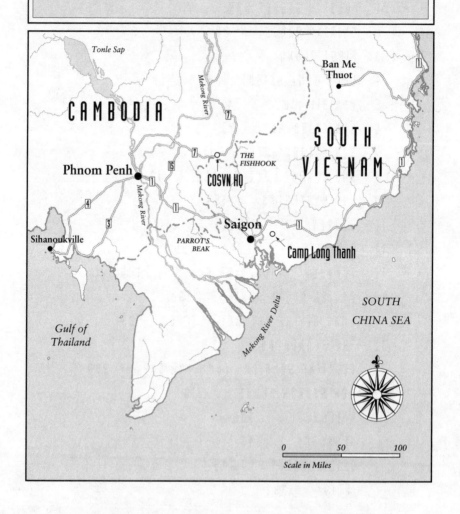

Scale in Miles

MU GIA PASS

BAN KARAI PASS

BAN RAVING PASS

NORTH VIETNAM

Gulf of Tonkin

Nakhon Phanom
[SOG Launch Site]

LAOS

911

912

92

Tchepone • • Khe Sanh

9 • Cam Lo

Area below

1

Hue • • Phu Bai

92

Oscar Eight
(NVA TRAIL HQ)

922

92

ASHAU VALLEY

• Da Nang

923

Saravan •

92

164

Kham Duc • 1 Chu Lai

165

THAILAND

Mekong River

BOLOVENS PLATEAU

• Chavane

SOUTH VIETNAM

96

Attopeu • Leghorn • Ben Het

The Bra • 110 • Dak To

• Kontum

Mekong River

0   50   100

Scale in Miles

CAMBODIA

19

• Pleiku

• Duc Co

1

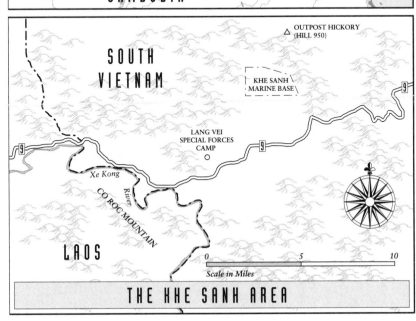

△ OUTPOST HICKORY
(HILL 950)

SOUTH VIETNAM

KHE SANH
MARINE BASE

9

9

LANG VEI
SPECIAL FORCES
CAMP

9

9

Xe Kong

River

CO ROC MOUNTAIN

LAOS

0   5   10

Scale in Miles

THE KHE SANH AREA

I'd like to have two armies: one for display with lovely guns, tanks, little soldiers, staffs, distinguished and doddering generals, and dear little regimental officers who would be deeply concerned over their general's bowel movements or their colonel's piles, an army that would be shown for a modest fee on every fairground in the country.

The other would be the real one, composed entirely of young enthusiasts in camouflage uniforms, who would not be put on display, but from whom impossible efforts would be demanded and to whom all sorts of tricks would be taught. That's the army in which I should like to fight.

JEAN LARTÉ GUY,
SOLDIER AND WRITER

1

COLBY'S SECRET WAR

It was a miserable sea yet navigable despite the looming islands and the swells that propelled the heaving 38-foot junk. February was well into North Vietnam's monsoon season, and when there weren't full-fledged typhoons there were squalls and showers, day after day, wretched conditions for small craft like this junk—but people must eat, so fish must be caught.

Despite the modern times—February 1961—the bobbing boat had been hand built in the Vietnamese tradition, crafted by the very half-dozen men who manned her. Wooden hulled and two masted, above deck she had just a small squarish wheelhouse aft, and like all North Vietnamese fishing boats, displayed proudly Communist red sails; they were her only propulsion. And because she lacked modern navigational instruments, her captain steered as had his ancestors for ten generations, by the stars. But in tonight's overcast it was not his knowledge of the heavens but his familiarity with the towering limestone islands around them that allowed him to steer closer to the seaside town of Cam Pha.

Two nights earlier they'd passed the glowing horizon that was Haiphong, North Vietnam's major port city, and this evening during a quiet sunset they almost could see the hazy mountains of Kwangsi Province, China, some 40 miles northward.

No other fishing boats braved tonight's squalls or teased the darkened reefs and shoals. On so miserable a night, surely no government craft could come to their rescue if they were swamped.

But on the other hand, neither would a Communist Swatow-class patrol boat stop them and make difficult inquiries, which actually was their main concern. Despite its authentic appearance, this junk had been built not in North Vietnam, but 800 miles away at Vung Tau, South Vietnam. And while the men who made and manned her were once simple fishermen, in more recent years they'd become refugees who fled the Communists; and even more recently they'd been trained by CIA paramilitary officers who also had financed this entire expedition.

When at last his junk reached calmer, leeside waters behind a jagged island, the captain called up a thin, middle-aged man from below. Several crewmen lowered over the side a small woven basket boat crammed with a radio and provisions, and off he went: Agent *Ares*, the CIA's first long-term North Vietnam–based operative, had been successfully landed.

The man to whom Agent *Ares* ultimately reported was as much his opposite as was imaginable. Catholic, Ivy League, with intelligent eyes behind horn-rimmed glasses, William Colby looked and sounded more like a corporate executive than the CIA's Saigon station chief. Comfortable in a bow tie and business suit on even the sultriest tropical days, the man who oversaw this expanding covert enterprise hardly appeared to be a rising CIA star and longtime veteran of the secret wars.

In 1944 then-Lieutenant William Colby had parachuted into Nazi-occupied France as one of the OSS's most elite operatives, a Jedburgh officer, to help the Resistance disrupt German defenses behind the Normandy beaches. A year later he was sabotaging Norwegian rail lines to prevent German units from reaching the Reich before its collapse. While several of his OSS colleagues became founders of U.S. Army Special Forces, Colby joined the new postwar civilian intelligence agency, the CIA. His career progressed steadily.

Soon after Colby's 1959 appointment to the ever more important Saigon station, there began a troubling reappearance in South Vietnam of old Communist Viet Minh fighters who had emigrated to the North in 1954, after the French-Indochina War.

At its April 1959 15th Plenum, the North Vietnamese Communist

Party Central Committee had voted in secret session to return covertly to South Vietnam thousands of such Viet Minh veterans. These infiltrators were to work with party cadres who'd remained in South Vietnam to execute a conquest intended from its inception to be deniable and thus undercut any rationale for foreign intervention. To infiltrate on such a scale, the Central Committee created a special Army unit, the 559th Transportation Group—the numbers commemorating its May 1959 founding—which in tandem with North Vietnam's Trinh Sat secret intelligence service would train people and move them southward. From his headquarters in North Vietnam's Ha Tinh Province, the infiltration commander, Brigadier General Vo Bam, cautioned, "This route must be kept absolutely secret." Therefore, when the first group headed south in August 1959, they wore untraceable peasant garb and carried captured French weapons.*

The returning Viet Minh marched 10 miles each day among busy detachments of Army engineers sent to improve and expand these simple footpaths they called the Truong Son Route because it meandered through a similarly named mountain chain. Westerners would call this network the Ho Chi Minh Trail.

CIA station chief Colby found gathering information about the Truong Son Route difficult. Indeed, this landlocked Laotian wilderness was largely unmapped, with misty valleys so blanketed by jungle that flyovers and aerial photos disclosed nothing. To find what was there required putting men on the ground.

The CIA recruited French coffee planters at Khe Sanh on South Vietnam's northwest frontier to travel every few weeks along Route 9 to the quiet village of Tchephone, Laos, 30 miles away. Despite keeping their eyes peeled, the planters brought back little intelligence because infiltration parties were small and crossed Highway 9 at night.

The incoming Kennedy administration expanded Colby's covert effort to detect Communist infiltration and insinuate an expanded network of CIA saboteurs and agents into North Vietnam. National Security Memorandum 52 authorized the CIA to employ Army Green Berets and Navy SEALs to train and advise the South Vietnamese who would execute Colby's covert missions.

---

*For the next sixteen years, Hanoi insisted it had no role in the fighting in South Vietnam.

Technically the Green Berets and SEALs weren't working for the CIA—they worked for CAS, an innocuous cover whose initials stood for Combined Area Studies. At the seaside resort town of Nha Trang, American Special Forces trained South Vietnamese 1st Observation Group commandos to explore the growing Ho Chi Minh Trail; during 1961 and 1962, the 1st Group mounted forty-one recon operations into the Laotian infiltration corridor, but its teams were too cautious to learn much. The CIA-funded Mountain Scouts penetrated Laos, too; however, these courageous but illiterate Montagnard tribesmen could not comprehend map reading and couldn't associate what they discovered with a recordable location.

Meanwhile, in Danang, the SEALs trained junk crews to land secret agents in the North and organized a civilian raiding force, the Sea Commandos, for hit-and-run coastal attacks. Soon the Sea Commandos began across-the-beach raids on North Vietnam, to plant a clever weapon designed by SEAL Gunners Mate Barry Enoch. Enoch rigged a packboard with four cardboard tubes—each containing a 3.5-inch antitank rocket—wired to a delay mechanism, so a raider could slip ashore at night, aim the packboard toward, say, a radar station, activate the timer, then paddle back to a waiting boat. The raiders would be long gone by the time the North Vietnamese got their sunrise surprise.

After several successes, some raider junks were intercepted by enemy Swatow patrol boats, whose automatic cannons and heavy 12.7mm machine guns made quick work of the flimsy wooden craft.

Although SEAL Gunners Mate Enoch devised a host of clever junk armaments—from hidden rocket launchers to .50-caliber machine guns concealed in 55-gallon drums—it soon reached the point that junks were just too vulnerable to ply North Vietnamese waters. The CIA began a search for faster boats, and turned as well to aerial infiltration via a new South Vietnamese Air Force unit.

To command the clandestine VNAF squadron that would penetrate the North, Colby sought out a flamboyant pilot with a thin Clark Gable mustache and a penchant for black flight suits. Though only thirty years old, already he was a colonel and commanded Saigon's Tan Son Nhut Air Base and seemed willing to fly anything, anywhere—but did that include piloting unmarked C-47s deep into North Vietnam, Colby asked?

The pilot smiled and said, "When do we start?" The gutsy flyer eventually would head his country's Air Force and go on to be South Vietnam's president—Nguyen Cao Ky.

Ky recruited his best pilots, but months of training would precede their first operational flight. To help them, the CIA brought in Nationalist Chinese instructor pilots with hundreds of missions over mainland China very similar to what Ky's men would fly—100 feet above the treetops, at night, under 30 percent moonlight.

CIA air experts at Takhli, Thailand, were tasked to help Colby plan the North Vietnam aerial penetrations; he couldn't have found a more capable group. Colonel Harry "Heinie" Aderholt, likely the most experienced special operations officer in the Air Force, had just finished the CIA's Tibet airlift, where unmarked C-130s had penetrated Chinese-occupied Tibet to parachute supplies and guerrillas to the pro–Dalai Lama resistance. On loan to the CIA for secret projects since the Korean War, Aderholt's Thailand-based organization had just been redirected to support the CIA's expanding guerrilla force in Laos, using Air America planes, when the infiltration analysis job was assigned.

Assisting Aderholt was probably the CIA's finest aerial infiltration planner, USAF Major Larry Ropka. Studious, intense, a perfectionist, Ropka had planned all the Tibet flights, and if not one plane was lost, it was largely because he applied his whole being to such a task.

With 90 percent of the North's population arrayed along its coastal lowlands and Red River Valley, Major Ropka could see that any approach from the Tonkin Gulf—the "front door"—was certain to be met by MiGs and antiaircraft guns. Therefore, he planned aerial infiltration routes through the less-populated mountainous border with Laos—the "back door"—where terrain masking and electronic confusion were most effective.

To improve the "back door," Ropka had Air America planes in Laos climb to 5000 feet, where they would appear on North Vietnamese radar, fly a "back-door" approach, then descend to low level, below radar, and turn back to Thailand. After dozens of false alarms, the North's air defense network would stop alerting fighters and antiaircraft units, and wouldn't be able to distinguish between Ropka's feints and the real infiltration flights, which were soon to begin.

Meanwhile, the agents to be inserted were being instructed at Camp Long Thanh, 20 miles east of Saigon, where Green Berets and CIA officers taught them intelligence and sabotage techniques, rough-terrain parachuting, weapons handling, Morse code and survival—skills to sustain them for years in North Vietnam.

By late spring 1961, the graduate agents were ready to join Agent *Ares,* who by now was regularly tapping out Morse code messages to a CIA communications center in the Philippines. But unlike *Ares*—a "singleton," or lone operator—the new operatives would land in teams of three to eight men. They would lack the luck of *Ares.*

The first airdropped group, Team *Atlas,* never came up on its appointed frequency; the plane that delivered them disappeared. Colonel Ky personally flew the next airdrop mission, inserting Team *Castor* deep in North Vietnam. Three months later Hanoi held a much-publicized trial for three *Atlas* survivors. Then Team *Castor* went off the air, and CIA handlers realized Teams *Dido* and *Echo* were under enemy control, so they were played as "doubles." The last team parachuted into North Vietnam in 1961, Team *Tarzan,* was presumed captured.

Despite such losses, at least Colby now had an infrastructure for conducting his secret war that he could improve and build upon. But something beyond Colby's control unexpectedly came into play: Two months after Agent *Ares* paddled ashore, another CIA expedition landed half a world away, in a debacle forever to be known by the name of its locale, the Bay of Pigs. The catastrophic failure of the Cuban-exile landing so embarrassed President Kennedy that he appointed General Maxwell Taylor to learn what had gone wrong. The Taylor Commission concluded the Cuba project had escalated beyond a size manageable by the CIA. It recommended a worldwide review of other CIA enterprises to learn if any had grown beyond intelligence operations, and if so, to switch them to military control.

William Colby's growing secret war fit the commission's criteria perfectly; during the summer of 1962 the CIA agreed to transfer these Southeast Asian programs to the military in eighteen months, dubbing it Operation Switchback. But on the very day scheduled for Switchback— 1 November 1963—South Vietnamese President Ngo Dinh Diem was overthrown. Then three weeks later, President Kennedy was assassinated, further delaying the transfer. And the military had yet to create a unit to absorb the CIA programs.

Meanwhile Hanoi stepped up its infiltration, causing Defense Secretary Robert McNamara to order a series of covert attacks on North Vietnam to "make it clear to the leaders of the North that they would suffer serious reprisals for their continuing support of the insurgency in South Vietnam." Under OPLAN-34A, issued 15 December 1963, McNamara intended to send only a symbolic message, limiting targets to "those that provide maximum pressure with minimum risk."

Despite McNamara's insistence that OPLAN-34A missions commence 1 February 1964, it wasn't until 24 January that Military Assistance Command, Vietnam (MACV), finally organized the covert unit to take over the CIA programs; soon it would be the largest clandestine military unit since World War II's OSS. Commanded by an Army colonel, it would include elements of all services, from Army Green Berets and Navy SEALs to USAF Air Commandos, operating as SOG, the Special Operations Group, a descriptive label that made a mockery of security. A few months later the unit was renamed, yet its acronym remained SOG, only now, SOG stood for Studies and Observations Group, a supposed gathering of quiet analysts devoted to academic study.

The Studies and Observations Group was not subordinate to MACV nor its new commander, General William Westmoreland; it answered directly to the Joint Chiefs of Staff (JCS) in the Pentagon, often with White House–level input. Only five non-SOG officers in Saigon were even briefed on its top-secret doings: Westmoreland; his chief of staff; his intelligence officer (J-2); the Seventh Air Force commander; and the commander of U.S. Naval Forces, Vietnam.

SOG's charter authorized operations from South Vietnam and Thailand into Laos, Cambodia and North Vietnam, with contingency planning for northern Burma and China's Kwangsi, Kwangtung and Yunnan Provinces, plus Hainan Island. Officially SOG would answer solely to an office in the Pentagon's high-status E Ring called SACSA, the Special Assistant for Counterinsurgency and Special Activities, a two-star general whose small staff responded only to the Joint Chiefs' operations officer (J-3), with unprecedented direct access to the Chairman of the Joint Chiefs. Any money SOG needed would be buried in the Navy's annual budget.

Heading SOG's secret war and bearing the title Chief SOG was a World War II paratroop officer who'd come into Special Forces in the 1950s, Colonel Clyde Russell. A veteran of combat parachute jumps in France and Holland with the 82d Airborne Division, Colonel Russell became Secretary of the Infantry School at Fort Benning, Georgia, then commanded the Europe-based 10th Special Forces Group, then the 7th Special Forces Group at Fort Bragg, North Carolina.

With OPLAN-34A allowing no time for contemplation, Russell's Saigon staff fell back on the tried and true and structured SOG like the old OSS, into air and maritime sections—because these are the ways agents are transported—plus a psychological operations section similar to the OSS Morale Operations Division.

The CIA offered Colonel Russell the agency's unique logistic channels for exotic hardware, such as suppressed weapons and wiretap devices, via the agency's top-secret Far East logistics base at Camp Chinen, Okinawa. Nearby was another office created by Operation Switchback, CISO, or the Counterinsurgency Support Office, which provided specialized logistics aid to SOG and Special Forces.

Another CIA contribution was a clandestine C-123 transport squadron from Taiwan, flown by Nationalist Chinese pilots, to replace the less capable Vietnamese-flown C-47s. Known as the First Flight Detachment, these four SOG airplanes bore removable U.S. insignia and formerly had flown with Nationalist China's top-secret 34th Squadron, which had been penetrating mainland China for more than a decade, inserting and resupplying agents and dropping CIA sensors. The 34th Squadron's U-2s had flown over China since 1960, spying on the Lop Nor nuclear test site and Kansu missile range. First Flight's C-123s had proved a tough target for SAMs and MiGs, penetrating the mainland two hundred times.*

Each First Flight plane had a backup USAF crew for flights in South Vietnam; the Chinese piloted deniable missions into North Vietnam and Cambodia. Though SOG's Chinese pilots carried South Vietnamese ID cards, they spoke hardly a word of that language, and only a handful of Vietnamese officials even knew they were in the country.

USAF Lieutenant Colonel Bill Rose spent two tours with First Flight,

---

*First Flight evolved from the Civil Air Transport Service (CATS), a CIA airline founded in 1949 to evacuate Chiang Kai-shek's followers to Taiwan. In 1954 CATS resupplied encircled French paratroopers at Dien Bien Phu, then in 1958 supported a coup attempt against Indonesian strongman Sukarno. CATS' thin cover side apparently became the well-known Air America while its deep cover side became Nationalist China's 34th Squadron.

eventually serving as its U.S. commander, and found the Chinese crews solidly professional. Another First Flight veteran, Colonel Don Radike, admired their guts, recalling, "We had one navigator, for example, who had been shot down on the Chinese mainland seven times and walked out every time. What could I possibly tell him about survival?"

In addition to the covert Chinese squadron, the CIA turned over its three-year-old long-term agent program, which by 1964 had airdropped twenty-two teams into North Vietnam. Of these only four teams—*Bell, Remus, Easy* and *Tourbillon*—plus the singleton *Ares*—remained intact.

At Camp Long Thanh, near Saigon, SOG inherited a couple of dozen agents-in-training, whom a SOG officer found "unmotivated, lacking any zeal to serve, and of generally poor, untrustworthy quality." As a SOG officer coldly confides, most trainees were "not capable of going anywhere and we had to get rid of them; at the same time, we couldn't turn them loose in South Vietnam because they'd been briefed and re-briefed on operations in North Vietnam." The solution was to do with them exactly what they had been trained and paid to do: parachute into North Vietnam. In May, June and July 1964, they were airdropped as Teams *Boone, Buffalo, Lotus* and *Scorpion*. All were captured. The few quality agents-in-training reinforced the in-place Teams *Remus* and *Tourbillon*. SOG began recruiting fresh agents for a twenty-one-week training program at Camp Long Thanh. It would be a slow start.

OPLAN-34A perplexed Russell, because deniable attacks on objectives having little military value did not make sense. "I don't feel that the objectives of OPLAN-34A were clearly spelled out," Russell later explained, "so we didn't know exactly what we were trying to do." But this was not his only problem.

Each proposed OPLAN-34A operation had to weave its way between Defense, State and the White House for approval, with each stop liable to change, restrict or delay SOG plans. Colonel Russell found this "a tremendous operational handicap," and complained that, "By the time we got it back, we were out of implementation time and the restraints were too many and too frequent."

Impatience was driving the program. McNamara had called for the first OPLAN-34A raid by 1 February 1964, incredibly, just seven days after SOG's founding. Such insistence instigated perhaps the strangest episode of Vietnam's covert war.

To support OPLAN-34A's hit-and-run coastal attacks, the CIA had replaced its old junks with 88-foot high-speed Norwegian Nasty-class PT boats, bringing in former Norwegian skippers to help SOG SEALs instruct the new Vietnamese crews. Developed for 47-knot runs from Norway's fjords to nip at passing Russian ships, the Nasty PTFs (Patrol Type, Fast) were light, heavily armed and bat-out-of-hell fast, the naval cigarette boats of the 1960s. Accustomed to tiny runabouts and junks, however, the Vietnamese simply couldn't master the Nastys' tricky high-speed maneuvers.

Within SOG's Naval Advisory Detachment—a dozen SEALs from Detachment Echo, Seal Team One; a few sailors from Boat Support Unit One at Coronado, California; and five Marine Force Recon men—were plenty of eager volunteers to crew the Nastys for raiding the North, but political deniability absolutely precluded using Americans; indeed, throughout the war no SEALs ever would be allowed north of the 17th Parallel.

But, a SOG staff officer shrewdly observed, *the Norwegians weren't Americans.* However, any Caucasian at the throttles of a covert boat in Asian waters flew in the face of plausible denial—How could a Norwegian possibly explain his attacking the coast of North Vietnam? But in the rush to get the raids under way the absurd became the acceptable; thus, due to impatience, SOG's first covert attacks on North Vietnam would be led by Norwegians.

On the night of 16 February 1964 three Norwegian-piloted Nastys attempted to land Vietnamese frogmen to demolish a bridge, but heavy coastal fire drove them away, aborting the mission. A few nights later another swimmer demolition was attempted, but it, too, failed, with eight Sea Commando swimmers lost.

By early summer the swashbuckling Scandinavian skippers began displaying a tad too much joie de vivre for their sedate SOG superiors. As one warned, "They were getting in trouble in Danang, and there were definite fears in Washington circles that the whole program would be blown because these . . . people were getting involved with Vietnamese girls and the police in Danang." With new urgency, Vietnamese boat crews were prepared to take over from the Scandinavians, but not before the latter got in a final few licks.

By July, SOG's Nastys and Sea Commandos had demolished five targets in North Vietnam, followed by two hit-and-run, over-the-beach attacks on 9 and 25 July. On 30 July, SOG launched its biggest bombardment ever, employing five Nastys against radar sites so far north they were closer to Haiphong than to Danang, an action SOG headquarters praised as "well executed and highly successful, with secondary explosions."

Two days later the boat crews were resting in Danang when word came that North Vietnamese PT boats had attacked the U.S. destroyer *Maddox,* in what became known as the Tonkin Gulf incident. Although he made no reference to the SOG raids, of which he was informed, President Lyndon Johnson warned Hanoi that another high-seas attack would have dire consequences, and ordered the destroyer *Turner Joy* to reinforce the *Maddox.*

SOG Nastys bombarded another coastal radar the night of 3 August, and the next day came a second alleged clash, which became the rationale for the Congressional Tonkin Gulf Resolution and U.S. retaliatory bombing. The Rubicon had been crossed.

Though conspiracy buffs and revisionist historians later would claim SOG "lured" the North Vietnamese into attacking the *Maddox,* nothing could be further from the truth. With entire regiments now headed south along an expanding Ho Chi Minh Trail, Hanoi already was committed to a widening war; a few small boat raids or destroyers passing near its coast were as nothing compared to North Vietnam's massive buildup in southern Laos.

But what was happening in Laos had remained largely a mystery in 1964. In April, Defense Secretary McNamara arrived in Saigon with another of his rush orders. "Out of a clear blue sky," a senior Special Forces officer reports, "I was asked how soon I could launch operations into Laos. I tried to pin [McNamara] down as to what kind of operations and what the mission would be, since nobody had enlightened me or tied it into our planning that we had already submitted." McNamara insisted the ARVN must recon west of Khe Sanh despite the Green Beret officer's warning that unmotivated, half-trained Vietnamese couldn't accomplish anything tangible without U.S. Special Forces leading them. McNamara agreed but still ordered the recon missions—code named "Project Leaping Lena"—and insisted they commence within thirty days. Despite hectic training, the first Leaping Lena teams could not be inserted until 24 June. Between then and 1 July, five teams, each with eight Vietnamese, parachuted into Laos. "We practically had to force them on the airplane at gunpoint," a disgusted Special Forces Colonel Charlie Norton reported.

Leaping Lena's results reached presidential adviser William Bundy in a terse report: "All of the teams were located by the enemy and only four survivors returned." The survivors' stories were shocked, confused and unreliable, although they reported crossing a network of trails and roads invisible from the air, some carrying truck convoys, and NVA everywhere.

More months passed with no significant intelligence from southern Laos despite telltale signs of a growing enemy presence. In early 1965, Air America pilot Jim Ryan photographed a new road from North Vietnam's Mu Gia Pass into the Laotian jungle, sheltered beneath camouflaged latticework; the war was entering an ominous new stage, with bicycles giving way to trucks and the Ho Chi Minh Trail to a road system.

On 8 March 1965, while television cameras recorded the first U.S. Marine combat troops wading ashore at Danang, there was a quiet celebration at SOG's Saigon headquarters. After years of inadequate intelligence, SOG at last was authorized to penetrate the Ho Chi Minh Trail, using not poorly trained, unmotivated Vietnamese but American Green Berets.

And SOG had a new chief en route to lead its secret wars, a highly respected Green Beret officer, Colonel Donald Blackburn, the legendary "headhunter" himself.

SHINING BRASS

New Chief SOG Colonel Donald D. Blackburn's World War II exploits had been lionized in a 1955 book, *Blackburn's Headhunters*, which two years later Hollywood turned into a motion picture, *Surrender—Hell!*

A U.S. Army adviser in the Philippines in 1941, Blackburn and a friend, Russell Volckmann, had escaped the Bataan Death March for the mountains of northern Luzon after the Japanese forced General Douglas MacArthur out of the islands.

During the Japanese occupation, Blackburn organized a clandestine spy ring and partisan training program among Filipino resistance fighters. Building secret jungle camps to train Igarote tribesmen—headhunters in the past century—his force soon was called "Blackburn's Headhunters."

When U.S. forces invaded Leyte in 1944, Blackburn's Headhunters came out in droves to scout for the Americans, help the Air Force find Japanese targets and rescue downed pilots. By the time Douglas MacArthur returned, the "Chief Headhunter" commanded 20,000 guerrillas and wore the eagles of a full colonel—the youngest full colonel in the U.S. Army.

The 1965 assignment of Blackburn, a senior Special Forces officer and one of the world's foremost guerrilla experts, as Chief SOG gave the organization instant crediblity with General Westmoreland, who was eager to penetrate the mysterious Ho Chi Minh Trail complex.

Nobody knew with certainty what was in Laos. Learning that would be the object of SOG's new operation, Shining Brass, which would form recon teams of tribal mercenaries led by U.S. Green Berets. To head Shining Brass, Blackburn chose Colonel Arthur D. "Bull" Simons, for whom "Bull" seemed a suitable nickname—everything about Colonel Simons was hard-charging tough.

During World War II, Bull Simons' 6th Ranger battalion was the eyes and ears of the 11th Airborne Division and led the way ashore on Leyte in the Philippines. During the Korean War the broad-shouldered Simons instructed trainees in hand-to-hand combat and close-quarters shooting at the Army's Ranger Training Center.

And Bull Simons knew southern Laos, where he'd recruited and trained Laotian Kha Tribesmen for the CIA in 1961–62. When the 1962 Geneva accords "neutralized" Laos, Colonel Simons and his covert Special Forces trainers withdrew.

While Marines began patrolling the countryside near Danang in the summer of 1965, and the U.S. Army's 173d Airborne Brigade and 1st Air Cavalry Division arrived in Vietnam, SOG's Shining Brass volunteers, from the 1st Special Forces Group, secretly began training on Okinawa. By late summer sixteen volunteers were ready, exactly the number required to man five U.S.-led recon teams, with one man to spare. Arriving in Vietnam, the Green Berets were mated up with their teams; as Blackburn conceived it, each recon team would be a mix of two or three U.S. Special Forces troopers leading nine local tribesmen to achieve a perfect complement of knowledge and experience. The Americans would bring a sophisticated perspective, the local mercenaries, a primitive one; the Americans had advanced technology, such as helicopters, and the tribesmen had ancient techniques, for example, silent ambush.

And though unstated, there was another factor in team composition: Since most members of SOG recon teams were indigenous, U.S. casualties, proportionally, would be reduced.

Initally, all SOG recon indigenous troops were Nungs, the special operations Gurkhas of Southeast Asia. Quite ready to let you know in a minute they weren't Vietnamese, the Nungs had emigrated to Vietnam from the southern reaches of China's Kwangsi Province. During the French-Indochina War, the Nungs had shown themselves to be furious fighters, especially as behind-the-lines operators. The South Vietnamese government regarded Nungs—as well as Montagnards and Cambodes—as inferior and didn't even draft them, so SOG found plentiful recruits. SOG's "indig" as they were called, were mercenaries, pure and simple, and well paid. The lowest-ranking Nung received monthly pay comparable to a South Vietnamese captain, about $60 U.S.

When the always clever Nungs learned they'd earn jump pay by submitting a parachute-school diploma, forgeries came in by the droves, so SOG Sergeant Major Paul Darcy decided to call their bluff and scheduled the "paper" paratroopers for a jump. "A lot of them showed great ignorance of how to get into a parachute," recalled Major Scotty Crerar, "but by golly, they all jumped."

While the Nungs and Green Berets trained, Colonel Blackburn was developing a master plan to employ them.

For Phase I, Blackburn's recon teams would explore southern Laos, identify NVA base areas and concentrations and direct air strikes on them. Meanwhile, SOG would recruit and train company-size raiding units to execute lightning heliborne strikes on key enemy facilities, such as truck parks, headquarters and matériel stockpiles, as quickly as the recon teams uncovered them. With tremendous aerial fire support, the raiding companies—or "Hatchet Forces," as Blackburn dubbed them—would land, sweep through and destroy a target and be gone before the enemy knew what had hit him. These destruction raids would be Phase II.

Then there was Phase III. Blackburn planned to recruit thousands of Laotian tribesmen to nip and slash the NVA at every opportunity, forcing the enemy to mass for security—thereby becoming better targets for even more air strikes and Hatchet Force raids. SOG would hit and harass the enemy at every turn.

But Blackburn's plan was opposed by the ambassador to Laos, William Sullivan, who severely restricted SOG's operating area to two small boxes along the South Vietnamese border, required any supporting air strikes to launch from Thailand, and forbade helicopter insertions— SOG recon teams had to walk into Laos, though they could be extracted by helicopter in an emergency.

Faced with Sullivan's restrictions, Blackburn could do little more than salute and do his best to make Shining Brass work.

While policy disputes boiled, Blackburn was arranging the transfer to SOG of a Vietnamese Air Force helicopter unit to support cross-border reconnaissance. He obtained the Danang-based 219th VNAF Helicopter Squadron, whose obsolete H-34 helicopters would become a SOG trademark.

Just because it was old, that didn't make the H-34 bad. "The best helicopter ever made for that [SOG operations] was the H-34," remembered Lieutenant Jim Fleming, an exceptional USAF helicopter pilot who flew SOG Hueys. "The pilot sat right on top of that big, 32-cylinder radial engine, and when you went in, you at least had some iron between you and them. And it was really rough and tough and rugged." How tough? "You could blow cylinders out of it and still get yourself home."

Because it was a tall ship, the H-34 could hover against a hill with one wheel and its blade wasn't as likely to hit as was a Huey's, allowing it to lift men from steeper slopes.

Inside, the bottle-nosed H-34s were grungy, filthy, oily birds, with exposed innards where Vietnamese mechanics had cut holes to get access to some part and never bothered to close it up. Each "Kingbee," as the H-34 was nicknamed, carried cases of pink hydraulic fluid and reeked of it, the overhead lines leaked it, the floors stayed slick with it. When enemy .50-caliber slugs hit its cavernous troop compartment it sounded like a washtub being beaten with a baseball bat, but this tub could take a lot of hits.

The H-34 had only one door, on the right side, which made it relatively blind on its left, especially to the rear. For armament, a Kingbee carried a single rusty World War II belt-fed .30-caliber machine gun hung from a bungee cord in the doorway, with a thousand rounds stacked in an old can under the gunner's seat.

The two most noted Kingbee pilots were known as "Cowboy" and "Mustachio." Mustachio's real name was Nguyen Van Hoang; his finely trimmed mustache gave him his nickname. Cowboy's actual name is forgotten, but his nickname arose from the Vietnamese aviator's preference for hand-tailored flight suits, usually in some odd camouflage pattern.

Neither impossible ground fire nor unflyable weather stopped Cowboy and Mustachio. Dozens of SOG men survived purely because "can't" was not in these pilots' vocabularies. "They were absolutely fearless," says Major Scotty Crerar.

With the Kingbees secured, SOG was ready for Shining Brass. In early September, Bull Simons established a modest Command and Control cell for Shining Brass in Danang, headed by Lieutenant Colonel Ray Call. Saigon soon began referring to Call's headquarters as "C&C," and this term took hold as SOG's internal designation for the unit conducting Shining Brass recon—later there would be Command and Control North, Command and Control Central and Command and Control South—but for now Lieutenant Colonel Call's headquarters was merely two room-size Conex shipping containers at Danang Air Base.

But Danang was far from the Laotian border, so Shining Brass needed a Forward Operating Base (FOB) to house recon teams, fuel helicopters and launch operations. A quick map study decided it: They'd locate the FOB with a Special Forces border surveillance A Camp at Kham Duc, 60 miles southwest of Danang, only 10 miles from the Laotian border. As secluded and desolate as the adjacent Laotian wilderness, Kham Duc sat in a bowl formed by jungled hills that held ground fog and rain for days and weeks, making the isolated camp probably the most weathered-in locale in South Vietnam. But despite weather problems, for the time being Kham Duc had to be the Shining Brass FOB.

To command the FOB, Lieutenant Colonel Call appointed Charlie Norton, a well-rounded Special Forces major, a veteran of Korean War partisan experience. And to direct SOG operations there, Bull Simons recruited one of the most remarkable officers in Special Forces, Finnish-American Captain Larry Thorne.

With an infectious zest for life, Thorne excelled as a scuba diver, skydiver, boxer, skier and first-class mountain climber. Born in Finland, he'd fought the Russian invaders in the Winter War of 1940, then spent four years leading missions behind Russian lines. Thorne earned every medal Finland could bestow, including three wound medals and the Mannerheim Cross, his country's highest award, for a convoy ambush that killed three hundred Russians with not one of Thorne's men lost. Aware of his superb special operations experience, former OSS chief "Wild Bill" Donovan personally interceded to get him U.S. residency.

Now Blackburn had an all-star team: Colonel Bull Simons to head Shining Brass; Lieutenant Colonel Ray Call at C&C in Danang; Major

Charlie Norton at Kham Duc; and Larry Thorne to oversee the first Shining Brass insertions. SOG's first five American-led recon teams, named for Iowa, Alaska, Idaho, Kansas and Dakota—were at Kham Duc finishing training.

Leading each team would be a Green Beret with the code number One-Zero, which became SOG's most prestigious title; any man appointed a One-Zero had proven his judgment under life-and-death stress. Throughout SOG, One-Zeros would be held in respect that verged on awe, because once on the ground, this was the man who must outwit everything the numerically superior foe could throw at his team.

The One-Zero's two Green Beret teammates also received numbers. The assistant team leader was the One-One, and their radio operator was One-Two. Other team members were Nung mercenaries, except perhaps for a South Vietnamese Special Forces lieutenant or other officer, attached to gain combat recon experience.

Each American also was given a personal radio code name, which soon evolved into everyday nicknames. For example, Master Sergeant Bill Grimes was called "Country," while Staff Sergeant Jim Bath became "Tub." Then there were "Pigpen" Ambrose, "Snuffy" Smith, "Roundeye" Stevens, and so on. This kind of rank-irrelevant informality appealed to SOG's recon men.

The One-Zero for SOG's first cross-border operation was Master Sergeant Charles "Slats" Petry, and his team was RT Iowa, consisting of seven Nungs, one ARVN lieutenant and a One-One, Sergeant First Class Willie Card. Lean and tall, with a genuine smile and an excellent reputation from Okinawa, Petry wasn't flashy or fast but as dependable an NCO as was to be found in all of Special Forces.

Petry's entire team was "sterile," meaning they wore no rank or unit insignia, and even their uniforms and rucksacks were Asian made and untraceable. They carried 9mm Swedish K submachine guns and Belgian-made Browning 9mm pistols, all of which, of course, had been acquired clandestinely so a serial-number check would lead nowhere.

And for the first time since World War II's 1st Special Service Force was issued the V-42 stiletto, an elite U.S. unit would have its own custom knife, an untraceable 6-inch-bladed weapon, designed on Okinawa by Ben Baker at CISO and manufactured clandestinely in Japan. Each American was issued this unmarked SOG knife.

If captured, Petry's men were to recite a flimsy cover story, that they'd stumbled into Laos while looking for a missing C-123 and had no idea they'd crossed the border. To support this fiction, SOG published special maps that shifted the border 10 kilometers west, something the worldly-wise Green Berets found ridiculous. "This will buy us about ten seconds," said Master Sergeant Billy Waugh, "because the other guys will be laughing too hard to shoot us."

Petry and RT Iowa were briefed extensively for their Shining Brass operation. Although Hanoi still denied it had a single soldier in Laos, by October 1965 its security, engineer and logistics troops there numbered at least 30,000, not to mention an additional 4500 men passing through each month on their way to South Vietnam. About two hundred truckloads of supplies rolled down the Ho Chi Minh Trail monthly, and by the fall of 1965 the Air Force already knew the enemy had spun its 900-mile road system the length of Laos, all the way to South Vietnam's Central Highlands. On 2 October 1965, fresh U-2 photos disclosed new roads in Laos, while other aerial photos showed new truck traffic.

RT Iowa's objective was Target D-1, only about 20 miles northwest of Kham Duc, where Laotian Highway 165 almost reached the South Vietnamese border, in the northern of the two boxes SOG was authorized to operate in. The rockets and mortars pounding the Marine and Air Force installations at Danang, it was suspected, came from D-1.

On 18 October 1965, American newspapers were reporting the 1st Air Cavalry Division's violent clash with the NVA 66th and 33d Regiment in the Ia Drang Valley, the first major U.S. ground combat of the war. But no one would read about the momentous, top-secret doings that day at Kham Duc.

Just after noon, RT Iowa's men opened their rucksacks and emptied their pockets for a final inspection to ensure they carried nothing attributable to the United States. Then while Petry's men test-fired their weapons, Major Norton and Captain Thorne brought the Kingbee and U.S. Huey gunship pilots, and a USAF Forward Air Controller (FAC), into the operations shack to plan their insertion.

RT Iowa's landing zone (LZ) would be a slash-and-burn area that looked like an old logging clear-cut from the Pacific Northwest. For thousands of years Laotian tribesmen had practiced the primitive agricultural technique of downing trees, then burning them to fortify the soil with ash; they'd grow row crops there until they'd exhausted the nutrients, then move on and do it again, leaving a patchwork of squarish clearings at various stages of regrowth across the countryside.

The plan was to insert at dusk so the enemy would have no daylight left to dispatch a reaction force or trackers, giving Petry's men a full night's head start. If they stumbled into enemy on the LZ, the Kingbees would swoop in to extract them while the Huey gunships fired miniguns and rockets.

First off at 5:45 P.M. was the FAC, a tiny Cessna O–1 Bird Dog spotter plane, flown by USAF Major Harley Pyles, with a Saigon-based SOG air liaison officer, USMC Captain Winfield Sisson, in his backseat. Minutes later, Pyles radioed that the weather was marginal, with clouds below the mountaintops and increasing ground fog. Still, he thought low-flying helicopters could weave around the worst of it. Pyles called for a launch.

If there was a song on anyone's mind as the three unmarked Kingbees cranked their engines, it had to be the current Johnny Rivers hit, "Secret Agent Man," whose first line, "a man who leads a life of danger," so fit a Shining Brass SOG trooper. Whether One-Zero, One-One or One-Two, indeed each had been given a number and his name taken away. Not only that, Petry and Card had turned in their dog tags, military ID cards, even their U.S. cigarettes, which were replaced by Asian brands. If they were killed and their bodies captured, the U.S. government would deny their identities.

At 6:00 P.M. the helicopters lifted off, Cowboy in the lead chopper, with Mustachio in the second bird. The third Kingbee, a chase aircraft to retrieve crew and passengers if Cowboy or Mustachio or a Huey gunship went down, carried only Larry Thorne, who was not about to stay behind at Kham Duc. In his lap he cradled a bolt-action Springfield M1903-A3 rifle, an obsolete weapon in this era of AK-47s and M-16s, but he'd always gone into combat with a Finnish Mosin Nagant or German Mauser so a bolt-action gun felt natural in Vietnam, too.

As the Kingbees and Huey gunships flew along, from horizon to horizon, all they could see was rolling, jungled hills, wild rivers and waterfalls. The weather proved especially hazardous, forcing them to weave between thunderheads and sunbeams, avoiding sporadic .50-caliber machine-gun fire. They took no hits.

Then the Kingbees spiraled into the appointed slash-and-burn, roared away and it was done. Petry and RT Iowa scurried into the wet jungle, all alone in the Laotian dusk.

The weather worsened. Thorne sent the first two Kingbees back, while he orbited near the landing zone in case RT Iowa ran into trouble. Cowboy and Mustachio reported low-level visibility so bad that they climbed to 8500 feet, above the clouds, and made it back to Kham Duc, followed shortly by the O-1 Bird Dog and the Huey gunships. Larry Thorne stayed until the team radioed that they were safe, then Thorne radioed that he, too, was headed back.

Larry Thorne was never seen again. In its first minutes, SOG's cross-border program already had swallowed up one of the finest officers in Special Forces and a whole Kingbee. And the day wasn't over. As long shadows edged across the valley around Kham Duc, the O-1 Bird Dog lifted off for Danang with Major Pyles and Captain Sisson. They, too, disappeared. In its first day, Shining Brass had generated three MIAs, not one of whom ever would be found.

By dawn Major Norton learned the sky had closed completely over both Kham Duc and Target D-1, with billowing clouds rising above 10,000 feet, higher than a helicopter or Bird Dog could fly.

Beneath the overcast and drizzle, RT Iowa found Target D-1 crawling with NVA, but the enemy soldiers seemed so preoccupied with their own labors that at first the team had an easy go of it. Enemy activity was everywhere, with many little base camps and trails. On the third day, after crossing many trails and bypassing enemy voices, Petry heard truck engines, so he maneuvered RT Iowa to investigate—and they bumped head-on into an NVA patrol. In the quick exchange of fire, Iowa's Nung point man collapsed, mortally wounded, and the chase was on.

Fighting the enemy was one thing, but the helplessness in the face of weather that shielded an aggressive enemy had Major Norton perplexed. "We couldn't get helicopters in there to get them out," he complained. Slats Petry was carrying along the Nung's body and gear, so RT Iowa was evading slowly. The NVA fanned out, searching high and low for them.

Two days later the weather broke, and Petry's force struck back with a high-tech vengeance, calling in thirty-seven sorties of F-105 Thunderchief fighter-bombers before the Kingbees lifted RT Iowa out. Then Petry went back with a FAC and called in an additional fifty-one sorties on targets he'd discovered, touching off "numerous" secondary explosions as bombs hit munitions stockpiles. The first Shining Brass operation unquestionably had been a success, yielding detailed information about the enemy and inflicting serious damage on him.

The next Shining Brass target was 10 miles away, another highway terminus just beyond the border, where large numbers of enemy congregated in sanctuary and stockpiled supplies for attacks into South Vietnam. Designated Target A-1, it had wide valley floors covered with head-high elephant grass, dangerous because a team could too easily be tracked through it.

Penetrating A-1 would be RT Alaska, with Master Sergeant Dick Warren, One-Zero; Sergeant First Class David Kauhaahaa, One-One; and Sergeant First Class Wilbur "Doc" Donaldson as One-Two, packing the radio. Warren was an "all business" team sergeant from Okinawa; his jovial Hawaiian assistant, Kauhaahaa, was mistaken for a Montagnard tribesman so often that he could not resist impersonating one for gullible strangers; and Doc was a bonus, a talented medic who volunteered to carry their radio.

On 2 November 1965, RT Alaska inserted into A-1 at dusk, but the enemy realized a team had landed. A stressful cat-and-mouse game followed, with RT Alaska silently bypassing and sideslipping enemy patrols.

They found a network of 5-foot-wide bicycle and foot trails coming in from nearby Laotian Highway 165, and NVA patrols—lots of patrols—sweeping and searching for them.

For three days, One-Zero Warren managed to bypass or hide from the enemy, but by the fourth day there were so many enemy troops that contact was inevitable. It came in a short firefight in which Alaska bested the NVA, hitting several without any recon men being hit. Then it was a foot chase.

"We kept running and running," Kauhaahaa, the One-One, recalls, "and then finally Dick and I decided to get up on the highest hill to make radio contact so we could be exfiltrated." Halfway up the steep hillside, their exhausted Nungs wanted to give up. "Bullshit," Warren admonished them, "we gotta keep going!" Pushing and threatening,

Warren got them to the top, which they found covered with elephant grass. While Doc Donaldson hurriedly attached a long antenna and contacted a FAC, the North Vietnamese streamed up and spread out, encircling them.

"They had us surrounded, oh my God," Kauhaahaa said.

Donaldson got a FAC overhead, an unarmed O-1 Bird Dog that reported fighters en route. The NVA hesitated to come into the elephant grass after RT Alaska; what were they up to?

Then smoke drifted across Alaska's position, and they heard the crackling sound of burning grass: The NVA had set it afire to push them into the open. They coughed and choked and had to shift positions but wouldn't come out.

Then a pair of F-105s arrived and turned loose 20mm Vulcan cannons, but the NVA stood their ground, shooting at both the fighters and into the burning grass. Another set of fighters struck with bombs, but the NVA didn't back off.

Then a lone Kingbee roared right over the shooting NVA and into the burning grass, Cowboy at the throttle. "He didn't give a damn, he came in under fire and picked us up," Kauhaahaa said.

In thirty seconds RT Alaska was away, not one man wounded, thanks to Cowboy. "No matter what position or what situation we would be in, he would be in to pick us up," the Alaska One-One says. "Cowboy was one of the best."

Warren, the One-Zero, went back with the FAC to direct eighty-two more fighter-bomber sorties against targets RT Alaska had located, destroying a bridge and thirty-six buildings, setting off ten secondary explosions.

For the second time, putting a SOG recon man with an Air Force FAC had made a particularly effective team; soon SOG reached an agreement with Seventh Air Force, cementing this relationship. Each day a 20th Tactical Air Support Squadron FAC, with the USAF code name Covey, would fly over southern Laos to assist SOG; in return, SOG would detail an experienced recon man to ride with the FAC, to help look for targets, select LZs, plan insertions and extracts, and stay in radio contact with recon teams. Called "Covey Riders," these SOG old hands saved many lives because they understood exactly what those on the ground were going through, resulting not just in an economy of language or effective use of air support, but an unanticipated psychological dimension that was hard to explain. "I know when I was down there," recalled One-Zero Lowell Stevens, "just to hear a voice gave me such a degree of comfort that I don't even have the words to explain it." When a team was running for its life, pursued by hundreds of NVA, there would come a Covey Rider's reassuring voice, calm and confident, "I've got you covered, partner, tac air's on the way, now tell me what's a-happenin'." Covey Rider Lloyd O'Daniels said, "You always had to make everybody believe—including the bad guys—that you were absolutely in charge of the situation." Covey Rider ranks would read like a One-Zero who's who: Paul Darcy, Billy Waugh, Bob Sprouse, Charlie Septer, Lowell Stevens, Larry White, Ken Carpenter, Bob Parks, Lloyd O'Daniels, Bill Grimes and Sam Zumbrun, to name but a few.

By early December 1965, Recon Teams Kansas and Idaho, too, had run missions out of Kham Duc. Like RTs Alaska and Iowa, Idaho had to fight its way out, then Bull Simons decided it was time to shift efforts elsewhere.

A few days later, on 11 December 1965, a swarm of twenty-four, eight-engined B-52 bombers struck Laos for the first time, dumping 2600 bombs into the area reconned by RT Iowa.

Meanwhile, Shining Brass had shifted southward, adjacent to South Vietnam's Central Highlands. Launching from the airstrip at Dak To, the SOG teams repeated their success from November, exploring the areas around Laotian Highway 110E to discover enemy base camps and high-speed trails leading into South Vietnam.

Target K-1 was a close-run thing for RT Kansas, which was hit so forcefully that the team split and two Nungs disappeared. Then during the second operation into this small southern box open to SOG operations, RT Idaho suffered SOG's first American ground casualty in Laos when one Green Beret was slightly wounded. RT Idaho also lost one Nung KIA. By the end of 1965, there'd been eight Shining Brass missions, six of them uncovering major North Vietnamese base camps, roads or caches.

"The more we sent teams in, the better our intelligence got," reports Major Norton. "At least we knew where the hot spots and the hot areas were and where big ground sightings were."

After each mission of about five or six days, the recon men were flown to SOG's Saigon headquarters to debrief. It was during these Saigon debriefs—lasting anywhere from a half day to several days—that at last American intelligence began to learn something of how the enemy operated in Laos.

The recon men explained, for example, there was no mistaking an enemy high-speed trail for an animal track or simple footpath. The North Vietnamese expertly built their trails as flat as if laid out with a mason's level, wide enough for two men to walk abreast, and when in use, not a twig or a leaf was to be found on its hard surface. Where an enemy trail climbed a hill, there were dug-out steps and bamboo handrails so well made that they were a marvel of handicraft.

Enemy roads were earthen and functional, hidden by meticulous camouflage, which made them all but invisible from the air. Instead of just bulldozing trees as most armies would have done, the NVA engineers wound the roads around to retain as many trees as possible. Where overhead gaps appeared, they tied branches of adjacent trees together or constructed bamboo trellises on which they'd place living plants or fresh-cut greenery. In some places the NVA transplanted whole trees.

NVA truck parks, base camps and way stations were hewn from dense forest, and care was taken to remove only a minimal amount of natural foliage. It was always a startling experience, SOG teams reported, to be wading through dense jungle then step into a cathedral-like expanse beneath a ceiling of woven treetops.

But the early debriefings sometimes generated resentment from recon men who'd narrowly escaped alive only to have their information doubted—and by rear-echelon noncombatants who condescendingly tried to tell them they hadn't seen what they reported. When one recon team said they'd heard tracked vehicles at night on Highway 110E, their civilian debriefer all but laughed them out of his office. "What kind of booze were you drinking up there, Sarge?" he quipped snidely. But the team got satisfaction a few days later, because an Air Force FAC flew over the area and found fresh tracked-vehicle tracks. "Then they got excited about it," the assistant team leader said. The fact was, intelligence analysts didn't know anything about Laos, the Ho Chi Minh Trail or North Vietnamese military forces. "For people down in Saigon," complained longtime recon man J. D. Bath, "if it wasn't in the book, then it couldn't be."

The classic case was that of a recon team that reported a convoy of elephants carrying provisions. After a Saigon analyst mocked the returning team's report, another One-Zero encountered elephants and brought back incontrovertible evidence—a plastic bag full of elephant dung, which he dumped all soft and squishy on the debriefer's desk.

Despite sometimes rocky relations with the debriefers, though, a lot of fresh insights flowed from the recon missions, probably the most important being a deeper understanding of the Ho Chi Minh Trail. It was now understood as a sort of circulatory system with its heart near Vinh, North Vietnam, from which major arteries flowed west across the mountains into Laos, then southward parallel to South Vietnam. Through these arteries truck convoys flowed southward, then eastward along major roads that formed infiltration corridors, toward the South Vietnamese frontier. As they neared the border, the roads splintered into a maze of high-speed bicycle and foot trails that, like capillaries, carried supplies and troops invisibly to the battlefields of South Vietnam.

Thanks to SOG recon, U.S. intelligence learned that the Laotian roads appeared unused because the enemy ran his convoys at night, and his trucks were so heavily camouflaged that they looked like rolling leaf piles. On overcast nights the NVA might run a hundred trucks in a convoy; on clear nights, when there was danger of air attack, they broke up into smaller convoys.

It was a slow start, but the enemy's Laotian sanctuaries were yielding their long-held secrets to SOG teams.

FIRST BLOOD

Early in 1966, Colonel Donald Blackburn's foremost concern was finding high-quality men to expand his successful Shining Brass recon operations. The new recon men proved themselves to Blackburn as "all just magnificent guys." One was a colorful soul, Master Sergeant Charles "Pops" Humble, a World War II veteran of the 1st Special Service Force, or as the Germans nicknamed it, the "Devil's Brigade," the joint U.S.-Canadian airborne-raider outfit from which modern Special Forces evolved.

When he arrived at SOG and learned he could carry any weapon he desired, Humble had to have a German Schmeisser submachine gun, the handy weapon sprayed at him in many a World War II firefight. He was a study in contrasts: One recon man said, "Charlie was as tough as woodpecker lips," while another recalled that Humble's tenor voice could sing "Danny Boy" with such feeling that "I practically had tears in my eyes."

Major Scotty Crerar thought the old NCO was proving a fine recon man, but one day Humble came into his office to announce, "Sir, I think I should be off the teams." "Why?" Crerar asked.

"I can do the work," Humble explained, "but it takes me too long to recover my breath when we're being chased, and I think it endangers the rest of my team."

Crerar realized that "that was more a consideration for others than for his own benefit." So "Pops" Humble ended up in supply and created two SOG traditions: First, when a man announced it was time he stopped running recon, no one said a thing. His peers understood the incredible stress and danger and respected an experienced man's decision when he said, "Enough." And second, when a former recon man like Humble went to a staff or support job, he did his absolute best to help, whatever it took.

When a recon One-Zero went to supply for, say, a suppressed Uzi submachine gun, instead of some self-important nitwit demanding justification, he found an old hand who'd used that weapon himself and not only fetched one instantly but shared his own experiences with it.

In early 1966, U.S. Ambassador to Laos William Sullivan eased his restrictions a bit, authorizing SOG helicopters to insert teams and expanding SOG's operational area so that instead of just two small boxes, the whole, 200-mile Laotian frontier could be crossed to a depth of 20 kilometers (about 12 miles).

To explore this expanded operational area, SOG began increasing its U.S.-led recon teams, which in mid-1966 jumped from five to an authorized twenty teams, plus several raider companies. To man all these new elements, Blackburn set up a Montagnard recruiting program.

The Montagnards—a French term, meaning "mountain people"— were South Vietnam's largest minority, organized along tribal lines somewhat like American Indians: The Jarai, Rhade, Sedang and Bru each had a distinct culture and history and homeland. Some tribes boasted a written language and Christian religion, while others were nomadic hunters and foragers who well into the 1960s still used crossbows. Each Montagnard tribe hand-wove cloth for sarongs and loincloths in its own unique pattern, somewhat as the Scottish clans did their tartans. Apart from their loincloths and brass-ring jewelry, Montagnards also could be distinguished from ethnic Vietnamese by their darker skin and stockier builds.

Proudly self-reliant and scrupulously honest, the Montagnards may have lived in simple huts but, like many poor people, they were generous and did not think themselves deprived. In some distant past they had populated Vietnam's coast, living much like the ethnically related Polynesians they so clearly resembled. The more sophisticated Annamese emigrated from China and forced the Montagnards into inaccessible hill country. Few Montagnards supported the Viet Cong, which they considered a Vietnamese institution.

SOG sent a number of American recon men to tribal villages, where they soon learned you didn't just mosey in and hire Montagnards. There was an etiquette about it. When Jim Hetrick and J. D. Bath arrived at a village, they were ushered through scurrying ducks and chickens to a communal longhouse on stilts, where a shriveled man squatted, said nothing and just sized them up. An old pipe hung from a gap in his teeth, and the elderly chief just puffed and puffed. Finally he waved them over.

Bath could sense an animosity but couldn't put a finger on it. Speaking through an interpreter, the recon men learned an American civic action team had dug a well for the village, but, the chief grumbled, the American leader had promised him a pipe and left without giving him one.

Fast on his feet, Bath widened his eyes. "So *you're* the chief we've been looking for! We're sorry we don't have it with us, but we know and we will bring it." The two Green Berets rushed to a PX and came back with two cans of Prince Albert tobacco and a couple of pipes, which they gave the grinning old chief. "We apologized that because of the war—him being a chief, he'd understand—that some things take time," Bath recalled. "The village was ours after that."

One of Bath's recruits had been an impressed bicycle porter in Laos, kidnapped by the NVA from his village and kept placated with assurances that the NVA were in radio contact with his village and that his family was just fine. Finally he escaped and found his family nearly starved—here was a man ready to fight, and the enemy's loss was SOG's gain. "Hell, he was a walking war library," Bath said. "He'd find things on the trail or cuts in trees and tell you exactly what they meant. Up to then, we'd never thought too much about it. Crossed lines on a trail meant, 'This path is booby-trapped, go this way.' All kinds of things."

Unlike most NVA soldiers, the Montagnards actually had grown up in the jungle. "It was like having a bunch of bird dogs around, these jokers were so good," Bath found. "They could see things grow."

For Bath and his fellow Green Berets, the word "Montagnard" was too long and too formal; soon it was shortened to "Yard." The Yards called themselves by single names—since *everyone* in the village *knew* Mit or Angao, why complicate life with surnames? But this presented a problem when Yards from different villages had identical names. RT California One-Zero Joe Walker solved it easily enough by dubbing two such men "Wo-One" and "Wo-Two," and within a few weeks their numerical surnames took.

The Green Berets did not think of Yards or Nungs as mercenaries, though that's what they were. Nor were they considered mere "employees," though a One-Zero could hire, fire, fine or give them bonuses; the relationship was more like a coach and an athletic team. For most Yards, pay was unimportant, and they frittered away their money within days of getting it. "They were like kids," a One-Zero recalled. "On payday they'd go downtown to a dentist and have these red and blue caps put on their teeth." They fought not for money but because they were proud of their tribe and village and detested the enemy; it was their natural inclination to fight Vietnamese, with only a slightly greater disdain for the northern variety. The animosity was mutual: Vietnamese called the Yards *moi*, which means "savage."

The Yards couldn't have cared less about South Vietnam as a country and felt no allegiance to some abstract paymaster like the United States, but they were loyal and ready to die for their recon teammates, American and Yard alike.

Training his team's Montagnards for recon was the One-Zero's responsibility, probably the first time since the American Civil War that a single leader recruited and trained the men he would lead into combat. Recon training proved a challenge to resourcefulness and patience because—in addition to unavoidable misunderstandings when instructing through an interpreter—most Yards had no formal education. A wise One-Zero therefore kept classes short and simple, repetitiously drilling his recruits in critical skills so they could be performed by rote. One effective technique I used was giving each Yard his own toy soldier; during tactics classes, I positioned the toys representing the Yards in a sandbox terrain model and was able to teach some fairly sophisticated maneuvers.

But the biggest mistake you could make was to underestimate the Montagnards. When Lloyd O'Daniels took over RT California, he led the team to a local range to evaluate how well they handled their weapons. Amid it all he paused, astonished. "All of a sudden I noticed, *they're* watching *me* to see how good *I* am!"

Rarely did a One-Zero need to dress down a Montagnard over some infraction; just a slight suggestion, and his Yard team leader or interpreter would straighten the wrongdoer out. Likewise, when the team needed a replacement, the Yards could be entrusted to find a suitable candidate.

But no matter how long the Yards were around SOG men, they still retained superstitions. One recon team leader, Ancil "Sonny" Franks, had a Jarai who grew sicker and sicker before his Yard teammates finally explained, "Witch doctor put curse on him." At their urging, Franks bought animals for sacrifice and sent the ailing man to the witch doctor with a modest honorarium. It worked, Sonny said. "Hell, he came back spry as a chicken."

The Montagnards found everything about America and Americans fascinating. On RT Washington I had one Yard, Knot, who could sit quietly watching Americans for hours, as though he were watching television. One evening he showed up at our team room door, knocked politely, and I opened it to find him locked at parade rest, in U.S. khakis and a green beret and spit-shined boots, begging Joe Quiroz and myself to inspect him, which we did with grave formality.

And he loved it.

About the same time that the Montagnards joined SOG, a new weapon arrived in SOG's arsenal. Based on the Colt CAR-15 survival rifle, it featured a barrel half the length of an M-16's and a collapsible stock—a deadly but compact weapon that fit a recon man's needs to a tee.

The Swedish K and other 9mm submachine guns always would be a part of SOG's armory, but after 1966 they became special-purpose weapons, usually employed only with suppressors.* It was a One-Zero's perogative to arm his men as he saw fit, and he had dozens of different weapons to choose among, from Soviet-made RPG rocket-propelled-grenade launchers to Walther PPK suppressed pistols. The CAR-15, however, would reign supreme as SOG's trademark; in fact, SOG recon would be the only unit armed entirely with CAR-15s.

That summer of 1966, as the new CAR-15s were arriving, SOG began executing a new mission: Bomb Damage Assessment (BDA), which required landing in an area freshly devastated by B-52 bombers to survey the results for the Strategic Air Command (SAC). It was without

---

*Though often called "silencers," these devices more accurately are now called "suppressors," since they reduce but do not eliminate a weapon's report.

precedent to use ground teams to examine strategic bomber targets; it had not been attempted in either World War II or Korea. Think of it: These targets were thought so concentrated with enemy as to justify hitting them with B-52s in Arc Light strikes, as they were code-named, and as quickly as the dust settled, American-led SOG teams landed right there among hundreds, perhaps thousands, of well-armed, hostile—and *upset*—enemy troops.

To watch a B-52 strike go in was an unforgettable experience, a withering spectacle almost too complex to visualize. Where just one 500-pound bomb strikes, a geyser of orange clay vividly shoots through the greenery; a concussion shock wave reverberates outward in billowing concentric rings that strip leaves and lift dust; dirty smoke drifts skyward; then, to make the earthquake complete, enormous trees collapse slowly inward and expose a fresh crater large enough to hold a small truck. That's *one* 500-pound bomb.

Multiply such a cataclysm by 109—the number of bombs in a single B-52—and imagine all these bombs crashing to earth in three seconds. The rumbling explosions overlap and churn up an area two blocks wide and more than a mile long, pounding destruction advancing on a front you can watch from the air.

And that's just one B-52. Each Arc Light involved an entire formation of the swept-wing bombers, anywhere from three to twenty-four aircraft—up to 2616 bursting bombs—a man-made maelstrom consuming as much as 2 miles by 6 miles, with the bombs bursting close enough to overlap each other, a rippling carpet of concussion, geysers and falling greenery that resembled the path of a tiller upturning a swath of thick grass. From their aircraft the BDA team would think, "God, what it must be like beneath that." SOG found out.

If you've ever seen what a tornado does to woodland, that's what they found, but with the bonus complication of fresh, loose-earth bomb craters everywhere. About half the time teams encountered NVA swarming from their subterranean bomb shelters like wasps reacting to their nest being whacked, and the fight was on. "They [SAC] thought that we'd find a lot of dazed and shaken people wandering around on the surface," Chief SOG, Colonel Steve Cavanaugh, (1968–70), recalled. Unless the bombs caught the NVA above ground, this was not the case.

When a BDA team had to fight, the Air Force's Strategic Air Command was happy because it confirmed the enemy was there in numbers. But too many Arc Lights hit nothing, due to faulty or old intelligence.

Despite their frequent ineffectiveness, though, the B-52s were doing an impressive job of exposing the Ho Chi Minh Trail's roads and paths simply by blasting away the heavy jungle. And though the enemy expanded his engineer troops to keep pace with the needed repairs, Arc Light craters and landslides often closed stretches of road temporarily.

Whether performing BDAs for SAC, confirming U-2 airborne photo intelligence or helping analysts determine how the Ho Chi Minh Trail operated, by mid-1966 SOG recon had established an unequaled reputation in the intelligence community for being able to go anywhere and do anything. Not since the French and Indian War had Americans operated so deep in an enemy-controlled wilderness.

By July 1966 SOG's Shining Brass program had conducted forty-eight missions into the enemy's heavily defended Laotian sanctuaries without losing one American in ground combat. There had been only eight Green Berets wounded, and not a one seriously.

It was too good to last.

That summer SOG shifted teams to Khe Sanh, to run targets in Vietnam's DMZ (Demilitarized Zone), a 14-mile-wide strip between North and South Vietnam, as well as west into Laos along the old unused Highway 9, which led across the border and 30 miles down a flat valley to Tchepone, a major NVA road hub.

Standing like a sentinel guarding the Laotian frontier was Co Roc, a 3-mile-wide limestone bluff that rose nearly 2000 feet above Highway 9. From Co Roc north in Laos was a region of karst limestone buttes, rising chimneylike from the jungle floor, some as small as factory smokestacks and others a thousand feet wide. The karst zone ranged 90 miles north, to the Mu Gia Pass.

Northward from Khe Sanh was nothing—not a road, not a village, not anything that spoke of man, not even a distinct landmark, just a hodgepodge of nearly identical hills, each rising about 1500 feet and together forming a uniform pattern like an upside-down egg carton, arrayed in a confusing sameness amid a spiderweb of shallow creeks. This was the terrain all the way up to the DMZ, some 15 miles away, and well into North Vietnam.

SOG launched teams into these areas from the little Special Forces A Camp beside Khe Sanh airstrip, a place almost as miserable and weathered in as Kham Duc, the original Shining Brass FOB.

This virgin territory gave up much information to the SOG teams. Among the early discoveries was "Bicycle Canyon," a narrow valley where the NVA made final adjustments to their portage bikes before sending them south. Captured NVA pack bikes were found to be heavy-framed two- or three-wheelers with wide balloon tires, somewhat like today's mountain bikes. Saigon analysts learned that a single bicycle carried nearly 500 pounds of cargo, far more than a man could carry. As the SOG men learned, a porter walked his loaded bike from one way station to the next, then rode it back for the next load. Like NVA truck drivers, a bicycle porter was assigned a fixed stretch of road or path and came to know it so well he could travel it even on dark nights.

Truck traffic west of the DMZ was heavy, with large convoys rolling every night unless an air strike closed the road; then, NVA bulldozers and laborers rushed to fill bomb craters and clear debris, repairing it so quickly that the Air Force sometimes found it hard to believe SOG reports of renewed use.

NVA troops heading south were self-sustaining so as not to burden their already overtaxed logistics pipeline. This meant soldiers walked rather than rode aboard trucks, and as they departed North Vietnam they carried their first several weeks' provisions. NVA troops stationed permanently along the Trail hunted wild game and grew crops to supplement their diet.

And everywhere, the SOG teams found, the enemy practiced astounding camouflage discipline. Were it not for the B-52 strikes, most roads would never have been visible from the air; base camps, truck parks and cache sites simply were impossible to discover except by ground reconnaissance.

The Khe Sanh teams came to rely on those two dynamic Kingbee flyers, Cowboy and Mustachio, who retrieved recon men under any kind of fire, in any kind of weather. Mustachio flew a remarkable chopper rescue one night in mid-1966, after a recon team was hit in its overnight position and managed to escape but, burdened with several wounded, seemed certain to be caught before daylight. American Hueys could not fly in darkness, and neither should the Vietnamese H-34s, but Mustachio announced he would give it a try. Since this was almost suicidal, he flew without a copilot or door gunner. In complete darkness, Mustachio found the team and got them all out despite heavy ground fire. "How he ever did it, I don't know," Scotty Crerar said. "The chopper came out with eighty-eight holes in it and the pilot's thumb shot off."

Tragically, a few weeks later Mustachio was flying RT Nevada back to Kontum when not far from Kham Duc his helicopter fell apart at 5000 feet. The old H-34's tail, designed to pivot for storage on aircraft carriers, had come loose, swung around and chewed the helicopter to pieces in midair, ejecting its passengers and crew to a nightmarish death. In addition to Mustachio and his crew, lost was RT Nevada—Master Sergeant Ralph Reno, Staff Sergeant Donald Fawcett and their Nungs— plus an operations officer, Captain Edwin MacNamara. SOG teams recovered all the bodies except Reno's.

Three weeks later, a recon team led by Sergeant Major Harry D. Whalen—the Kontum NCOIC—inserted west of Khe Sanh. Whalen may have been the FOB sergeant major but he preferred a rucksack and a CAR-15 to a desk and in/out box.

During the third day of their mission they needed water, so they climbed down the back slope of Co Roc to a wide stream. Whelan waved over his assistant team leader, Sergeant First Class Delmer "Outlaw" Laws; and Specialist Four Donald Sain, the team radio operator. Laws and two Nungs would get water first, Whelan whispered, and he and Sain would cover them.

He and Sain stayed slightly back while the forward party began filling canteens. As Whalen leaned toward Sain to whisper to him, Sain's face exploded in a burst of AK-47 slugs. There wasn't even time to return fire—hundreds of bullets cracked the air, slapped the ground, ripped through leaves. Whalen dove off the riverbank. The Nungs and Laws jumped into the water, too, and headed downstream, away from Whalen, but there was too much fire to follow them, so he sloshed upstream as hard as he could. The NVA were everywhere, their numbers doubling every ten seconds—it must have been a company—one hundred men—swarming, leaping into the water, shouting, splashing behind him, firing at nothing and everything. Whalen saw a place where the grassy bank overhung the river, and without thinking he dove into it.

Gasping to catch his breath, Whalen pressed himself as far back into the shadow as he could and tried to stay motionless. AK-wielding gunmen sloshed past, then stopped, circled back and slowly began a detailed search, reconning here and there with a burst of bullets. Miraculously, the slugs slapped the water and ricocheted around Whalen, but not one hit him.

Whalen dared not pull his survival radio, because the enemy was all around him, just a few feet away. He wondered what had happened to Laws and the Nungs.

Then he heard the first scream. He wasn't sure if the voice was Nung or American, but it definitely was an agonized human cry, not 30 yards away. Whelan's first instinct was to rush out, CAR-15 blazing, and kill all these bastards, or at least die trying. But he paused. That's exactly what they wanted him to do—so they could kill him and wipe out the whole team. No, Whalen vowed, never.

There was a rifle shot, a pause, then a different voice cried out. Whalen realized the North Vietnamese had executed one man and begun torturing another. A few minutes later there was a second shot and a fresh agonized cry.

Whalen heard more screams—peaking, haunting cries. More NVA walked past, scanning the bank, alert, ready. A brave man, Whalen began to feel a terror he'd never before experienced; his hands and knees spasmed so that he thought the searchers surely would hear him.

Whalen waited there, motionless, until long after dark, then waded upriver. Eventually a chopper came in and got him, alone.

Up to now the North Vietnamese had been dealing with fleeting shadows that ambushed them, planted mines and called air strikes on their encampments; now they learned who these will-o'-the-wisps were. Sain's and Laws' bodies yielded maps, codes, radios, CAR-15s, everything. At last, the NVA had something concrete to study and plan countermeasures against.

Two days later, SOG inserted a body-recovery team led by Master Sergeant Billy Waugh and Major Gerald Killburn. They found Sain's body exactly where Whelan told them they would. The NVA had left it crudely booby-trapped with a hand grenade, which Waugh deactivated, then slid the young One-Two's remains into a body bag. Delmer Laws' body was not found.

At the Kontum FOB, there was a somber mixture of sympathy for

Sergeant Major Harry Whalen, who hardly had spoken, and grief over the lost men, Delmer Laws and Don Sain. No one wanted the anguish of a memorial ceremony, especially seeing how badly Whalen was taking it, but something had to be done, so the recon men just gathered at the NCO club. There were drinks, some toasts, a few funny stories retold. After hours of anecdotes and toasts, someone proposed they sing a song, a fitting one for lost companions, fine Green Beret recon men who'd given their all. It was a sort of taps, a closure; everyone in the club stood and sang, slow and sad. The song was "Hey, Blue."

> I had a dog and his name was Blue.
> Bet you five dollars,
> He's a good dog, too.
> Hey, Blue,
> You're a good dog, you.

Several succeeding verses recalled Old Blue's life, loyalty and companionship, qualities like those that bonded the recon men to each other. Then Old Blue died, and in that final verse, instead of calling the dog's name over his grave, all those gathered substituted the names of their lost comrades and sang sadly:

> Sain and Laws and Fawcett, too.
> And Reno, Thorne and MacNamara, too.
> Hey, friends,
> You were good guys, you.

As the war continued and SOG losses mounted, verse after verse of names were added, which, like an oral history, reminded succeeding rotations of recon men who had gone before them. It was SOG's most solemn tradition.

The night they sang "Hey, Blue" to Laws and Sain, people eventually wandered away, some to be alone and think, others to prepare for missions and a few to lose themselves in drink. Sergeant Major Whalen followed the last course.

To the great disappointment of those who admired him, Whalen's drinking did not stop. "One of the things that got to him was that Charlie [the NVA] knew he was in the area, and they kept kicking these guys to make them scream and holler," recalled J. D. Bath. "But he was a super guy and I really thought the world of him."

Whalen also bore the onus as the first One-Zero to leave a man behind, creating a monumental case of survivor's guilt. If someone had called him a coward, Whalen could have beaten hell out of him and been done with it. But how do you fight yourself?

Each night Whalen would sit at the bar in the club, brooding, and get drunker and drunker, then with no warning, push his stool over backward, knocking himself senseless.

No one knew what to do. In a burst of levity, the recon guys nicknamed him "Crash" and tried to joke him into stopping. But Whalen kept drinking himself into oblivion.

This was a fine soldier, loved by everyone, but nothing could stop those haunting screams in his head. Then one night, as Crash slid onto his bar stool, some recon NCOs crowded around him and before Whalen could stop them, they'd snapped a Huey seat belt to the stool and to two newly installed clips on the bar so, as one of the NCOs recalls, "he'd get whiplash, but he wouldn't hit that floor." Tragically, though, Whalen's drinking still did not stop. "He carried those two guys in his rucksack for a long time," J. D. Bath said regretfully.

The U.S. government could not tell the families the truth of where Sain and Laws had died. The families were only told that their loved ones had died in South Vietnam, a small lie that planted the seeds of postwar MIA conspiracy claims. "The sad thing about losing anybody over there," said a later Chief SOG, Colonel Steve Cavanaugh, "was that you never could give credit to those people for what they were really doing. Those were bold and heroic operations and you could never give credit for those kinds of things. You could write them up for a Silver Star or DSC [Distinguished Service Cross] or something like that and you had to waffle around it and it sounded like they'd gone out on a cookie bake of some kind—'Lost on a reconnaissance mission in South Vietnam.'" Official accounts so diminished SOG's true dangers that most awards were at least one degree below their legitimate level.

The same security concerns prohibited distributing SOG's most critical intelligence for fear the source and means might be revealed, but when he thought American lives were at stake, Scotty Crerar followed his conscience. "A couple of times we violated our directions and didn't report it [intelligence] only to Saigon; we told the American units who were on the friendly side of the border, 'Hey, there is some big stuff right across the fence.'"

There were other problems. "Our teams would be out on the Cambodian border and just getting the hell shot out of them," recalled a senior SOG officer, but they couldn't call upon regular Army units for help. By the time SOG intelligence was filtered through all the necessary clearance and an American division completed its extensive planning and logistics preparations, the NVA were long gone. Colonel Blackburn once quipped to the 1st Division commander, "It's strange as hell. Your guys can't find the enemy and we can't get rid of them."

Eventually SOG solved its intelligence distribution problem by creating a mythical Loatian partisan organization, the FGU or "Friendly Guerrilla Unit," to which Shining Brass information could be attributed. Once scoured of clues to its true origin (sterilized) and routed through MACV, the FGU information was widely distributed to American units with no mention of SOG.

In the fall of 1966, Lieutenant General Lewis W. Walt, III Marine Amphibious Force commander, requested SOG's special recon help in and near the DMZ. During the just-completed Operation Hastings, the Marines had pushed two NVA divisions back toward the DMZ, then occupied two dominating positions just south of there, Con Thien and a hill mass dubbed the Rockpile.

These two outposts attracted masses of NVA and continuing artillery fire from the DMZ. There was great uncertainty about where the two NVA divisions had gone, and some evidence the enemy was massing to seize South Vietnam's two northernmost provinces. The hills around Khe Sanh and the DMZ were so alive that Marine recon teams found it impossible to stay on the ground. Was the enemy massing, falling back, reinforcing, what? And where was his artillery? General Walt needed to know.

When SOG's recon teams packed their rucksacks to go north and support the Marines, they carried along a new item—wiretap devices. Over the past year, SOG teams had discovered dozens of enemy telephone lines along roads and trails, but until now they didn't have wiretaps and cassette recorders. These taps could produce intelligence of inestimable value because landlines often carried messages too sensitive to transmit by radio—plus they might yield important clues for decrypting radio messages.

However, the NVA's ability to detect taps electronically was so great that, at least initially, any team that planted a tap was living on borrowed time. Eventually, the CIA supplied induction tap devices, which used rubber-coated pads over the wire to glean a recordable signal from its electrical field. The CIA induction wiretap was not electronically detectable.

Yet these operations remained fraught with hazard, because a landline phone system meant an NVA regiment or division was in the vicinity.

Wiretaps began with SOG's USMC support missions that fall of 1966, when General Walt's staff selected seventeen targets in the DMZ and adjacent areas in Laos. The first three SOG teams averaged less than three days on the ground, and two had to shoot their way out. The next three teams managed to avoid contact for just two and a half days; then all three fought quick engagements and escaped, with one team bringing back a POW.

On 28 September, an aggressive enemy force nearly overran a team near Khe Sanh, splitting the Americans and Nungs; Staff Sergeant Danny Taylor and two Nungs were never seen again.

Five days later, Recon Teams Colorado and Arizona were inserted by Marine helicopters near Khe Sanh. RT Colorado, with Sergeants Ted Braden, Jim Hetrick and J. D. Bath, went in first, just north of the Ben Hai River on the western end of the DMZ.

The choppers went back, picked up Master Sergeants Ray Echevarria and Jim Jones, One-Zero and One-One, plus Staff Sergeant Eddie Williams, One-Two, along with their Nungs, and again flew north, this time just 7 miles. Riding with a Covey FAC overhead was Sergeant Major Paul Darcy.

The CH-46 Sea Knight carrying Arizona made it safely into the LZ and had just lifted away when the enemy opened fire from 360 degrees, all the way around the LZ. Arizona had landed amid an entrenched NVA unit.

Heavy fire pinned down the team and kept the Marine helicopters at bay, with one bird taking fifteen hits. Just 15 miles away, RT Colorado radio operator Jim Hetrick heard Echevarria's voice on the radio screaming, "Come and get us! You've got to come and get us!" Despite air strikes around them the heavy enemy fire couldn't be suppressed.

Finally RT Arizona One-Zero Echevarria's voice came back, calm. "That's it, guys," he announced. "It's all over. Don't come in. You haven't got a chance." Echevarria said they would never get out. "When I quit talking, put the shit right on us," he told Covey Rider Darcy.

Minutes later U.S fighter-bombers dumped their bomb loads across RT Arizona's position. There were no further radio transmissions. Outnumbered almost one hundred to one, the team had been swallowed whole, the first entire SOG team lost to the enemy. Of the seven helicopters that tried to retrieve RT Arizona, six were hit, as was an A-1 Skyraider. Amazingly, none was shot down.

Three days later, RT Arizona's Yard interpreter was extracted, alive. He told debriefers he had evaded capture with the team One-Two, Staff Sergeant Eddie Williams, after Echevarria and Jones were mortally wounded. Williams had taken an AK-47 bullet through his thigh and sapped his strength climbing a cliff, after which he took shelter in a cave and told the interpreter to get help. A few minutes later the interpreter heard AK fire and explosions near the cave, then total silence.

A month later, an enemy POW told interrogators he'd seen a black man with a wounded thigh, hands tied behind his back and a noose around his neck, being led through villages for public mockery until he was too ill to walk. Then he was executed.

Only three months had passed since recon men first gathered to sing "Hey, Blue" and already its final verse was crammed with names—Thorne, Laws, Sain, Reno, MacNamara, Fawcett, Taylor, Echevarria, Jones and Williams—and 1966 was far from over.

Meanwhile, RT Colorado's mission had been a resounding success. Not only did the team uncover several NVA base camps, but they emplaced SOG's first wiretap and brought back seven cassettes of North Vietnamese phone conversations.

SOG wiretaps soon were recognized as incomparable intelligence sources. And despite the dramatic losses of recon men, SOG One-Zeroes were winning more than they were losing, particularly two who seemed to be able to pull off anything, Master Sergeants Jerry Wareing and Dick Meadows. General Westmoreland was so impressed by both that he gave them direct commissions and cited them by name in his memoirs.

Under Wareing, RT Ohio had a recurring problem: "Wareing's team quit en masse every time he came back," Major Scotty Crerar said. "He did such hell-raising things that they would quit."

Several times RT Ohio bumped into enemy right on their insert LZ, but instead of asking to be extracted to land elsewhere, Wareing fought his way through. "Wareing pulled that a couple of times," Crerar reports. "Good instincts; he pulled it off."

A man of death-defying audacity, Wareing brought back almost a dozen enemy prisoners from Laos, a record bettered only by RT Iowa One-Zero Dick Meadows.

They were a study in contrasts. Where Wareing was instinctive, Meadows was methodical. "Meadows did everything meticulously, everything was rehearsed. You could have taken a film of [his] mission preparation and used it as a training film," Major Crerar recalled.

When he came to Shining Brass in 1966, Meadows had been a professional soldier nineteen years, though he was only thirty-four. Born in a dirt-floor moonshiner's cabin in West Virginia, Meadows had lied about his age to become a fifteen-year-old paratrooper in 1947, then so distinguished himself in Korea that he was that war's youngest master sergeant.

Before an operation, Meadows would build a terrain map in the dirt, then have his whole team—Americans and Nungs—memorize the prominent features, all the LZs, streams and rally points. Then they'd take turns reciting the plan and pointing to sites in the model. "He would work them hard," Crerar said.

Much of Meadows' reputation came from his ability to capture prisoners; he held SOG's record—thirteen POWs snatched from behind enemy lines.

Despite his great emphasis on planning, though, Meadows could act with boldness when it was needed. He once had RT Iowa hidden beside a trail when five NVA strolled up and stopped right there for lunch. Meadows emerged and announced, "You are now POWs." Three of the NVA started for their AKs and Meadows shot all three dead instantly. The other two proved compliant.

Meadows also had a knack for being in the right place to make history. In 1966 he proved North Vietnamese Prime Minister Pham Van Dong a flagrant liar. Early that year, Pham adamantly insisted not a single North Vietnamese soldier was fighting in South Vietnam.

Lying beside Laotian Highway 110E, RT Iowa was watching North Vietnamese soldiers and porters file past when their One-Zero decided to take a chance. At great personal risk, Meadows pulled a Pen-EE camera from his pocket, crawled forward and snapped a whole roll of photos from such close range that the clicking shutter almost got him killed.

Then Meadows and his One-One, Chuck Kearns, crawled back beyond enemy earshot and Meadows decided on an even more dangerous gambit; in Kearns' rucksack was his personal 8mm motion-picture camera, which he'd brought along on a lark. Meadows crawled perilously close to the highway and began rolling. He shot a few perfectly exposed frames of each man who came into his viewfinder. For an hour Meadows lay there and recorded hundreds of heavily armed North Vietnamese marching alongside porters toting military supplies.

The color film was rushed to Washington. Chief SOG Colonel Jack Singlaub, who had taken over from Colonel Don Blackburn in April 1966, had Meadows personally present his findings to General Westmoreland, who could not help but praise Meadows and SOG.

Meadows' footage was shown before a closed-door briefing of select members of Congress who needed convincing that Hanoi was lying about its involvement in South Vietnam.

A few months later, Meadows went into a heavily patrolled area west of Khe Sanh and penetrated an enemy cache containing new artillery pieces and fire-control equipment. The howitzers were too big to carry back, so he photographed them, then stripped them of sights.

Again Chief SOG had Meadows brief General Westmoreland. The intense young master sergeant presented Westmoreland a souvenir: A Soviet-made artillery sight from the Laotian cache. As General Westmoreland noted in his memoirs, it was such evidence "which finally prompted the State Department to relax its restrictions on firing into the DMZ."

Deeply impressed by the sincere, quiet-spoken Green Beret, Westmoreland recommended Meadows for a battlefield commission, promoting him to the rank of captain.

It was only logical that Chief SOG chose Dick Meadows to lead SOG's first American operation into the heartland of North Vietnam.

4

CODE NAME BRIGHT LIGHT

Lieutenant Dean Woods' crippled A-1 Skyraider had limped within sight of the South China Sea, but the U.S. Navy pilot couldn't squeeze another mile out of her. Woods reached for the yellow handle between his legs and pressed himself back tight and one tug later he was flying in space, his ejection seat falling away.

For miles around, any North Vietnamese soldier could see Woods' propeller-driven Skyraider plunge and explode as his parachute drifted west into the hills.

The tree in which Lieutenant Woods landed was on a heavily jungled ridgeline about halfway between Vinh and Hanoi and almost 30 miles inland, overlooking rice paddies and dikes and villages. Lieutenant Woods realized he was between the two bomb-pocked highways that carried supplies from Haiphong's docks to the Mu Gia Pass and the Ho Chi Minh Trail. Both roads, he knew, would be crawling with troops; only about 15 miles away was the provincial capital, Thanh Hoa, which was certain to have a large garrison.

Woods turned on his emergency radio but the failing light told him he would see no rescue this day, 12 October 1966, so he put some distance between himself and his telltale chute draped in the tree and found a place to hide for the night.

It looked hopeful the next day. Escorted by A-1 Skyraiders and high-flying Navy F-4 Phantoms, a Sikorsky SH-3C Sea King helicopter whirred above the ridgeline until, at last, the crew chief could see Woods waving his arms beneath the heavy canopy. While the A-1s strafed approaching enemy patrols, the hovering Sea King lowered an extraction rig from its winch, but the harness kept snagging in the trees. By the time it was clear this would not work, there was not enough station time left to talk Woods to an open area where the helicopter could land, nor enough daylight to fly out to sea, refuel and return.

They wished him good luck until the next day. But the next day heavy fog and clouds blanketed the jungle around the Navy pilot, making rescue impossible, although a Navy plane communicated with him. All day, aircraft stood by, but the weather never broke.

Out in the South China Sea, Seventh Fleet Commander Admiral Leroy Johnson decided he could not just stand by with one of his men in such jeopardy. That night, Admiral Johnson cabled General Westmoreland in Saigon, requesting a small force to land in North Vietnam, search for the young aviator and fight through any enemy that tried to interfere.

Westmoreland phoned Chief SOG Colonel Singlaub. While Singlaub made preparations, political approval was sought, reportedly all the way to President Johnson. With that approval, Chief SOG called upon the best man he could imagine to lead the mission, One-Zero Dick Meadows.

It was midnight by the time a Navy C-2 Greyhound transport delivered Meadows and his reinforced RT Iowa to the heaving deck of the USS Intrepid, and it was just as well since the thirteen heavily armed SOG men did not want to arouse unwanted speculation.

This was the first mission under the code name Bright Light—top-secret rescues of Americans from behind enemy lines—ever to be attempted in North Vietnam. But once again the weather refused to cooperate, and the SOG men could do little more than pace and hope for a break. It did not come.

Beneath the shielding cloud cover, the North Vietnamese continued searching for Lieutenant Woods, who was now suffering through his third day without food. Enough time had passed that the NVA had trucked in additional 37mm and 57mm antiaircraft guns to engage

American rescue helicopters when they came, as the enemy knew they would. Several companies of NVA had arrived to reinforce the local militia.

The next morning the clouds scattered, and just before dawn a pair of Navy Sea King helicopters lifted from the *Intrepid*'s deck with Meadows and RT Iowa aboard. As the North Vietnamese coast took shape, there was an uncomfortable realization that ahead was a modern air-defense system whose radars already were tracking their approach and alerting antiaircraft units and ground forces who'd had four days to prepare for them.

When the helicopters crossed the coast, the sky exploded with antiaircraft shell bursts, but the Navy pilots expertly weaved between the worst of it. Minutes later they could see the heavily forested ridge where that very moment the NVA were converging on the downed flyer. After several false insertions to confuse the enemy, one Sea King inserted RT Iowa about 800 yards from Lieutenant Woods' hiding place. Meadows made a beeline for the ridge.

Lieutenant Woods could hear buzzing planes and helicopters and the booming of antiaircraft guns, but his greatest concerns were more immediate: Brush was breaking nearby, and he could hear shouts of excited soldiers.

Meadows and his men moved fast and had closed to a few hundred yards when they received a sickening radio report: The Navy pilot was captured. Had they traveled 500 miles only to come up 200 yards short? "A cautious soldier would have taken his men to the nearest extraction point and departed enemy territory," Colonel Singlaub says. "But Meadows was not overly cautious."

Coming upon a major trail, Meadows decided to set up an ambush and capture a prisoner. A few moments later an NVA officer and three enlisted men walked up, alert, still searching for Woods, apparently unaware he'd been captured.

Perhaps they expected a lone, injured pilot with just a pistol. They were astonished when Meadows stepped from the dense foliage and leveled his AK-47, calling a friendly good morning. As one, they went for their guns, but Meadows shot first, killing all four in one blur. While his men searched the bodies, Meadows radioed for an exfil, and soon they were flying away, although their helicopter was sprayed by gunfire and eventually had to ditch near an American destroyer. From this, their first Bright Light mission, every SOG man made it out.*

It could be said Bright Light was Colonel Harry "Heinie" Aderholt's personal creation. Six months earlier, USAF General Hunter Harris, Pacific Air Force commander, had challenged the experienced special operations officer to develop a concept: What to do *after* a Search and Rescue (SAR) effort came up empty-handed and one or more Americans were still evading, missing or taken prisoner. A recent Air Force study had found that 47 percent of all failed SARs resulted from slow reaction time by helicopters. If a rescue bird could reach a downed airman within fifteen minutes, the chances of rescue were good, but if retrieval took more than thirty minutes, the downed airman's chances fell precipitously.

Colonel Aderholt decided a single office should handle all post-SAR responsibilities, and it should be in SOG since this was the only joint service agency with assets and authorization to operate secretly throughout Southeast Asia. The Joint Chiefs agreed and, on 16 September 1966, authorized Aderholt to head SOG's OPS-80 section, to track MIAs, locate prison camps, attempt rescues and even offer bribes and ransoms to get Americans released. Because OPS-80 needed to coordinate with many non-SOG entities, it would operate behind its own special cover, the Joint Personnel Recovery Center (JPRC), a supposed staff section in MACV.

More than anything, though, Aderholt wanted to raid POW camps and liberate Americans.

The very day Dick Meadows landed in North Vietnam, a teenage Viet Cong defector had offered to help SOG plan its first JPRC Bright Light raid. The seventeen-year-old defector had emerged from the swampy forest of the Mekong Delta on 30 August and told U.S. interrogators his camp held an American POW. When questioned, he seemed to recognize the name "Jackson." USAF Captain Carl E. Jackson had been MIA since his C-123 was downed southwest of Saigon on 27 June 1965.

---

*After the war, Meadows met Lieutenant Woods, who'd spent six years as a POW, and presented him with the Tokarev pistol captured from the NVA officer he'd wished good morning on the trail.

After aerial photography and even a polygraph seemed to confirm the youth's claims, the bureaucracy slowly moved forward until, at last, five weeks after he defected, SOG's Joint Personnel Recovery Center became involved. Working alongside Bull Simons' staff, Colonel Aderholt and JPRC planned a heliborne rescue for one week later, which involved everyone from the IV Corps senior adviser to the Seventh Air Force commander and eight different sections of the MACV staff. Colonel Aderholt felt overwhelmed by bureaucracy.

Meanwhile, in Kontum, Operation Crimson Tide, a company-size rescue, was in preparation. SOG headquarters appointed a special mission commander, Captain Frank Jaks, who as a teenager in his native Czechoslovakia had been an anti-Nazi resistance fighter. After the Communists seized power in 1948, Jaks came West and, under the 1952 Lodge Act, which offered U.S. citizenship to 12,000 East European refugees for enlisting in the American Army, he signed up and went into Special Forces. He served his first Vietnam tour in 1963, earning one of the war's earliest Purple Hearts, and was now on his second tour.

Short of Green Beret leaders for his third Nung platoon, Jaks took on two volunteers for the mission, Sergeant First Class Charles Vessels, a former recon man, and Sergeant First Class Fred "Huckleberry" Lewis, a Special Forces engineer who had been constructing the SOG base at Kontum. Friendly and easygoing, Huckleberry had a country way about him, and with an old straw hat propped above his freckled face, he needed just a piece of straw dangling from his teeth to perfectly impersonate the Twain character. Because the camp was about finished, at last Huckleberry could do what he'd come to SOG for in the first place—fight—and what better operation than rescuing an American POW?

Early on 18 October, Jaks' raiding company and the VC defector were at the Kontum airfield, but the C-130 assigned to airlift them was delayed. When finally they landed at Soc Trang, the staging base in the Mekong Delta where they married up with their lift helicopters, they were four hours late.

There was no real briefing. During a fast open-air chat, an American IV Corps adviser showed Jaks a map of the woodline containing the POW camp, 90 miles north of Vietnam's southern tip. The colonel said it would be lightly guarded by a dozen men at most, with no other enemy units nearby, and estimated they would be in and out in twenty minutes. The colonel offered no real intelligence, just suppositions so limited that Jaks felt "it was almost going in blind."

Jaks had an uneasy feeling. Six weeks had passed since the young VC had defected, and it seemed everybody and his brother knew about the rescue mission. On a hunch, Jaks decided to carry a double load of ammunition. It was a wise decision.

In most raids it would have been preferable to land atop or as close as possible to the objective, but fearing an ambush, Jaks elected to land all three platoons, aboard twelve Hueys, on a large LZ about 500 yards away. Only a shallow canal and thin brush stood between the LZ and the camp, and they could cover that in minutes.

Hurriedly, Jaks boarded his men, and the three parallel lines of four Hueys each lifted away and turned south. Twenty minutes later the Hueys descended, but just before reaching the LZ, one string of four birds, carrying Huckleberry, Vessels and the third platoon, shifted east. Apparently the Huey commander found the LZ too small to land all twelve helicopters simultaneously, and the third Huey formation set down across the canal, in another LZ, perfectly located at the edge of the camp.

As Jaks and his two platoons landed, hellacious fire erupted 500 yards away, at the other LZ, but there was fire here, too, so he could do little but organize his first and second platoons and hope the best for the third platoon.

Jaks couldn't raise Vessels or Lewis on the radio.

The Huey carrying Huckleberry Lewis and a squad of Nungs, had flown into the intersecting fire of .50-caliber machine guns; the affable Green Beret fell from the aircraft, mortally wounded, and the bird crashed.

The other Hueys disgorged their passengers and flew clear but SFC Vessels and his Nungs came under intense small-arms fire. Jaks heard a dozen mortar tubes coughing rounds as fast as they could be dropped, the shells falling viciously on the other side of the canal. But Jaks and his two platoons were pinned down.

There should have been slow-flying A-1 Skyraiders overhead, but inexplicably the Air Force sent F-100 Super Sabre jets, and they were worse than no support, trying to drop heavy bombs beneath the low cloud cover. When the bombs hit close enough to be effective, they hit friendlies. By the time Skyraiders finally arrived it was too late for the third platoon. And the sun was setting.

Jaks and his two platoons withstood probing attacks all night and at dawn finally fought their way across the canal. Most of the enemy had fled. They found Huckleberry Lewis and clusters of Nungs lying dead on the LZ. Apparently Charlie Vessels had gathered the last of the Nungs and made a final stand in a little cemetery; he was found among another cluster of bodies. The entire third platoon had been killed or seriously wounded.

Jaks later learned Lewis and Vessels and their forty Nungs had landed in front of two full Viet Cong battalions, nearly one thousand enemy, supported by mortars and heavy machine guns. "And all we had was carbines," said Jaks.

Perhaps the family and friends of Captain Carl Jackson—who have never heard of SOG's top-secret raid—will appreciate the sacrifices made to try to rescue him. He remains MIA.

After Jaks' men returned to Kontum, the superstitious Nungs refused to set foot in the annihilated platoon's barracks; its ghostly silence stood as a haunting testament to the consequences of faulty intelligence. Several Green Berets poured kerosene on that empty structure, tossed a match and watched the flames build. Then they joined the rest of the men in the NCO club for toasts to Lewis and Vessels and a rendition of "Hey, Blue." In honor of the Twainsian character whose hands had helped construct it—Fred "Huckleberry" Lewis—the club that night was christened the Huckleberry Inn.

Only a week later, SOG realized its first Bright Light success, almost an act of divine redress, because the successful mission was led by Captain Frank Jaks. A SOG Bird Dog spotter plane flying deep in Laos saw an F-105 Thunderchief fall from the sky and a parachute drift to earth. The fighter-bomber had been hit by antiaircraft fire over North Vietnam.

A SOG officer in the Bird Dog, Major Frank Sova, radioed the Dak To launch site, "I can see the parachute and I'm closing in on it. I see him landing, he's out of the chute. And he's into the bushes. Can you crank something up and go get him?"

The officer in charge at Dak To, Captain Jaks, plotted the downed pilot's location—70 miles away, beyond the Ho Chi Minh Trail, in an area infested with NVA. Worst of all, the location was well beyond the maximum range of the Hueys.

Jaks huddled with his Huey crews and challenged them to devise some means to stretch their helicopters' range. In a display of ingenuity, the crew chiefs loaded 55-gallon fuel drums and a hand pump aboard one bird, so they could land on the way back—God knows where in Laos—refuel and return to Vietnam.

The sun was low on the horizon when the Hueys took off. By the time they spotted the flyer's pen flares arcing in the near darkness, they could see hundreds of NVA closing in on him.

Sergeant First Class Luke "Grady" Nance, Jr., a Special Forces medic aboard one Huey, saw NVA only 100 yards away when the downed pilot leaped aboard. "When he got in that helicopter, I'll tell you, he was one happy fella," Nance says. The pilot looked around in awe and shouted, "Gosh, I didn't know we had Army aviation out here." He was told to forget what he'd seen.

Halfway back to Vietnam, the Hueys turned on their landing lights, settled into a grassy field somewhere in Laos, rolled out the 55-gallon drums, pumped like crazy, then off they went. When Jaks put the rescued pilot on a C-130 to Saigon, "he was as happy as could be." Jaks was too. Colonel Aderholt notes with pride, "That was the first-ever night pickup of a downed pilot."

Few USAF and Navy aviators were aware SOG teams would go into Laos and North Vietnam after them. To preserve any chance of success, Bright Light had to be an unadvertised service, and it remained one of the best-kept secrets of the war.

Declassified records don't clearly disclose how many downed aviators saw SOG teams materialize like guardian angels to rescue them from behind enemy lines. My best estimate is several dozen, and double that if you add aircrew who were downed and rescued while supporting SOG operations. There was an equal number of body recoveries, which, while no occasion for joy, at least gave families positive proof and something to bury, providing at least a degree of mercy.

Large numbers of NVA troops and heavy antiaircraft fire was typical for Laotian Bright Lights, but the North Vietnam ones were always worse, given the greater distances and sophistication of enemy defenses, which at times included SAMs and MiGs. One North Vietnam Bright Light, led by Sergeant First Class Glen Lane, was within sight of Hanoi when another SOG man hollered to Robert "Squirrel" Sprouse, "What would you do if you saw a MiG right now?"

"Well, I'd shit," Squirrel hollered back, according to Staff Sergeant Robert "Spider" Parks, another volunteer. The other man pointed. "Well, you'd better start shittin', because there's a MiG." Fortunately, the MiG was more interested in their fighter escort than in the helicopter. Despite the Communist fighter, they pressed on to where the downed pilot had been evading, but found such heavy ground fire that the CH-3 Jolly Green couldn't land.

Marauding MiGs also aborted a North Vietnam Bright Light for Staff Sergeant Eulis Presley's recon team, which was attempting to reach the Red River Valley. Every time they entered North Vietnamese airspace, they had to turn back because MiG-21s came up to intercept them.

In this case, as in many Bright Lights, tactical problems arose because time lags delayed insertion. JPRC remedied this somewhat by obtaining SOG recon teams for one-week Bright Light duty, literally "strip alert" since they were packed and ready to go, twenty-four hours a day, within 50 feet of an airstrip where Jolly Green helicopters or a C-130 would pick them up. The only notice team members got was their One-Zero walking out of the operations shed and shouting, "Grab your shit, let's go!"

Teams on Bright Light duty usually "went heavy," bringing along every team member and switching some CAR-15s for M-60 machine guns and even a 60mm mortar. Beyond additional ammunition, they carried extra first-aid gear, rappeling harnesses and helicopter extraction rigs. While these teams might be employed for any kind of Bright Light rescue, most often they went after downed airmen or to look for missing SOG men.

Bright Lights were the most consistently dangerous SOG missions, not just because teams went behind enemy lines into an area bristling with antiaircraft guns, but because the enemy could lie in ambush for them. The enemy often turned on a captured pilot's survival radio's beeper or laid out his marker panel to draw rescue aircraft into a trap. In some cases, a North Vietnamese soldier would don a captured pilot's flight suit and helmet, fire pen flares and wave, then collapse. When a rescue helicopter came in to get him, it was blown to bits by antitank rockets. In several instances SOG Bright Lights were aborted at the last minute when a downed pilot managed to slip an odd word or two into his radio conversation, tipping off his rescuers that he was in enemy hands.

Sergeant Steve "Jade" Keever, who rappeled from a hovering Huey into thick Cambodian jungle above a crashed aircraft, gives some sense of what Bright Light men faced: "[When you] get out on the skids of a helicopter, knowing that you're going to rappel down and you cannot see anything but the tops of trees—you have no idea what's down at the bottom of those trees or underneath that canopy waiting for you." But there was no option.

Once the men were on the ground, heavy antiaircraft fire might drive away the helicopters. A Green Beret medic who rappeled onto a crash site tied his rope to a tree to prevent the Huey's departure—which was only sick humor, since the crew chief could cut the line in a second.

Helping airmen downed in North Vietnam remained a subject of unending SOG planning, since only SOG among U.S. agencies had assets in North Vietnam—its agent teams—as well as the only clandestine cargo plane flights into the North's interior.

SOG's capabilities in North Vietnam had been expanding apace with the rest of the war. By 1966, SOG's Nationalist Chinese aviators of the First Flight Detachment were penetrating North Vietnam's night sky almost monthly. In addition to parachuting supplies and reinforcements to the five established agent teams, First Flight had inserted another three teams. Even the Kingbees got into the act, in November 1965, when they landed Team *Romeo* in the southern panhandle, near Mu Gia Pass. The four new agent teams plus the five surviving ex-CIA teams—*Bell, Easy, Remus, Tourbillon* and the singleton, *Ares*—gave SOG nine teams and 112 agents in the enemy's heartland.

SOG had reinforced all the old CIA teams except *Ares,* with some so expanded that they were almost small platoons. SOG was planning to reinforce *Ares* by sea, the same way he'd been infiltrated nearly five years earlier, but using high-speed Nasty boats.

During the three years the CIA managed the agent team program, eighteen of twenty-three teams were lost, mostly upon landing; by contrast, excluding the malingerers SOG purposely dumped into North

Vietnam in the spring of 1964, SOG had lost not one team, although a few individual team members had been lost in parachute accidents or clashes with NVA patrols. It was an impressive turnaround.

But could SOG really entrust these teams with a sensitive and dangerous task like Bright Light? Beyond concerns that some teams might have been captured and "doubled," there were serious doubts that agent teams had the mettle for such work.

SOG sought authority to establish a resistance movement in North Vietnam and combine it with a SAFE areas program. SAFE was the acronym for Selected Areas for Evasion, and the program evolved from a Strategic Air Command plan to recover nuclear bomber crews from remote regions of the USSR, in turn an idea not without precedent.

During World War II, the American OSS and British Special Operations Executive (SOE), working with Tito's guerrillas, maintained enclaves deep in Nazi-occupied Yugoslavia for bailouts and emergency landings. Likewise, during the Korean War the CIA had guerrilla bands on many offshore islands where crippled planes could ditch and fliers could bail out.

SOG wanted similar SAFE areas west and north of Hanoi, where pilots could bail out and receive medical aid, food and protection, then be retrieved by helicopters from Laos. When properly armed and supported by tac air, SOG's SAFE area guerrillas could defend their zone; if confronted by a powerful force, they'd just melt away.

But for political reasons, SOG was denied the authority to raise a North Vietnam resistance movement, even though it would have saved some downed pilots. Similar proposals for SAFE areas in Laos, too, were rejected by the U.S. ambassador in Vientiane, William Sullivan.

SOG still did what it could to enhance the survival chances of downed Americans. One major contribution was running special recon missions along the Laos–North Vietnam border to identify escape routes. During one such mission lasting nineteen days, Sergeant First Class Bob Howard explored small east-west valleys to find out-of-the-way mountain passes through which U.S. evadees in North Vietnam's panhandle could escape safely into Laos.

SOG also sought to create SAFE areas in its own assigned slice of Laos—the 12 miles adjacent to South Vietnam—where many U.S. planes were shot down while bombing the Ho Chi Minh Trail. However, nearly every tribal village in the area had been long abandoned, their Kha and Katu inhabitants fleeing westward to avoid impressment as NVA road repair crews and porters.

Another SOG Bright Light contribution came via its unique USAF transport unit, the 90th Special Operations Squadron (SOS), whose MC-130s were the war's only aircraft outfitted with the Fulton Recovery System (Skyhook).

Assigned directly to SOG, the 90th SOS MC-130s were the most advanced transport planes in the world, with secret electronic countermeasures and computerized navigation instruments for penetrating heavy antiaircraft threat areas. As well, the 90th SOS planes employed radically new, top-secret night-viewing sensors, Forward-Looking Infrared (FLIR), that rendered the darkest night daylight-clear on a TV screen, and even could see through rain or fog and into foliage.

A SOG MC-130 was distinguished by its black-and-dark-green paint job, removable U.S. insignia, and a 20-foot Fulton Skyhook yoke swung back against its nose; wherever these black planes appeared, real spook stuff was under way. Nicknamed "Blackbirds," the SOG MC-130s typically taxied to some out-of-the-way airfield corner to pick up troops packing strange submachine guns or unload men in North Vietnamese uniforms who scurried into unmarked civilian vans and sped away.

The 90th SOS had arrived in Nha Trang, South Vietnam, in December 1966, from Ching Chuan Kong AFB, Taiwan, where they'd been based for several years.*

The 90th SOS led a secret double life, in daytime flying seemingly routine transport missions in South Vietnam and at night airdropping supplies to agent teams in North Vietnam, or parachuting SOG recon teams along the Ho Chi Minh Trail. By 1967 the 90th SOS Blackbirds were logging four night resupply flights into North Vietnam each month. "If they went down in North Vietnam," one 90th SOS veteran recalled, "the story they were to tell was that they had equipment malfunctioning, which resulted in a navigational error." To give this credibility, the Blackbirds carried phony flight plans, although it would have made little difference to the North Vietnamese.

The 90th SOS worked closely with SOG's Nationalist Chinese–flown

*The unit arrived as the 15th Special Operations Squadron.

First Flight planes, dividing these clandestine flights among them.

Despite their sophisticated navigation aids and electronic counter-measures, a SOG navigator said, their success resulted from careful route planning and meticulous navigation, while the electronic wizardry was just gravy. "I never felt in any particular danger," Colonel Don James, a Blackbird pilot, reported, although the North bristled with antiaircraft guns, SAMs and MiGs. But those large, lumbering C-130s were not exactly nimble fighters, and any penetration of North Vietnam was hardly a casual thing. Unlike SOG's First Flight Detachment, the 90th SOS would not fly North Vietnam's skies without loss.

But it was the amazing Fulton Skyhook that gave the Blackbirds a special role in Bright Light operations. In the final scene of the James Bond thriller *Thunderball,* a Skyhook-equipped plane lifted Bond and a female companion from a rubber raft. This was exactly what Skyhook had been conceived to do: exfiltrate people from a spot where no airplane could land. To accomplish this, a special canister was dropped from the Blackbird, containing a balloon, two tanks of helium, a 1500-foot cable and attached combination suit/harness. It took about fifteen minutes to don the suit, inflate the helium balloon and get the cable up; meanwhile, the C-130 swung forward its nose-mounted, hydraulically operated 20-foot yoke, which formed a wide V-shaped jaw. The pilot flew that jaw right into the cable beneath the balloon—which broke away—snatching up the passenger at 125 mph. The recovered man was then winched into the C-130's tailgate. It was like bungee jumping in reverse.

Cofunded by the CIA for agent extracts, and by the Strategic Air Command to lift pilots from SAFE areas in the USSR, the Fulton Recovery System was designed by Robert E. Fulton, Jr., descendant several times removed of *the* Robert Fulton who had invented the world's first practical steamboat.

Skyhook had been used in the real world in several CIA operations prior to its arrival at SOG. In one, a Soviet military detachment had been operating a meteorological station on the Arctic ice cap but was suddenly withdrawn when that part of it broke away as an iceberg, leaving behind their sensors and instruments. The CIA parachuted in a two-man team to recover the gear, but the iceberg began breaking up before a ship could reach them. At the last possible moment the CIA's air branch airdropped Skyhook kits and snatched the men out with a Fulton-rigged B-17.

What was it like accelerating to 125 mph in one second? USAF Colonel Bill Page, SOG's senior air staffer, extracted for a demonstration, found it "a pretty good thrill." SOG's most distinguished Skyhook passenger was Chief SOG Colonel Jack Singlaub, the first man to be extracted in-country when the MC-130s arrived. The pickup went perfectly. "The only thing I regretted was I hadn't told the pilot where to fly after he had me dangling out behind," Singlaub recalled. "I could see that we were flying over War Zone D, not more than a thousand feet up—the most heavily enemy-populated part of all South Vietnam."

Skyhook was best suited for clandestine extracts, not for lifting people away under heavy antiaircraft fire or with hostile ground forces pursuing them. "To get a guy out of somewhere with a Fulton Recovery System took a lot of planning," explains former SOG Blackbird pilot Colonel James. "He had to be in an area where he could put this balloon up, which would alert everybody around him."

Colonel Bill Page agrees, adding, "It was almost impossible to use because by the time you fly over the guy on the ground, drop him the equipment, have him send the balloon up, make a big turnaround to come in and snag the balloon, my God, every bad guy in the world would be on top of you."

Despite this, SOG Blackbird crews several times braved great hazards to go after downed pilots in North Vietnam and Laos. In one case, the downed pilot had his balloon inflated but he'd forgotten to consider nearby obstacles he might hit when snatched up. It took a few moments to reposition himself, then he radioed he was ready, and the Blackbird turned in for its run just as NVA soldiers swarmed over the pilot. It was the same story each time the Blackbirds attempted such rescues.

POW rescue attempts by SOG ground forces, too, did not fare well. There were sixteen POW rescue raids in JPRC's first full year of operations, 1967, but SOG liberated just twenty ARVNs and not a single American. In each case, SOG anticipated finding Americans but discovered they'd been moved just before the raid. The failure to bring out any Americans was chalked up to bad luck and the enemy's simple security practice of moving them frequently.

But there was treachery, too, though it would not be discovered for years.

PRAIRIE FIRE

In March 1967, the code name for SOG's Laos operations, Shining Brass, was switched to Prairie Fire to confuse outsiders who'd learned its original designation.

"Prairie Fire" also was a term used by outnumbered SOG teams in danger of being overrun. When a team radioed a Covey FAC that it had a "Prairie Fire Emergency," Covey would hail the USAF airborne command post—a C-130 orbiting above Laos, called Hillsboro in daytime and Moonbeam at night—and minutes later Air Force, Navy and Marine fighters began stacking up to support the endangered team with phenomenal combat firepower.

Exorbitant as SOG's casualties became, they would have been even worse had it not been for this extraordinary air support. This high priority was obtained largely due to the persuasive efforts of SOG's third chief, Colonel Jack Singlaub. The first Chief SOG to serve a two-year tour, 1966–68, he'd spent much of his Army career in special operations. During World War II, he'd been a "Jed"—an OSS Jedburgh Team member. Jed was the most prestigious title in U.S. WW II special operations, comparable to SOG's One-Zero. The Jeds were liaison teams that parachuted into occupied France to help the resistance demolish bridges, ambush German convoys, seize prisoners and guide Allied units.

Singlaub was one of the few OSS operatives to serve in Asia, too, making a parachute jump onto Hainan Island, China, to assist in the release of American POWs just after V-J Day. Fellow Jed Bill Colby left the OSS as a major and went with the new civilian intelligence agency, the CIA, but Singlaub stayed with the Army and opted for Special Forces when it came into being.*

After World War II, Singlaub twice was loaned to the CIA for highly classified Asian operations, first in Manchuria, to run an intelligence net against Mao's Communist forces; then during the Korean War to serve with a special operations unit similar to SOG, the CIA-affiliated Joint Advisory Commission, Korea (JACK).

As the 101st Airborne Division's G-3 (operations) officer in the 1950s, the future Chief SOG earned the personal respect and friendship of his division commander, Major General William Westmoreland. In Vietnam their relationship was close enough that every Monday morning, the commander of U.S. Forces in Vietnam spent two hours at SOG headquarters being briefed personally by his old G-3.

USAF Colonel Bill Rose, a senior SOG air officer, says Singlaub didn't hesitate to criticize even three-star generals during MACV staff briefings if it was the right thing to do. "He was a ball of fire. He did a fine job," Rose said. With Westmoreland's solid support, Singlaub's emphasis could be upon new technologies and new projects. Singlaub imbued SOG with the OSS spirit of his old French Maquis days, when the Jeds had admonished, *surprise, mitraillage, évanouissement*—"surprise, machine-gun, vanish."

After doing exactly that, a 1967 SOG operation in Laos brought Singlaub into conflict with a Washington bureaucracy that did not share the Jeds' famous enthusiasm. It began when a helicopter gunship popped a few rockets at a fleeing NVA. Unknown to the gunship pilot, an enormous cache covered the whole hilltop. One rocket hit an explosives bunker which "went nuclear" with such force it almost brought the helicopter down. A hastily assembled platoon led by Master Sergeant Bill "Country" Grimes, inserted and swept up the hill. What they found was *awesome*.

Stacked under the trees were tarp-covered, 220-pound bags of rice,

*Despite a contrary official lineage, Special Forces' true precursor is the OSS.

piled five bags wide, four high, as far as they could see. They counted, calculated and—what a find!—it was 500,000 pounds, *250 tons*, enough rice to sustain an NVA division at least six weeks. When that lucky rocket hit the cache's ordnance bunker, local NVA security guards had run for their lives.

One by one, the SOG men dragged down each 220-pound burlap sack, sliced it open and dumped it out, a time-consuming task. They tried to burn the rice with diesel fuel, called A-1s to napalm it, even urinated on it. "We cut damned rice bags from 11 A.M. in the morning until dark, and still had rice bags in front of us," recalled J. D. Bath. They spilled so much rice "it looked like it had snowed on the side of that hill."

For two days they took turns fighting NVA and dumping rice. Fortunately, the region's major NVA infantry units were 35 miles away, in South Vietnam's Plei Trap Valley, fighting the U.S. 4th Infantry Division during Operation Sam Houston. Still, the platoon barely got out before a large NVA relief force arrived, a skin-of-your-teeth escape.*

In Saigon, Colonel Singlaub was proud his men had discovered one of the war's largest rice caches and done their damnedest to destroy it. A little later, though, there were reports of NVA soldiers in South Vietnam with burned rice in their rucksacks, the apparent salvage of the SOG raiders' handiwork. This sent Singlaub right up the wall. There must be a way to destroy rice when SOG men found it, a simple, permanent technique or treatment to do the trick. He put his SOG science staff to work on it.

They came back with exactly the unconventional solution Singlaub thrived on: Contaminate the rice with Bitrex, "an odorless chemical that made rice so bitter it was virtually impossible to swallow." Bitrex had a magnitude greater effect than alum, the closest similiar compound, and could be mixed with water and poured as a liquid. Bitrex could be applied quietly, without attracting enemy attention, making it ideal for a recon team. It was not intended to poison the enemy, just destroy his food, so it did not violate the "Law of Land Warfare."

Washington was aghast at SOG's proposal. What clinched it was when the Pentagon had a rat injected with Bitrex and, of course, the ro-

*Several men were recommended for awards, J. D. Bath recalled, but the unit clerk fell behind in his typing, so he tossed the paperwork and went home to the States.

dent croaked. Singlaub argued that he did not intend for the NVA to *eat* Bitrex, which was all but impossible—indeed, he was convinced they would *not* eat it. But he was overruled.

Another idea that Singlaub championed did reach fruition although this one came from a recon One-Zero. First Lieutenant George K. Sisler had found an almost vertical peak in southern Laos, and personally carried photos of it to Singlaub with a proposal to occupy it, telling him, "I am absolutely certain that I could stay on top of that rock indefinitely."

Colonel Singlaub liked initiative, innovation and skydiving, and the young lieutenant had all three going for him; Singlaub had first met Sisler years earlier as a competitive skydiver. As for the peak, it truly dominated southern Laos and, as Lieutenant Sisler explained, from its top could be relayed radio messages from recon teams, thus solving a deadly problem. The NVA had figured out SOG's modus operandi and had begun allowing teams to land unmolested, then waiting for the helicopters to fly well east so intervening mountains cut off the teams' radio transmissions. Then the NVA hit them. A radio relay site also would be a big help at night, when teams had no one to communicate with them.

U.S. Ambassador to Laos William Sullivan didn't want any part of it. After a month of cablegrams between Saigon and Vientiane, finally a compromise was reached, and Sullivan allowed one small SOG team to use the pinnacle, provided they were armed with obsolete World War II–era weapons. They occupied the peak on 15 January 1967.

Code-named Leghorn, the SOG radio relay site was only days old when the NVA hit a just-inserted team minutes after they could no longer radio the helicopters; from his commanding perch, Sisler called back the aircraft, which plucked the team safely away.

Leghorn proved a useful observation post until the NVA figured out what could be seen and masked it. When conditions were right, men atop Leghorn heard NVA bulldozers repairing bomb damage on the road network 6 miles away, but not with enough precision to direct air strikes.

After ten days, Sisler's men flip-flopped with another team, which arrived on the birds that carried his team out; Leghorn was only intended to be a temporary outpost, but SOG would occupy it continuously for five years, with a small security detachment and radio operators eventually replacing the recon teams.

Almost overnight Leghorn became a "must-see" for passing U.S.

fighters, whose pilots would sneak up at low level, then kick in after-burners and flash past low overhead. But aviators found the peak more than a curiosity: For the first time there was a place they could bail out in southern Laos where friendlies might hear their distress call and ensure that they were rescued.

They were not Leghorn's only visitors. General Westmoreland had absolutely forbidden Singlaub to accompany a recon team into Laos, but that didn't stop the Chief SOG from stripping off his rank and name tag and spending a day atop the peak. Westmoreland later learned of Singlaub's Laotian escapade and "damned near died," but admitted, "I should have guessed as much, Jack."*

Just after his ten days atop Leghorn, Lieutenant Sisler volunteered to accompany a SOG platoon going into Laos to assess a B-52 strike. For Sisler, the BDA (Bomb Damage Assessment) also was an opportunity to try out one of SOG's new "toys," a revolutionary rocket pistol he'd just been issued, called a Gyrojet.

A private initiative to bring small arms into the space age, the Gyro-jet pistol was made mostly from stamped steel and plastic and weighed only a few ounces. It fired a thumb-size 13mm mini rocket, propelled by solid fuel that gushed from two little canted holes in its base, spinning it like rifling. Leaving the barrel at 1300 feet per second, the rocket emitted a noisy *whoosh* like a Roman candle. Firing it generated almost no recoil, and it wasn't very accurate, but it impacted with impressive effect. In one test, a rocket round punched through an old truck door and into a water-filled 55-gallon drum, almost exiting its opposite side. SOG men also test-fired it through sandbag walls and even tree trunks.

The BDA platoon was commanded by Captain Edward Lesesne, assisted by Sergeant First Class Leonard Tilley, a respected recon man, with Sisler going along for the experience. They inserted near Laotian Highway 96 and hardly had left the LZ when a reinforced NVA company assaulted, threw them back and almost overran them.

The SOG men put up such a fight that the enemy fell back, then Lieutenant Sisler realized two wounded Montagnard tribesmen were almost

*Actress Martha Raye, a solid supporter of Special Forces, was smuggled to Leghorn in 1970. After singing a couple of songs and kissing each Green Beret, she was whisked away on the Huey that brought her. She never said a word publicly of her deliciously unauthorized visit to SOG's most secret site.

within the enemy's grasp. Sisler raced out, lifted one man and was running with him when the NVA launched a second assault, directly toward him. The Green Beret laid the Yard down, destroyed a machine gun with a grenade, then killed three NVA with his CAR-15. Sisler retrieved the second Yard just as a forty-man NVA platoon attacked, and all alone, he assaulted them, shooting and throwing grenades. In that desperate solo melee, he undoubtedly fired his remarkable Gyrojet pistol, too, much to the enemy's amazement, no doubt, when tiny rockets smashed into their comrades, hitting like .50-caliber machine gun slugs.

Almost single-handedly, Sisler repulsed that platoon-size NVA attack. Meanwhile SFC Tilley organized the rest of the men and called in tactical air support to within 50 feet of their position. But there was no place for extraction helicopters to land, so they had to move. Then an RPG antitank rocket detonated near Lesesne, shredding his thighs and groin, and instantly he was almost bleeding to death. Everyone around Lesesne was hit, too.

Tilley expertly directed air strikes that at last forced the NVA back, and gunships arrived to escort the Hueys that would extract them. George Sisler stood to direct the gunships; then a sniper's round cut him down. He died there.

It was only because of Tilley's leadership and skill that anyone came out. Lesesne recalls, "We were all crawling toward the landing zone. How we got to the landing zone, I don't know." They brought Sisler's body with them. Twice Tilley went back after wounded men and once charged directly into the enemy, which so astonished the NVA that they fell back. Despite heavy ground fire, no aircraft were lost during the extraction.

When Lesesne recovered enough to sit in his hospital bed, he wrote up both Tilley and Sisler for the Medal of Honor. Sisler's award was approved and presented to his widow and two young sons a year later; his was SOG's first Medal of Honor.

Many SOG men thought Tilley, too, deserved the medal; instead, the heroic sergeant received America's second highest award, the Distinguished Service Cross (DSC).

After Sisler's death, his One-One, J. D. Bath, was teamed up with a new One-Zero, Captain Richard Legate. A month later he was dead, too.

• • •

There seemed to be a whole lot more singing "Hey, Blue," and it was no illusion. There had been a sea change—SOG recon was becoming more dangerous, though no one would realize why for some time.

NVA countermeasures had improved since the early Shining Brass days, when there'd been no special effort to oppose recon teams. Now every few months the NVA added another twist until by mid-1967 the enemy's Laotian defenses were redundant, layered and in depth.

NVA defenses began with one- and two-man "LZ Watcher" teams that surveilled likely insert LZs, which they correctly saw as lifelines. "There wasn't much you could do to change it," Lieutenant Colonel Charlie Norton noted. "We were dependent on helicopters, you needed to have an LZ."

The NVA couldn't cover every piece of open ground in Laos. Master Sergeant Billy Waugh thought they assigned a 2.5-square-mile area to a single watcher and positioned him on high ground in the center. Several teams found watcher platforms on tall trees that oversaw enormous expanses.

RT Illinois One-Zero Steve Keever once flushed two uniformed NVA LZ Watchers when his landing Huey's propwash exposed them. The door gunner's M-60 machine gun and Keever's CAR-15 eliminated the watchers, then the Huey shifted to an alternate LZ.

SOG teams kept finding 4-foot-wide holes scooped out of Laotian hillsides. The Yards explained they were listening devices. "You could dig out a hole and sit beside it, and if the choppers were coming," J. D. Bath recounts, "even before you heard them with your ears, you'd hear the vibrations out of that hole."

When an LZ Watcher spotted a helicopter landing, he reported it by phone or runner, or rang a large brass gong; nearby NVA base camps or truck parks beat their own gongs or fired signal shots to relay the alarm.

Sometimes the NVA dispatched trackers, which in the early days were Laotian hill tribesmen, who displayed good woodsmanship but poor tactical sense; they were hunters rather than warriors. Other times the NVA sent out people to follow a team at a safe distance and clack bamboo sticks together, or fire signal shots to try to drive the team toward an ambush or away from an imporant NVA installation.

The NVA also used "Trail Watchers"—just like they used LZ Watchers—to detect SOG teams when they crossed. A major NVA advantage was their perfect knowledge of trails, which SOG men discovered only when they came upon them by chance. In a flat-out race to an LZ, the NVA often outran teams because the SOG men headed cross-country, while the NVA dashed down high-speed trails.

The enemy sometimes employed Radio Direction Finding (RDF), plotting a team's radio to within perhaps 200 yards. Although SOG never found an RDF site in Laos or Cambodia, the evidence was simply too strong to doubt their presence. For example, Sergeant First Class Newman Ruff one night spent hours radioing South Vietnam–based artillery to hit NVA convoys, then moved 300 yards away to sleep. No sooner did his team finish moving than mortar fire pounded his old position, which was then swept by NVA troops. That certainly was an RDF fix.

NVA dismounted patrols didn't go into the jungle unless trackers already knew a team's whereabouts, although platoon-size elements swept the jungle beside convoy routes each evening at dusk, in search of SOG ambushers. At night the NVA posted sentries at each road curve, perhaps 300–500 yards apart, who'd fire signal shots if they detected a prowling SOG team or the sound of approaching aircraft—then the trucks would pull to the roadside or into dugout revetments.

However the enemy located SOG teams, the next step was always the same: Bring in as many troops as he could, as fast as he could. The reaction force might be rear-echelon logistics soldiers grabbed because they were nearby; inexperienced NVA on their way to South Vietnam; or, the toughest of all, seasoned NVA infantry resting across the border between battles in Vietnam. The NVA reinforced fast since several infantry battalions always were but a half-day's march away; they'd fan out to saturate the team's area with sweeps, ambushes and blocking forces.

SOG men learned how a hunted animal felt, because that's how the NVA pursued them. Signal shots, shouts and clapping hands were as much to panic a team as anything else, like Indian beaters banging on pots and pans to drive a tiger into a waiting rifleman's sights. Except the recon men kept their heads and resisted moving in the direction the NVA seemed to want them to go. It required tactical acumen to slip around the noisemakers, but the options were few. Some teams boldly charged the noisemakers and shot their way through; when this worked it was brilliant, when it failed, it seemed the height of stupidity.

Teams sometimes were found because they bumped into an NVA patrol but that was only the beginning of their troubles. In a hot area, ten minutes later a company-size reaction force arrived; unless you disappeared or were extracted, you could count on another company getting there in a half hour, and they kept arriving, particularly if you'd bloodied their noses good.

The enemy sometimes trucked in reinforcements, usually after dark to avoid air attack. Many a recon team thought they'd given the slip to the NVA and were comfortably asleep in their night position when the sound of halting trucks and dropping tailgates slammed them right in the gut.

But these make-do reaction forces weren't responsive enough, apparently, so the NVA added yet another defensive layer in the form of "Route Protection Battalions" and "Rear Security Units," which were infantry units permanently assigned to the Ho Chi Minh Trail to patrol against SOG recon and Hatchet Force operations.*

Assuming a SOG team managed to avoid or fight through all these impediments, the enemy still had a chance for a final blow on the team's extraction LZ by repositioning 12.7mm antiaircraft machine guns once the team's location was first suspected.

An NVA battalion's two dozen 12.7mm machine guns typically were dispersed to cover as many LZs as possible over an area 5 miles in diameter. His heavier flak guns—23mm, 37mm and 57mm—were situated to protect roads and major base areas from bombing attacks, which is why the roads were so dangerous: Operating there brought a team's choppers into the sights of the enemy's heavy antiaircraft guns. Even if an objective was near a road, the team inserted at least a ridgeline away to give their helicopters cover from concentrated flak fire.

When watchers or trackers confirmed a team's presence, the NVA toted their two dozen 12.7s into a closer, 2-mile radius to try to cover every possible departure LZ. More than one SOG team thought they were home free only to have their exfiltration helicopter riddled by freshly repositioned 12.7mm machine guns.

By 1967, the enemy had implemented all these defensive measures in Laos and committed well over 25,000 soldiers to defend his sanctuaries and the Ho Chi Minh Trail; add to this NVA units coming down the

---

*During WW II, the Soviets had formed identically named units within the NKVD— precursor to the KGB—to combat German raiders and saboteurs behind their lines.

Trail or resting in Laos after battle, and the number of soldiers occasionally doubled. Even so, the NVA's score wasn't very impressive; SOG kept about fifty Americans roaming Laos at a time, meaning each man was tying down at least five hundred enemy troops, and the NVA couldn't catch even half the teams.

Maybe the loss of that enormous rice cache was the final straw, but something changed dramatically in 1967, only SOG didn't realize it immediately. There'd always been incentives for the NVA to hunt down SOG men, the oldest being a special medal for killing Americans, the *Huan-Chuong Dung-Si Diet My* (Order for Heroes Who Destroy Americans), nicknamed the "American-Killer Award," presented in three classes, apparently to distinguish a killer of one American from a mass killer.* To sweeten the pot, a captured document disclosed, the NVA added a bounty of 10,000 piastres—several months' pay—for a living or dead SOG man, a severed head being adequate proof to collect.

But these incentives could not explain what had happened in the case of Master Sergeants Sam Almendariz and Robert Sullivan.

In mid-July 1967, they, along with Sergeant First Class Harry Brown and five Nungs, were on a recon mission near Laotian Highway 922, about 60 miles due west of Hue, when they were ambushed—not by men firing weapons but NVA who leaped out of nowhere. One NVA wrestled Sullivan's CAR-15 away from him, shot him dead, spun around and shot the team's One-Two, Brown, through the shoulder, even as another NVA shot Almendariz dead.

Brown and half the team broke away and ran like hell; then Brown managed to get off a radio message.

At Khe Sanh, the surviving half of that well-known flying dynamic duo, Cowboy, climbed into his H-34 helicopter as soon as he got word about Brown, and three SOG men jumped aboard after him, Master Sergeant Charles "Skip" Minnicks, that perennial recon man, Billy Waugh and Captain Oliver Brin.

Though they had no gunships or fighter support, Cowboy slowly trolled his Kingbee above the treetops until, peering into the brush below, they spotted Brown and several Nungs. Cowboy tried to squeeze into an LZ so tiny his rotors chewed into overhanging branches; then

---

*The star-shaped medal featured an NVA soldier stepping on an object labeled "U.S."

slugs started thumping into the old Kingbee, and finally Cowboy had to abort the landing. At Khe Sanh they refueled and examined the Kingbee, which sported several bullet holes but was still flyable. No rational pilot should have taken an already shot-up helicopter back out there, especially with no fire support, heavy ground fire, a tiny LZ and no other aircraft to retrieve him if he went in.

Cowboy ordered his copilot and door gunner to stay at Khe Sanh and brought along only the insistent Skip Minnicks. At the LZ, Cowboy again descended into that narrow hole and hovered while Minnicks leaped off; an AK bullet passed completely through Cowboy's neck, but somehow he flew the Kingbee with one hand and slowed the bleeding with the other, while Minnicks dragged the wounded Brown aboard, and off they went.

Billy Waugh still shakes his head at that display, and though Minnicks, too, showed real valor, Cowboy's bravery astounded him. "I thought he should get the Medal of Honor," Waugh said.

Miraculous though that rescue was, it was what happened to Almendariz and Sullivan that was the subject of much post-action review. They had not been bushwhacked by typical NVA, not even combat-seasoned NVA; no, the ambushers were superbly camouflaged, flashed out of nowhere like ninjas, employed martial arts and tried to take at least one American alive. Carefully planned and crisply executed, the attack had to have been rehearsed. SOG men had never before encountered NVA quite like these.

Four months earlier—about as long as it would have taken a new unit to travel down the Trail—Ho Chi Minh had attended a ceremony in Son Tay, 30 miles west of Hanoi, to congratulate the first graduates of a unique new school. This date, 19 March 1967, coincides with that cited by postwar North Vietnamese publications as the organization date for "Special Operations Forces in the Vietnamese people's war."

And it's the same date that North Vietnam's only paratroop unit, the 305th Airborne Brigade, (which by no small coincidence was based at the same town, Son Tay), was disbanded. Clearly, the North Vietnamese had converted their Soviet-trained parachute unit into a new, special-operations organization.

The 305th's soldiers were hand selected, well trained and much better equipped than an ordinary NVA unit. And they were true believers, North Vietnam's most politically reliable force, the equivalent of Nazi Germany's elite SS units. More than half the 305th Brigade's paratroops became "sappers," the suicidal night infiltrators renowned for penetrating American base camps, wearing only shorts and carrying satchel charges. Sappers were respected and feared throughout South Vietnam.

Unknown to American intelligence, another 305th Brigade element became special counter-recon units whose mission it was to hunt down and kill SOG teams. This idea wasn't entirely new. During the French-Indochina War, the Communist Viet Minh's 421st Intelligence Battalion existed solely to track down French commandos and tribal mercenaries of the top-secret Groupement de Commandos Mixtes Aéroportés (GCMA), which fought behind Communist lines.

The new NVA unit's overlap with sappers was verified when twice SOG teams were hit in their night positions by NVA stripped to shorts who came in silently with only AKs and grenades, the well-established sapper's modus operandi. In the first instance, all the Americans were killed; in the second, all were missing: MIA were Staff Sergeants Gunther Wald, William Brown and Donald Shue.

It appeared that one enemy counter-recon battalion roamed between the area just west of Khe Sanh and Tchepone; another battalion likely operated between South Vietnam's Ashau Valley and the major sanctuaries 20 miles west of there; and a third battalion patrolled the southern Laos–northern Cambodia region.

Accompanying the new counter-recon units were NVA soldiers trained as trackers and stationed at strategic points along the Ho Chi Minh Trail, to be called in whenever the NVA discovered evidence of a SOG team's presence. Enough tracker teams were available that less than twenty-four hours after a U.S. bootprint was found near the Laotian POW camp holding U.S. Navy Lieutenant Dieter Dengler—halfway between Mu Gia Pass and Tchepone—multiple tracker teams arrived to hunt the SOG men down.*

Trackers would have been bad enough, but some came with "man's best friend"—*dogs*. The NVA dogs weren't true bloodhounds but rather

---

*The recon team eluded its trackers; Lieutenant Dengler later escaped, the only U.S. Navy pilot to make his way out of Laos.

ordinary beasts taught simply to follow a scent, which they did competently. Not as numerous or available as human trackers, the dogs apparently were dispatched from important NVA base areas.

One-Zero Joe Walker was one of the few recon men to carefully observe an approaching tracker dog. Walker found it a "little old bug-eyed, ugly looking dog, but the sonvabitch could smell a bit. Not real well, but he was tracking me." He disposed of both dog and handler a moment later.

The most complicated cat-and-mouse game I'm aware of pitted a North Vietnamese counter-recon company against RT Maine, in a three-day contest distinguished by the enemy commander's persistence, patience—and fatal overconfidence.

It began like many a recon mission, with Maine's One-Zero, Staff Sergeant David Baker, his One-One, Sergeant Sherman Miller, and One-Two, Sergeant Mike Buckland, and five Yards, creeping through an NVA base area when they were picked up by trackers. Baker led Maine through a couple of evasive turns, a sideslip and a double-back; it should have shaken the NVA off but didn't.

Instead, one enemy platoon, then another, arrived, formed a line and began sweeping the jungle. Baker sidestepped one platoon, then circled around behind the second.

They heard nothing that night, but again the next morning trackers and platoon-size forces swept behind, beside and in front of them. Baker would advance cautiously, fall back, pause, advance again, dancing between his determined pursuers. By late afternoon a pattern was discernible: The NVA commander was attempting to push them east, where they'd be pinned against a steep ridge or forced into open ground. Baker did his best to resist, but inevitably RT Maine was being herded in that direction.

That night the SOG men lay low, but the pattern continued at dawn. All morning Baker did double-backs and side steps, but now the NVA commander ordered his company into a single formation, with two platoons reaching out in a Y to ensnare the SOG men, the third platoon following in reserve. Baker could sense the noose tightening. He saw but three options: become fatally pinned against the ridge, be pushed into open country or, before he ran out of maneuvering space, take back the initiative and attack.

Baker opted to attack more than one hundred NVA.

Late that morning, he came upon a decent ambush site, an open expanse his pursuers would have to cross; he hustled Maine to where the far woodline dropped off about 20 feet and arrayed them in a linear ambush. Soon they heard the NVA approaching, but they halted just out of sight, apparently for lunch. Most of the enemy stayed in the far woodline, but one platoon fanned out along the clearing, almost to where RT Maine lay in ambush. Then Baker's men couldn't believe their eyes: Nine enemy soldiers walked to within 10 feet of them, sat down and started eating—it was the company command element, complete with radio operators and two Chinese advisers. It was a tempting target, but Baker didn't like all those other nearby NVA, so he signaled his men to stay motionless.

They did for about forty minutes. Then a Montagnard grenadier pulled his .45 pistol and cocked it. With that metallic "click" all nine enemy stopped talking and turned their heads. Two reached for their AKs.

The instant Baker fired, all RT Maine let loose, and not three seconds later all nine enemy soldiers were dead and the SOG men were running for their lives. A hundred AKs returned fire but it went high because RT Maine was sliding downhill without looking back. The real lifesaver was that they'd decapitated the enemy by killing not just the commander and his two Chinese advisers, but the three platoon leaders who'd joined them for lunch.

An hour later, RT Maine was extracted with only two men wounded slightly, and at last Baker's interpreter could tell him that over lunch the enemy officers had been boasting that they'd have at least one American POW by nightfall.

The new counter-recon units made life more hazardous for SOG men, but there was a discernible difference in enemy attitude, too. Until 1967, SOG's men had fought a rather ordinary cross section of NVA—everything from rear-echelon clerks to hard-core infantry—but the politically reliable counter-recon units added zealotry to the contest. That's the best explanation for what happened to One-Zero Sergeant First Class Paul Miguez.*

It began when a Covey FAC overflying southern Laos reported, "I've got somebody screaming on the radio."

*Miguez, Glenn and Pilton are pseudonyms.

A youthful voice pleaded, "Please, please, come and get me!" The FAC calmed him enough to learn he was alone, split from his team, but he couldn't explain what had happened.

A recon team led by Miguez, along with SFC Bill Pilton, his One-One, and a young specialist four, Mike Glenn, their One-Two, had been in Laos three days. A former Marine, Miguez had a previous tour with Project Delta, the 5th Special Forces Group's in-country long-range recon unit; both Pilton and Glenn were relatively new. Miguez realized their insert had been observed by LZ Watchers but thought he'd shaken them.

Apparently not.

Another One-Zero, Sergeant First Class Fred Zabitosky, had been extracted from a nearby target that day, and he'd heard the pleading voice, too; he was at SOG's Dak To launch site when word came to insert a Bright Light rescue team. To Fred's disgust, the Bright Light team leader—a non-Special Forces NCO from a conventional unit who'd mistakenly volunteered for SOG recon without knowing what it was—invented excuse after excuse to avoid launching.

A veteran recon man on his second SOG tour, Zabitosky shook his head and announced, "Screw it, I'll go, let's go get 'im."

By the time his Huey got to the area, another Huey had extracted the young man whose voice had been on the radio, using a McGuire rig, a sort of rope swing, dropped through the jungle canopy. Zabitosky's Huey tried three times to land where Miguez's team had inserted, but heavy fire erupted each time; their damaged aircraft barely made it out, then had to autorotate at Dak To.

That evening, Zabitosky heard a fantastic story. The young specialist four, Glenn, had come out with just his clothes, he explained, because the NVA had taken everything else away from him. Still shaken, he described how the NVA had forced him to talk on his radio, then put him in the McGuire rig.

If this was true, why didn't they shoot down the Huey, which should have been child's play? Because they *wanted* him to get out, he said, so he could tell what happened to Miguez.

The NVA had suprised the team that morning, he said. They'd been overrun so fast that no one got off a shot, although the One-One, Pilton, managed to escape. The rest were captured.

An English-speaking NVA officer told Glenn to watch carefully, then they cut Paul Miguez's belly open, and his intestines fell to the ground. The officer took a flamethrower from one of his men, stuck the nozzle in Miguez's stomach and literally melted him alive, burning him horribly while the young specialist four watched.

The NVA officer told him to tell his Green Beret friends that this is what waited for them in Laos.

A number of recon men doubted the story, thinking perhaps the One-Two had hallucinated; but they knew never to discount anything. A visiting SOG lieutenant colonel from Danang badgered the traumatized youth, even called him a coward. Then he turned his bile on Zabitosky, demanding to know why he hadn't landed, and when he was told the Huey had been shot full of holes, he called Zabitosky a coward, too.

"OK, Colonel," Zabitosky said, "tomorrow morning I'm going back in there with nothing but three Americans and three Yards, some body bags and ammunition. And if you would like your first tour of Laos, seeing as you have not been to Laos, I want you on the lead ship with me."

The colonel went along but tried to scrub the insert when they took ground fire; Zabitosky already had talked with the pilot, who disregarded the colonel's pleas—after all, *Zabitosky* was the operation commander, *not* the colonel. The colonel did not get off the helicopter with the recon team.

But miraculously, another circling helicopter spotted the missing One-One, Pilton, and extracted him.

Meanwhile, Zabitosky found the team's back trail, followed it 600 yards to a hill crest, looked over and could see gear strewn where the team had been overrun. A little farther on he found black streaks where a flamethrower had scorched the ground and trees, then just ahead something was smoldering. It turned his stomach.

The hideous, sadistic murder of an unarmed man surprised Zabitosky, who explained, "That was the first time I ever knew the NVA to do anything like that."

Several Montagnards lay there, too, burned to death.

It was another dangerous day before Zabitosky got Miguez's body out; enemy pressure was so great he had to abandon the Yard bodies.

Chief SOG personally relieved the bellicose colonel.

Paul Miguez, who displayed incredible courage while his captors burned him alive, was posthumously awarded the Distinguished Service Cross.

SOG recon men saw the Miguez incident as proof of what lay in store for them if captured alive; such inhumanity was borne out again and again, with particular confirmation coming from the June 1967 Hatchet Force raid in Target Oscar Eight.

About 25 miles northwest of South Vietnam's Ashau Valley, Oscar Eight encompassed the Highway 922 turnoff from Highway 92. More USAF planes were downed at that road junction than any place in Laos, which isn't surprising since burrowed deep into the hills of Oscar Eight, defended by belts of antiaircraft guns, was North Vietnamese General Vo Bam's 559th Transportation Group's forward headquarters—the Ho Chi Minh Trail's control center.

Both SOG and the Air Force had suspected as much, with USAF intelligence determining Oscar Eight contained the largest depot outside North Vietnam. Sergeant John Meyer, who ran recon near Oscar Eight, recalled, "the area was really hot. I mean, every team that went in there got the shit shot out of it." Just before the 1967 raid, U.S. signal intelligence each day detected 2300 radio messages emanating from there to North Vietnam, a volume unparalleled throughout Laos. General Westmoreland believed an NVA Field Army headquarters that controlled all enemy operations in South Vietnam's I Corps was located there.

Oscar Eight's terrain favored the enemy, with the only suitable LZs in a wide bowl, surrounded by jungled high ground containing antiaircraft guns and bunkered infantry.

The raid began with a dawn Arc Light by nine B-52s. Flying Covey, Master Sergeant Billy Waugh watched nearly a thousand 500- and 750-pound bombs walk across Oscar Eight, setting off fifty secondary explosions. Incredibly, the bombs had barely stopped falling when he could see NVA running from their shelters to roll fuel barrels away from a fire. Waugh radioed SOG Lieutenant Colonel Harold Rose at Khe Sanh, "I've got people out here scurrying around. That sonvabitch is *loaded.*" As the smoke cleared, nine Kingbees and five USMC CH-46 Sea Knights landed a Nung Hatchet Force company.

The Arc Light temporarily silenced the flak, but hardly had the raider company arrived when NVA soldiers were *everywhere,* surrounding the one hundred SOG men who had taken cover in a few bomb craters. They began calling in gunships and tac air danger-close.

Then NVA flak opened up, hitting an A-1 Skyraider; when his wingman flew beneath him to check damage, an updraft bounced them together. The undamaged A-1's propeller cut off the other's tail.

On the LZ, Sergeant First Class Charles Wilklow was horrified to see the tailless A-1 plunge into the ground. No one ejected. But his attention as quickly returned to the Nungs and Americans crowded around him in a bomb crater, raked by fire and surrounded by hundreds of NVA. The Hatchet Force company had enough firepower to cut down any NVA assault, but not enough to themselves assault the NVA. It was a perfect stalemate lasting all afternoon, then all night.

Not long after dawn, helicopters supported by a dozen fighters took off from Khe Sanh to retrieve the company. After the fighters strafed and dropped cluster bombs, two USMC Huey gunships passed low overhead—both were shot down. Then a Kingbee went in, and it burst into flames and crashed.

Next, a USMC CH-46 settled among the bomb craters, took some hits but lifted safely away with almost a platoon aboard. Then flak connected with an Air Force F-4 Phantom fighter, which plowed into a hillside, bursting into a greasy, orange fireball.

On the LZ, three Green Beret NCOs, Charles Wilklow, Ron Dexter and Billy Ray Laney, readied the next chopper-load of Nungs, and when the second Marine CH-46 came in, they and two dozen mercenaries leaped aboard and returned the heavy ground fire as they lifted away. Riding with Covey overhead, Billy Waugh wished that Marine chopper into the air, but streaming tracers stayed right on it.

Inside the CH-46, Wilklow could see bullets punching both sides of the aircraft; then one pilot was shot, and it veered out of control, hit the trees, spun violently, fell 100 feet and broke in half. Enemy fire didn't let up a bit.

Injured and dead Nungs were piled everywhere, but somehow Wilklow scrambled to his feet and shot at the nearby NVA, who were riddling the wreckage with bullets. He saw Billy Laney was chest-shot, crumpled over and probably dead; he couldn't see Ron Dexter. Then the Marine door gunner beside him was shot in the head and slumped over his gun.

Wilklow took a slug in his right leg and rolled out of the chopper. One pilot materialized, said he had to go back inside and get something; he never came back. With shouting NVA all around, the Green Beret couldn't wait; unable to walk, he began crawling. He was light-headed from blood loss and had to remind himself to check ammunition; he had none left so he buried his CAR-15.

By then firing had stopped. Strength almost exhausted, he forced himself to crawl a few more yards, then collapsed and looked up and for the first time noticed an NVA soldier watching him from 60 feet overhead, sitting on a wooden platform beside a 12.7mm machine gun, smoking a cigarette, his feet swinging over the edge. Superbly camouflaged gun platforms were in trees all around him, and now Wilklow could see he'd crawled right into an enemy base camp and NVA were everywhere. And he was too weak to resist.

High overhead in the FAC plane, Billy Waugh shook his head at the black smoke billowing where five aircraft had crashed. Not even half the Hatchet Force had been lifted out; from this point on, all they could do was watch for evading survivors.

Charles Wilklow, too weak to move, expected to be seized, but the NVA soldiers merely walked over, saw his condition and left him there. They didn't tend his wounds and gave him nothing to drink, sentencing him to death by indifference. Wilklow passed out.

By the time he awoke his web gear had disappeared and he'd been dragged a few yards into a clearing, an orange panel laid out beside him. NVA machine guns covered the spot, in hopes U.S. helicopters would come to his rescue. All day, Wilklow stayed motionless in the tropical sun, resolved to appear dead so no one would fall for the trap.

While SOG aircraft looked for any sign of the missing men, Wilklow watched the NVA carry away several American bodies, then mount their heads on stakes like trophies. American POWs were led past, but he couldn't tell who they were. Lack of food and water kept his mind hazy; he slipped in and out of consciousness.

He awoke the second day to see two Caucasians in civilian clothes watching him from a distance. They were escorted by an NVA officer. He concluded they were Russians.

The Green Beret thirsted mightily, but the NVA offered him no water; he probably would have died that second day but he lapped up water from a muddy puddle. Enemy soldiers strolled over and urinated in the puddle, chuckled and walked away.

Then there was the Pig, an NVA private whose nose had been cut off, leaving him just two grotesque holes in his face, like a pig's snout. Such disfigurement was an ancient punishment for lying or thievery; this outcast teased and taunted Wilklow, relishing the chance to lord it over something even lower, a dying American. The Pig's hideous, haunting gaze was there for hours at a time, and Wilklow had nightmares about it.

By the third day, Wilklow was indeed dying. It rained on him for hours, and he shivered uncontrollably, exhausted as hypothermia set in. The NVA gave him not a crust of bread, not a rag to bind his wounds, and he drank only from the urine-scented puddle.

On the fourth day he squirmed when he saw maggots crawling in his open wound. Shriveled up and shaking, Wilklow barely clung to life; the NVA no long even bothered watching him. His usefulness was about over; perhaps he'd look convincing one more day and maybe they had one last chance to lure in a helicopter.

That night the last of Wilklow's strength began slipping away, and he knew he was on the verge of death. Like many people facing that abyss, his thoughts went to his family, to his wife and three children. He saw his little nine-year-old daughter Kathy's face; and Charles, seven; but especially he recalled Randy, his three-year-old, and how he'd cried and tugged on him, begging Daddy not to leave them all for something dangerous called Vietnam.

Charles Wilklow was not a religious man, but for the first time in his adult life he prayed—fervently prayed—for God to help him live to see his family again. If only he could find the strength to move. In the darkness, cold rain pelted his face. He felt a twinge of energy somewhere, and though he couldn't stand, he forced himself up on all fours—pain almost consumed him, yet that God-given pain jolted him into consciousness. He moved his good knee forward, dragged his bad one, gingerly at first; then again. He repeated the movements, then faster, again and again, and with each yard hope grew a little. Weak, feverish, several times he had to pause and sometimes passed out, but he always woke up and started again.

The pain kept him going. He fell face-first and slid down a rain-slicked hillside. The pain surged, but Wilklow kept going. He hallucinated that men were watching him; he forced himself back into reality. By sunrise he must have crawled and dragged himself nearly two miles.

That morning several NVA, eating breakfast from aluminum rice bowls, walked past the little puddle where Wilklow should have been lying. The American wasn't there. Unalarmed they looked beneath some bushes, then noticed scrapes in the soft clay where the American had dragged himself—one shouted, and in an instant the whole camp came alive to a clanging gong. Dozens of NVA dropped their rice bowls and grabbed AKs, then streamed out after the escapee.

The sun was high when Wilklow heard a plane, crawled into a small opening and, miraculously, found a cloth panel the NVA had missed when emptying his pockets; he waved it weakly, rolled over and slipped into feverish sleep. Sometime later, a shadow above him blocked the sun. If they were going to kill him, Wilklow could not resist, could no longer even crawl away.

A face began to take shape—the hideous Pig? No, the face was *black,* a black American who shouted, "Charlie! Charlie!" and two strong hands lifted him, those of SOG Staff Sergeant Lester Pace, who'd just rappeled in, a one-man Bright Light team. Pace dragged the dehydrated and nearly dead Wilklow to a nearby LZ. Then the sound of whirring rotors, and a Kingbee appeared, and they were rising, ascending from that place of horror. And rushing air bathed Charles Wilklow back to life; he shook and sobbed and tried to talk, but he could not.

Later, General Westmoreland visited Wilklow at the Danang evacuation hospital, spoke a few private words to the emaciated NCO and pinned a Purple Heart to his pillow.

In all, twenty-three Americans were lost in Oscar Eight—SOG raiders, Air Force pilots and Marine helicopter crewmen—plus twice that many Nungs. Of the six American MIAs, Hanoi admitted capturing only a door gunner, USMC Lance Corporal Frank E. Cius, Jr. After his 1973 release, Cius told Ron Dexter's brother, Ted, that the Green Beret had been captured and died while in enemy hands.

These incidents of 1967 not only made SOG men aware of the enemy's improving capabilities but told them what lay in store if their foes captured them. *Eventually, fifty-eight SOG Green Berets were MIA in Laos and Cambodia—Charles Wilklow was the only one ever to return.*

DANIEL BOONE

Ted Wicorek bounced in the little Bird Dog spotter plane's backseat, snapping photos from an open window; his were the educated eyes of a former SOG recon man turned aerial photographer. He found interesting what lay beneath him.

Through his viewfinder, Wicorek was focusing on northeast Cambodia's Highway 19, a hard-packed dirt road, two lanes wide, obviously heavily traveled, but there was practically no civilian presence visible—no towns or villages, no people walking or leading animal-drawn carts on the road, no automobiles or trucks or bicycles, hardly anything. "That's the thing that was amazing," Wicorek concluded. "Here's this beautiful road, and there were no vehicles in daytime."

A much better road than the nearby Laotian Ho Chi Minh Trail, northeast Cambodia's Highway 19 was, for political reasons, immune from U.S. bombing or ground attack, *and it led nowhere*—it headed due east and petered out about 5 miles from South Vietnam's border. Why? Twenty miles farther on lay Pleiku, the most important town in South Vietnam's Central Highlands, along with east-west Highway 19, long a Communist target as they sought to cut South Vietnam in half.

In October 1965, just 12 miles southeast of Cambodian Highway 19, in the Ia Drang Valley, the U.S. 1st Air Cavalry Division lost 304 troopers KIA to two NVA regiments that had traveled on and been supplied across the Cambodian road. When the Communists broke off the engagement and fled 5 miles west, they entered "neutral" Cambodia, where they were protected from U.S. action. In 1966 Highway 19 was secretly connected to nearby Laotian Highways 110 and 96, meaning the Ho Chi Minh Trail did not end in Laos but clandestinely extended south into Cambodia. By late 1966, SOG recon men in southern Laos regularly watched NVA trucks, overloaded with troops, turn in to Cambodia, and once across that border, the NVA knew they were secure even from SOG's prying eyes.

To some extent the Vietnamese Communists had operated from Cambodian soil since the early 1960s, but these infractions grew to wholesale proportions after Cambodia's ruler, Prince Norodom Sihanouk, closed the U.S. embassy in Phnom Penh in May 1965, eliminating diplomatic cover for CIA intelligence-gathering efforts and thus concealing his secret duplicity.*

While SOG recon and Hatchet Force men were risking their lives to raid rice caches in Laos, the NVA secretly purchased rice from the Sihanouk government. It was no small-scale enterprise: North Vietnam bought 55,000 tons of rice annually from Sihanouk, plus another 100,000 tons from Cambodian farmers—62,000 *truckloads of rice*— without running the Laotian gauntlet of air attacks and SOG ambushes and raids. Each truckload of rice purchased in Phnom Penh allowed the NVA to fill another southbound truck on the Ho Chi Minh Trail with rockets, ammunition and grenades to kill Americans.

Sihanouk also secretly opened his country's major seaport, Sihanoukville, to clandestine arms shipments. Though they lacked proof, already by 1966, MACV's senior intelligence officers estimated a thousand metric tons of Chinese military hardware had slipped surreptitiously through Sihanoukville to enemy sanctuaries on Vietnam's frontier.

MACV Commander General Westmoreland found himself at odds with Johnson administration officials who refused to criticize Sihanouk because they hoped to woo him from Hanoi. After Lieutenant General Stanley Larsen, commander of U.S. forces in central South Vietnam, told

---

*Years later, writing from exile, Sihanouk admitted he closed the embassy to disrupt CIA operations.

reporters the enemy was operating from the safety of Cambodia, Defense Secretary Robert McNamara declared the evidence insufficient. When reporters went back to General Larsen for clarification, the chagrined officer could only smile and say, "I stand corrected."

In early 1967, both General Westmoreland and Admiral U. S. Grant Sharp, Commander in Chief, Pacific (CINCPAC), urged that SOG be authorized to infiltrate recon teams into Cambodia. Washington's political process finally shook it all out in May 1967, and Project Daniel Boone was born: SOG was off to Cambodia, with the State Department's "grudging authorization," according to Chief SOG, Colonel Jack Singlaub, and with restrictions tighter even than on SOG's Laotian Prairie Fire operations. Daniel Boone meant penetrating the territory of an unsympathetic regime, so Washington demanded deniability—*absolute* deniability. Under no circumstances were SOG teams to be given tactical air support; it was better to lose a whole recon team than have one F-4 Phantom documentably bomb Cambodia. If an American was captured, just as in the popular TV show *Mission Impossible,* the U.S. government would disavow his actions, perhaps even declare him a deserter. As in the early Shining Brass days, all weapons and gear would be of foreign manufacture and unattributable to the United States.

The SOG teams would be limited to gathering intelligence; there would be no offensive actions—no ambushes, no mining, no raids—and SOG could engage the enemy only for genuine self-defense, because SOG recon men might mistake Cambodian soldiers for NVA; both carried AK-47s and wore plain green uniforms. "That's why we had to be so careful," First Sergeant Billy Greenwood explained. "You'd be trailing a bunch of people and you weren't sure if they were Cambodes or North Vietnamese."

Only to take prisoners could SOG men initiate contact, and then policy limited it to "isolated groups of two or three VC/NVA."

Helicopter gunships were the only aerial support authorized, and they could fire only in self-defense or to help a team break contact, using machine guns and rockets. No incriminating bomb craters were to mar Cambodia's countryside.

Daniel Boone operations initially were targeted into Cambodia's thickly jungled but heavily occupied northeast, adjacent to South Vietnam's Central Highlands. The first Cambodia penetration came off without serious incident; but the second mission, executed on 15 June 1967, was described by the recon One-Zero who led it, Sergeant First Class Lowell Wesley Stevens, as "the longest day in my life."

Inserting by unmarked Kingbee helicopter on a heavily forested ridge that jutted 100 yards into Laos, One-Zero Stevens, his assistant team leader, Sergeant Roland Nuqui, and four Nungs dashed up a steep slash-and-burn LZ into the jungle only to hear voices and signal shots. They'd been spotted.

Instead of spending five days sneaking eastward in search of two roads, several enemy base camps and assorted artillery positions, they could only hunker down and hope for the best. NVA were converging all around them.

Setting aside his suppressed Swedish K submachine gun, Stevens took up the radio handset and reported, "We've got bastards all around us. Request immediate extraction."

In most situations that would have been enough, but there was an inexperienced SOG major with the FAC overhead—in fact, the officer wasn't Special Forces qualified, wasn't even airborne qualified, had no combat time and would never have had his job but for high-level bureaucratic inanities.

The ignorant major thought Stevens was crying wolf and would not turn the Kingbee around to retrieve the team. He wanted more proof. Stevens heard NVA leaders shouting to their soldiers, herding them uphill into advantageous firing positions.

Technically, Stevens and his men belonged to Project Omega, which on paper was a 5th Special Forces Group organization. The 5th SFG's Projects Omega (Special Forces Detachment B-50) and Sigma (Detachment B-56) were formed supposedly to recon remote areas in South Vietnam, but actually they represented an attempt by 5th Group's senior officers to wrest Cambodian cross-border operations away from SOG; correctly anticipating that Project Daniel Boone would be approved, the Group's senior officers formed Omega and Sigma in hopes of winning the Cambodia project. Instead, the Joint Chiefs transferred Omega and Sigma to SOG. Caught in the middle were dozens of Green Beret recon men like Lowell Stevens who didn't give one damn about bureaucratic rivalries but had to deal with the fallout, such as this incompetent major.

At Stevens' urging, the major finally had four American Huey gunships strafe the woodline around the slash-and-burn, and when they didn't draw ground fire the cocksure officer was convinced Stevens was running scared. With disgust in his voice, the major radioed, "OK, send in a helicopter and we'll call it a day."

Because the slope was so steep, the Kingbee that went in carried an American to help lift the recon men aboard, a tall, lanky, master sergeant, Ben Snowden. Friendly, quiet and a good soldier, Snowden was an old Vietnam hand and well respected, and it was his welcome hand that reached from the hovering Kingbee above Stevens.

Just as Stevens lifted up his Nung point man to Snowden, "there let loose such a volume of fire as I've never heard since," the One-Zero said. While the men on the LZ jumped for cover, the chopper rocked groggily back and forth but somehow lifted away. The Kingbee made it back to SOG's Dak To launch site where, riddled with sixty-eight bullet holes, its engine out, it slammed into a ditch.

From his cover, Stevens raised his head, looked uphill and for the first time could discern a gully and a cave. Protruding from the cave was the NVA machine gun that had hit Snowden's Kingbee. It had ceased firing as soon as the helicopter left.

Now Stevens realized they were after the helicopters. "They didn't want us. They could have got us on square one. They could've shot me sitting in the door coming in."

Fortunately, Stevens and his men were not actually in Cambodia but 100 yards into Laos. Covey brought in a pair of A-1s that dropped bombs and strafed danger-close, forcing the enemy back.

A Kingbee made a few low passes and didn't take fire, so it swung around and touched down, and the whole recon team rushed it and jumped aboard. It was about 30 feet in the air when that NVA machine gun reappeared at the cave mouth and its concentrated fire shot the tail rotor off, spinning the bird wildly around until it flipped and slammed in on its side, its shattered rotors flailing the earth, kicking up a momentary dust storm.

Inside the crashed Kingbee, Stevens lay among a mass of rucksacks and squirming bodies; despite his daze he saw high-octane gas streaming everywhere and he knew any second it would torch up. He jumped up, grabbed the edge of the open doorway and pulled himself out, sitting atop the H-34's side; he could make out three NVA and the machine gun that had brought the Kingbee down. Whether awestruck or compassionate, the Communist gunners stopped firing for a few seconds. That was all that Stevens needed. With adrenaline inspiration, he snatched up his Nungs and the Vietnamese door gunner and heaved them like rag dolls to safety. Meanwhile his One-One, Roland Nuqui, ran around, kicked in the cockpit Plexiglas and dragged the pilots out.

Amazingly, not one of the nine men was dead, and only the Vietnamese door gunner's wounds were serious. As they low-crawled into the jungle the machine gun resumed firing, but by then Stevens had arrayed everyone securely in a small perimeter. But they had to be extracted soon or they were doomed. Only one flyable Kingbee remained, and it had to leave to refuel.

To make matters worse Covey, too, went to refuel. The only air support left was an unarmed Bird Dog carrying recon man Joe Woods. The Bird Dog made simulated gun runs to keep the enemy occupied.

But it was a propeller-driven A-1 Skyraider from the Pleiku-based "Spads" that saved the day. While the Kingbee and Covey refueled, Stevens carefully described to the A-1 pilot the exact heading to the cave containing the deadly machine gun. Then the A-1 rolled in, banked almost vertically to release a shiny canister that spun end over end just above the team, smashed through limbs and leaves, bounced once then spewed 50 yards of jellied gasoline into the small cave mouth, and PHOOOMPFFFFF!—the napalm flashed blackish orange. Scratch one machine gun.

Looking up at that sharpshooting Skyraider, Stevens saw what looked like dust flicking off its skin and realized other enemy machine guns were stitching it with slugs. A second later the plane belched smoke. Stevens watched the A-1 nose up, saw the canopy fall away and the pilot eject. Stevens clenched his Swedish K so hard it shook in his hands, but wishing and hoping were no help; the parachute drifted into the NVA positions.

The A-1 pilot was lost—whether he died in captivity or was killed immediately, Stevens never learned.

Momentarily helicopters appeared—gunships, and the remaining Kingbee, flown by the Vietnamese pilot who'd taken sixty-eight hits and crash-landed the other bird at Dak To. He had insisted on flying because he knew the LZ.

With the deep shadows of sunset falling across the hillside and this one final H-34 available, everyone understood there'd be just one chance; the gunships let loose almost their entire loads in a couple of withering low-level passes. Then came the Kingbee. It seemed anticlimatic after six hours of shooting and bombing and strafing, but they got out with only minimum ground fire.

At Dak To, Stevens and Nuqui and the Nungs climbed from the Kingbee, exhausted and sweating but euphoric because their team had come through without losing a single man. Stevens lifted a silent toast to the unknown A-1 pilot. Then Lowell Stevens saw a body bag and learned Ben Snowden was dead, riddled by nine of those sixty-eight bullets that hit the first Kingbee. He'd probably died even while he hovered 6 feet over Stevens on the LZ.

In honor of the lanky master sergeant, about a hundred SOG men gathered that night and sang "Hey, Blue." In memory of this first man lost in Daniel Boone, they named the new recon company office at Kontum, Snowden Hall.

Within a few months, the SOG teams penetrating Cambodia had proved their worth. The new teams discovered dozens of enemy trails, roads, phone lines, base camps and caches. For the first time, U.S. intelligence could assemble a comprehensive picture of where the NVA were in Cambodia and what they were doing.

Cambodia's extreme northeast, which protruded like a 30-mile peninsula between Laos and South Vietnam, may as well have been North Vietnamese territory, the NVA so heavily dominated it. In this dense rain forest the NVA did anything they wished, and their roads secretly networked with the Laotian Ho Chi Minh Trail.

Down around Highway 19, opposite South Vietnam's city of Pleiku, there began a zone 50 miles long so devoid of water that SOG troopers called it "the Wasteland." Unable to sustain enemy occupiers, this was an area the NVA transited on foot while infiltrating farther south to more inhabitable places. The Wasteland formed a major demarcation: North of here, all enemy supplies came via the Ho Chi Minh Trail; south of here, most supplies came via secret shipments to the port of Sihanoukville.

South of the Wasteland grew triple-canopy jungles, where the NVA concealed major sanctuaries that paralleled South Vietnam's III Corps region. The NVA and VC based three or four infantry divisions here, north and northwest of Saigon.

One area with particularly heavy enemy concentrations, where Cambodia protruded 10 miles into South Vietnam, near Loc Ninh, was called the Fishhook. It was in the Fishhook, U.S. intelligence learned, that the Viet Cong concealed their overall headquarters, the Central Office for South Vietnam (COSVN).

A larger and more dangerous salient was the Parrot's Beak, which pointed daggerlike at Saigon, only 30 miles away. Sitting astride the major Saigon-Phnom Penh highway, the Parrot's Beak's open rice paddies and thin woodlines offered little concealment for base camps, so the enemy staged from here only for short periods, then slipped back north to havens in the Fishhook.

Cambodian villages dotted the Parrot's Beak, making it all but impossible for SOG teams to move in daylight without being seen. SOG teams still reconned the Parrot's Beak when essential, but so risky were these politically sensitive penetrations that each had to be approved by the Joint Chiefs and State Department, sometimes even by the White House.

Most Cambodian penetrations were in the Fishhook and Tri-border area, northwest of Pleiku. It was against the latter that SOG focused teams in the fall of 1967, not far from where U.S. troops were drawn into the war's costliest confrontation yet, the Battle of Dak To.

While the U.S. 173d Airborne Brigade fought its way up the bloody slopes of Hill 875 southwest of Dak To, several SOG teams slipped into Cambodia, 5 miles west, to support the American paratroopers—though, of course, this was so highly classified that not even the 173d commander knew of it.

One such SOG foray, led again by One-Zero Lowell "Roundeye" Stevens, this time with Sergeant First Class Ken "Shoebox" Carpenter as One-One, walked into Cambodia from southern Laos to search for a mysterious road supplying the enemy on Hill 875, and to learn whether the NVA was reinforcing or withdrawing.

Stalking eastward across Cambodia for two days, Stevens' exasperated team searched high and low for the invisible road with no luck. It was during a noontime break the third day that Roundeye noticed the trees beside them seemed to form an odd pattern. "I stepped out on this thing," Stevens explained, "and I'm standing there looking at trees and leaves on the ground, but there's something that isn't right about this place. But finally I see *it's a damned road* . . . a road. And it followed the contours."

Stevens and Carpenter found soft earth around the tree trunks and, looking up, they could see where the NVA had lashed together the highest treetops with vines. "This is unreal," Roundeye whispered to his partner, so unreal that he hesitated to report it. Positioning his men in an overlooking bamboo thicket, Stevens set up to surveil the strange scene.

Just after dark they heard the sound of distant truck engines, coming their way, barely moving. About 10 P.M. several dozen men materialized like ghosts in the moonlight, silent, making no noise; the work parties lined up with bamboo poles, lashed them on either side of trees 18 inches in diameter, ten coolies per side. It reminded Lowell Stevens of a movie about Egyptians building the pyramids as he watched the coolies heave up the trees and scoot them aside with little choppy steps, leaving a path just wide enough for a truck to squeeze past.

A half hour later, the Green Beret NCOs watched an NVA truck convoy crawl past on the road's circuitous bed. As the Russian-made trucks headed toward Hill 875, they could make out rice bags and wooden crates of ammunition but no soldiers. Clearly, the NVA were resupplying but not reinforcing.

About 4 A.M. the trucks returned. This time the cargo at first looked like heaps of tree limbs, but in the stark moonlight Stevens got a better glimpse and recognized the protruding forms as arms and legs locked in rigor mortis—whole piles of NVA bodies frozen in death—grim testimony to the 173d Airborne Brigade's combat effectiveness and a sign that fighting on Hill 875 was nearly done.

Just before dawn the coolies returned with their bamboo poles, dragging and pushing the trees back into place. Finally another crew walked by with sacksful of leaves, which they scattered to cover the truck tracks.

By sunrise the road was gone.

That morning Roundeye and Shoebox and their Nungs walked the camouflaged road, photographed its hairpin turns and marveled at this feat of engineering. "It was magnificent to me how anybody could do something like that," Stevens said later.

Just before noon their point man unexpectedly stepped onto a trail and waved Stevens forward. As Roundeye began inspecting it, four NVA walked over a rise 20 feet downtrail. Stevens lifted his AK as he made out a long column beyond the four men, but only the tops of the others' heads were visible. When at last the NVA point man saw Stevens, he gasped—perhaps in a final introspective moment about the fatal stupidity of carrying his AK slung while walking point.

Stevens let loose and dropped all four North Vietnamese. The rest of the enemy column was too shocked to react and did nothing. Stevens, Carpenter and their four Nungs ran for all they were worth, with not a single shot fired after them. Five minutes later there were a few signal shots, but that was all.

And what would the NVA think? What could they prove? Like most SOG teams in Cambodia, Stevens' men all carried AK-47s, so it was only spent Communist cartridges that the NVA found scattered around their four dead comrades, while the SOG team escaped without trace.

SOG's Cambodia program had put Hanoi over a barrel: The enemy couldn't publicly protest SOG's presence without admitting their own illicit presence, and a private complaint to Prince Sihanouk would be an admission they couldn't defend their own sanctuaries. The NVA could do nothing except vent themselves on SOG teams, if given the chance.

It was the State Department that generated most Cambodian political impediments, not the North Vietnamese. When former First Lady Jacqueline Kennedy visited the ancient Cambodian temples at Angkor Wat in 1967, the State Department had SOG halt its penetrations in hopes of a diplomatic breakthrough. When nothing came of it, SOG resumed operations into an expanded 20-kilometer depth, though the populous Parrot's Beak still required case-by-case clearance. Even if it cost the lives of an entire recon team, tactical air support remained absolutely forbidden.

That fall of 1967, and into early 1968, SOG formally absorbed the 5th Special Forces Group's old Projects Omega and Sigma, whose men, on loan to SOG, had been penetrating Daniel Boone targets. The teams were stationed at a new SOG base at Ban Me Thuot for missions into Cambodia, and at Kontum for missions in both northern Cambodia and southern Laos. SOG's Danang headquarters, with FOBs at Phu Bai, Khe Sanh and Kontum, became Command and Control North (CCN). Its recon teams were named after states and snakes, for example, RT Anaconda or RT California. The Ban Me Thuot organization was named Command and Control South (CCS), and its teams named for tools, e.g., RT Saw or RT Hammer.

It was early in the new year, 29 January 1968, that SOG had its first Cambodia MIA, Sergeant First Class Charlie White, scheduled to rotate home just three days later. Operating in northeast Cambodia, his team had made contact, shot their way free and made it to a tiny opening, where ropes were dropped from a hovering Huey. A Special Forces medic, Charlie White was an enormous African-American, built like an NFL lineman, 6 feet 4 inches and 280 pounds.

When he put his massive form into the extraction rig, and the chopper started lifting away, he turned upside down, and about 25 feet in the air he fell out. Because of the many enemy soldiers nearby, nothing could be done that night to look for him.

A Bright Light team with Sergeants First Class Fred Zabitosky and Dallas Longstreath III inserted the next morning, rappeling into the same LZ Charlie White was attempting to be extracted from. They found tracks where the NVA got in line and swept up the hillside, then discovered a place where all the tracks came together at one spot. There some bamboo had been crushed, apparently by White's fall. There was no blood on the ground. By the tracks they determined the NVA had left as a single party, but the bootprints were too intermixed to determine whether White's larger tracks were among them. A full day behind, and the area crawling with NVA, the SOG men couldn't even contemplate trying to follow them. Zabitosky's Bright Light team was extracted.

The Defense Department all but declared Charlie White dead, but Fred Zabitosky—who had climbed that Cambodian hillside looking for Charlie—came out convinced the huge NCO had survived his fall and been seized by the NVA. What they did with him we can only speculate, for Hanoi denied any knowledge of him.

In the case of another Cambodia MIA, First Lieutenant Harry Kroske, Jr., we know exactly what happened. Kroske was one of a few Ban Me Thuot–based CCS officers running recon, and as One-Zero of

RT Hammer he soon acquired a reputation for audacity. When young Specialist Four Bryan Stockdale became his new assistant, Kroske announced, "I have a hell of a reputation for getting people killed. Does that bother you?"

Stockdale had not volunteered for Special Forces and SOG to evade the draft. "This is my kind of guy," the gung-ho trooper thought.

RT Hammer was slated to recon the major NVA base area nicknamed the Fishhook near the suspected Viet Cong headquarters, the Central Office for South Vietnam (COSVN). They'd go in with just two Americans and four Nungs.

After a few days' training, they took off from the SOG launch site at Bu Dop and inserted late in the afternoon.

Their LZ was dangerously open grassland, so they hustled for the cover of a thick patch of jungle a quarter mile away; once there, Lieutenant Kroske told Stockdale to make a radio check. While the young specialist four set up, the One-Zero and his Nung point man crept forward to examine a major trail they'd spotted from the air as they landed.

Stockdale completed his radio check as the sound of their choppers faded in the east. Sunset was only a half hour away, and Stockdale thought they'd find a place to hide for the night, probably in this thick clump of jungle.

Suddenly there was a quick burst of automatic fire, then another, then a hail of fire, all of it 50 yards away, where Kroske had gone with the point man.

Stockdale pulled together the rest of the team just as the point man ran up amid even heavier fire. When Stockdale asked where Kroske was, the panicky point man shouted, "Lieutenant *fini!*"

Stockdale may have been just an E-4 and new to recon, but he knew you didn't take an excited Nung's word, so despite the danger he dashed forward to find Lieutenant Kroske. The Nungs were so petrified that not only did they fail to follow him, they ran off.

The young Green Beret had dashed just a few yards when cracking bullets forced him to his hands and knees. AKs raked the earth around him. "The fire was kicking up so much dirt that I couldn't even lift my head up," he reported.

Stockdale would later learn his One-Zero had walked up on three

NVA, one of whom he wanted to take prisoner. Kroske shot two and waved over the third, but the last NVA jumped into the grass, fired wildly and hit Kroske three times in the stomach and chest. Now, under heavy fire, the specialist four managed to crawl close enough almost to touch Kroske's body, shouting at him to no avail. Then four NVA leaped up in the nearby grass and let loose with AKs. Bullets smacked the earth all around Stockdale but miraculously did not hit him. He knew there was nothing more he could do. His withdrawal was almost cut off by a squad of NVA maneuvering around his flank. Then he heard shouts on two sides.

Reaching the edge of the jungle again, he ran back to where he'd left the Nungs, but they were long gone, and the shooting, shouting NVA were right on his tail. Stockdale couldn't go forward because another group of NVA had outrun him and already turned to sweep back toward him. With NVA closing behind him, the Green Beret dashed in the only direction left, right across a wide field of shoulder-high grass, crossing it so quickly that the enemy assumed he was still in it as squads of NVA streamed right and left around it. Hiding just beyond them, in an island of thick jungle about the size of two football fields, Stockdale watched dozens of NVA form a cordon around the grass field.

Then they set the grass on fire to flush him out or burn him alive.

Though he tried repeatedly, Stockdale couldn't raise anyone on his radio. As the flames built, he could see the NVA watching the field as if they'd cornered an animal and this was great sport; they didn't care whether they took him dead or alive, flushed him or burned him or shot him.

Stockdale lay motionless, waiting for it to get dark, muffling his coughs as smoke drifted around him. Despite the shock of losing his team leader, the apprentice recon man rationally concluded he couldn't allow himself to give in to impetuous action; his sole chance was to outthink this numerically superior foe. It might be dark right now, he thought, but come morning they'd sweep the area thoroughly and find him. He had to move. In the light of the dwindling flames he could make out rows of NVA silhouettes sweeping the burned grass for him, on line, alert, AKs ready at port arms.

Except for trying to raise someone on his radio, Stockdale lay there quietly, patiently, for five hours, until midnight. All the while the NVA soldiers kept talking and maneuvering in front of him, with some even calling out in accented English, "GI, we know you there!" Another voice promised, "Come out, you die, you die!"

By now the fire had exhausted itself, and the scorched earth should have cooled and the enemy become less attentive, so Stockdale decided it was time to cross the burned field. He low-crawled the 100 yards of ash-covered ground, creeping so slowly and quietly that it took more than two hours. All the way he heard voices and saw patrols pass within yards of him. But what most alarmed him were the NVA he spotted with flashlights, walking elbow to elbow, scouring the ground for any sign of him.

Somehow Stockdale made it between, around and past the many NVA, who'd grown so bold that they'd begun yelling, laughing, even whistling. Once across the field, he scurried into a woodline, then crawled a few yards forward until he found himself pinned between two converging trails with NVA voices on both.

That was it; Stockdale was trapped.

Despite his best efforts, he figured they'd find him, he'd put up a hell of a fight and that would be the end of it: Two more SOG recon men vanished, another mystery to contemplate in the NCO club and to lie to families about. But not if Bryan Stockdale could help it.

Now for the first time since the firefight he heard a voice on the radio. His heart jolted. He fumbled to cover the handset so the nearby NVA wouldn't hear it. Just barely within range, Stockdale contacted a FAC putting in an air stike back in South Vietnam, and whispered his predicament. The FAC assured him he'd relay the message, to which Stockdale added a warning: "You better come get me at first light—or not come at all."

The young Green Beret spent those final two hours of darkness watching the burned field and the congregating NVA who awaited the dawn. Their shouts kept promising, "We kill you!"

In the predawn darkness of Ban Me Thuot, 80 miles away, a unique U.S. Air Force unit, the 20th Special Operations Squadron (SOS), launched a half-dozen camouflage-painted Hueys to rescue the isolated Green Beret. With tail numbers removed and U.S. markings painted over, their only insignia was a stenciled green hornet on their tails. Hence the 20th SOS nickname, the "Green Hornets." Like the comic book character, behind their masked identity these top-secret Green Hornets, SOG's Cambodia flying unit, worked clandestinely for good. In fact, they were the only USAF combat unit flying Hueys in Southeast Asia.

But before the Air Force helicopters could reach Stockdale, with daylight just cutting through the morning mist, the hidden Green Beret detected two NVA walking back and forth across the burned field. Then they froze, pointed to the ground and shouted excitedly. They'd found his snakelike trail, where he'd crawled through the ashes the night before, and now they were pointing directly to where he lay hidden. More NVA came on the double.

By now Stockdale could hear the Green Hornets' whopping rotors, but there was no time left. He took careful aim and with two shots dropped both NVA trackers. There was hell to pay with what seemed to be a whole platoon opening fire. For a couple of minutes young Stockdale fought an intense one-man defense against assaulting NVA, but before they could sweep over him, the Green Hornet gunships rolled in.

It took three hours of gunship runs, with the birds rearming many times, before at last a Green Hornet troopship dropped a McGuire rig rope and harness through the trees, then lifted the Green Beret to safety.

Harry Kroske's family learned of his death even though his body was not recovered. And with a bit more seasoning young Stockdale became the RT Hammer One-Zero. He led the team with distinction for almost two years, establishing himself as one of CCS' most respected team leaders.

The Green Hornets, as in Stockdale's case, were the prime reason a lot of SOG men came out of Cambodia alive. "They had great esprit and really did some great jobs," said Colonel Jack Singlaub, the Chief SOG who arranged to have the 20th SOS reassigned from base security duties to SOG.

The 20th SOS was SOG's only U.S. helicopter unit whose crews lived with the SOG men they supported. Although officially based at Cam Ranh Bay, the Green Hornet birds and crews rotated every ten days to the CCS camp at Ban Me Thuot, which did a lot for developing rapport. There probably was not another unit in Vietnam whose helicopter crews became personal friends of the men they inserted and extracted.

The 20th SOS flew the F-Model Huey, which, a 20th SOS pilot said, "wasn't made for combat, it was made for hauling toilet paper and military policemen to missile silos in North Dakota." Though the F-Model's turbine was fragile and a maintenance nightmare, it also generated considerably more power than Army Hueys, which meant it more quickly escaped hot LZs and carried more people, features well suited to recon operations.

And unlike Army Hueys, which typically were piloted by nineteen- and twenty-year-olds, these Air Force Hueys were flown by career majors and lieutenant colonels in their thirties and forties, many on a final assignment before retirement.

Half the Green Hornet Hueys were configured as gunships with rocket pods and unique hand-controlled miniguns; the latter proved extremely effective. "Best damned gun system over there," CCS recon man Ben Lyons thought, because the pilots could focus on flying their aircraft while two gunners turned their six thousand-round-per-minute guns to meet the target: They fired during the approach, while passing the target and even pivoted the guns to shoot backward after passing. When a Cobra gunship's minigun jammed, the Cobra went home for repair. If a Green Hornet minigun jammed, the gunner put on an asbestos glove, spun the barrels to clear it, then resumed firing, all in less than ten seconds.

The Green Hornet gunships pioneered their own tactics, too, especially firing techniques to exploit their handheld miniguns—like "three-sixties": Hovering above a team, the pilot would spin his bird in a 360-degree pedal turn with both miniguns shooting straight down to form a circular wall of fire. "I don't give a damn who you are, you're not getting through that," a former recon man said.

One young Green Hornet troopship pilot, Lieutenant Jim Fleming, had a tough time adapting to this organization with its high esprit and firmly established pecking order. A swaggering lot, the gunship pilots thought themselves the chosen few. Knaves flew troopships, these knights of the gunships reminded him. It was the swashbuckling gunships that came in spewing lead and rockets to save the day, then the second-class troopships, like airborne taxis, went in to pick up the team—at least that's what the gunship crews liked to say.

Worse yet, the twenty-five-year-old Fleming was a lowly lieutenant in a world of thirty-five-year-old majors and lieutenant colonels. Though elevated to aircraft commander (AC) after five months of combat flying, he may as well have been driving a dump truck, according to the gunship pilots. The rivalry irked the proud and skilled junior officer though he said little about it. He just tried to do the best job he could.

Any SOG team that a Green Hornet pilot inserted was "his." That is, if he put them in, he pulled them out, with the four Green Hornet troopships dividing the teams among themselves. Even if a particular Green Hornet commander and his bird were scheduled to rotate back to Cam Ranh Bay, they'd not depart before extracting "his" team.

It was only Fleming's second day as an AC that he was tested in a life-and-death contest. Flying with a new copilot, Major Paul McClellan, Fleming started his day routinely. That morning Fleming inserted RT Chisel in Cambodian Target Tango-51; there was no ground fire, so the recon men began moving quietly toward a wide river they were to surveil for enemy boat traffic.

The Green Hornets returned to Duc Co, the small Special Forces border camp they'd launched from, refueled, ate lunch; then in midafternoon another team climbed aboard and they flew far south to slip them into Cambodia.

By now RT Chisel had set up overlooking the river, lying in thick brush along a bend. Led by Staff Sergeant Ancil "Sonny" Franks, who'd run recon almost a year, RT Chisel included his One-One, Sergeant Charles Hughes, and three Montagnards. They were accompanied by Green Beret Captain Randolph Harrison, the new CCS Recon Company commander, there to acquaint himself with what his men did.

While the rest of the team improved camouflage, Sergeant Hughes erected a wire radio antenna to extend their range. It was barely set up when an NVA force hit RT Chisel.

Hughes radioed for help but there was no response.

The inherent danger of a river-watch mission, especially on a wide stream such as this, is that the position is untenable if detected. One-Zero Sonny Franks realized he was trapped. There was no place to go except the river, and they'd be cut down before they were halfway across it.

Hunkered down in a small, half-moon-shaped washout, they had decent cover but couldn't hold out very long. By the growing fire, Franks could tell more NVA were arriving by the minute. The enemy had them surrounded on three sides, pinned against the water. The recon men set off a couple claymore mines, and that helped, but for how long?

Hughes tried the radio again.

Thirty miles away, the formation of five helicopters was returning to Duc Co after inserting the second team. Not one of the helicopters could hear RT Chisel's anxious calls for help.

But flying higher in his Cessna O-2 Skymaster, their FAC, USAF Major Charles Anonsen, thought there was something familiar about a fuzzy transmission; snapping off his other radios he turned up the volume and—yes, it sounded like RT Chisel, but the signal was so broken up that he had to fly west before he could make it out.

By now the NVA were thickly ringed around Chisel, peppering the bank above them with machine-gun and AK fire. Sonny Franks' men narrowly beat back several assaults.

Anonsen's plane was close enough now for clear communications; by the time he'd located RT Chisel's position the two Green Hornet gunships and three troopships were arriving, too. There was one big problem, though; after the long flight they barely had enough fuel for anything but a quick pickup.

First they had to push the enemy back. Major Anonsen directed the two gunships to make runs around the team; Green Hornet rockets and minigun fire were returned by heavy fire from all sides. Orbiting overhead, Lieutenant Fleming saw the gunships knock out two 12.7mm heavy machine guns only 200 yards from RT Chisel, but the NVA filled the sky with such intense fire that one gunship shuddered, then its engine died, but its pilot, Captain Dave Miller, somehow landed the bird in a nearby clearing. As soon as Miller's skids touched Cambodian soil a Green Hornet troopship swooped in for the four crewmen. Already low on fuel, the rescue helicopter then headed straight for Duc Co.

Sonny Franks' men still held their horseshoe defense, but they were being pressed toward the river's swift, wide waters. They tossed grenades and blew more claymores.

The Green Hornets had been overhead just two minutes, and already one gunship had been shot down and another bird had flown away with the retrieved crewmen. Now a third helicopter, another troopship, was below minimum fuel and had to depart. That left just two helicopters:

Jim Fleming's Huey and a gunship commanded by Major Leonard Gonzales. They, too, were dangerously low on fuel.

The firefight surged around the cornered team, but they doggedly held on thanks to fire discipline and the cover of the riverbank. But six men couldn't hold out much longer against this large NVA force.

Major Gonzales' gunship rolled in and pickled rockets all around the team; he took heavy fire coming out, and Jim Fleming noticed him trailing smoke. Gonzales' bird had been hit, though he thought the aircraft was flyable.

Out of station time and almost out of ammunition, Fleming had to go in after RT Chisel immediately or fly away. No one would've said a word if he had announced his fuel was simply too low. Leaving made more sense than attempting a pickup with a Huey flying on fumes. But young Fleming had inserted RT Chisel, they were "his" team, his responsibility.

He told the FAC he was ready to go in. To mask his approach from ground fire, the FAC led Fleming's Huey around a low hill, then talked him toward the river. Fleming banked so hard his rotor pointed almost vertically, then he skimmed full-throttle just above the water, running a gauntlet of AK and machine-gun fire while his copilot and door gunners shot at NVA and scanned for Chisel. He nosed the Huey into the bank where the team should have been, but just then the NVA hit RT Chisel in such strength that every recon man was too busy shooting to run for the bird.

One-Zero Sonny Franks' mind flashed back to a nightmarish vision of a Green Hornet crashed and afire. Only weeks earlier Franks and his team had braced themselves as the Green Hornet they rode smashed through treetops, broke apart and burst into flames. The passengers and crew scrambled to safety except one young Air Force gunner whose arm was pinned in the burning wreckage; by the time his desperate crewmates began hacking at his arm with their puny survival knives it was too late. The 2000-degree inferno pushed them away, and they watched transfixed as a living man, their friend, was reduced to ashes. The vision tore at Sonny Franks' guts.

Then another NVA assault almost rolled right across the tiny team, and Lieutenant Fleming heard their radio operator scream, "They've got us! They've got us! Get out, get out!"

Fleming pulled pitch, backed away from the bank and began climbing out; not 50 feet away one of the team's claymore mines detonated and the whole helicopter crew saw an NVA's body thrown in the air.

Fleming radioed, "What's going on down there?"

"We blew them back," Sergeant Hughes explained, "but we're out of claymores and can't hold out much longer."

Orbiting at a safe altitude, Fleming took stock of the situation. Their backs against a river too wide to swim and too open to rush across, RT Chisel could last only another few minutes. There was maybe an hour of daylight left, not enough time to get more helicopters or refuel at Duc Co and return.

Fleming radioed the FAC, "We'll give it one more try."

The gunship pilot, Major Gonzales, said, "I'll make one more pass over 'em, give 'em everything I've got, but then I've got to get out of here."

Fleming fell in behind the gunship, Gonzales swung low, salvoed his remaining rockets and let those miniguns moan and groan until the barrels warped.

At first Fleming couldn't find the team, yet he knew he was getting close because the volume of bullets ricocheting across the water increased. Then the right door gunner shouted above his chopping machine gun's roar, "There he is!" and Fleming saw one Montagnard leap in the river, sloshing from shore as four men jumped in right behind him.

Seeing all that fire, Franks thought surely the helicopter would be shot down or the pilot would pull out, but the Huey just came right over and hovered. Despite bursts of AK fire and exploding rockets, Fleming held that bird rock-steady in what the Air Force later called "a feat of unbelievable flying skill."

Fleming's right door gunner, Fred Cook, kept firing with one hand while pulling men aboard with the other. "Oh, I loved him," One-Zero Franks said of Fleming. "Every one of 'em there, there wasn't none of 'em flinching."

From the cockpit, Fleming saw more NVA trotting and crouching along the riverbank; he could do nothing but hold the aircraft stable and warn his door gunners. His left door gunner, J. J. Johnson, was giving them everything he had, then his gun jammed.

Bullets shattered the Huey's windshield and a bursting RPG antitank rocket raked the helicopter's skin, but Fleming held that bird level and snug up to the riverbank. "He was just steady as a rock," Sonny Franks said. At last five recon men were aboard, but the last man, Captain Randy Harrison, wasn't there.

With bullets slapping the water all around his helicopter, Fleming finally told himself that was it, they had to get out before a slug hit the turbine and dropped his Huey right there in the river. Even though he knew Randy Harrison best of all these men, he had to leave or they'd all be done for. Taking up the collective, he began pulling back from the bank—and there was Harrison's face above the bushes, as he sprayed fire at an unseen NVA a few feet behind him. The lanky captain ran four strides, jumped in the water, stroked twice, and Fred Cook managed to grab his hand just as Harrison snared a rope ladder. They lifted away, dragging the Green Beret captain in the water, AKs firing and rockets bursting all around. Then several hands heaved Harrison aboard, and Fleming catapulted them above the trees.

Ten seconds later they were away and it was peaceful again.

Fleming and his copilot had been so focused they hadn't noticed their shattered windshield until air rushed in; the Huey's fuel gauges read EMPTY when they landed at Duc Co.

After shutting down his engine, Fleming climbed out, took his helmet off, wiped the salty sweat from his eyes and looked up at the slowing rotor. Suddenly two big hands grabbed his head, and Randy Harrison shouted, "You sweet motherfucker!" then stuck his tongue in the startled Green Hornet pilot's ear.

A couple months later, Fleming returned from R&R only to be told to keep his bags packed—he was being shipped home three months early. Even the swashbuckling gunship majors and lieutenant colonels gathered round to shake Fleming's hand and congratulate this "mere" troopship pilot. Fleming began to grow angry at the practical joke until the truth sank in and he realized everyone was serious.

First Lieutenant James P. Fleming's presence had been requested by the President of the United States. He'd been awarded the Medal of Honor and would be SOG's lone Air Force Medal of Honor recipient.

The Green Hornet gunship pilot, Major Leonard Gonzales, was awarded the Air Force Cross.

"They were great people," says RT Chisel One-Zero Sonny Franks.

7

SOG'S DARK ARTS

One sunny morning in mid-1967, four North Vietnamese fishermen were working the calm waters near Hon Mat Island, 150 miles south of Haiphong, North Vietnam. As they strained to drag aboard their crude net, one fisherman stood, shielded his eyes and stared to the horizon— yes, there was a foaming white wake, glowing brightly in the midday sun and bearing down on them. The other three men looked, too, and already the wake had segmented into three wakes behind three distinct shapes, gray and close to the water, getting nearer by the second.

In five minutes three strange boats fanned out and screamed past, then one turned back, cut engines and drifted alongside. A dozen Vietnamese men waved AK-47s at the fishermen, and all they could do was raise their hands.

Two strangers jumped aboard their boat. While one blindfolded and bound the fishermen, his partner announced in a North Vietnamese accent, "We are your brothers!" The fishermen offered no resistance when they were herded aboard the strange gunboat, which got under way immediately.

"We are your brothers!" a voice shouted above the roar of the engines. "The Sacred Sword of the Patriot League!"

What was this? Could it be? There had been many secret patriotic societies in colonial days, but they had been purged decades ago. And these men called them "brothers," not "comrades" as the Communists did.

Several hours later, the bound fishermen could feel the boat slow and sensed they were in calm water. Then their captors ceremoniously pulled away the blindfolds, and what the fishermen saw made their heads swim: In a small cove stood an ordinary-looking North Vietnamese fishing village, except a bamboo stockade encircled it, as in the old anti-French liberation war days, and over it flew not the North Vietnamese Communist flag but the large blue-and-white banner of what they had been told was the Sacred Sword of the Patriot League (SSPL).

"This is liberated territory," their guide boasted as they pulled up to the dock. "You are welcome here, brothers." Friendly people swarmed onto the dock and beckoned the new arrivals to share their dinner.

And what a feast! Pork, shellfish, spring rolls—more food than they'd seen for fifteen years. Then they all sang sentimental ballads the Communists had outlawed. The fishermen might have forgotten they were in North Vietnam except Patriot League men walked guard and issued repeated warnings not to violate blackout rules.

For two weeks the fishermen did nothing but eat, talk about the old days and learn about the Patriot League's liberation program. The League men knew all about corrupt Communist Party officials by name; it was a fresh breeze to hear such things.

Even as the war raged around them, they learned, the SSPL was organizing, recruiting and insinuating their people into positions across the country. They boasted of other enclaves like this, and hidden camps in the hills, with some villages secretly controlled by patriots. They even had their own clandestine radio that broadcast almost every day.

On their final night, the fishermen were talked to individually and given the names of SSPL contacts. Then they committed to memory secret recognition signals and meeting places and learned how to receive instructions via clandestine radio broadcasts.

At the dock the next morning, each man was given a gift package of items in short supply in North Vietnam—fishhooks, thread, cloth—and a transistor radio. Then as the whole village waved, the gun boat that had brought them cast off and—for security reasons—the crew again blindfolded their passengers.

After watching the boat disappear from the dock, one Patriot League man walked back toward the village, but he bypassed the bamboo stockade and went on until he came to another cove, from which it was clear this was not the mainland at all but an island. Cu Lao Cham Island. As any map of the Vietnamese coast discloses, Cu Lao Cham Island is well *south* of the 17th Parallel, near Danang. And in the island's second cove flew not the Patriot League banner but the Stars and Stripes, above a small SOG compound.

It was all trickery.

Operating as Project Humidor, the false village and the SSPL were the war's most elaborate continuing deception, conceived in SOG's den of the devious, the Psychological Studies Branch (OPS-33), the only U.S. element in Southeast Asia practicing those darkest of deceptive arts, black propaganda—vile, bold, often terrible lies that are falsely attributed.

Patterned after the old OSS Morale Operations Division, OPS-33 operated behind such heavy security that few Americans in Asia had any idea of its existence, which was absolutely essential since any trace of SOG's hidden hand would destroy a deception's effectiveness.

No small-scale effort, SOG's covert propaganda operation had a 1967 budget of $3.7 million and a staff of 150, about half of them Vietnamese civilians, the other half U.S. military, plus a dozen CIA officers.

The key to a successful black propaganda campaign was to develop a general theme upon which to hang all sorts of individual operations. As in any kind of deception, the SOG propagandists found, it was fastest, easiest and most effective to reinforce what the enemy already believes or suspects rather than try to convince him of something entirely new. For instance, since the North Vietnamese feared and hated the Chinese, black propaganda could aggravate these tensions.

For example, SOG manufactured stories that Chinese troops in North Vietnam were romancing the wives and girlfriends of faraway NVA soldiers; implied that the Chinese were supplying poor quality ammunition; suggested Peking was bleeding its Vietnamese comrades merely to send a political message to America. There was a grain of truth in each story, making them credible.

An almost crippling limitation, though, was that the same U.S. policy that precluded establishing a resistance movement in North Vietnam prevented SOG from stirring up the populace to overthrow its Communist government. There were some fine distinctions, however, because SOG was allowed to create a *false*, or "notional," resistance movement, the Sacred Sword of the Patriot League.

The Patriot League deception resulted partly from an analysis of what to do with the high-speed Norwegian Nasty boats once American planes began bombing North Vietnam: the boats weren't needed for retaliatory raids anymore, and by 1966 the enemy realized SOG's coastal threat would never grow beyond pinprick strikes, so their diversionary effectiveness had declined, too.

Their great speed made the Nastys a key contributor to Project Humidor, for they traveled so fast that the blindfolded fishermen miscalculated time and distance and believed they were still in North Vietnam.

The operation on Cu Lao Cham Island—called Paradise Island by the Americans—was run directly by OPS-33, and like all its brainchildren, the technical touches were superb, from architecture to accents. The illusion worked.

Along with lots of food, SOG fed their guests lots of false clues concerning conspiracies, secret agents and saboteurs, to be passed along to the enemy counterintelligence officers who were certain to debrief them. SOG's experts interlocked these clues with other evidence—from phony radio transmissions sent to nonexistent agents, to secret instructions hidden in a fisherman's gift bundle—for enemy counterintelligence officers to discover and collate. On top of all this, SOG agent teams planted Patriot League leaflets along North Vietnamese roads and trails, while First Flight C-123s airdropped resupply bundles to phantom resistance units. The harder enemy intelligence pursued these phantoms, the more confused they became, for a while even suspecting the Soviets of being the Patriot League's secret sponsor.

Though many fishermen undoubtedly were deceived, the links between the Nasty boats and U.S. were too well known.

Yet North Vietnamese counterintelligence could not ignore Project Humidor because of its sheer scale; by 1967, SOG's secret island processed twenty-seven kidnapped fishermen each month, and any one—or all—might return as sincere spies or saboteurs.

Integrated with Project Humidor were several other deception programs, the largest being SOG's so-called Poison Pen Letters, which attempted to implicate North Vietnamese officials by inventing apparent evidence of espionage and disloyalty.

Drawn up in Saigon, the Poison Pen Letters were posted to North Vietnam from Hong Kong and places as far away as Africa and New Caledonia. In 1964, SOG was mailing two hundred such letters per month, growing by 1966 to five hundred per month.

Most candidates were targeted solely because analysts found some means to incriminate them, which SOG accomplished, using an extensive, sophisticated database that contained, say, a profile of the mayor of Vinh or the name of a clothing shop facing the lagoon in downtown Hanoi.

The scheme might involve sending the target a birthday card from Paris, perhaps with a microdot message hidden under the stamp, *but it's not his birthday*. Even if North Vietnamese authorities let him receive the card—and certainly he would not look under the stamp—his pseudo instructions were so vague that surveillance would find his ordinary activities suspicious.

Perhaps the most devilish double cross ever devised was to examine a target's typewritten correspondence, have a micromachinist duplicate his typewriter's distinctive typeface, then produce and post a series of incriminating letters that—enemy experts would attest—could *only* have been typed on his typewriter. The British Secret Service perfected this technique in the early 1940s and employed it to frame Nazi agents in South America.

Another kind of Poison Pen Letter was correspondence that was *barely* suspicious—such as an envelope with a Paris return address but a Hong Kong postmark—just odd enough to ensure that a censor would open it and sweep it with six brushes, each containing a different chemical solution for exposing hidden messages. To his astonishment, since he so rarely found anything, a secret message would materialize warning, say, that an agent had been arrested outside Hanoi (which SOG knew to be true) and the letter's recipient must prepare to continue the lost agent's mission. The message was just nebulous enough that counterintelligence could fit it into any pet theories or conspiracies they wished. To further incriminate the recipient, perhaps a few hundred dollars were deposited in a Hong Kong bank in his name, or a bundle of gold coins given a known double agent for him. Or maybe a fisherman kidnapped by the Patriot League was told if ever he needs help, place a chalk X on a telephone pole that just happens to be across the street from the targeted official's apartment building.

Most letters were much simpler, just correspondence that alluded to the recipient's anti-Party criticisms, incriminating enough to put the recipient in a difficult position. Mere suspicion was enough to lock up almost anyone, who, at the hands of a Communist interrogator, was liable to confess and incriminate others. To the target's relatives and friends, each unjust arrest verified the regime's brutal character, setting off a chain reaction that spread through the entire society.

The most obscure and potentially most controversial of SOG's black psy ops was its secret funding of South Vietnamese anti-Communist and pro-U.S. front groups, a small effort that cost about $100,000 in Fiscal Year 1967. Little has been disclosed concerning SOG's role with front groups but it probably included the typical activities: sponsoring speaking tours for enemy defectors and massacre survivors; subsidizing conventions; underwriting printing and mailing of publications; and financing everything from rent to phone bills so useful organizations could disseminate their message.

A less politically controversial SOG black psy-op effort was the widespread forging of enemy documents, which were then fed back into the enemy's own distribution channels to confuse and manipulate him. Enough Viet Cong and NVA documents had been captured that the CIA's master forgers could replicate anything published by North Vietnam, right down to the exact papers, watermarks and inks. To help SOG accomplish these frauds, the CIA maintained special catalogs of various North Vietnamese and Viet Cong officials' signatures, letter formats, code names and bureaucratic jargon.

Few of these forgeries would have had much effect if SOG, via its CIA connections, had not been able to insinuate them directly into the enemy's distribution channels, especially through the Cambodian-based Central Office for South Vietnam (COSVN).

In at least one case, U.S. media unwittingly reported the contents of false documents, unaware they were SOG's handiwork. In 1971 the South Vietnamese government gave U.S. reporters what it honestly thought were enemy documents captured in the Central Highlands that claimed floods had so devastated the North that Defense Minister Vo Nguyen Giap had ordered thousands of troops back home. SOG had planted these forgeries to cause NVA in South Vietnam to worry about their families and desire to return home to help them. Although Hanoi hollered long and hard that the story was untrue, the American press never realized the documents were SOG forgeries.

A covert program of much wider influence was SOG's "Black Radio," which was aimed at the ordinary North Vietnamese civilian and soldier.

One North Vietnamese who defected in South Vietnam complained bitterly to American interrogators that the last straw came when Radio Hanoi "repeatedly announced the names of students sent to Poland, Korea [and] Red China for advanced study. This certainly was an injustice I could not tolerate. How could these privileged students be blessed with advanced study abroad while I was dying in this strange land, unnoticed. . . ."

Although there probably was a lot of truth to it, the "Radio Hanoi" story that pushed him into defecting quite likely came from Number 7 Hong Tap Street, Saigon—SOG's top-secret Black Radio office.

As was the case with so much in the secret war, Black Radio was limited by what the U.S. government would sanction. It was specifically forbidden to suggest the overthrow or destruction of the Hanoi government, though by definition black propaganda is not attributable. Despite these restrictions, SOG's Black Radio wizards were deviously clever.

One program involved a supposed clandestine radio. Listeners were told the broadcasts originated in North Vietnam and the radio had constantly to be moved to evade the North's security services, although it actually used studios and transmitters in South Vietnam. In midprogram there'd be an excited shout or two, then breathless, the announcer would explain that Communist forces were approaching and the station had to close down. A few days later he was back on the air, explaining how close a call it had been.

In Project Jenny, a U.S. Navy EC-121 aircraft broadcast SOG radio programs while flying off the North Vietnam coast, a technique that confused enemy radio direction finders and, because the radio wasn't far away, tended to overwhelm local station signals.

SOG's primary Black Radio technique was called "surfing," which means transmitting alongside a real station's frequency to capture listeners who mistakenly think they've tuned to the real station. Another technique was "hitchhiking," or coming up on the same frequency as the real station just after it signs off and using its call sign.

Enemy intelligence realized SOG was playing radio games but the goal was not to fool Hanoi officialdom but to carve a chasm between the Communist leadership and ordinary peasants and soldiers. These unsophisticated listeners were SOG's true radio audience, and by reaching them SOG encouraged and exploited doubts, reduced efficiency and undermined political reliability.

SOG's greatest material limitation in these radio games was a shortage of transistor radios in enemy hands. The solution was simple enough: SOG built its own radios, code-named Peanuts, which were CIA-designed and manufactured in Japan. Like anything having to do with OPS-33, the Peanuts radio was fiendishly clever. No matter how carefully you turned a Peanuts frequency dial, the real Radio Hanoi was lost in preplanned static, but right there, just a hair away and clear as a bell, was SOG's "Radio Hanoi." There was some speculation that the CIA had done in Vietnam what the British Special Branch had done with similar radios they planted among Communist insurgents in Malaya: Some contained hidden homing transponders, allowing the radios to be tracked electronically.

Peanuts radios were inserted using ruses like "lost" rucksacks or packages left behind on buses in Viet Cong areas; Nasty boats floated hundreds ashore into North Vietnam; U.S. recon teams planted Peanuts radios in enemy base camps or left them along trails; and C-130 Blackbirds airdropped them into North Vietnam, inserting eight thousand in 1967.

Blackbirds also airdropped another SOG black psy-op product into North Vietnam, so-called gift kits, like those given the abducted fishermen, dreamed up by American women office workers at CISO on Okinawa. "Let's give them a yard of cloth, real cheap cloth," they suggested, "about ten cents' worth, with some thread and a needle."

Learned psy-ops experts protested that the cloth could be used to make uniforms. Not *this* cloth, the women explained, showing a yellow-and-red, three-stripe psychedelic pattern that resembled South Vietnam's flag. There was just enough cloth to make diapers or a child's shirt, which CISO deputy Ben Baker found particularly inspired. "Imagine the secret police trying to take a kid's only shirt off his back," he said. "The mother will kill them with a broom."

The CISO women also designed a child's ball, its rubber impregnated with South Vietnam's national colors. Ben Baker found it all amusing. "Can you imagine taking them away from kids?"

Black propaganda items often were planted in Cambodia and Laos by U.S.-led recon teams, the primary type being "Soap Chips," which were forged letters supposedly from families in North Vietnam to soldiers in the South. Hand planted on NVA bodies or left beside heavily traveled trails, the letters were folded over and over as if read and reread—some soldier's treasured message from home.

The themes were clever. For instance, a letter could term a Tet (New Year) dinner a "feast" but describe such minimal fare that the reader could only wonder what food was available back home.

In early 1970, shortly after Ho Chi Minh's death, SOG teams inserted fraudulent "Happy Tet" cards bearing the message "Best wishes and success." Supposedly from a high North Vietnamese official who implied he was Ho's heir apparent, and coming well before the Party Central Committee had selected a successor, the cards seemed a usurper's attempt to wrest power and were intended to doom his chances.

SOG also continued a long wartime tradition of damaging an enemy by counterfeiting his money.

During World War II, the United States had printed large numbers of German Reichsmarks to fund intelligence operations, because the genuine article was hard to obtain. But fearing retaliation, U.S. policy has been to restrict counterfeiting to limited intelligence uses rather than engage in it on a scale intended to wreck an opponent's economy.

It wasn't very difficult to forge North Vietnamese paper money, which lacked modern counterfeiting safeguards. Indeed, North Vietnamese currency designers thought there was little likelihood anyone would duplicate their money since, like other Communist money, it had no value beyond North Vietnam's borders. In addition, the Party stringently controlled internal printing presses, leaving the only real threat from SOG or the CIA.

Cutting technically perfect plates and printing North Vietnamese "funny money" proved a snap for Okinawa-based experts who'd mastered their craft duplicating all sorts of foreign documents and credentials.

For those running recon, the top-secret counterfeit currency most often inserted was code-named Benson Silk, an NVA scrip, or kind of occupation money. Mostly it was carried as a secondary rather than a primary mission, with our intelligence officers instructing, "If you get a chance, plant some of this stuff." Benson Silk was tightly controlled, signed out on a hand receipt and usually carried only by the One-Zero.

It was planted mostly to confuse the enemy: A North Vietnamese intelligence officer coming upon a small fortune on a dead NVA soldier would have to ask, *How had he acquired all this money? Was he a thief? No. Then he had to be a U.S. agent and therefore this wasn't an ambush but a prearranged meeting that went bad! How could the comrades in his squad not have known—unless they, too, were traitors?* and so on. The enemy was meant to chew this over and over and never be quite sure.

And insidiously, even if the enemy determined this money was counterfeit, his paranoia was aroused all the more: How much other money was counterfeit, too? Interestingly, Hanoi did not complain publicly about these money games, though certainly its leaders realized SOG was counterfeiting North Vietnamese currency; a defector reported Hanoi could throw no stones because the North Vietnamese were duplicating South Vietnamese money on an even larger scale.

But polluting the enemy's currency was as nothing compared to SOG's most successful salting operation, Project Eldest Son, at various times also code-named Italian Green and later Pole Bean, which insinuated into the enemy's supply system cleverly sabotaged AK-47 and mortar ammunition that blew up in his weapons, killing or wounding his soldiers.

The genesis of Eldest Son was in the fertile mind of that old OSS operative Chief SOG Colonel Jack Singlaub, who explained, "I was frustrated by the fact that I couldn't airlift the ammunition we were discovering along the [Ho Chi Minh] Trail." A typical cache contained far more ammo than a small team could carry away; it could not be destroyed with fire. And explosives would only scatter small-arms ammunition, not damage it.

Singlaub reports, "Initially I thought of just booby-trapping it so that when they'd pick up a case it would blow up." Some kind of mercury switches or timers would have worked, but it would have been difficult and time consuming for recon men to open ammo cases and plant booby traps without leaving a trace.

At almost the same time Singlaub was wrestling with the problem of ammo caches, a reader's letter in *American Rifleman* magazine suggested the very solution he came up with: Booby-trap the ammunition *itself*.

Singlaub had his CIA deputy use agency channels for a quick feasibility study. A short while later Singlaub was invited to Okinawa for a demonstration; a bench-mounted AK-47 was loaded with one Eldest Son round, then he was invited to pull the string attached to its trigger. He was awed because "it completely blew up the receiver and the bolt was projected backwards, I would imagine that would be into the head of the firer. It appeared to be very lethal—I was convinced that it was."

Each recon team carried a few Eldest Son rounds, usually as loose AK cartridges or a single round in an otherwise normal full AK magazine. These were not so much for inserting in caches as planting on the bodies of ambushed enemy soldiers, which was the least detectable means of insertion.

Eldest Son 82mm mortar ammo typically came in heavy crates of four rounds, so teams didn't carry it as often; still, I recall twice toting such cases during recon operations, and to our surprise we witnessed an enemy platoon carry one case away.

Probably the cleverest Eldest Son insertion was performed by SOG SEALs in a Mekong Delta canal, where they filled a sampan with tainted ammunition, shot it tastefully full of holes, then spilled chicken blood over it and set it adrift upstream from a known Viet Cong village, making it look as though its Communist crew had fallen overboard in an ambush. The Viet Cong took it hook, line and sinker.

But the bulk of Eldest Son ammunition was disseminated in other ways, probably the biggest being the construction of false caches in areas known to contain real ones. Special teams were created at SOG recon FOBs in Danang and Ban Me Thuot just to build these false caches. It was while on such a mission that a Danang Eldest Son cache-building team was lost on 30 November 1968, generating more Special Forces MIAs than any other SOG cross-border operation. Led by a happy-go-lucky Hawaiian, Major Samuel Toomey, this seven-man, all-U.S. team and a dozen cases of Eldest Son 82mm mortar ammo were aboard a Kingbee helicopter 20 miles west of Khe Sanh when a single 37mm antiaircraft round hit the chopper. The effect was catastrophic. An eyewitness reported, "There wasn't anything bigger than a cigarette butt that hit the ground. It just went off like a nuke." In addition to Toomey, missing were Lieutenant Raymond Stacks and Sergeants Klaus Scholz, Arthur Bader, Richard Fitts, Michael Mein and Gary LaBohn.

Beyond the human loss, the incident generated a scathing reaction from Vientiane when the U.S. ambassador learned of it; SOG headquarters had tried to slip the operation past him, and hadn't sought his approval. The embassy's protest was so strong, recalls Chief SOG Colonel Steve Cavanaugh, that it "almost stopped the whole Eldest Son Progam."

But Eldest Son's successes spoke louder and more convincingly than could any parochial argument. And the proof of its effectiveness rolled in.

For instance, on 6 June 1968, U.S. 1st Infantry Division soldiers came upon a shattered AK-47 "found beside the body of an NVA soldier" who'd died while firing at the Americans. It seemed a great mystery to them why his weapon had exploded, since his AK magazine was half empty, suggesting that nothing could have been obstructing the muzzle. Paratroopers of the 101st Airborne Division similarly found a dead Communist soldier grasping his exploded rifle, while Captain Ed Lesesne reports seeing a photo at SOG headquarters of a dead enemy soldier with his AK's bolt blown out the back of his weapon "and right through his eye socket."

SOG's booby-trapped mortar rounds proved effective, too. American 25th Infantry Division soldiers discovered a whole North Vietnamese mortar battery destroyed, with dead gunners sprawled around four peeled-back tubes. In another incident, a 101st Airborne Division firebase was taking mortar fire one night when there was an odd-sounding *boomphf* from a facing hillside, after which firing abruptly stopped. A sweep the next morning revealed two dead enemy soldiers, a split tube and blood trails going off into the jungle.

Eldest Son ammo was getting into enemy hands, and as the reports came in, SOG initiated the program's next phase: its black psy-op exploitation. One "Viet Cong" document—forged by SOG, of course, and insinuated through secret agents to the Viet Cong's National Liberation Front (NLF)—tried to make light of exploding weapons, declaring, "We know that it is rumored that some of the ammunition has blown up in the AK-47. This report is greatly exaggerated. It is a very, very small percentage of the ammunition that has exploded. . . ."

And through Eldest Son, SOG was tossing salt in that Chinese-relations wound, attributing the faulty ammunition to Red Chinese sources. "Only a few thousand such cases have been found thus far," was the theme of a number of forged North Vietnamese documents as quoted by a senior SOG officer. One forgery concluded, "that while our allies, the Peoples Republic of China, may be having some quality control problems, these are being worked out and we think that in the future there will be very little chance of this happening."

That "in the future" hook was especially devious, because any NVA soldier looking at the lot numbers on his ammo cases could see all of it had been manufactured years earlier, and due to the natural lag of shipping from China and transporting it down the Trail, no really new ammo could possibly reach NVA combat soldiers for a long, long time.

Eldest Son impacted at enemy command levels, too, Colonel Cavanaugh reported. "We had communications [intercept] evidence, anyway, that that thing [Eldest Son] was worth its weight, because warnings were issued throughout the NVA to be careful of this and do that and this." The enemy actually thought it was a manufacturing problem, not sabotage.

To make sure the word got out—not just to the enemy but also as a warning to American soldiers—SOG arranged for cautionary notices on Armed Forces Radio and TV. But the concerns about endangering U.S. personnel were no deception: MACV issued Directive 381–24 which forbade "the employment of captured weapons and munitions other than by special mission personnel." News reached the weekly civilian Stateside tabloid *Army Times,* which warned GIs in August 1969 that "numerous incidents have caused injury and sometimes death to the operators of enemy weapons," the cause of which was "defective metallurgy" or "faulty ammo."

Inevitably, the enemy realized something was happening to his ammunition, but this was still psychologically useful since it caused him to fear any ammo cache that U.S. recon teams had found.

Word about Eldest Son was leaking out so extensively by mid-1969 that *Time* magazine reported, "Special Forces have been accused of . . . slipping doctored ammunition, designed to explode on use, into enemy caches." SOG men chuckled at such naïveté, since *Time* thought this "illegal" and the work of rogues.

Related to Eldest Son were a few specially built booby-trapped items SOG teams inserted in Laos, not for their destructive effect but to inspire certain enemy reactions. For example, recon teams left behind booby-trapped 35mm cameras so enemy soldiers would find them and pass them along to their intelligence officers; when opened, of course, they blew up.

The least suspicious booby trap I ever handled was an Okinawa-built, one-quart canteen that even contained a liquid you could hear sloshing if you shook it. Under the cap was a time-delay activation switch. Once the switch was flicked—the next time the cap was unscrewed—*ka-pow!* Like the camera, it was intended to deter the enemy from stripping gear off recon men's bodies.

To deter the enemy from using captured American radios, CISO manufactured special booby-trap kits for PRC-25 FM sets, the standard type carried by U.S. and ARVN units as well as SOG recon teams. These were packed with plastic explosive and a detonator that went off when the radio was switched on.

Bob Howard, one of SOG's most accomplished recon men and a Medal of Honor recipient, came up with his own technique to instill a bit of caution in enemy soldiers posted to watch landing zones in Laos. He took an old footlocker and painted it bright red; then he packed it with about 80 pounds of aging TNT that was starting to sweat nitro, dual-primed it with five-minute-time-delay detonators and left it on his insert LZ.

He led his team off into the jungle, then circled back to watch what happened. "Sure enough," he said, "people were coming from everywhere, running out to get that footlocker. And I actually think some of them were in the process of opening it when it went off. I mean, that bastard blew a hole in the ground, it blew shit for a quarter of a mile, that's how much TNT we had in it."

Probably the most elaborate dirty trick was the brainchild of Sergeant Major Paul Darcy, who scrounged an unflyable two-seat U-17 spotter plane, then rigged it with smoke grenades and had a helicopter carry it over southern Laos one overcast morning. Darcy and another man played a radio game, simulating messages from a stricken plane until finally came a panicky voice, "He's going down! He's going down!"

Darcy ignited the smoke grenades, then the helicopter released the old aircraft, which fell through the clouds streaming smoke and "crashed" in the jungle.

Eventually the enemy reached the wreckage, found the smoke grenades and realized he'd been had—but when the next real plane went down, perhaps he wouldn't respond quite so fast, which would improve chances of a Bright Light team getting there first.

But the most mind-blowing dirty trick I ever saw was conceived by my good recon friend Floyd "Pigpen" Ambrose. He went all the way to Bangkok to have printed a poster of his own design, showing a nude, large-breasted Asian woman, which he'd tack on trees beside major enemy trails.

Imagine the shock of an NVA soldier, raised under a straitlaced Communist orthodoxy that prohibited pornography, who came upon Floyd's poster—not to mention the provocative headline, which boldly asked in Vietnamese, "Who's sleeping with your wife, and has she got jugs like these?" As the message grew more inflammatory, the print became smaller, luring the engrossed soldier closer—and closer—and he'd forget caution and step right on the small mine Floyd had planted and lose a foot.

Due to these and other SOG black psy-op tricks, one can hardly wonder at the confused reports that flowed up and down the enemy chain of command, and the fevered attempts to reassure everyone that headquarters was on top of it. Could the NVA publish a bulletin to beware of red boxes left in the open? They might as well have issued a bulletin, Beware of *everything*.

Though the exact effects remain unmeasurable, there can be little doubt SOG's black propaganda yielded results. The closest SOG ever came to learning its impact was in Paris in May 1968: As a precondition to peace talks, Hanoi's negotiators insisted that the U.S. put an end to its black psy-ops programs, especially that despicable Sacred Sword of the Patriot League.

RUN THROUGH
THE JUNGLE

By late 1967, nearly every other SOG cross-border mission made contact, with about half the contacts leading to live-or-die shoot-outs against vastly more numerous enemy. NVA forces in Laos and Cambodia had climbed above 100,000 with 40,000 of them detailed as Ho Chi Minh Trail security; another 100,000 NVA passed down the Trail that year en route to South Vietnam. Against these enormous numbers, SOG typically fielded thirty or forty Americans at once in Laos and Cambodia.

Major Ed Rybat, SOG's FOB 1 commander at Phu Bai in 1967–68, recalls the stress. "I was almost getting nightmares. Every time we went in, *ba-ba-ba-ba-boom-crack-bang*. FOB 1 took a hell of a plastering during my time up there—we took 51 or 52 percent casualties on operations."

At least half the time, though, SOG teams successfully penetrated enemy redoubts to wiretap, ambush, kidnap, mine and surveil the North Vietnamese, and fought their way out despite abysmal odds. How? Take the case of RT Maine's adventure in southeast Laos.

It was late morning when RT Maine's H-34 Kingbee dodged drifting rain squalls to land on a slash-and-burn clearing about 15 miles inside Laos, near Highway 165. Additional troop helicopters, gunships and A-1 Skyraiders hung back just beyond earshot, ready to intervene in case of trouble.

One-Zero David Baker was first man off the Kingbee, followed by Mike Buckland, his One-Two, with the radio, then the One-One, Sherman Miller, and five Montagnards. The Kingbee lifted away.

Baker headed for a woodline, then froze—everyone froze—just ahead were bunkers and milling groups of NVA. Baker backed away, turned for another woodline and saw it, too, bristling with men and heavy earth-and-log bunkers—NVA soldiers were *everywhere*.

RT Maine was totally surrounded on an open LZ, outnumbered perhaps twenty to one by an entrenched enemy, overlooked by heavy machine guns whose bolts they now heard slamming shut. By any reckoning, Baker and his seven men had about ten seconds to live. Buckland tersely radioed Covey, "Have inserted into a major unit and not yet engaged. Stand by."

But the NVA just stood there watching, some only 20 yards away. Baker made a shrewd observation: The NVA had bomb shelters, not fighting bunkers. These lacked firing ports, so the NVA couldn't shoot from inside and had to climb out even to see, silhouetting their heads and shoulders like targets in a shooting gallery.

Meanwhile a half-dozen enemy leaders marched from deeper in the bunker area with an indignant "we'll-get-to-the-bottom-of-this" air about them. Perhaps, just perhaps, RT Maine's unmarked Kingbee had been mistaken for a similar-looking Soviet-made Mi-4, used by the North Vietnamese. One-Two Mike Buckland smiled, waved and called out reassuringly in Russian.

More NVA were standing atop bunkers now, craning necks like gawkers at a traffic accident. They didn't even point their AKs at the team. Baker, Buckland and their Yard point man kept their CAR-15s low and let the NVA officers approach to the edge of the woodline, only fifteen paces away. Then all three opened fire and snuffed them in two seconds. The NVA command element was gone.

Stunned NVA machine gunners grabbed their heavy 12.7mm guns but did not fire, unable to believe what had happened. That's where they died, shot down by the fast-firing recon men. So astounded were the NVA that the SOG men fired a full ten seconds before the enemy shot back, but then it turned into a melee.

More NVA climbed into view, and RT Maine cleaned the bunker tops again, this time dropping twenty men. But their luck was almost gone. Seeking cover, Baker hustled his men a few steps into a knee-deep depression, just enough to lie belly-down in while heavy fire crisscrossed above them. Astonishingly, the NVA began shooting at each other!

Hugging terra firma, the SOG men shot low to ensure hits while the confused NVA fired high, hitting each other. Newly arriving NVA didn't understand at whom or what they were supposed to fire. Baker called in gunships and told them to strafe any treeline.

Manned by replacements, the two 12.7mms fired, but they'd been emplaced as antiaircraft weapons and their muzzles couldn't be depressed low enough to hit RT Maine—they were pummeling their own bunkers. A pair of A-1 Skyraiders rolled in with cluster bombs and 20mm cannons just as an NVA squad assaulted the SOG team: The NVA were dead before they'd gone 10 yards.

On a shouted command, another NVA squad rushed out but made it only 20 yards before CAR-15 fire knocked them all down. Covey offered to attempt an extract, but Baker said no, not until the NVA were dead or pushed back.

Fire was coming closer now. Bullets smacked into the rucksacks behind which Maine's men had taken shelter, then a bullet tore a URC-10 radio from Baker's hand. The NVA launched three human-wave assaults, and each time they got closer before Maine's fire cut them down; Baker told Covey to bring napalm in close or they'd be overrun. Another fifteen NVA jumped to their feet, shouting and dashing and firing just as an A-1 rolled in.

Then a bouncing 750-pound napalm canister split apart so close it spewed petroleum-smelling globs on RT Maine's rucksacks and weapons and on Mike Buckland's hands and shirt. An instant later the napalm burst hot orange all around them and set ablaze rucksacks and a Montagnard's CAR-15. They felt the air sucked away as black smoke blocked the sun, and inside its shadow fifteen Vietnamese human torches staggered and collapsed, "a horrifying sight," Buckland called it.

The napalm globs on RT Maine's men did not ignite. Buckland recalled a verse from Isaiah: "When you walk through fire, you shall not be burned." The Skyraiders had knocked out the heavy machine guns, and at last, bloodied and burned, the NVA fell back.

A Kingbee nearly out of station time snatched away RT Maine; Baker's men had been on the ground forty-two minutes and had fired nearly four thousand rounds and had thrown fifty grenades. They'd been too busy fighting to count, but a likely fifty enemy lay dead, and twice that many wounded. Against this heavy loss, Baker alone was wounded, superficially, by grenade fragments.

What's significant in RT Maine's encounter is not that they were lucky but that luck's contribution was secondary. Though odds often seemed dismal, as in Maine's case, it was the One-Zero's job to turn the odds around through shrewd judgment and tactical skill. Realistic training, mastery of weapons and understanding the enemy were the bedrock that made this possible. It began with solid mission planning.

Contrary to how Hollywood depicts such things, a SOG operation was not laid out in a thirty-second huddle aboard an aircraft en route to a target. The process began a week before insert with a warning order that gave the One-Zero an execution date, target and mission description. Later, the team's Americans sat through a formal briefing, then the One-Zero overflew the target to select LZs, shoot photos and get the lay of the land. Next came days studying maps, intelligence reports and aerial photos. Then the One-Zero formulated a detailed plan that he briefed back to his FOB commander. The One-Zero had tremendous latitude, a freer hand, thought Major Henry Gole, a SOG staff officer, "than most senior officers in conventional forces." And there was premission training: If it was a wiretap, for instance, the team brushed up on operating tap gear and rehearsed security formations they'd used during the tap. Finally came the draw of mission-specific gear, packing it all up, followed by the One-Zero's equipment inspection, then a quick weapons test firing.

Every aspect of SOG recon procedures was intensely thought through to push out little edges, a thousand little edges that, cumulatively, yielded the kind of decisive advantage that brought RT Maine out alive. Recon men had to outrun, outshoot, outmaneuver and outthink the best Hanoi threw at them. Mastery of weapons was the starting point.

Chief SOG Colonel Jack Singlaub said, "It is my view that a guy who has 100 percent confidence in his ability to use his or any weapon doesn't have to worry about his personal safety. He can concentrate on his mission."

Applying Colonel Singlaub's observation, SOG men practice-fired at least every other day. After firing a CAR-15 extensively, its three-round bursts seemed to dance from its muzzle. You hit targets not by aiming but by *thinking* about aiming. Reflexes became so blazingly fast that the act preceded the thought—I once drew, shot and dropped an NVA faster than I could recognize him, and only afterward did I realize that he already had his AK trained on me when I drew.

But a recon man required presence of mind. RT California One-Zero Joe Walker once had an NVA let loose full-auto just 30 yards away; Joe instantly fired back at full-auto but didn't connect in two bursts, so he knelt, flipped to semi-auto, aimed—in a flurry of flying lead—and dropped the NVA with one shot. Most men would have "sprayed and prayed."

Every item a recon man carried was deliberately positioned. Reload magazines went on his left side, grenades on the right, compass on the left wrist so he could extend his arm away from a steel weapon for an accurate reading without taking his right hand off the grip. Reload magazines were positioned so even on the move he could drop an empty magazine with one hand, pull a full one with the other, slam it into his CAR-15 without even looking, slap the bolt release with the left palm and continue firing. With practice, reloading took less than three seconds.

Recon men straightened grenade pins and wrapped them once with tape so that even if wounded in one arm they could pull pins with their teeth, just like in the movies. And every bit of gear was muffled with tape or rubber bands so it generated no rattle, clank or noise of any kind. There was a rule, a lesson, a reason, for everything they did— *everything*.

SOG's top-secret world evolved its own ethic, an unspoken code tempered by danger, duty and loyalty. The One-Zero was the most knowledgeable and experienced man on the team. Even if outranked by his One-One or One-Two, the One-Zero was god. When he declared his team had to be extracted, his judgment was not usually questioned. As Major Scotty Crerar observed, "If he's wrong, if we find out he's lost his nerve, we'll change him. But don't second-guess him from here."

The One-Zero was the first man off the helicopter going in, and last man on coming out. If a point man was overwhelmed by fear, the One-Zero walked point himself. He led not by force of rank or intimidation, but by example. Indeed, a SOG team was a free association of volunteers who chose to serve together.

Medal of Honor recipient Bob Howard explained: "It's kind of hard to put into words, but it's like having somebody that you love. If you served [in SOG] and you were willing to die, you wanted to have a person there you would not mind dying for or dying with. A lot of people don't understand that."

There was great assurance in looking over, narrow-eyed and tense, your thumb easing the CAR-15 safety off, to see your partner's eyes just the same, both knowing that no matter the fury about to be unleashed he would not run off and leave you, nor would you leave him. That's not cheap talk. When ten times as many NVA as anyone should reasonably fight suddenly appear, eons of evolution and every bit of common sense screams *Run!* Afraid? Beyond words. But you stay and fight.

Leaving behind a live, wounded man was all but inconceivable, but teammates forced each other to vow not to risk their lives for their dead bodies. Yes, SOG teams left American bodies if they had to—better that than give their foes more lives. To give such an order, and I've given the command myself, leaves no remorse, just regret at its necessity. SOG survivors always felt they carried their teammate's spirit back with them.

Devotion to mission was an ethic, too. A recon man's duty was to accomplish his mission *and* survive, in that order.

Those who operated well in SOG's environment earned the highest compliment, "He's good in the woods." When One-Zeros talked among themselves, their highest assessment was, "I'd take him on the ground with me." Like notches on the butt of a six-gun, a SOG man's cross-border missions measured merit: Until he had three missions he shouldn't open his mouth; after five missions, he could be relied upon to tell a war story honestly; ten made him seasoned and probably a One-Zero; fifteen and he was running out of luck; twenty and it was hard to explain why he was still alive.

Based upon the military logic that your best men handle the most difficult tasks, mission success earned you a more dangerous assignment next time, until, as One-Zero "Squirrel" Sprouse used to say, "We're bein' run to death." Often that's where it led.

In RT Hawaii's case, their nemesis became Target Juliet Nine, the most hostile piece of real estate in southern Laos. One-Zero Bill DeLima and teammates Glen Uemura and Lonnie Pulliam barely escaped their first time in Juliet Nine, but their One-One, First Lieutenant Jim Ripanti, was killed. A few months later, Juliet Nine again was the scheduled target, and since they knew the area, Uemura, as acting One-Zero, and DeLima got the mission, bringing along Ripanti's replacement, Specialist Four Dennis Bingham. Hit by a reinforced company, Uemura and DeLima barely made it out, and this time bloody Juliet Nine took young Bingham's life.

Not long afterward Bill DeLima declared his willingness to go *anyplace* but Juliet Nine and insisted he could not go back into that hellhole. Yet even as he spoke he knew he'd go if assigned. Recon men always did.

One-Zero Ken McMullin recalls, "You'd absolutely not want to run that mission, not at all. Scared to death. But I'd rather die than have my friends think I was chickenshit."

But SOG's behind-the-lines domain was not every man's cup of tea. Sergeant First Class Sammy Hernandez had a recon man weep on his shoulder after a narrow escape, begging not to go back into Laos. The man quit.

"When I saw him at [Fort] Bragg years later, at the bar, he always put his head down when he saw me come in," says Hernandez, "I told him, 'Hey, buddy, you don't have to do that, you have nothing to be ashamed of.' Some people can do it, some people can't. I am never going to be the guy to say, 'Hey, you don't have the guts to go out on those patrols.' You'll never hear that from me."

Explains Captain Jim Storter, "There are some people that once they hear the helicopters go off in the distance, their ass gets so tight they can't breathe. When it gets quiet and you're on your own, a lot of people can't handle it." Adds the Kontum FOB commander, Lieutenant Colonel Galen "Mike" Radke, "You can't train a man for that, he's got to be born into that."

Like Ben Lyons, who explained, "I just got a charge out of being in the other guy's backyard."

A few longtime recon men couldn't quit if they wanted to; like compulsive gamblers, they'd so often wagered their lives that anything else became hopelessly boring. We called it, "getting recon in your blood," a danger-induced adrenaline rush that inspired ever-greater risks; the more missions you accumulated, the harder it was to stop. Eventually, most such men wagered once too often.

Everyone respected the dangers; that's why they trained so hard, why they finessed tactics. The basic tactic for bettering a numerically superior foe was Immediate Action (IA) Drills, which worked something like a bantamweight boxer bloodying a heavyweight's nose with a surprise flurry of punches, then exploiting the subsequent ten seconds of amazement to head for the hills. IA Drills were carefully orchestrated, rehearsed, then mastered.

An IA Drill "trigger" was one shot, usually fired by the point man, though even if the enemy fired first the drill was executed the same way. Odd-numbered men jumped one step right, even men one step left, and faced the direction of fire whether hit from back, front or side. The man closest emptied his weapon full-auto at the enemy in three-round bursts, then dashed between his arrayed comrades to lead the team away in the opposite direction. The split second the first man's weapon was empty, the next man picked up the slack, also firing full-auto; then he, too, ran down the middle, after the first man. And so on. To exaggerate a team's firepower, they fired only tracer rounds in their first magazine.

The result was one long continuous burst backed up by exploding 40mm projectiles, tear gas and white phosphorous grenades, then a one-minute time-delay claymore planted by the last man. From first shot to last was thirty seconds or less, a shocking blur of bullets and explosions that seemed ten times the fury possible for a mere six or eight men to unleash. Between operations, recon teams rehearsed live-fire IA Drills several times per week.

SOG men constantly looked for new devices or techniques to enhance IA Drills. While I was One-Zero of RT California it occurred to me that a bugle sounding a charge would unnerve the NVA, but I couldn't find a bugle, nor anyone who could be relied upon to pucker amid a firefight. Then I recalled the Freon-powered air horns at high school football games. Perfect! My father shipped me an air horn, which I spray painted black and carried into Cambodia, taped to my web gear.

On our second day in Daniel Boone, Rex Jaco, John Yancey, Galen Musselman and I walked into an L-shaped ambush by about twenty NVA firing AKs, machine guns and rockets. We squatted down and returned fire but we were almost pinned. I reached for a grenade but my hand found the air horn. I depressed its plunger for a full fifteen seconds: AHHHHHHHHHHHHH-OOORRRRRRRRRR!

When I lifted my finger you could hear a pin drop—the NVA had run away! We escaped from what could have been doom, without a scratch. But tricks like that work only the first time.

No force, no matter its size or armament, stood a chance against SOG IA drills—*for thirty seconds.* After that, no matter how slick your IA Drill, God found himself on the side of the big battalions.

A competent One-Zero anticipated enemy contact and mentally rehearsed his reactions, continually revising his thoughts to fit shifting circumstances. If we're hit right now, where's the nearest LZ? What do I do if we take fire from uphill versus downhill, or at our same elevation? Should we fight through or flee? If there's a trail atop this hill, are we far enough below the crest that passing NVA won't hear us? Where's the nearest defensible terrain? Where's our next rally point in case we're split? Upon contact the team would be executing their One-Zero's plan while the enemy was only reacting.

Preferably, though, SOG teams practiced such stealth that there was no contact. In a full day, a team often advanced only 500 yards—that's only 50 yards per hour, which translates to just one step per minute. During that minute, you scanned front and sides; carefully eyeballed anyplace an enemy soldier might lurk; trained your CAR-15 at the spot where contact might erupt; examined the ground where you'd next place your foot; paused; smelled; listened; delicately pushed aside a vine with your left hand; tested the ground ahead with one toe; slowly shifted your weight to the forward foot; eased the vine behind you and ensured it didn't catch on your rucksack or web gear; paused; listened; looked around again; lifted your trailing foot and gently brought it up to your other foot. You repeated this process hour after hour, exactly; you became immersed in tiny, deliberate actions, patient acts that so occupied your mind that there was nothing but the present—this step, this minute, this place. Consciousness soared.

Silence was not a virtue, it was *the* virtue. If a Yard or American snapped the tiniest twig, his teammates' glaring eyes damned him for endangering the rest. A few such infractions and the perpetrator was off the team.

Camouflage was simple but effective: Just before an operation each man put on his field gear—rucksack, web gear, hat, scarf, weapon— over unmarked, "sterile," jungle fatigues. Teammates took turns spray painting each other with black streaks to tone down the edges and blend it all together. For their shadowy world of deep jungle, stepping from shadow to shadow, this camouflage pattern fit in superbly. They applied camouflage stick to their faces and touched it up hourly during breaks; some men took it one step further and dyed their blond hair black.

During a five-day mission they spoke only in whispers, but most often they communicated by hand signals, facial expressions and body language. A nod, a click of the tongue, a raised eyebrow, a shrug, tipping or shaking or nodding the head, an inquiring glance.

Your Montagnard point man freezes, one foot suspended midstep, his left hand signs "V-C," then he eases that foot to earth. He turns slowly, gives you, his One-Zero, a smile like Sylvester the Cat espying Tweety Bird, meaning the enemy is lax, few in number and vulnerable—and his wide, happy feline eyes look to you for the nod to eat Tweety Bird.

And then there was instinct. Modern life so celebrates intellect that we ignore instinct, but when recon men "felt" something—danger, anticipation, anxiety, hackles rising on their neck—they thought it a subconscious warning. Some hints might be too oblique to be articulated but were to be considered real nonetheless. It could be the gut feeling that someone's watching you, or an overwhelming foreboding about climbing a hill. Recon men learned to trust their instincts.

It was instinct and woodsman skills that saved the day for RT Illinois. After evading trackers and an aggressive NVA platoon for two days, deep in Laos, One-Zero Steve Keever paused for a break on a hill beside his One-One, Larry Predmore, and One-Two, Dan Ross. "Pretty soon, Larry Predmore taps my leg and he points downhill," Keever recalled. "Being the knowledgeable outdoors person that he is, he sees an owl come out of a tree and fly up the hill toward us a little bit, alight in another tree, and turn around and look."

A longtime Minnesota hunter, Predmore knew owls don't take wing in daytime unless disturbed, and by no coincidence, this owl had been flushed from their back trail. Predmore had a bad feeling about it. Signaling the others to be still, he raised his CAR-15, and his front sight met the curious face of an NVA tracker who looked up to his doom. The One-One dropped him and several other NVA, Illinois executed an IA Drill, then they ran for it. Between Predmore, the IA Drill and tactical air strikes, they accounted easily for a dozen NVA, while RT Illinois suffered not one minor wound.

A wise One-Zero assumed from the moment he landed that the enemy was scouring for any sign of his team and therefore he tried to eliminate evidence of their passage, a process called "sterilizing." It was the assistant team leader's job to sterilize their back trail, picking up flotsam, intertwining foliage and obscuring footprints. Some RTs became fatally lax: Two overrun teams were found by Bright Light teams simply by following candy wrappers and cigarette butts from their insert LZs to the places they died—or it can be said, to the places the NVA so easily slaughtered them.

Yet even after careful sterilizing, creating false trails and deftly changing directions, teams still sometimes picked up trackers. Then the basic countertactic was "buttonhooking," circling back to observe your own back trail. Or you could leave mines.

Mining a back trail was easy using the M-14 "toe popper," a mine that was the diameter of a soda can but only one-third as long and weighing less than a quarter of a pound. Designed to injure one foot—hence its nickname—the toe popper was compact and carried by the dozen. Toe poppers were great for alerting you to shadowers, as RT West Virginia found during one mission. While slogging through thick jungle, One-Zero Ron Knight noticed his Nungs had to sit atop a wide mahogany log then pivot their legs over to cross it; Knight wedged a toe popper under the bark, right where they'd crossed. "And we probably hadn't gone 300 or 400 meters and I heard that boy pop, and you never heard such screaming. So we got somebody."

Another countertactic was more direct, though riskier: Ambush the trackers with a suppressed weapon. It works fine in the movies, but if the enemy gets off even one shot it discloses your location to nearby enemy forces and the race is on. One-Zero Richard Gross had evaded NVA for several days in the heavily occupied Ashau Valley when one morning he spotted a tracker a few yards below him in a gully, so preoccupied studying the ground that his M-1 carbine was slung over his shoulder. "He's looking right and left, right and left," Gross said. Gross began unholstering his silenced .22 High Standard pistol—then the tracker looked up and made eye contact. "And he grabbed that damned carbine, and I had my CAR-15 lying right there, picked it up, and *boom*. Had to, didn't have any other choice." Gross hoped the tracker was alone, but several NVA platoons arrived, and a long firefight ensued. Fortunately Gross lived to tell the tale.

Doing the unexpected also could shake pursuers. With trackers close behind, One-Zero Joe Walker and RT California reached a major highway. To lose the trackers Walker did the unthinkable: At high noon he trotted 2 kilometers down Highway 110. It was *pok*-time, the Vietnamese equivalent of siesta, and they came upon not a single NVA. The trackers couldn't find a track on that hard-packed clay surface, and besides, they *knew* no Americans would go down the road.

Dog-assisted tracker teams proved tougher to counter, but the handlers often relied too heavily on their furry friends to alert them to danger. In Cambodia, Ben Lyons' recon team had an oddly ironic tracker dog encounter. Out of water, his team crept to a creek and spotted a handful of approaching enemy. Lyons' men lay low. The NVA had a dog, which began barking. "I could hear an NVA talking, didn't understand what he was saying," Lyons said. Then one Communist soldier almost stepped on Lyons' Yard point man, who opened fire, cutting down the dog and several NVA. After the mission, Lyons asked his point man what the dog handler had said just before he shot him. The Montagnard chuckled and reported, "He say, 'Don't worry, dog! I know Americans are near!'" Lyons shook his head. "And that's the *last* thing that sucker said."

After experimenting with various concoctions to confuse tracker dogs—red pepper, exotic fragrances—SOG settled on CS tear gas powder, which teams carried in plastic bottles and shook out like talcum powder.

John Meyer, One-Zero of RT Idaho, had to employ every trick in the book to escape NVA hot on his trail in Target Echo Eight, a particularly dangerous place just west of the Ashau Valley. He had just set up an ambush on Highway 922 when a toe popper on his back trail exploded. Seconds later two heavy diesel engines started up and tracked vehicles rolled out of a base camp a half mile away. "Then things got real hairy," Meyer said.

A reinforced NVA platoon came down the highway, alert, eyes scouring the bushes, as the two tracked vehicles swept back and forth through the thin brush. Then RT Idaho heard a dog barking behind them. In full daylight Meyer risked everything to dash his men across the road, then headed into deep jungle to find a place to hide overnight. Again he heard that damned dog. His One-One laced their back trail with CS powder. Then they heard another dog, this one nearer, on their left flank.

RT Idaho waded quietly along a stream, emerged and scattered more CS powder, then went back in the stream, continuing to move long after dark. They heard a dog howl when it got a good whiff of CS powder. Finally they climbed a steep bank and set up a perimeter. Meyer's point man climbed a tree and in the darkness could make out dozens of flashlights scouring the stream banks and back trail, but RT Idaho was safe. "Going back through that stream saved us," Meyers decided.

Because trackers would come running when distinct American bootprints were discovered, SOG devoted considerable effort to disguising boot soles. The CIA research and development technicians at Camp Chinen, Okinawa, came up with the cleverest solution, boots with human barefoot soles. But when tested, the heel-less boots couldn't grip, they lost authenticity with wear and, besides, they were uncomfortable. A great idea that didn't pan out.

The next brainstorm was to replace Vibram soles with tire treads to resemble Ho Chi Minh sandals, but many NVA by then were wearing sneakerlike Bata boots, which had their own distinct pattern. CISO acquired Bata boots in Hong Kong, and some teams wore them despite the boots' weak arches and reduced ankle support.

Many SOG teams wore portions of enemy uniforms to confuse the NVA and gain a few seconds' advantage during a chance contact. For instance, CCS One-Zero Bob Graham's entire team wore NVA pith helmets; many One-Zeroes attired their indig point man in NVA uniform complete with chest-style web gear and AK-47.

Some teams went whole hog, outfitting themselves entirely in NVA clothes, weapons and gear, despite the fact that the "Law of Land Warfare" sanctions executing disguised men. The advantage was significant: *Anyone* a SOG team encountered was a bad guy, while the enemy had to figure out just who you were.

One-Zero Ron Knight's NVA-uniformed RT West Virginia once inadvertently walked right into an ambush, but an uncertain NVA called, "*Ei be do?*" (Who goes there?) This was followed by another shout on Knight's flank, "Americans! Americans!" But Knight and his One-One,

Larry Kramer, were already firing and shot their way out of it. "But I'm convinced," Knight said, "if we hadn't been in those NVA uniforms, it would have been all over for us."

Ron Knight also experienced the flip side of mistaken identities. After a tough afternoon of ground assaults and gunship duels against 12.7mm machine guns, a Huey managed to brave the fire and land. RT West Virginia piled aboard, and Knight gave thumbs-up to the door gunner to lift off, but they didn't go anywhere. Knight hollered to the door gunner, "What are you waiting for?" He replied, "You've still got some people out there . . . " and pointed to several men dressed identically to Knight's men, trotting toward the Huey. "Fire 'em up!" Knight screamed, and both shot furiously, allowing the Huey to escape the approaching NVA.

Like uniforms, team armament was wholly a One-Zero's call. SOG stocked about forty different kinds of U.S. and foreign weapons. Team leaders strolled into supply and simply fit firearms to any task; the atmosphere was casual. Many teams amassed their own arsenals, with the average about three guns per man, but some men acquired over a dozen apiece, everything from belt-fed machine guns and rocket launchers to snub-nose revolvers.

One weapon unique to SOG recon was the sawed-off Chinese RPD machine gun. Chopping off the RPD's bipod and barrel at the gas port reduced its length to just 32 inches and cut its weight to only 12 pounds while shifting its center of balance to the drum magazine. The drums were modified to hold 125 rounds rather than 100—every other one a tracer—and a circular slice of linoleum was inserted to eliminate rattle. The SOG RPD was compact, balanced, lightweight and so controllable you could almost write your name with it. It was superb.

Some teams, such as RT New York under Ed Wolcoff and RT California under Joe Walker, carried two RPDs, plus Soviet RPG antitank rocket launchers, rifle grenades, even a 60mm mortar—quadruple the firepower of a conventional unit this small. Plus the SOG teams integrated these heavy weapons into IA Drills.

Another item unique to SOG was the golfball-sized Dutch V-40 grenade, called "minigrenade." Each weighed just 3.5 ounces yet spewed four-hundred-plus fragments; it could be thrown a long, long way, and ten could be carried in a single shirt pocket.

Recon men carried any number of odd weapons, from sawed-off shotguns to flail-like Okinawan *nunchakus*. One-Zero Ed Wolcoff armed himself with a meat cleaver (no kidding) whose blade he thought would mesmerize an enemy soldier, giving Ed a slight edge. Although he brought the cleaver to the field, his theory was never tested. I'm convinced that had the Indiana Jones movies existed back then, some recon man would have worn a fedora and packed a bullwhip to crack at the NVA in Laos.

But the award for the most peculiar weapon actually employed has to go to CCS One-Zero Robert Graham, who'd experimented with Montagnard crossbows but found them underpowered. He told his Yards on RT Pick about the quality bows made in his native Canada, so on a whim he had a friend of his father's ship a 55-pound bow from Simpson's, the Canadian branch of Sears.

A veteran bow hunter, Graham tipped his arrows with razor-edged broadheads. He trained with the bow until he could consistently hit a 6-inch circle at twenty-five paces. Then his team was slated for a prisoner snatch mission near the enemy's suspected field command headquarters (COSVN), in Cambodia's Fishhook. Just for safety's sake, he also carried a sawed-off M-1 carbine.

Inserting with Sergeant Mike Crimmings ("another crazy Canadian," according to Graham), Staff Sergeant Frank Oppel, a new lieutenant and two Montagnards, they soon found a perfect ambush site. But before they were ready some NVA stumbled into them, shooting erupted and they had to rush back to their LZ.

Pinned in a bomb crater, they soon found themselves practically out of ammo, and Graham became frustrated then angered at their predicament. AKs kept cracking rounds over their heads as the NVA maneuvered into position. Finally Graham had had enough and jumped up with his bow. "I yelled as loud as a I could and fired exactly where the flashes were coming, and got back down again." Then Graham looked around wide-eyed at his teammates, amazed at himself—and even more amazed because the firing had stopped.

He flung a few more broad-headed arrows, then a Green Hornet Huey arrived to extract RT Pick. Graham is humorously philosophical about it. "I'm sure there's a bunch of guys sitting around a bar up in Hanoi today, and they're all saying, 'Yeah, you think you got one! I was out there one time and I had this guy yell, jump up and fire an arrow at me. No, no *really!*'"

Though they didn't go as far as using bows and arrows, SOG aircrews experimented and modified, too, adapting their weapons to fit this unique fighting environment. For instance, Sergeant Charlie Dodge, a Huey crew chief, reports he and fellow 57th Assault Helicopter Company gunners squeezed another one hundred rounds per minute out of their machine guns by inserting a nickel behind the buffers and inserting a second recoil spring. "I'm sure the armorer would probably tell you that won't work, but it worked great," Dodge said.

From cannibalized guns and scrounged parts, the 57th men custom built their own M-60s, replacing the bulky buttstock with a simple plastic cap and attaching an infantry-type pistol grip for a much more compact, easy-to-wield gun. An ordinary C-Ration can was modified to replace the feeder ramp, which, combined with a heavier feeder spring, allowed them to connect *seventy* belts, for seven thousand rounds per gun, one awesome amount of firepower.

One source of unending pride to crew chiefs and gunners, "a big morale builder," was their authority to use "free guns," that is, M-60 machine guns free of any pintle mount, just hanging from an overhead strap, which enabled them to engage faster with deadlier fire—although this created a danger of losing control of a gun and hitting one's own aircraft or crew. "It was a kind of sign of your competence and we were really proud of it," Dodge said.

Aircraft tactics and insert techniques were developed, too, some quite elaborate. For instance, SOG teams inserted on tiny LZs, seemingly too small to handle a helicopter, which made it unlikely enemy LZ Watchers or tracker teams covered them. Some teams were inserted by "flip-flop," that is, pulling a team at the end of its five-day mission and simultaneously landing a fresh team on the same LZ. The new team would lie low for a few hours, then sneak away. One variation on this was a "stay-behind," with a recon team accompanying a Hatchet Force for several days, going into hiding when the Hatchet Force lifted away, then creeping off for its own recon mission.

Sometimes helicopters would fake an insert on a nearby LZ to draw the enemy away from the real LZ while a team landed there. Such dummy landings weren't attempted often, however, since fake inserts were as dangerous to crews and aircraft as real ones.

But SOG's cleverest diversionary tool was an airdropped firefight simulator called "The Nightingale Device." Named after the bird whose song captivated Chinese emperors, the Nightingale was a CIA product reminiscent of the papier-mâché paratrooper dummies rigged with firecrackers and dropped over Normandy on D-Day. Mounted on a 4-by-3-foot mesh screen, the Nightingale had powder trails leading to clusters of firecrackers and cherry bombs, which mimicked the peaks and pauses of a real firefight lasting about ten minutes. Add an acid-delay pencil to its ignitor and a Nightingale could go off several hours or several days after emplacement. It was used mostly for false inserts, but there were other uses.

Medal of Honor recipient Bob Howard used a Nightingale one night for perhaps the most astonishing firefight of the war. His team had shadowed an NVA battalion along Laotian Highway 110, then watched from a hilltop while the enemy set up a night encampment—a lucrative target, but low overcast precluded a tactical air strike.

Then Howard's assistant team leader, Robert "Buckwheat" Clough, held up two Nightingales he'd tied to his rucksack for faking an extract, which hadn't proved necessary. Clough offered an amazing proposal: After dark he and one Yard would creep inside the NVA position, leave the Nightingales with a two-hour time-delay, then sneak back. Howard thought it "unbelievable," but if Buckwheat wanted to go for it, well, all right.

It took seven hours of slow, stealthy movement, but Clough and one Yard crept among the five hundred NVA, activated the two-hour time-delay fuse, then rejoined their team. "All at once, these damned devices started going off and it was the biggest firefight I've ever heard in my life," Howard recalled. "This son-of-a-bitch goes on for at least an hour and a half or two hours, and it's starting now to break light." Eventually enemy officers got their men to stop their wild shooting and flee, probably fearing an air strike. When Howard passed the empty bivouac, "It was unbelievable," he reported. "We found dead bodies everywhere."

New insertion/extraction equipment improved operations, too. First Sergeant Norman Doney took aluminum cable ladders off Chinook helicopters and adapted them to SOG Hueys, which allowed teams to land or come out wherever a Huey could hover 28 feet above the ground, forcing the enemy to disperse LZ Watchers.

But the most revolutionary emergency extraction development was the McGuire rig, invented by the man whose name it bore, Special Forces Sergeant Major Charles McGuire. The rig was simply a 100-foot rope with a 6-foot loop at the end and a padded canvas seat; you rode it just like a playground swing seat.

A single Huey carried four McGuire rigs, or "strings" as they were called, two on each side. Not only were they faster than any winch, but four men could be lifted at once. All the pilot had to do was rise vertically until his string passengers were above the jungle canopy, then fly away. A team could be lifted through any canopy hole wide enough for the crew chief to see the ground. Strings could not be used on Kingbees, though, because they caused a serious balance problem to the H-34.

During an extraction the Huey pilot had to hold his bird at a steady treetop hover while his crew chief, lying on the aircraft floor and peering down, directed him over the hole by intercom. After dropping the ropes the crew chief watched the recon men climb into the seats, then told the pilot when to lift up—a dangerous few seconds, because the ropes could become snared in the trees or a sudden barrage of fire could threaten the aircraft. Sergeant Charlie Dodge of the 57th Assault Helicopter Company explained, "If you got in trouble with the strings, the crew members would have to cut them. That would be the only way the aircraft could fly free. It didn't matter if anyone was on the ends of the strings or not; if you had to cut the ropes in order to save the aircraft, you cut the ropes. That was understood by everybody."

Riding strings felt a bit like being Peter Pan, a magical climb, better than any elevator, but your weight soon shifted to the crotch, eventually cutting off blood flow to your legs. There you were, swaying below the Huey, 3000 feet above the jungle, the air rushing past at 90 knots.

USAF Lieutenant Colonel Dean "Stretch" Ballmes, a Pleiku-based A-1 pilot, will always remember the first day he saw anyone ride a McGuire rig. Piloting his Skyraider, he rushed to a Laotian hillside where a SOG recon team had been run to ground by an NVA company. He found the team in a bomb crater, frantically flashing a signal mirror, just as the NVA launched an all-out assault. Ballmes and wingman Don Dineen rolled in with cluster bombs, but they hit too close. "Damn!"

Ballmes told himself, "that's going right through the bomb crater!"

The team was not hit. After the team was safely lifted away in McGuire rigs, Ballmes dumped the rest of his ordnance, then climbed up behind the Hueys to fly back. Looking up through his canopy at the odd spectacle of men riding McGuire rigs, Ballmes almost had a heart attack when the team One-Zero suddenly hung upside down, swung like a chimp on a trapeze, waved to Ballmes and shouted into his radio, "You sweet motherfucker!"

Though many recon men's lives were saved, several men were injured or killed when dragged through trees or when they fell from strings. An especially tough case was that of Lieutenant Jim Bircham, lost 15 November 1968. Birchim and a young Special Forces NCO had been lifted out in darkness after a long day of running firefights against determined NVA pursuers. Both were wounded but managed to lash themselves together in the only McGuire rig they could find; they would hold onto each other. The Huey lifted safely away but had to fly through a heavy tropical storm so violent that at times the whole aircraft shuddered. It was pitch-black.

When the storm-shaken helicopter finally descended back in South Vietnam, a waiting party rushed to the mass of ice-laden clothes and gear in the McGuire rig but found only the unconscious, shivering young NCO, rope burns cut deep into his hands where even his super-human grip had been insufficient to hold Lieutenant Birchim. "He had terrific rope burns," recalled his recon company commander, Captain Ed Lesesne. "It was an impossible human task to do what he did but I'm sure he feels guilty as hell that he dropped him."

Jim Birchim's body was never found.

After several McGuire rig fatalities, First Sergeant Norman Doney added a wrist slip loop, which helped, but men still fell.

Eventually three instructors at the 5th Special Forces Group's RE-CONDO School developed the solution, the STABO rig, an acronym for their names: Major Robert Stevens, Captain John Knabb and Sergeant First Class Clifford Roberts. The STABO rig replaced a man's web gear with a special webbed harness. To be extracted, the soldier unfastened two straps on his belt's back, swung them between his legs and snapped them securely in front. When the helicopter dropped a rope with a special STABO yoke, he snapped it onto two rings, one at each shoulder, and away he flew.

It was ingenious. Not only did the STABO rig hold its rider securely, but it left his hands free to use weapons.

Another tactical subject given much thought was countering enemy attempts to hit teams at night, for the NVA realized teams seldom had radio contact with anyone after dark. Therefore, like a rabbit taking cover in a brier patch, at dusk a recon team squirmed into the thickest, thorniest foliage it could find, preferably on the side of a hill to make enemy night sweeps difficult to control. Team members lay so close in a Rest-Over-Night (RON) position that each man touched the man on either side, a whole team in a space so small the NVA wouldn't imagine they could be there, which was the idea. The NVA would have to step on them to find them.

Your rucksack was your pillow, and you slept in your web gear, just opening the belt and propping it behind you so it naturally fell back into place when you sat up. Your weapon was never beyond your grasp.

Before dark the One-Zero squatted beside each man and pointed from one tree to another to designate his share of the perimeter, describing where to throw grenades and where to emplace his claymore mine. Because of back-blast danger, the U.S. Army warns against positioning claymores closer than 50 feet, even for entrenched soldiers. SOG claymores were but 15 feet away, on the opposite side of trees so back blast would be absorbed. Why so close? A distant claymore might be found by NVA searchers who'd follow it back to the team, or turn it toward the team without discovery.

When a team was hit in the RON, likely it was because trackers had followed them, then fetched special counter-recon troops who operated confidently in darkness. Typically it began with one or two NVA letting loose with AKs in hopes the recon men would shoot back or blow a claymore, pinpointing their position.

I can close my eyes and still see a night in Laos with Medal of Honor recipient Franklin Miller, Glen Uemura and Chuck Hein. A counter-recon unit came after us. Without the slightest warning, an AK not 40 feet away suddenly ripped the air. Illuminated by his 3-foot muzzle flame, I watched the NVA turn his head round and round, watching for our tiniest reaction. All that kept me from squeezing the last ounce from my CAR-15 trigger, aiming squarely at his head, was the certainty that hidden nearby were dozens of NVA ready to pounce. His commander offered this poor sap's life, but we weren't takers. It was a long, hard night.

Relaxing at night might mean death: Better to stay uneasy, alert, easily terrified, with the tiniest sound jolting you awake, your heart pounding. It might be a passing tiger, but it might be an NVA counter-recon platoon crawling up on you.

By dawn you were packed and ready to go, sitting in an outward-looking circle, quietly eating rice, watching your claymores and waiting for Covey's morning radio check. After that, you recovered your claymores and were on your way.

If you were hit in daytime, you'd dash about 200 yards, then shift into evasive movement to shake off pursuers. You traded speed for minimizing what trackers call "sign." If you moved quickly you might gain distance but you left a detectable trail.

Evasion often was preferable to a footrace, because the enemy carried less gear and could outpace you on parallel trails or relay word ahead via radio and telephone. Stopping was hazardous. A thirty-second head start might become a clean escape, while just ten seconds wasted could mean encirclement and annihilation. In a hot target, an additional forty-man platoon of NVA joined the search every ten minutes after contact—even more troops when there was a major trail or road nearby.

Sometimes teams abandoned rucksacks to gain speed, like a lizard giving up its tail to a closing predator; once unburdened it seemed a team could fly through the jungle, while the enemy couldn't help but pause to examine his windfall. This could prove his undoing. With pursuers gaining on him, Bob Howard once tore off his shirt, threw it across a bush and left a few toe poppers in front of it. Sure enough, three minutes later he heard two toe poppers go off, and that ended the pursuit.

When you had wounded men and couldn't move fast or far, then you grabbed defensive terrain, such as a hilltop or bomb crater, stacked reload magazines and fought it out. You hoped you were beside an LZ so you could exfil as quick as tac air reduced or pushed back the enemy. But you had to get out soon or the NVA would rush in a one hundred-man company and 12.7mm machine guns. If your fight lasted overnight, by dawn they'd have trucked down 37mm antiaircraft guns and hordes of ground troops.

The NVA tried to get so close that air strikes would endanger the team as much as them, but being a fatalistic lot, SOG men called in tac air anyhow, sometimes right across themselves, chancing accidental death from the air rather than certain death from the NVA. In conventional units, medals were given to those who'd call in air strikes on themselves; in SOG, it was an ordinary affair. Desperation inspired risks that the NVA would not match. Ken "Shoebox" Carpenter's team once found itself hotly pursued by NVA that kept pushing them toward a cliff, where at last they seemed pinned. Then Kenny and his Yards held hands and jumped into the treetops 30 feet below, crashing through foliage, bouncing violently between branches and spraining a few ankles, but by God, they all hit the ground alive. Not a single NVA had the inclination to follow them.

After five days facing such dangers deep behind enemy lines, meticulous in every act, deliberate in every step, seldom even whispering, hunted day and night like an animal by hundreds, sometimes thousands of enemy, a SOG man's mental focus wore down, fuzzing the keen edge so crucial to his survival. He had to come out. And then he needed a one-week stand-down to unwind and recharge before running that deadly gauntlet again.

During stand-down recon men did as they wished, when they wished. They'd lounge around the NCO club in cutoff bluejeans and tennis shoes. Harvey Saal once arrived in such filthy fatigues that the Phu Bai club manager announced, "I will not serve you in the club dressed like that." Fair enough. Saal went outside, stripped and returned buck naked demanding service—and he got it.

If an entertaining poker game was under way and it was closing time, they'd extend the club hours, a practice that so exasperated the Danang club manager that one night he tossed a tear-gas grenade under a card table. Five minutes later the whole group was back, playing poker *in gas masks.*

I remember one afternoon joining a conga line of recon men—drunk, sober and in between—that spontaneously formed up, snaked its way around the compound and into the club, chanting, *"Cha-cha re-con, cha-cha re-con."* It was crazy.

But that craziness was not restricted to SOG's remote bases. On stand-down, recon men could travel anywhere in South Vietnam and stay at SOG safe houses in Danang and Saigon, or at the 5th Special

Forces headquarters in Nha Trang. The evening might begin in a genteel enough way, with lobster and French onion soup at the Hotel Nautique, but deterioration via alcohol and debauchery inevitably followed. Recon men lived like there was no tomorrow because often there wasn't. Yet they kept a sense of humor.

The best running gag concerned the hilariously obnoxious Walter Shumate, a superb SOG and Project Delta trooper. It began inauspiciously when a Green Beret gave candy to a Vietnamese girl and told her, "Here you are, my dear. My name is Walter Shumate." Not much, but the snowball had begun rolling.

Word spread to attribute everything and anything to Walter. A guy would win a bet and while scooping up his winnings he'd boast, "You should've known better than to bet against Walter Shumate!" Or after beating the crap out of some Marine, the victorious pugilist would holler from the bar doorway, "If any of you bastards wants a piece of me, my name is Walter Shumate!"

Tales of Shumate's dares, threats, boasts and fame (infamy?) spread across South Vietnam, perhaps the world. His became the name most often entered in seedy hotel registers, exceeding even those standbys "A. Lincoln" and "G. Washington," with no two signatures even faintly similar. What robust staying power this Shumate possessed, for he signed out more Taipei prostitutes than any ten men! What a specimen!

And when word of some new misadventure filtered back, the real Walter would declare, for instance, "I have never been to Hong Kong in my life." But the truth was that he basked in the notoriety.

First Sergeant Billy Greenwood understood the antics. "When you're out there face-to-face with a man and either you kill him or he kills you, it's pretty tough. There's no such thing as getting acclimated to it. And when a man comes back to a secure area he does strange things. It's like a pressure cooker: There's got to be a little valve to let this pressure off, and that was our means of letting it off."

When a recon man did too much screwing around on stand-down—and too many SOG superiors had to cover for his antics—he was told to get back into the field and earn his redemption.

And the best redemption from the worst trouble was to capture a prisoner, or as SOG troopers said, "to pull off a snatch."

9

THE SNATCHERS

The SOG mission that most demanded ingenuity and audacity was snatching enemy prisoners. By hook and crook, by trickery and device, by technology and technique, SOG men aspired to perfect their kidnapping craft, developing more skill in this artful science than at any time in previous military history. Rewards and accolades were heaped upon successful snatchers, and with good reason: There is no intelligence source so fruitful as a freshly snatched prisoner.

Taking a prisoner meant a free R&R to Taiwan aboard a SOG Blackbird on maintenance rotation, a $100 bonus for each American and a new Seiko wristwatch and cash to each Nung or Montagnard. Despite the incentives, during the entire war SOG teams snatched fewer than fifty prisoners from Laos and Cambodia.

Hunting was good in the early days: In 1966, SOG's first full year of Laotion operations, recon teams seized twelve prisoners; it remained fair in 1967, with ten NVA snatched; but new enemy counter-recon units and expanded security forces proved their worth by 1968 when seizures tumbled to one; and in 1969, not a single NVA prisoner was brought out of Laos. SOG teams snatched just eighteen prisoners from Cambodia between 1967 and 1970.

A snatch meant initiating contact in dangerous areas, against forces that usually outnumbered your team. And when you grabbed someone, the prisoner slowed your pace while other NVA chased all the harder, knowing you had one of their own.

Snatch tactics were a subject of endless NCO club debate but it essentially came down to three options: disabling the candidate with a carefully placed gunshot; knocking him senseless with explosives; or just plain grabbing him.

A gunshot was tricky because it was difficult to incapacitate but not kill your target. For this reason many teams preferred SOG's least powerful suppressed weapon, the .22-caliber High Standard Model H-D pistol.

In early 1969, Master Sergeant Norm Doney, One-Zero of RT Florida, took careful aim with a .22 High Standard at an NVA approaching him on a side road near Laotian Highway 110.

Minutes earlier, Doney had positioned a three-man Nung security team in a curve 50 yards down the road, telling them to block any reaction force so he could disable and capture a passing NVA.

RT Florida's only other American, Sergeant Joe Morris, stood by at a rally point 100 yards in the jungle, in radio contact with Covey. SOG helicopters were nearby, inserting another team just minutes away; conditions seemed ideal.

Soon a nice husky NVA appeared. Doney let him approach to 10 feet, then plugged him in the thigh; he collapsed, dropping his AK. Perfect! But unknown to the One-Zero, around that curve a long line of NVA troops followed, visible to Doney's security men, who, instead of shooting to buy their leader time, turned and ran so noisily that the NVA column opened fire.

Doney, his interpreter and an ARVN sergeant were standing over the wounded NVA when their teammates rushed past, running for their lives. The ARVN sergeant and interpreter ran away, too.

Then an exploding RPG rocket knocked Doney to his knees, peppering him with shrapnel. The would-be prisoner leaped for his AK but Doney groggily managed to shoot first, popping him several times with the suppressed pistol, killing him. With NVA advancing up the road, Doney rejoined Joe Morris and ran to an LZ, where they found the rest of their team. While awaiting extraction, they heard a truckload of troops drive up; an air strike destroyed it. Then Hueys swooped in and pulled them out.

Yet they'd been so close! After chewing asses all around, Doney decided to repeat the ambush, and what better spot than that very curve! Exactly one month later, RT Florida crept up to the same spot, this time with a third American, Sergeant Bill Stubbs, but an NVA happened along and spotted Stubbs, who drilled him. With the cat out of the bag, they had to run for it again.

A few weeks later another recon team passed the curve and found the enemy had posted a sign, warning, Danger Zone Ahead! And sure enough, the team noted, whenever enemy troops passed Doney's ambush site, they'd fire a few magazines into the bushes like kids whistling past a graveyard on a spooky night. It made RT Florida proud, but not as proud as had they snatched a man.

Of SOG's various suppressed weapons, the .380 Walther PPK automatic pistol with Sionics suppressor was popular. Compact and extremely quiet, it fired standard .380 ammo loaded for subsonic velocities, which eliminated the bullet's "crack" in flight. "So quiet," One-Zero Newman Ruff recalls, "that the first time I went out and played with it I kept hearing these funny noises and finally rather than look at the target I watched the gun when I fired it and the funny noise was the shell cases hitting the ground."

But most of SOG's suppressed weapons weren't pistols but submachine guns, used to eliminate trackers and sentries, and occasionally to attempt snatches. I carried a suppressed 9mm Swedish K submachine gun when I went into northeast Cambodia with RT Illinois to assess one of Henry Kissinger's so-called secret B-52 raids, in hopes that if we came upon a small party of bomb-disoriented NVA, I could dispatch all but one and we'd take him prisoner. Instead, we bumped head-on into an NVA unit, exchanged fire and had two of our indigs hit bad. Ben Thompson, our One-Zero, dragged them toward an LZ while my other U.S. teammate, George Bacon, and I delayed the enemy. When George fired his CAR-15, enemy soldiers ducked and dove; when I fired my silenced Swedish K, it had virtually no effect. They didn't know I was shooting! But that wasn't all.

When finally we rejoined the team, a lone NVA suddenly popped up and almost got me, but I dealt him a solid torso burst and he went down. When a Huey landed to evac our wounded, I rushed past where the NVA had fallen and saw that he'd crawled away with his AK. It may have worked well for snatches, but the suppressed Swedish K lacked a lethal punch for ordinary firefights.

But another SOG submachine gun had great lethality despite its suppressor: The .45 caliber M-3 "Grease Gun" retained deadly terminal ballistics because its hefty 230-grain slugs weighed twice as much as 9mm cartridges. An OSS product, the M-3's muffled muzzle generated sound only a few decibels above that caused by the firing mechanism alone. It was heavy, over 11 pounds, yet some SOG men preferred it because the M-3 held steady with almost no muzzle rise. One of SOG's legendary One-Zeros, Jerry "Mad Dog" Shriver, often carried a suppressed Grease Gun.

An acquaintance of Shriver's, RT Hammer One-Zero Jim Mackay, brought a suppressed Grease Gun along for a prisoner snatch in the Fishhook region of Cambodia.

Just three hours after insert, Mackay, his One-One Bryan Stockdale, an American accompanying them and four Yards came to a series of high-speed trails. Cargo-laden bicycles rolled past, and loud voices called out from several directions; they found a bundle of communications wires 2 inches thick. "We knew there was something pretty major around," Stockdale recalled.

One-Zero Mackay figured they'd better attempt a snatch immediately and get away fast. While Stockdale radioed a nearby FAC, Mackay arrayed the team along a trail and cocked his Grease Gun. They'd take the next man coming down the trail.

The FAC radioed the SOG launch site at Bu Dop, 50 miles away; USAF Green Hornet helicopters headed for the Fishhook.

RT Hammer hadn't lain there five minutes when along came a lone enemy soldier, his AK slung because his hands were full of canteens. When he was just 10 feet away, Mackay took aim at his leg, squeezed the Grease Gun trigger—but the bolt lurched to the magazine lip and jammed there, making a loud *thunk!* The startled NVA dropped his canteens, but just as quickly two RT Hammer Yards pounced on him and, with Stockdale, dragged him into the bushes, handcuffed and blindfolded him.

Mackay came over to help and set down his errant Grease Gun—and the bolt snapped forward and popped one shot into Stockdale's leg, under the knee. Stockdale felt the pain, thought he'd been hit by some distant gunman, then he noticed smoke wisping from the M-3's suppressor. He soundly cursed out his One-Zero. However, he found just a grazing wound; he could walk and, fortunately, no one had heard the shot. Soon the Green Hornets were overhead and RT Hammer escaped without a hitch.

Two of SOG's other suppressed "snatch" guns were British in origin, developed by England's World War II Special Operations Executive (SOE), which ran agents, resistance groups and saboteurs into Nazi-occupied Europe. One was the WELROD pistol, the first ever purpose-designed suppressed handgun; indeed, the WELROD was just a 14⅜-inch tube, the front half a suppressor and the back half its rotary bolt action. The grip was simply a rubber-wrapped Colt .32 auto magazine. Since each round was chambered manually, the WELROD generated absolutely no sound from slide movement or escaping gas. It was so quiet that a World War II agent could sit behind his quarry in a darkened theater, fire a shot and walk away without anyone the wiser; the OSS found it "most effective when used with the muzzle against the target." While SOG men thought it impressively quiet, it was not accurate beyond about ten paces, which, combined with its low rate of fire, made it more suited to assassinations than prisoner snatches. Nevertheless some teams employed WELRODs.

SOG's other British firearm was the suppressed Sten Mark IIS submachine gun, with its distinctive side-mounted magazine. The Sten had practical appeal for snatching: It disassembled into three components you packed in your rucksack so your primary armament was a more powerful CAR-15 or AK-47, and you broke out the Sten only at the ambush site. But, reflecting its economical manufacture, the Sten lacked accuracy.

Sten often accompanied SOG teams into Laos and Cambodia, and it was an attempted snatch in Laos that saw perhaps the most tasteless employment of a suppressed Sten in SOG history. Those involved shall remain nameless.

The team was sent in to surveil a river, beside which they found a large trail, so the team leader decided to kill two birds: He laid out a snatch ambush at a spot from which he could surveil the river, too. After a few hours, six NVA crossed the river and walked right into his ambush—but by now it was clear many other NVA were nearby. The One-Zero dared not start a firefight.

But the NVA squad stopped right there, dumped rucksacks and five of them stripped to their skivvies, then jumped in the water. One NVA remained behind to guard their equipment and AKs, hardly a dozen feet from the One-Zero; it began to drizzle and the NVA guard donned a plastic poncho. The recon men heard more NVA voices; sooner or later, they'd be spotted—they had to quietly eliminate this lone NVA guard and sneak off.

The One-Zero put his Sten sight on the NVA's head, but then he noticed a peculiar expression on the man's face and a bouncing movement beneath his plastic poncho. The man was masturbating. Out of some peculiar sense of decency, the One-Zero held his fire but trained his Sten on the soldier's head until the man was finished; then the One-Zero fired two silent shots, and the guard slumped forward, forever euphoric. In ten seconds the SOG team was gone, having created one of SOG's truly great campfire stories.

Sometimes just plain aggressiveness yielded prisoners. Captain Ed Lesesne, Kontum's recon company commander in 1968, emphasized snatches but found a real reluctance among the teams to assume the extra risks, so he accompanied a team into Laos to snatch an NVA himself. A few hands predicted failure, noting Lesesne's teammates were reservists from the Florida-based 20th Special Forces Group.

But Lesesne and the reservists performed like seasoned pros, creeping up on a major enemy supply dump secured by a hundred NVA. For three days they lay beside a trail, watching passersby, until they found an NVA who went back and forth several times a day.

Lesesne sent the others to secure the escape route to a nearby LZ, keeping just one American with him for security. Like clockwork, here came the lone NVA; the recon commander raised his unsuppressed M-16. "I shot him in the leg," Lesesne recalled, "jumped on him and stuck a morphine injection in him, gagged him and tied his hands with plastic restraints."

Lesesne's teammate, Sergeant First Class George Hunt, gunned down three NVA drawn by the shot, then a machine gun opened fire from a bunker only 30 yards away, forcing them behind a termite mound. The Green Beret captain chucked one grenade to throw the gun crew off balance so he could take time to deliberately hurl a second one; it rolled right into their bunker, silencing the gun. Then Lesesne and Hunt rejoined the team and fifteen minutes later flew away with SOG's first Laotian prisoner in nine months.

SOG's search for the perfect snatch weapon was a never-ending quest. Chief SOG Colonel Jack Singlaub had great interest in tranquilizer darts, "like you would shoot at a tiger if you wanted to brush its teeth or something." But he found himself butting heads with Pentagon officers who voiced technical objections that masked an aversion for anything remotely connected with chemical warfare.

Singlaub raised the tranquilizer issue in a mid-1968 meeting with the four service chiefs in the Pentagon's Joint Chiefs conference room. "They asked about NVA reaction to SOG helicopter insertion of recon teams, and they wanted my opinion on the ability of SOG teams to capture valuable NVA officers on the Trail. I pointed out the Pentagon's refusal to authorize tranquilizer darts for this very purpose. [Army Chief of Staff Westmoreland] made it clear the matter would be reconsidered."

It was. Several SOG teams subsequently tested tranquilizer guns but learned the same thing that veterinarians did when anesthetizing dangerous animals: By the time dosage is sufficient to incapacitate quickly, it's enough to kill, while safe dosages act so slowly that the subject remains a threat to anyone within reach. The SOG men were compelled to gun down the NVA hit by darts or watch helplessly as they died from the anesthetic.

When tranquilizer darts failed, SOG tested another chemical incapacitator—Mace, the nonlethal spray used by police. But a few recon men had been Maced during Stateside barroom brawls and warned it was not always effective.

Some snatches were accomplished the old-fashioned way. Down in Cambodia's Fishhook, RT Pick One-Zero Everett Cofer and One-Two David Zack planned to cover while One-One Bob Graham seized a passing NVA. It was a dangerous place, with the jungle so heavily occupied that they watched an NVA unit stack arms for morning exercises. "We were being superquiet," Graham said.

One-Zero Cofer selected a spot on a trail between two battalion base camps, meaning a thousand NVA were within a half mile. Hardly had they set up when flank security signaled a man was coming. There wasn't time for anything fancy: Graham jumped out and punched the soldier "right between the eyes." He collapsed, three recon men leaped on him and covered his mouth while the team interpreter whispered, "Your silence or your life!"

The soldier opted for life. It turned out he was a kidnapped South Vietnamese pressed into enemy service and so happy to be free that he dredged up every scrap of information he could recall. "It was a good catch," Graham said.

Not quite so lucky was another team leader I shall not identify beyond his code name, Fat Cat, who planned to step out on a trail and grab a lone passing NVA. When Fat Cat stepped out, he found *two* NVA and instantly had to shoot one in order to subdue the other. It seemed a success, with Fat Cat's team outrunning NVA pursuers, reaching an LZ and being extracted.

The truth came during interrogation. After responding negatively to a litany of questions, the exasperated NVA private finally protested, "Why do you keep asking me things I don't know? You should have asked the colonel."

The interrogater blinked. "What colonel?"

"Why, the one your commando killed on the trail."

Alas, Fat Cat would be known as the man who shot a colonel to capture a private.

Far more frequently employed than fisticuffs were explosives, laid out as a demolition ambush. In theory, the blast would knock the target off his feet, wrench his AK from his hands and render him temporarily senseless.

But the unpredictability of blast effects always left demo ambushes a sort of grab bag—you never knew what you'd find after the smoke cleared. Captain Ed Lesesne accompanied a snatch mission in which the demo went off exactly as the One-Zero had planned, knocking five NVA off their feet—and all were dead.

SOG's most sophisticated demo ambushes employed Astrolite, a unique liquid explosive whose existence was not publicly known at the time. A by-product of NASA rocket-fuel research, Astrolite had the remarkable property of detonating anything you soaked with it—such as the dirt on a trail—and came in two plastic bottles you combined on the spot. "Once you mixed it together, the stuff was so damned unstable that you had to either use it right away or get rid of it," explained Captain Bill O'Rourke, a SOG Hatchet Force commander who used Astrolite in Cambodia.

"We created a thing we called a 'gate' by pouring this liquid down both sides of the trail, making a rectangular box with a space in there for our target," O'Rourke said. "Once the individual we wanted was in that space, *boom!*" After snatching a party of three NVA this way, O'Rourke's men were rewarded with a week in Taiwan.

The NVA had a reputation for fanatical resistance, but it was seldom that NVA prisoners turned out to be fanatics. A hot meal, shower and fresh clothes typically opened an intelligence spigot. Take the case of a prisoner brought back from Cambodia by Jerry "Mad Dog" Shriver. When CCS intelligence NCO Dale Libby asked the prisoner his job the little man thrust out his chest and boasted, "I'm a killer!"

"Well, who do you kill?" Libby inquired. "I kill Americans!" the prisoner growled. The interrogation continued. "How many Americans have you killed?" The little man's thin shoulders sagged. "Well, none, yet."

Libby stopped the interview, took him to the mess hall, got him a plate piled with food, which he wolfed down, then took him over for a shower. "You could see his . . . eyes change. He got fed, he got clothed, nobody beat him."

Later the prisoner admitted his whole adult life had been one catastrophe after another: kidnapped by the Communists, wounded in a B-52 strike, underfed in Cambodia, beaten for minor infractions, bedridden with malaria, then captured by his enemies. The SOG men nicknamed him "Charlie Brown."

When his interrogation ended several days later and he was turned over to the military police for transport to a POW camp, Libby watched them drive away. "And Charlie Brown looked back like a puppy leaving home," Libby said.

But there was another kind of NVA, the hard-core-to-the-death type. A CCN recon team snatched such a man west of the DMZ along an enemy fuel pipeline running out of North Vietnam. Making it safely to an LZ, they asked the prisoner, a sergeant, how many NVA were in the area. "One million," he snapped. According to Captain Jim Storter, "They'd caught the baddest son-of-a-bitch in the NVA army, their

'Sergeant Rock.'" Like a chained animal, he struggled against his plastic wrist restraints.

American Hueys dropped the team McGuire rigs, but they had nine men and only eight rigs, so they looped the prisoner's plastic restraint through a wrist loop and sat him on the burly One-One's lap, facing him. Off they went.

They gradually climbed to 2,000 feet and ten minutes later could make out the Khe Sanh airstrip in the distance. But sight of the American base panicked the NVA prisoner, who began struggling like a man possessed, ramming his head into the One-One, kicking and pushing them away from the others.

Swinging pendulumlike beneath the Huey, the One-Zero sailed past his struggling assistant and smacked the prisoner, but that agitated him all the more, and astoundingly, he snapped the plastic restraint as the One-One seized him in a headlock. Then the prisoner twisted away and bit the One-One's arm; the American pushed the NVA's head back, which started him sliding off the One-One's lap. The NVA began nipping like a mad dog and trying to pull grenades off the One-One's web gear. All that was holding the wriggling NVA was the One-One; then the prisoner bit into the muscular Green Beret's neck, and that was the last straw. Despite the team leader's shouts, the One-One held the NVA's head with both hands, jerked him away from his bleeding neck, shouted "Fuck you!" and let him go.

It would make for nice sentiment to say how deeply impressed they were by the NVA's suicidal devotion, but truth is, the One-Zero's greatest regret when he saw the NVA crash through the treetops was losing out on a free trip to Taiwan.

On his fourth try to snatch a prisoner in Cambodia, One-Zero Mike Cooper—not his real name—laid a hasty ambush along a trail, just as a bicycle happened along. His Nungs inadvertently shot the bicyclist. A quick search of the body yielded nothing of value, so Cooper took a closer look at the bicycle. He'd never known anyone to bring back a bicycle, so, grabbing the handlebars he wheeled it into the jungle.

Cooper encrypted a situation report into three-letter groups, but without bothering to encrypt "bicycle," and transmitted it to a FAC, who relayed it to Ban Me Thuot, where a radio operator decrypted it.

Cooper's message described the contact and reported one enemy KIA, but the message's last two groups puzzled the radio operator: It seemed to say, "Have captured," followed by the unencrypted word "bicycle."

Captured a bicycle? No way! The radioman scanned his daily code-word list, but "bicycle" wasn't there. Maybe Cooper had mistakenly used a previous day's code word. When he checked it, the radioman's jaw dropped—"bicycle" meant *general*—Cooper had captured an NVA general! The radio operator called the FAC on secure voice scrambler and said, "Have Cooper confirm, he has a 'bicycle,' he has a North Vietnamese general."

The Air Force pilot raised Cooper and requested, "Confirm, you have a North Vietnamese *bicycle,* repeat, home plate needs confirmation, *you have a North Vietnamese bicycle.*"

Reclining against an old termite mound, his feet propped against the two-wheeler, Cooper lit a cigarette and looked for a manufacturer's seal on the frame, but heavy paint obscured the inscription. "I think it's North Vietnamese," he radioed, "but it might be Chinese. Can't tell for sure."

Even as the radio operator got confirmation the CCS commander rushed in, the rumor already having rocked his office. "Is it true? Cooper actually has a *general*!?"

Just to be absolutely sure, the radio operator contacted the FAC yet again. "Home plate wants to confirm, I repeat, *confirm,* team has a 'bicycle' and it's intact, over."

The inane questions were starting to irritate Cooper. The seat was worn a bit and maybe it was missing a spoke or two, but it was certainly usable. "Listen," he snapped, "the bicycle's fine now, but if you don't come get us pretty quick I'll put a couple bullets through it and dump it here."

The FAC switched to secure voice, barely containing himself. "Team leader *confirms,* he has an unwounded general officer and he wants out ASAP or he'll shoot him himself."

That was enough for the CCS commander, who ordered, "Give me the direct line to Saigon." In two minutes Chief SOG was in the know; he flash-messaged MACV headquarters. What a catch! This would be SOG's greatest triumph!

Had there been time, a thousand men and a hundred helicopters would have gone after the general, but by now the enemy would be massing, too, to retrieve him. This was no time to tarry. The CCS commander would lead the pickup personally. Not an hour later a formation of Green Hornets circled in wide orbit over Cooper, who was instructed, "First aircraft is for the bicycle, only the bicycle."

Gunships whisked past at low level, trying to draw fire, then came a Huey that hovered a foot off the ground. Beckoning arms waved from the Huey, and Cooper left the woodline, wheeling the bicycle; and all the while his commander kept looking beyond Cooper, right, left, everywhere but at the two-wheeler. The lieutenant colonel shouted, "Where's the bicycle?" Cooper sat it on the skid and beamed, "Right here."

"No, dammit!" the lieutenant colonel repeated, "I mean the . . . the *bicycle!*" But as he grasped the handlebars his eyes widened and the horror sank in. As the Huey lifted away the officer must have wanted to throw that bicycle at Cooper.

But the bicycle made it safely back to the SOG compound at Ban Me Thuot, where for the rest of his tour Cooper rode it in grudging defiance of a torrent of guffaws. At higher levels there was enough embarrassment to go around so nobody pointed a finger at anyone else.

Even a failed snatch attempt could have combat effect. Probably the most successful ambush of the war resulted from a failed SOG prisoner snatch. Staff Sergeant Ralph Rodd's RT Colorado had lain beside a Laotian trail a half day when they heard approaching enemy, but they soon realized there were far too many NVA to attempt a snatch. Rodd counted almost three hundred men—then a whistle blew and they stopped, formed ranks right in front of RT Colorado's eight claymores, stacked arms and opened their rucksacks for lunch.

Just 5 yards away, the RT Colorado men dared not even breathe. Then an NVA soldier stepped off the trail, undid his fly to urinate and saw a Montagnard. Instantly, Rodd's men detonated all eight claymores, emptied their CAR-15s, tossed grenades and ran with such abandon that the six of them were plucked away from six different LZs. Not a one was wounded. We can only imagine the horrendous NVA casualties, for they did not return Rodd's fire for five full minutes.

Though SOG attempted numerous snatches, rarely did SOG teams target a particular person. One such mission began in early 1970, in the conference room of General Creighton Abrams, then commander of U.S. forces in Vietnam. The Seventh Air Force commander, General George Brown, and Abrams' senior intelligence officer, Major General Phillip Davidson, were discussing USAF reports of heavy night truck traffic in southeast Laos. It was perplexing. How were these convoys reaching South Vietnam? What was their cargo and where was it going? Without precise answers, American B-52 strikes were little more than darts tossed at a map. General Abrams turned to Colonel Steve Cavanaugh: Wasn't there something SOG could do?

Chief SOG Cavanaugh promised Abrams he'd look into it.

Back at SOG headquarters, Cavanaugh's staff suggested sweeping southeast Laos with recon teams, but the area was so full of NVA that half the teams would be discovered. No, what Chief SOG wanted was something more precise, tailored, a single operation with enough priority and support to get the job done.

It hit him like a flash. "You know," Cavanaugh announced, "one of the big things we could do is grab somebody from a truck." It was brilliant—a convoy driver had to know the location of truck parks, supply dumps, major headquarters, his cargo, every bit of information Seventh Air Force and MACV wanted. Yet Cavanaugh realized the odds were terrible, with enemy security so vast and ubiquitous that not a single prisoner had come out of Laos in all of 1969. Though he voiced optimism before his subordinates, privately Cavanaugh believed, "In my wildest imagination I never thought that we would succeed."

Cavanaugh met with the FOB 2 commander, Lieutenant Colonel Frederick T. Abt, charging him with selecting his best men to ambush a North Vietnamese convoy and seize a truck driver, "a mission that required a hell of a lot of expertise and skill," Chief SOG added. Abt had permission from the U.S. ambassador to Laos to send in ten Americans, triple the normal complement.

To lead what became Operation Ashtray, Abt appointed Major Frank Jaks, his most experienced officer. Already well into his third year in Vietnam, Jaks had led SOG's first Bright Light POW rescue attempt in 1966.

Picking from among FOB 2's top five recon teams, Major Jaks accepted eight volunteers: Oliver Hartwig, Daniel Ster, Ray Harris, John

Blaaw, Tim Lynch, Forrest Todd, Bill Spurgeon and John Grant.

They trained at SOG's Naval Advisory Detachment SEAL base in Danang, where their first challenge was determining how to halt a truck without killing the driver. "There was nothing in our manuals, nothing anywhere," Jaks said. John Grant, the team demo man, tested various explosive charges before deciding upon five claymores in a series, arrayed in a crescent to focus their blast and collapse a truck's front wheels.

After seven days of planning and rehearsals, the Operation Ashtray men inserted into southern Laos.

On the third night they lay beside Highway 110 and watched four convoys, each with more than twenty trucks, roll by. The next night, split into two elements—one led by Jaks, the other by Oliver Hartwig—they were ready to snatch a driver.

Hartwig's element struck first, ambushing the last truck in a seventeen-vehicle convoy, but the combined mine blast and team small-arms fire killed the driver. Meanwhile Jaks' element hit another truck. Daniel Ster went after the driver, but a second truck rolled up, loaded with NVA firing over the the cab. The SOG men silenced the NVA guards, but not a single NVA was left alive to capture. There were no friendly casualties.

Early the next morning they were lifted away amid only light ground fire. Although no prisoner was seized, Jaks' men had destroyed three trucks and killed or wounded about a dozen NVA.

"The first [snatch] was damned near successful," Colonel Cavanaugh concluded, "it could have gone." After briefing General Abrams, Chief SOG decided it was worth a second try.

That night in the NCO club, fresh back from Stateside leave, I listened to the Operation Ashtray men recount their ambush. Several One-Zeros, including myself and Willie McClod, volunteered for Operation Ashtray II. A few days later it was decided at some high level that Jaks was too knowledgeable an officer to risk capture a second time. Instead, I was selected to lead Ashtray II, which would be a two-team mission combining my RT California and RT New Hampshire, under Captain Fred Krupa.

Although Krupa outranked me—I was a staff sergeant—he was fairly new, while already I had fourteen months running recon and more than a dozen cross-border missions. Not once during our time together did Krupa try to pull rank.

The other six Americans were our respective teammates, all NCOs: Rex Jaco, John Yancey, Richard Woody, Paul Kennicott, R. Michael Grace and David Galaso. Additionally, we'd bring four Montagnards for a total of twelve men.

Each day we planned, and each night we brainstormed in the NCO club. We studied past snatch attempts in which the prisoner was killed and concluded that merely having him dead-to-rights didn't assure success: You had to exploit that momentary edge and seize him so quickly he had no option but to submit.

For the assault itself, our biggest man, John Yancey, would carry just a Browning 9mm pistol so he'd have a hand free to grab the driver while Krupa covered him. Meanwhile, Richard Woody would clear the back and I'd dash around the truck's hood, eliminate the assistant driver, then help Yancey from inside if the driver put up a struggle. Once we tripped the ambush, our security teams, 100 yards away on each flank, would block the road.

What if the driver was chained to the steering wheel, as agent reports alleged? Looking like a ninja-mechanic, Yancey would carry 10-pound bolt cutters slung over his back. And if guards aboard the truck fired, we'd kneel and shoot upward to avoid cross fire and hope ricochets didn't get us. To be ready for any option, we rehearsed assaulting a truck traveling right or traveling left.

But what happened *after* the snatch concerned us, too. We had reports of an estimated battalion base camp just 500 yards from our ambush spot, and who knew what other NVA installations were nearby? We had to confuse and delay the enemy to buy time to get deep into the jungle with our slow-moving prisoner.

So I developed what we dubbed "goody bags"—each man would carry a small canvas bag containing five time-delay devices he would ignite and scatter during our withdrawal, leaving behind a virtual minefield of fragmentation, white-phosphorous and tear-gas grenades that would cook off randomly for forty-five minutes. Every time an NVA started into the jungle, it would seem, another device would explode, spewing dangerous fragments or white phosphorous amid a cloud of tear gas.

And we'd set the truck afire with thermite and explosives, creating a beacon for air strikes, while our big bonus, loitering in orbit just over the horizon, would be a Thailand-based AC-130 Spectre gunship, whose 20mm and 40mm guns would devastate Highway 110 as we withdrew.

We rehearsed the ambush over and over. I was an unyielding taskmaster, but everyone understood so there wasn't the slightest gripe. These weren't unwilling draftees but seasoned Special Forces soldiers, most on their second tour in Vietnam, although several were new to recon. We walked through our first rehearsals, then a bit faster, finally at real time in daylight, then real time with live fire, then walk through at night, real time at night and, for the final dress rehearsal, live fire at night. By then we could hit the truck, clear it and seize a driver in less than ten seconds.

We were ready for the Super Bowl.

When Krupa and I briefed the plan to Colonel Cavanaugh in Saigon, he sat back in his chair, thoughtfully silent for thirty seconds, then announced we first must conduct a short, two-day recon of the area we'd flee through after the ambush, to ensure we didn't rush into a hidden enemy base camp. Krupa led this quick mission, which slipped in and out without incident, while I finished last-minute preparations. Two days later, our combined twelve-man team inserted by helicopter.

Except for a few signal shots and skirting an abandoned bunker area, our first two days were uneventful. The second night, about 10 P.M., I awoke and sat up, straining my ears—yes, I heard trucks, about a mile away—six, maybe ten of them. In the shadows around me, I realized everyone else was sitting up, too, listening but saying nothing. We all knew, tomorrow was our night.

Midway through the next day's slow, silent movement we reached Highway 110. Krupa and I crept forward and found fresh truck tracks on the hard-packed, single-lane road. Two out of three recon missions never made it to such a heavily defended highway, and here we were within 2 yards—a very spooky feeling.

This was a poor ambush site, a thin bamboo grove on the downhill side of the road, almost no cover or concealment—yet I was convinced it was our *best* choice, betting that the enemy thought this so unlikely an ambush spot that they wouldn't sweep it or post guards along it at night.

Late that afternoon we radioed a code word to Leghorn, the SOG mountaintop radio relay station, which, as per our plan, would cause the Air Force to orbit an AC-130 Spectre gunship just over the horizon, ten minutes away, ready to chew up the road with 20mm Vulcan cannons and 40mm ack-ack guns when truckloads of NVA came rushing after us.

At dusk I gave each American a "Green Hornet," a powerful SOG-issue amphetamine, which, like the old OSS "B Tablet," ensured twelve hours' stamina, which I knew we'd need.

It was still daylight when I made my next notebook entry: "1920 [7:20 P.M.]—One vehicle passed headed east-to-west. Contained some troops and large wooden boxes." Beneath mounds of foliage lashed to the truck, Rex Jaco saw flat armored sides, probably a Soviet-made armored car carrying security troops. It sailed clean by.

Then I wrote, "1925—Second truck passed headed east-to-west. Believe it was empty." I actually saw the driver's smiling face while he downshifted; his truck was covered by bamboo lattice and piled high with leafy branches.

With daylight almost gone, I signaled our flank security teams—led by Jaco on our left and Kennicott on the right—to advance to the road and emplace claymores. Next, our assault team crept up—Krupa, Woody, Yancey and myself. With barely enough light to see, I laid out three claymores in a crescent, aimed at a prominent tree across the road. In the dark I'd watch for the truck's front tire to align with that tree, then blow the mines. Typically for a SOG operation, we lay barely 15 feet from the nearest claymore, danger-close. I made a final scribbled entry in my notebook: "1930—Moved into location. Will ambush the next truck regardless of contents or direction."

Then we stayed facedown beside the highway and waited almost two hours. Had the enemy spotted us and canceled his convoys? Just before 2130, the sound of a truck's engine grew gradually louder until it seemed to roar like an approaching locomotive. A tire rolled directly before me and KABOOM!—I blew the mines and shouted, *"Assault!"* Instantly, Yancey, Krupa, Woody and I rushed the Soviet-made GAZ-63 truck that had lurched to a halt in front of us. Flash-blinded in one eye from watching the detonation, I'd just have to shoot left-eyed.

I dashed around the hood, ready to kill the assistant driver—there was none—then covered as Yancey jerked the driver like a rag doll out the opposite door, threw him to the ground and pinned him while Krupa slid plastic restraints on the stunned man's wrists. The driver sobbed in broken English, "No kill, no kill." Yancey gladly threw away his bolt cutters.

I'll never forget the amazing vision of Fred Krupa with his Kodak Instamatic and flashcubes, standing in the middle of the notorious Highway 110, flashing away as I tossed a satchel charge in the truck and placed a time-delay thermite grenade on its hood. Seconds later I shouted, *"Withdraw! Withdraw!"* which Woody backed up with two whistle blasts, as rehearsed—then a hidden enemy soldier shot Woody, bad, through both arms.

Jaco took hold of Woody and led him back toward the rally point. Krupa and Yancey dragged away the prisoner.

That left only me at the truck. I had to buy time for the rest to get a head start, so I began exchanging fire with several enemy soldiers. Meanwhile our Flank Security men were igniting time fuses for the forty assorted grenades that would go off over the next forty-five minutes, to hit other trucks as well as confuse and delay the many North Vietnamese soldiers converging on the ambush site.

At the rally point, Galaso—a Special Forces medic—patched Woody up as best he could. Despite great pain (both his forearms had been shattered by AK slugs), Woody refused morphine for fear it would slow us down. He was one tough trooper.

As I backed away, I could hear NVA shouting and shooting from the road, taking cover behind the ambushed truck—then the 5-pound satchel charge went off, killing the lot of them. It was time to call in the Spectre and show these guys what firepower was. Krupa radioed our mountaintop radio relay site only to learn the *Spectre was not on station.* No explanation was offered, and we had no time to ask. With more NVA at the road and shouting, and signal shots in the distance, we had to get out of there.

While we were running for our lives, back at FOB 2 in Kontum, the staff vacillated. Lieutenant Colonel Abt had rotated back to the States that very morning, leaving an officer of questionable competence in charge, who thought it just fine to wait until morning to do something. But Sergeant First Class Lloyd "OD" O'Daniels, already angered to learn no Spectre had arrived, snapped, "Bullshit. Let's get a helicopter to take us up to Pleiku and go out there tonight [with a Covey FAC aircraft]."

It was midnight when O'Daniels flew across the border but he had no trouble finding us—he could see the beacon of burning trucks from 10 miles away. Here we were, in deep trouble, but true to his light-hearted nature, OD radioed the badly wounded Woody, whom he owed money from an R&R. "Woody," he said, "I told you I was going to screw you out of that $150 one way or the other."

While we ran through that pitch-black jungle, OD used the flames of burning trucks to direct pair after pair of U.S. fighters, continuously bombing the ambush site, the road and our back trail until just before dawn. We paused only twice all night, to treat Woody or check the prisoner's restraints.

Our air assets launched in darkness to arrive overhead at the very crack of dawn—Hueys from the 57th "Gladiators" Assault Helicopter Company, escorted by Cobra gunships from the 361st "Pink Panthers" Attack Helicopter Company. Just before the Hueys came in, a pair of A-1 Skyraiders made one last pass, dispensing cluster bombs, and, as O'Daniels reported, "they dropped it right on top of you. And I thought, 'Oh, shit, I've wiped them all out.'"

But God was with us that morning, for although cluster bombs exploded in all directions, as close as 5 yards, not a man was hit. Then the Hueys swooped in and we were gone—we'd made it out, driver intact, Woody seriously wounded and myself with minor shrapnel wounds.

After our tumultuous welcome on the Kontum helipad, we barely had time to drop off our gear in the RT California team room when the recon first sergeant told me a SOG Blackbird would arrive in ten minutes to transport the prisoner and me to Saigon. Sure enough, ten minutes later I was leading the blindfolded and handcuffed NVA onto a C-130. We were the only passengers.

Because this was all improvised, the Blackbird dropped us at Saigon's Tan Son Nhut civilian terminal instead of the out-of-the-way Air America ramp. Unshaven, with traces of camouflage stick smeared across my face, I led the handcuffed but no longer blindfolded prisoner across the tarmac. Once he saw the amazing reality of a modern, bustling airport he became a bit antsy. To reestablish perspective, I put the muzzle of my

.45 automatic to his head and held it there as we walked the 100 yards to the military terminal. He calmed right down, but the rear-echelon types at the terminal took one glance at the scene—a haggard me approaching with a .45 pressed to a bound captive, and suddenly they remembered they had to go someplace else. In ten minutes an unmarked SOG commercial van arrived to take us away.

Mission done, I began to thirst mightily for a cold beer, then I learned SOG's deputy chief, USAF Colonel Ross Franklin, and I had an important appointment: General Abrams wanted to see us. After a shower and haircut for me, Colonel Franklin and I traveled to MACV headquarters, where we were ushered into a small amphitheater.

I've never since seen such a gathering: Around that horseshoe table sat seven two-, three- and four-star generals, and in the middle, chewing a cigar in his high, leather ship-captain's chair, was General Abrams himself.

For ten minutes I recounted the operation, step by step, and I recall, when I described how the cluster of NVA shooting from behind the truck were snuffed when it blew up, there was a chuckle around the room. When I finished, Abrams shook my hand and asked that I pass his congratulations to all the Ashtray II ambushers, and he meant it. Abrams' kind words surprised me, for he had a reputation for being rabidly anti-Special Forces. Later, Colonel Cavanaugh explained: Despite his biases, Abrams was a fighting man and respected courage under fire, no matter where he found it.

An hour after briefing General Abrams I was in an air-conditioned nightclub, trading toasts with friends from SOG headquarters; my only regret was not celebrating with my ambusher comrades that night. Looking over Saigon's lights from that rooftop bar, I lifted my glass in a toast to them all.

Ours was one of just three prisoners SOG brought out of Laos that year, and the only enemy soldier specifically targeted, then successfully captured, in SOG's history. Chief SOG Colonel Cavanaugh later called Ashtray II "undoubtedly our most successful operation where we had visualized doing something, planned it, then had it done."

A few months after Ashtray II, a SOG platoon operating near Highway 110 snatched a wounded NVA soldier who reported truck drivers still feared darkness and the American "night commandos" who might kill them, or worse yet, steal them away, never to be seen again.

Severely wounded, Richard Woody was stabilized then medevaced back to the U.S. He fully recovered. Although Paul Kennicott came through our ambush unscathed, he was badly wounded almost a year later while reconning 5 miles from where we hit that night convoy. He, too, was medevaced.

John Yancey, who dragged the driver from the truck, later received the Distinguished Service Cross for single-handedly defending a badly wounded comrade, David "Baby Huey" Hayes, against NVA attackers for more than an hour until a rescue force arrived. I thought he deserved the Medal of Honor.

One of Delta Force's earliest counterterrorists, John landed at Desert One in Iran in 1980 during the failed hostage rescue attempt. Later, due to another Delta Force trooper's error, John was killed in a live-fire training exercise. He is still missed.

Just over a year after Ashtray II, Fred Krupa was leading a company-size SOG raid on the Cambodian border when he fell from a hovering helicopter after being hit by an AK round. I was directly overhead, flying Covey. Although we put in many air strikes and tried to launch a rescue mission, we never got Fred back. He remains missing in action. God bless him.

BLOODY '68

By early 1968, Khe Sanh, where the U.S. presence had begun as a simple A Camp and SOG, FOB had become the western anchor of DMZ defenses, held by the 6000-strong 26th Marine Regiment. Surrounding them were 20,000 NVA, pounded day and night by U.S. artillery, fighters and B-52s. SOG's presence at Khe Sanh and the role played by its cross-border missions from there went publicly undisclosed.

Inside the base perimeter, SOG's fifty U.S. and five hundred indigenous personnel were dug in, just like the Marines, withstanding up to fifteen hundred rounds of incoming artillery and rockets per day.

Outside Khe Sanh, in those incredibly dangerous hills, prowled recon men from SOG's FOB 1 at Phu Bai who uncovered targets for air strikes, wiretapped phone lines and emplaced sensors.

To bypass the monsoon squalls that closed the Laotian border west of Khe Sanh as solidly as a wall, some teams launched from SOG's top-secret "back door," Nakhon Phanom (NKP) Air Base in Thailand, 145 miles away, completely across Laos. Seven SOG Americans operated the NKP launch site, working with the USAF 21st "Pony" Special Operations Squadron, sister unit to SOG's 20th SOS Green Hornets. Since January 1967, the Ponies had supported SOG agent teams in North Vietnam, CIA operations in northern Laos and then late that year began inserting American-led SOG teams in Laos. The Thai launch option proved important in early 1968, when SOG helicopters could not operate from the besieged Khe Sanh airfield.

One continuing SOG target was Co Roc, the dominant terrain feature west of Khe Sanh, a 3-mile-wide bluff whose 1800-foot limestone cliffs signaled each dawn with a rosy glow ten minutes before sunrise. Just a half mile into Laos and safe from Marine ground attack, Co Roc was honeycombed with caves and tunnels sheltering enemy artillery pieces. Recalled one recon man who penetrated Co Roc, Rick Bayer, "They had steps cut in the mountain you could walk down. They had bamboo poles with candles where they could march their troops up. They had trails coming off the main trails all over that mountain."

On 12 January 1968, RT Indiana was ambushed on Co Roc's reverse side. The team broke contact and evaded through a deep gully but somehow the One-One, Staff Sergeant Jim Cohron, and two Nungs became separated from the others. Cohron's teammates made it to a small knoll where they vainly tried to raise him by radio. They barely made it out themselves. Cohron disappeared.

Eventually U.S. intelligence concluded RT Indiana had been hit by the NVA Dong Nai Regiment, which, signal intercepts disclosed, had interrogated an American determined to be Cohron. To this day, Hanoi denies any knowledge of the Iowa-born Green Beret.

Five miles west of Khe Sanh, in the shadow of Co Roc on the Laotian border, lay South Vietnam's most distant (from Saigon) outpost, Lang Vei Special Forces camp, commanded by Captain Frank Willoughby. As NVA strength grew in early 1968, the camp's 282 Montagnards were reinforced with another Yard company and additional Green Berets.

RT Indiana walked into Lang Vei one night in late January after being chased several days near Co Roc. One-One Rick Bayer sought out Lang Vei's team sergeant, Bill Craig, with a special warning: RT Indiana had seen tank tracks! Furthermore, when they waded across the nearby Xe Kong River at dusk, they found the NVA had surveyed the river and marked off suitable fording sites. Bayer had no doubt the NVA were going to bring tanks into South Vietnam.

"When we got flown down to Saigon for debriefing," Bayer recalls disgustedly, "I was called a liar."

Also disgusted was his Phu Bai FOB 1 commander, Major Ed Rybat. "We'd send the reports in and they'd say, 'No, you're wrong. These are earthbuilding [*sic*] tractors or bulldozers.' Now I'm an old tanker and I know a damned tank track, and those were PT-76s."

In Saigon, Chief SOG Colonel Jack Singlaub was convinced the NVA was staging tanks for a strike. MACV ignored his warnings.

Just after midnight of 6 February, Marines in Khe Sanh's western trenches heard a mechanical groaning in the wind, like a chain saw revving—*tanks!* At Lang Vei the ground shook as eleven PT-76 tanks and an NVA infantry battalion supported by 152mm howitzers stormed into the tiny camp. Flamethrowers flashed while the tanks' 76mm guns shattered bunker after bunker. More than half the camp's Montagnard defenders died in their positions, emptying M-1 carbines and machine guns at the oncoming tanks. The Green Berets managed to destroy more than half the PT-76s with 106mm recoilless rifles, but hastily supplied M-72 LAW antitank rockets failed miserably. Captain Willoughby and a handful of holdouts locked themselves in the camp's command bunker while a PT-76 climbed atop it, spinning one track to try to dig them out like a badger tearing at a gopher hole.

Chief SOG relayed word of the attack to MACV, "And the J-2 flat out *refused* to believe it. He just said, 'There are no tanks in Vietnam.'"

When a SOG delegation at Khe Sanh forwarded Lang Vei's request for a relief force, Colonel David Lownds, the 26th Marines commander, "refused the request and said that he would not sacrifice any American lives," recalled recon man Harvey Saal. "He just glared through us like an X-ray machine and dismissed our thoughts as so much bravado."

"It is true that we had an agreement to go to the aid of Lang Vei in the event it was threatened with being overrun," conceded Major Jim Stanton, Khe Sanh's Marine artillery coordinator, "but the situation at the combat base deteriorated so quickly and so completely that it should have been obvious to anyone that we could no longer guarantee their security."

Aides woke General Westmoreland twice that night with news of the Lang Vei attack. Colonel Francis Kelly, the 5th Special Forces Group commander, urged him to dispatch a relief force, but Westmoreland hesitated to override the Marine command. Privately, Westmoreland saw the refusal to send in a rescue force as the final act in a dispute between his headquarters and the Marine Corps; he ordered a conference with Marine commanders in Danang that very morning.

By sunrise at Lang Vei the NVA were trying to blow the door of the American-held bunker with satchel charges; when that failed they tossed grenades and tear gas down a vent. Choking men pressed their faces to cracks and gasped for air. An NVA officer promised, "Give up and we will not harm you." The ARVN commander and several Vietnamese officers scrambled out, only to be summarily executed. Then explosive charges rocked the bunker and knocked all eight Americans unconscious.

Arriving in Danang, General Westmoreland immediately ordered Marine Lieutenant General Robert Cushman to provide helicopters to lift a SOG rescue force from Khe Sanh into Lang Vei. Reviewing what had been transpiring in I Corps, Westmoreland grew "more and more shocked at things that virtually begged to be done yet remained undone." He issued orders to Cushman's subordinates, violating the Marine chain of command and ruffling such feathers that he heard about it from the Joint Chiefs. Westmoreland wrote, "That was the issue—the one issue—that arose during my service in Vietnam to prompt me to consider resigning."

At Khe Sanh, Major George Quamo and Master Sergeant Charles "Skip" Minnicks could see smoke rising in the distance as they called together the recon teams. Quamo recited the dangers of going into Lang Vei, then asked, "OK, who wants to go?" A dozen Americans grabbed their CAR-15s, assembled thirty Nungs and Yards, then climbed aboard the Marine choppers.

The Marine command's attitude affected the pilots, who showed no enthusiasm to rescue "a bunch of gooks" at Lang Vei. Shocked to see the destroyed tanks and collapsed buildings, they kept circling and circling in their big CH-46s. Finally Major Quamo demanded that his command chopper go in and at last they all landed.

Fanning out, the SOG men trotted bunker to bunker, searching for survivors. Thousands of NVA were nearby but stayed hidden, fearing U.S. air strikes.

Most surviving Americans owed their lives to Sergeant First Class Eugene Ashley, who died that morning leading repeated assaults to push the NVA from Lang Vei; he was awarded the Medal of Honor. Several wounded Americans survived because Lieutenant Quy, an ARVN, raced his jeep through the enemy to retrieve them.

The SOG men assembled the U.S. survivors and as many Montagnard wounded as they could carry and called in the Marine helicopters. As the rescue force lifted away, RT Alabama One-Zero John Allen saw an American dash onto the airstrip waving his arms, but there was no going back—he was left to his fate. The abandoned Green Beret, Dennis Thompson, survived five years as a POW. Of the twenty-four Special Forces defenders at Lang Vei, Major Quamo's SOG men brought out fourteen, all but one wounded.

Lang Vei had shown the enemy what losses awaited them at Khe Sanh: Of the eleven attacking tanks, seven were destroyed, with two more probables, plus 250 North Vietnamese dead—a full-scale ground assault on Khe Sanh would have been disastrous.

SOG's greatest contribution to the Seige of Khe Sanh was also its greatest Laotian achievement of 1968, uncovering a major enemy stronghold and munitions stockpile near Co Roc. "As a result," a SOG report notes, "an Arc Light [B-52] strike was conducted, resulting in continuous secondary explosions over a two-hour period." General Westmoreland in his memoirs described how the big bombers hit a "military headquarters in a limestone cave inside Laos, believed to be the North Vietnamese headquarters controlling the forces around Khe Sanh if not the entire northern region [of South Vietnam]." He noted, "radio traffic from the headquarters ceased for almost two weeks, there was evidence of considerable confusion in the North Vietnamese command in the north, and no major attack developed at Khe Sanh during Tet."

In late March, while the 1st Air Cav began its push to break the Khe Sanh seige, RT Asp inserted 25 miles to the northwest to track the withdrawing NVA. Led by Sergeant First Class George Brown, with Sergeants Charles Huston and Alan Boyer, RT Asp was suddenly hit by a massive NVA force.

A Kingbee going in for Brown and Huston was driven off by intense ground fire. Another Kingbee spotted Alan Boyer and dropped him a rope ladder, which he snatched amid a hail of fire. But the ladder mount broke, apparently hit by a bullet, and Boyer slid back into a sea of NVA.

None of them was heard from again.

Two hundred and five Marines and soldiers died during the seventy-seven-day Khe Sanh siege. NVA dead were estimated at 10,000 to 15,000. As things wound down, Major George Quamo, who led the Lang Vei rescue, left Khe Sanh aboard a SOG plane which disappeared in bad weather while bound for Danang.*

A few weeks later SOG's Khe Sanh FOB closed, its personnel reassigned in SOG and its launch-site role shifted east-northeast to Mai Loc.

On the last day of March, President Johnson suspended bombing above North Vietnam's 20th Parallel: This meant only North Vietnam's southernmost 150 miles remained subject to air attacks, and all air attacks would end on the eve of the November elections. Previously there had been a cost in manpower, vehicles and cargo for each mile they flowed south, but now a sizable length of that route became immune from attack. North Vietnam soon began running one-hundred-truck convoys in broad daylight across rebuilt bridges and repaved roads, freeing thousands of engineers and antiaircraft units for transfer to Laos, where they expanded the Ho Chi Minh Trail.

As fighting declined around Khe Sanh, other SOG teams were penetrating Cambodia to learn whether the enemy was back in his sanctuaries after the Tet Offensive. On 2 May 1968, a SOG recon team led by Sergeant First Class Leroy Wright inserted into Cambodia's Fishhook, 75 miles northwest of Saigon, for an area recon mission. Going in with Wright were Staff Sergeant Lloyd "Frenchie" Mousseau, One-One, and Specialist Four Brian O'Connor, One-Two, along with nine Nungs.

Watching them launch that morning from Quan Loi was an old friend of Wright's, Sergeant First Class Roy Benavidez, a heavy-set Yaqui Indian, a likable, teddy bear–type, who did support jobs at the launch site. As the Hueys faded in the west, Benavidez shook his head respectfully, awed by the kind of bravery it took to operate behind NVA lines.

Soon after landing, Wright's team hit an enemy squad and shot its way clear. A half hour later, the ram fought through a full platoon and got back to the insert LZ, but so many NVA fell upon them that heavy fire pinned them and forced away rescue Hueys. One gunship was shot down.

*Major Quamo's remains were recovered in 1974.

Several NVA companies blasted away at them with mortars, RPGs and machine guns. Then a lone AK round struck Wright in the head, killing him instantly; Mousseau and O'Connor were shot several times, while half their Nungs lay dead around them with the rest wounded. Unable to move, they were about to be overrun.

Gathered with others at the launch-site tent at Quan Loi, Roy Benavidez listened to radio messages from the FAC and helicopter pilots and grew more upset by the minute. Leroy Wright was shot; Frenchie Mousseau was shot; Brian O'Connor was shot—all their Nungs were wounded or dead. A brigade of the U.S. 1st Infantry Division was within shouting distance, but they couldn't go into Cambodia after the SOG men. Not even a Bright Light team was available. *Somebody had to do something!*

Weakened by loss of blood, Brian O'Connor heard a Huey coming in but could barely move; in the helicopter doorway, a hefty figure made repeated signs of the cross, tossed out a medic bag, then rolled to the ground. It was Roy Benavidez, a one-man Bright Light team who'd volunteered so spontaneously that he didn't even bring an M-16, just the bowie knife on his belt.

Benavidez snatched up the medic bag and dashed 75 yards through withering enemy fire. *Crack!* An AK slug hit his right leg. He stumbled and skipped but convinced himself he'd only snagged a thornbush and kept running, then dove into the brush pile where Wright's men lay.

With one look, Benavidez could see that Wright was dead, while Frenchie Mousseau had a serious head wound. O'Connor was coherent but barely able to crawl. Benavidez bound their wounds, injected morphine and, ignoring NVA bullets and grenades, passed around ammunition he'd taken off several bodies and armed himself with an AK. Then Benavidez directed air strikes and was calling in a Huey when an AK slug hit his right thigh, his second wound.

When the Huey landed, Benavidez gave his AK to O'Connor and struggled to bring along Wright's body. Something threw him to the ground—he'd been shot through one lung, his third gunshot wound. Benavidez almost passed out but somehow pulled himself back to his feet to see the Huey lying on its side, destroyed, a pilot and one door gunner dead.

Coughing blood, Benavidez stumbled onto the LZ to help survivors get free before the Huey's gas tanks exploded. While mortar shells burst everywhere, he called in Phantoms danger-close. Benavidez was shot yet again. He tried to ignore it.

Five minutes later he took still another slug.

And another gunship was downed.

Then amid heavy gunship supporting fire and another air strike, a lone Huey came in for one final extraction attempt. On board was Staff Sergeant Ronald Sammons, a Green Beret medic, who helped Benavidez carry and drag injured crewmen from the crashed Huey and recon men to the helicopter. Benavidez hefted Frenchie Mousseau over his shoulder and staggered toward the chopper, walking past a fallen NVA. The enemy soldier rose up and clubbed him in the head with an AK, knocking Benavidez to his knees, then the berserk NVA butt-stroked him in the face and turned to thrust at him with a bayonet. Instinctively, Benavidez pulled his bowie knife, but not before the bayonet poked completely through his left forearm. Benavidez threw his body against the North Vietnamese and drove his knife into his side with such force that he couldn't pull it out. He left the NVA there, dead, the knife hilt pointing skyward, and stumbled to the Huey, pushed Mousseau aboard and snatched up a fallen AK. Then two more NVA materialized and he shot them both. Powerful hands dragged Benavidez aboard and the Huey lifted off.

Bleeding almost into unconsciousness, Benavidez lay against the badly wounded Mousseau and clasped his hand. Just before they landed at the medevac hospital in Saigon, "I felt his fingers dig into my palm," Benavidez recalled, "his arm twitching and jumping as if electric current was pouring through his body into mine." Then Frenchie Mousseau died.

Wright and Mousseau received the Distinguished Service Cross posthumously. Benavidez spent almost a year in hospitals to recover from seven major gunshot wounds, twenty-eight shrapnel holes and a bayonet wound. Credited with saving eight lives, his incredible bravery was written up, but the paperwork was lost. Congress passed special legislation thirteen years later and retired Master Sergeant Roy Benavidez was flown to Washington, where President Ronald Reagan draped the Medal of Honor around his neck.

• • •

Only one day after Benavidez's May 1968 rescue, RT Alabama inserted in Laos, 15 miles beyond the Ashau Valley, to emplace a wiretap. Led by Staff Sergeant John Allen, with Specialist Five Kenneth Cryan, One-One, Private First Class Paul King, One-Two, and six Nungs, RT Alabama was penetrating an area thought to conceal an entire NVA division that had been pushed into Laos when the 1st Air Cav had swept the adjacent Ashau.

As they neared the LZ, Allen's men saw bunkers, trails and hootches flash past beneath the trees. There was no sign of NVA at their insert LZ, so Allen radioed the customary "Team OK" and started his mission.

They'd traveled an hour when Allen's sixth sense—the product of twenty missions into Laos and one North Vietnam Bright Light—reared up. Allen whispered to his One-One, Ken Cryan, "This don' look right, don' smell right, just don' *feel* right." Taking a Nung with him, Allen slipped forward to investigate.

They had crept about 250 yards when the foliage opened into a man-made clearing with upper tree branches tied together as natural camouflage. In the middle stood an elaborate bamboo and palm-leaf house, clearly a major NVA headquarters, with soldiers coming and going. Beyond it, dug into a hillside, was a tunnel so wide two men could enter abreast. Allen snapped a half-dozen photos then crept back to RT Alabama.

One-One Ken Cryan reported several NVA had passed nearby; thinking them trackers, Allen decided to shake them off. Then they heard shouts from their left and brush breaking on their back trail.

Minutes later the point man led them across a fresh high-speed trail, probably a route into the headquarters they'd just discovered. With enemy voices only 50 yards behind them, Allen increased the pace to a light trot. They crossed another trail, and to their right heard shouts and crashing brush, answered by more shouts to their rear. Allen went to a full run and pivoted the team up a steep hill. Then the enemy opened fire, wildly spraying the area with AKs and machine guns, and as one, RT Alabama emptied their CAR-15s in quick bursts. Cryan collapsed, holding his right thigh. He grunted he'd be all right but couldn't stand, and Allen grabbed him, ignoring his plea to be left behind. One Nung took an AK hit center chest and slumped to the ground, dead; his fellow Nungs carried him along.

With Paul King behind him calling fruitlessly on the radio, Allen forged through the brush, scanning for anything that looked defensible. He spotted a bomb crater 50 yards uphill.

"Cover me!" Allen shouted, tossed a grenade downhill to buy a few seconds, scooped up Cryan, then charged straightaway to the crater, rolling into it with the rest of the team behind him.

The bomb had impacted perpendicularly to the hill, making the crater almost a ledge, the upper lip blocking fire from uphill, the lower lip forming a small parapet. The surrounding terrain favored defense, with the foliage blasted clear for 10 yards on one side, while on the other, a washout formed a natural obstacle that, combined with the landslide below, gave them all-around fields of fire.

It wasn't perfect, but given their situation, it was a godsend. Allen spread an orange panel at the crater bottom.

King turned his attention to the casualties. The Nung tribesman, he saw, was dead. Then, tearing open Cryan's bloodied pants, King saw an AK round had smashed his femur. He feared the shattered leg would have to come off; for now, King injected morphine, not using too much so that Cryan would remain conscious.

Meanwhile, Allen and the Nungs hurriedly stripped grenades from their web gear and stacked them in the soft earth. Then Allen collected two dozen 40mm grenade rounds the Nungs carried for his pistol-sized, sawed-off M-79 grenade launcher.

They'd been in the crater two minutes when a line of NVA broke from the woodline below, charging uphill. Three grenades and several entire CAR-15 magazines sprayed over the lip forced them back. Then higher up the ridge an RPG round crashed harmlessly. Allen's sawed-off grenade launcher dispatched the rocketeers as three NVA scrambled across the ravine, too late to benefit from the supporting RPG. Allen dropped them with as many shots from his CAR-15.

Then all was quiet; a stalemate began.

Periodically the team heard NVA soldiers, and the Nungs responded as Allen had taught them, by carefully lifting the spoon from a hand grenade, waiting two seconds, then lobbing it in a high arc so it would airburst above the enemy. This went on more than an hour, with NVA probing toward them and Allen directing his defense with quick peeks from the top of the crater. At last King looked up from the radio and shouted, "I've got Covey!"

Allen slid down and grabbed the radio handset. "Handle things topside," he told King, and had started to talk when the young medic peeked over the edge of the crater. Allen opened his mouth to shout, but at that instant a bullet struck King, flipping him backward, his skull blown away. Allen tenderly laid Paul King at the bottom of the crater; RT Alabama now had two dead men.

Covey announced tac air was en route. It would be close, Allen thought, but tac air would clear the way for a rescue helicopter.

Then the sky teemed with fighters. A pair of F-4 Phantoms dropped 500-pound bombs, then more Phantoms arrived, followed by F-100 Super Sabres and A-1 Skyraiders. Pass after pass riddled enemy positions with cannon fire, cluster bombs and napalm.

Then Hueys arrived, but the lead helicopter pilot radioed, "Is it secure down there?" Allen laughed. "Secure? Hell no, it ain't secure. An' the longer you wait the worse it's gonna get. But I think their heads are down."

"Then we can't go in," the Huey pilot announced and Covey argued with him, but it was no use. "Listen," Allen offered, "you bring in some napalm, damned near right on top of us. Then right away, *right away,* come in with the Huey. OK?"

Grudgingly, the pilot agreed.

A pair of A-1s rolled in with napalm, which flashed hot and dirty orange, so close Allen could feel the air sucked from his lungs. He peeked over the edge; the only NVA he saw were running away or dead on the open ground.

"Are you sure it's secure?" the pilot demanded.

"Fuck no, it ain't secure, but that's as good as it's gonna get. We just pounded hell outta 'em, an' they're runnin' away."

The Huey dropped low, off in the distance. "But I still see people over here and over there," the pilot complained.

"Jesus Christ!" Allen pleaded, sensing the chances of escape evaporating with each second's hesitance. "They're runnin' away, runnin' away. Come 'n' get us, dammit!" Covey yelled, too, and at last the pilot agreed to come in.

As the Huey cleared the trees 100 yards away it took a few rounds of ground fire and, ignoring the marker panel Allen waved, accelerated and climbed away.

By now the helicopters were low on fuel and it was almost dark.

Covey put in more air strikes until there wasn't enough light to direct them. "I'll be back after first light, John," he promised and almost added, "if you last that long."

Allen shut off the radio to conserve batteries. He considered abandoning the bodies and slipping away during the night but he couldn't carry Cryan and move quietly. And the enemy knew that if they couldn't overwhelm RT Alabama that night, there'd be another rescue attempt at dawn.

If they survived the night.

It was entirely dark now, and Allen worked hurriedly. First he low-crawled to emplace four claymores, which he could detonate from the crater, along likely approaches. Then he checked Cryan's leg, loosened the tourniquet and injected more morphine.

That done, he warned his Nungs not to fire in the darkness because muzzle flashes would attract enemy fire; instead, they would throw grenades, silently and with no warning.

A half hour later they heard footsteps below the crater and dispatched the unseen enemy with hand grenades. Then crunching pebbles signaled NVA approaching on the right. Allen blew a claymore. Then it started again, but with machine-gun fire raking the crater's lip, followed by an RPG rocket crashing into the ground nearby. Then, nothing.

Many times that night they responded to crunching leaves or a low whisper with grenades and claymore mines. Using his M-79 as a mini-mortar, Allen lobbed 40mm rounds toward likely NVA positions. Miraculously, they kept the enemy enough off balance to prevent a concerted attack from reaching their crater.

It was nearly dawn when Allen checked Cryan's tourniquet again and told him not to worry. His One-One was weakening, and the pain grew so bad that Cryan requested additional morphine. Then it was false dawn, and Allen spoke to each surviving Nung, applauding the fine job he'd done. Only one had been slightly wounded.

Then the enemy launched an all-out assault with intersecting machine-gun fire and whole salvos of RPG rounds, while NVA infantry fired and advanced toward the crater. A Chicom grenade plopped in, but a Nung tossed it back. Another bounced in, and Allen heaved it out. Two more grenades fell in, and these, too, were thrown back before they could detonate.

With the assaulting troops almost at the crater, it was the moment of truth. To stay low in the crater would have allowed the enemy to come right over the top; yet to expose themselves to the enemy's withering fire was suicide. Allen had no choice.

"Now!" he shouted, and he and the five Nungs rose up, cutting down a line of NVA seconds before they would have overrun them. Allen dropped down again into protective cover and fought off shock as he surveyed the result. Seconds earlier, he and five Nungs had jumped up; not a half minute later, only he and one Nung were still alive. RT Alabama, which had inserted a day ago with nine men, was down to himself, the badly wounded Ken Cryan and one Nung. All the others lay around him, dead.

After the last man's death rattle stopped, Allen numbly dragged his teammates to the bottom of the crater—thoughts welled up and nearly overwhelmed him. Allen had to fight the urge to cry for his dead friends and comrades. But his work wasn't done, he told himself, and he regained control.

Allen froze. Beside him was a Chinese hand grenade; how long it had been there, he didn't know. Delicately he tossed it away.

Then Covey was overhead and the sky was abuzz with aircraft. But as the first pair of fighters learned, RT Alabama was circled by antiaircraft guns—six 12.7mm machine guns ringed the crater at 500 yards, and beyond was another ring, this of heavy 37mm flak guns that had been trucked in during the night.

When a Phantom swooped low, 37mm guns opened up, tracking him until he erupted in a fireball. Other fighters concentrated on the antiaircraft guns, then Covey brought in more air strikes around the crater, then the guns opened up again.

At last fire slackened, but by now both Covey and the choppers were too low on fuel to attempt a pickup. While they returned to Vietnam to refuel and rearm, a Skyraider pilot brought in more air around the besieged team. At one point the gallant A-1 pilot—his own ordnance totally expended—opened the canopy of his propeller-driven plane and swooped just above Allen, tipping his wing 45 degrees and emptying his revolver at the NVA. In spite of the tense situation, Allen could not help but admire that crazy bastard and swore he'd buy him a drink one day.

When Covey returned he resumed the aerial pounding until, at last, an extract could be attempted, using USAF Jolly Green helicopters. The lead Jolly Green pilot told Allen he couldn't land on the steep hill and instead would lower a three-seated jungle penetrator, but due to altitude he could lift just two men.

"But the goddamn penetrator is built for *three* men!" Allen shouted into his handset. "We got *three* men down here!"

The pilot was insistent. Allen looked at Cryan, too groggy to speak anymore, and at the diffident Nung, who would do whatever he ordered. "Send the goddamn thing in," he radioed.

A pair of A-1s roared overhead, miniguns and cannons groaning, as the penetrator landed. Allen lashed in Cryan, while the Nung slid into the adjacent folding seat. He leaned his face close to Cryan's and shouted, "See yuh at Phu Bai!"

The Jolly Green lifted upward. One bullet smacked the Nung. And another. A round struck Cryan. And another. Blood trickled down on Allen's upturned face, then it fell freely and still the enemy fired—not a round at the Jolly Green, all of it at his teammates. *"Noooo!"* Allen screamed as he watched the helicopter slip away, a line of deadly tracers following his men, their shirts flying open and arms flailing the air. "You bastards, *bastards!*" Allen screamed. *"Dirty fucking bastards!"*

Then it was quiet again. Allen couldn't understand: Had the enemy fired at the helicopter, they might have knocked it down. But they held back, giving false hope, then sadistically shot his men. "I'm making a run for it," Allen announced to Covey.

Covey pleaded with him to wait for more air. He'd talked to the Jolly Green and Allen's teammates had only been wounded. "It's no use," Allen insisted. "I'm makin' a break for it."

"But where will you go, John?"

The vision of his men hanging helplessly while bullets tore into them was fresh and horrible. "I dunno, but I can't stay here, I can't cover everything by myself. Get all the air you've got left and dump it all around me, right on top of me, all of it at once. *All* of it."

Covey protested but there was no time left. Allen slid deep into the crater, wedging himself between the bodies, and held his hands over his ears while the ground shook and dust and clods of earth fell around him. Then the bombing stopped. Allen checked his CAR-15; it was empty. Dumping his useless web gear, he found two 20-round magazines in a Nung's gear, slipped one into his weapon, the other into his pocket. For the first time, he noticed a thin washout at the bottom of the crater, just wide enough for him to squeeze into the open. A pair of F-4 Phantoms screamed past with afterburners to divert attention.

Grabbing the radio, Allen shinnied into the open and raced madly downhill, directly into an NVA who suddenly stood up; Allen shoved his CAR-15 into the man's belly and pulled the trigger. Seconds later he was in a woodline and another NVA swung an AK toward him but never finished—and still Allen ran. Mistaking him for a fellow NVA, another soldier watched the SOG recon man run toward him and Allen dropped him, too, replaced his spent magazine and kept going, never even looking sideways.

Allen jumped into a chest-high washout and followed it 100 yards downhill. To his right a 12.7mm machine gun opened up at a passing fighter, its five-man crew so intently watching the aircraft that they didn't see Allen level his CAR-15. In two seconds they were dead and he was running again.

From the excited shouts behind him, he knew the NVA realized an American had escaped and were after him. Adrenaline drained, and gasping, he came providentially upon a small, cavelike washout, just large enough to crawl into. He checked his last magazine—three rounds left, with a fourth in the chamber. There was no hope, no possibility of escape, so there was no need for fear or remorse, and once he accepted this, a tremendous calm settled over him. The only remaining matter was the number of enemy soldiers he could take with him, which, if he restricted himself to semi-auto fire, meant three—with the fourth round for himself. He was in control again.

Allen slid the radio out to raise Covey. "How are my boys doing?" Allen asked.

"Medics say they're going to be just fine, John, just fine. But we've got to get you out of there, too." Squeezing himself into that tight hole, Allen had fighters blanket the whole hillside with 20mm fire, machine guns, rockets and cluster bombs. Though Allen warned against it, a Kingbee roared above the treetops and dropped a rope near him.

A 12.7mm machine gun opened fire, pummeling the Kingbee until it tipped into the jungle and exploded. Allen knew there were no survivors. After calling in air on the gun, Allen ran farther down the ravine, directing still more air to his front. Then Covey said an American Huey was inbound with a McGuire rig.

Ground fire erupted, and Allen prayed the Huey would pass by, but the pilot pressed on. The Huey suddenly went out of control and sailed past, enemy tracers following it as it dove and crashed into the valley below. Allen was sure that more men were dead.

He had to regather his wits. He'd been heading east, toward the border—maybe that's what the enemy expected. He called in another air strike, this time to the north. When the last bomb exploded, he was up and running north; then he called air south and kept running north. He repeated the tactic several times over the next two hours, until he came upon a large open field. At last a Kingbee spiraled in and Allen ran for it, ran for his life.

There was no enemy fire. Within an hour they were landing at Phu Bai; it was as if Allen were coming out of a trance. All he could think about was visiting Cryan and the surviving Nung at the evacuation hospital.

Allen's recon comrades rushed to his Kingbee to thrust a beer into his hand, but strangely, not a word was offered. Their glances conveyed a truth none could express, that Covey had not admitted, though John Allen had known the truth all along. Later Covey would explain, he had to lie because, had Allen known Ken Cryan and the Nung had died— each man riddled by more than thirty slugs—he might have thrown his life away. Allen understood, though this overwhelming truth sapped his last strength: *Except for John Allen, RT Alabama no longer existed.**

The losses did not stop with RT Alabama. The Covey Rider who supported RT Alabama, Sergeant First Class John Robertson, was killed—fifteen days later and only 10 miles from where RT Alabama was lost—when a rocket hit the Kingbee he was riding.

• • •

Then three days after that, RT Idaho inserted not 5 miles from there. That afternoon One-Zero Glen Lane and One-One Robert Owen had a brief conversation with Covey, explaining they couldn't talk because

---

*Though many thought John Allen deserved the Medal of Honor, a jealous NCO reportedly confessed years later to manipulating the paperwork so the award was downgraded to a Silver Star.

NVA were all around them. It was the last anyone ever heard from RT Idaho.

RT Oregon went in to search for Idaho and found a place where concussion grenades had exploded; Lane and Owen probably were incapacitated and captured by NVA counter-recon specialists. A large NVA force hit RT Oregon and, with every member of the team wounded, they narrowly escaped.

RT Idaho's loss was the last event in Colonel Singlaub's two-year tour as Chief SOG; his final contribution, he believed, was ensuring he had a suitable replacement. One night, Singlaub phoned an old UCLA classmate in Germany with the 8th Division to announce proudly, "Steve, I've nominated you to take my place." On the other end, Colonel Steve Cavanaugh asked, "Where?"

"Why, SOG!"

Cavanaugh paused then asked, "What's SOG?"

Singlaub's choice was a wise one. As a young paratroop officer in World War II, Steve Cavanaugh had made two combat jumps with the 11th Airborne Division, fighting the Japanese in New Guinea and the Philippines. His second jump was on a North Luzon drop zone secured by Don "Headhunter" Blackburn's guerrillas.

Cavanaugh had served a 1961 Vietnam tour as the country's senior U.S. Army training officer, then had run the Special Warfare Development Branch at Fort Bragg's JFK Center. He went on to command the Germany-based 10th Special Forces Group, then, being groomed for higher command, he was appointed 8th Division chief of staff. And now the boy who'd dreamed of being a professional soldier would head his country's largest and most secret special operations organization since the OSS.

Cavanaugh arrived at SOG's new Saigon headquarters, a coverted hotel on Rue Pasteur, the old MACV headquarters Westmoreland vacated when he moved to a new Tan Son Nhut complex. While offering useful advice, Singlaub issued a warning about *that damned patch*: A few SOG men had scribbled a design on a cocktail napkin and had it run off at a local tailor shop. It featured a Green Beret skull in a yellow shell burst with Air Force wings and a Navy and Marine anchor. It compromised the whole operation, complained Singlaub. "Look at the thing! It's no 'Studies and Observations' patch!" Cavanaugh found the patches a lost cause, though he insisted that men visiting Saigon wear sterile uniforms.

Despite his lofty position, Cavanaugh was always supportive, almost a fatherly figure and a real listener, respected by the recon men, whose advice he often sought.

That summer of 1968, under Chief SOG Cavanaugh, SOG refocused its operations across the border and tapered off in-country missions except in the Ashau Valley, which remained a SOG haunt.

Situated beyond a barrier of imposing mountains that masked it from coastal enclaves 40 miles away at Phu Bai and Danang, the Ashau Valley stretched 25 miles northwest to southeast on the Laotian frontier. Two miles wide in places, the Ashau's flat bottom was grassy and so open it was eerie; flying overhead you could feel eyes following you. Two abandoned airfields and three ghost camps haunted the valley floor, while its major road, Highway 548, connected with Laotian Highway 922. From adjacent Laotian base areas the NVA built a network of forty high-speed trails into the valley. Northern Ashau's Tam Boi Mountain contained immense chambers hewn from solid rock and fitted with heavy iron doors, so well constructed that they withstood B-52 strikes.

On 3 August a reconstituted RT Idaho, led by One-Zero Wilbur Boggs, inserted into the Ashau Valley about 10 miles from where the old RT Idaho had vanished on 20 May. Boggs' One-One, Specialist Four John Walton, was an accomplished poker player, friendly, intelligent and a talented medic capable of surgery. Idaho's One-Two was a new man, Private First Class Tom Cunningham.

Not long after insertion, swarms of NVA descended on RT Idaho, and soon One-Zero Boggs was seriously wounded, two Yards were dead and the team immobile, hopelessly encircled by NVA so close Walton could see smoke drifting from their cigarettes.

With his team about to be overrun, young Walton did the only thing he could and called an air strike practically on top of RT Idaho, which hit friend and foe alike. The NVA fell back. It took every bit of Walton's medical skill to keep his wounded teammates alive, though Tom Cunningham would lose a leg. That anyone made it out is attributable to Walton's courage, cool head and medical ability. He was awarded the Silver Star.

Brigadier General Donald
Blackburn, Chief SOG, 1965–66.
(Photo by the author)

Major General Jack Singlaub, Chief
SOG, 1966–68. (U.S. Army Photo)

Colonel Steve Cavanaugh,
Chief SOG, 1968–70. (U.S.
Army Photo)

Colonel John Sadler, Chief SOG,
1970–72. (U.S. Army Photo)

"The Bra," a heavily defended area along Laotian Highway 96, after it was hit by repeated B-52 strikes (Photo by Ted Wicorek)

Laotian Highway 110, a heavily defended North Vietnamese Army convoy route and major conduit on the Ho Chi Minh Trail. (Photo by the author)

Kham Duc Airfield, October 1965. SOG's first U.S.-led Laotian mission. One-Zero Charles Petry (center), Captain Larry Thorne (left) and Kingbee pilot, "Cowboy" (right). (Photo courtesy Charlie Norton)

SFC Jerry "Mad Dog" Shriver, MIA after SOG's top-secret raid on COSVN headquarters. (Photo by Jim Fleming)

(*below*) Captain Frank Jaks and Viet Cong defector just before SOG's first attempted POW rescue, 1966. It proved to be a horrible trap. (Photo courtesy Frank Jaks)

(*below*) RT Iowa One-Zero Dick Meadows (third from left), SOG's most accomplished prisoner snatcher. (Photo by Charlie Norton)

SFC Fred Zabitoski receives the Medal of Honor from President Nixon. (Dept. of Defense Photo)

(above) While an SFC in SOG, Colonel Robert Howard three times was submitted for the Medal of Honor. Today he is America's most highly decorated serviceman. (U.S. Army Photo)

SFC Charles Wilklow, the only SOG man to escape enemy captivity in Laos. (Photo courtesy the Wilklow family)

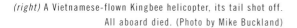

Snatched by McGuire rig "strings," four men of RT Maine escape Laos for the safety of South Vietnam. (Photo by Clarence Long)

(right) A Vietnamese-flown Kingbee helicopter, its tail shot off. All aboard died. (Photo by Mike Buckland)

RT Maine fights for its life, surrounded on a Laotian landing zone, while Cobra gunships pound North Vietnamese Army bunkers beyond them. (Photo by Mike Buckland)

A SOG recon man's gear included a CAR-15, twenty-one magazines, handgun and an assortment of full-size and "minigrenades." (Photo by the author)

(top above) The High Standard H-D suppressed pistol, SOG's most popular suppressed handgun. (Photo courtesy Jim Phillips)

(above) The "toe popper" mine, a handy counter-tracker device. (National Infantry Museum Photo)

(left) Enemy countermeasures included radio direction finders, as shown here, plus human trackers and bloodhounds. (Photo from the author's collection)

(above) Dug in on this hilltop above Laotian Highway 110 on the Ho Chi Minh Trail, a SOG Hatchet Force blocked enemy road traffic. (Photo by Ted Wicorek)

(left) SOG's top-secret Laotian mountaintop outpost, "Leghorn," as viewed from a passing aircraft. (Photo by Mike Buckland)

(below) Heavily entrenched SOG Company B withstood day and night attacks. Here, a radioman calls air strikes on the enemy, while Rich Ryan observes. (Photo courtesy Rich Ryan)

(above) Enemy forces became so numerous by 1969 that SOG teams preferred small, seemingly unusable landing zones, like this one in Laos. (Photo by John Renegar)

(left) A SOG recon man rides a STABO rig out of Cambodia, 3,000 feet above the jungle. (Photo courtesy Ben Lyons)

(below) SOG skydivers train at Camp Long Thanh for the world's first HALO combat jumps. (U.S. Army Photo courtesy Jim Storter)

Back home in Arkansas, the young Green Beret's enterprising father was transforming his drugstore chain into the world's largest family-owned retail system—Wal-Mart. You'd have to tie wild horses to billionaire Sam Walton's son John, a humble sort, to get him to talk today about his valiant wartime service and the lives he saved that desperate day in the Ashau Valley.

It was that same month of August 1968 that brought the war to SOG's CCN headquarters where a misperception had reigned that danger lurked in faraway areas but not among Danang's sprawling bases. At 3 A.M. on 23 August, more than one hundred NVA sappers penetrated the CCN compound, tossing satchel charges and blasting away with AKs. For the next three hours, Green Berets and SEALs from the nearby SOG Naval Advisory Detachment compound combated the NVA raiders. By dawn it was over and the terrible toll was visible: Fifteen Special Forces officers and NCOs died that night, the greatest single-day loss of Green Berets in Vietnam. Sixteen Nungs, Yards and South Vietnamese were dead. Some thirty-eight enemy were killed and nine captured—all wounded. Among the dead NVA was a cook's helper from the mess hall, apparently their inside agent.

When Chief SOG Colonel Cavanaugh flew in that morning to assess the damage he came upon a detail carrying away Master Sergeant Gilbert Secor's body—not a year earlier Secor had walked into his office in Bad Tölz, Germany, to volunteer for another tour in Vietnam. Watching them carry Secor away, killed in his sleep by a satchel charge, Cavanaugh thought, "What a senseless way to die."

To this day there's an unresolved debate about that sapper attack, whether it was targeted to disrupt SOG cross-border activities, or whether the NVA saw CCN as just another U.S. compound worth raiding. Because the raid hit just as the bombing halt enabled the NVA to shift troops and equipment from North Vietnam into Laos to expand the Trail, many are convinced that the Danang attack was a deliberate strategic attempt to cripple SOG at a critical time.

Despite the Danang sapper attack, teams continued penetrating Laos, and that fall of 1968 there was no recon man luckier than Sergeant Lynne Black, Jr., a recon One-One. On 5 October his team landed in central Laos, and almost right away they were hit by numerous NVA, with their One-Zero, Staff Sergeant James Stride, killed in the first burst.

In danger of being overrun and unable to drag Stride's body, the team split, with the enemy in pursuit.

All day Black and two Yards played hide-and-seek with the enemy, twice fighting their way through their pursuers. "They literally ran right through the NVA," said recon man John Meyer. "It happened so fast, the NVA didn't realize what was happening."

Finally a USAF Jolly Green helicopter from Thailand hovered overhead and lowered a three-seated jungle penetrator. Black helped the two Yards climb in, then their missing One-Two arrived, so he put him in the third seat; Black would wait on the ground while they were winched aboard.

Masked by the noisy aircraft, two NVA crept up and lunged at the young Green Beret, AKs almost pressed to his belly. With that sweet sound of freedom swirling only 100 feet overhead and its umbilical cord on its way back down, Black grabbed one AK barrel and held it down while his other hand seized the second soldier's AK, jerked it away and crashed the butt over the NVA's astonished head. As quickly, Black twisted the first AK free, smashed it wickedly into the NVA's face, leaped on the hoist and rode upward while USAF door gunners ripped the countryside with miniguns.

As the Jolly Green lifted away, Black felt the heavy bird bounce from an RPG rocket impacting its armored belly, but the pilot squeezed over the next ridge and made a controlled crash in an open field. Another Jolly Green retrieved them all, and at last they were away, alive and free.

Stride's body was never recovered.

Bill Copley was not as lucky as Lynne Black. A few weeks after Black's escape, a recon team in southern Laos was hit by a party of NVA led by trackers. In the exchange of fire, Copley was badly wounded and cried out, "Help me, I'm hit!" A teammate carried Copley on his back as far as he could, then he fell. He tried to administer first aid but to no avail. Copley's face showed signs of approaching death. Rapidly closing NVA forced the teammate away. A Bright Light team later found only blood where Copley had lain.

By the end of the year, singing "Hey, Blue" had become nearly a weekly event and almost every building at CCN in Danang had been named for dead and missing men such as Bill Copley.

In 1968—excluding the August Sapper attack and Khe Sanh casualties from incoming fire—CCN lost 18 Americans KIA and 18 MIA, the equivalent of fifteen recon teams. CCN had fewer than fifteen active recon teams. Combined with the 199 SOG Americans wounded in Laos that year, that meant that every single SOG recon man was wounded at least once in 1968 and about half died. The terrible truth became clear: *SOG recon casualties exceeded 100 percent, the highest sustained American loss rate since the Civil War.*

11

A PALE BLUE RIBBON

Each SOG Forward Operating Base (FOB)—Danang, Phu Bai, Kontum and Ban Me Thuot—was assigned about a dozen U.S.-led recon teams. Only about six teams were combat-ready at any given time because casualties had depleted the other six teams. Therefore, half the teams constantly were recovering and retraining while the other half performed hazardous missions until casualties made them combat incapable.

By early 1968, Kontum-based RT Maine was approaching the end of that six-month active mission cycle, and to One-Zero Fred Zabitosky, readying for his final recon mission, it seemed he'd cheated the grim reaper. This wasn't because "Zab" hadn't given the NVA plenty of opportunities to end his twenty-six years of life. As older, more experienced teams fell by the wayside, Zab had shown tactical skill that made him worthy of tougher missions; RT Maine's assignments had grown incrementally more hazardous. His assistant team leader, Staff Sergeant Doug Glover, didn't just sense the growing danger, his body bore testament to it: He had been seriously wounded on each of their last two missions. While Glover mended, Zabitosky had led two perilous Bright Lights, recovering a One-Zero's body after the NVA captured, tortured and burned him to death in Laos, then searching for Charlie White, who'd fallen off a McGuire rig in Cambodia.

Now, ominously, Zab's final target was "The Bra," the river curve where Highway 110 split eastward from the Ho Chi Minh Trail's major north-south route, Highway 96. Across The Bra flowed all NVA troops, supplies and weapons for South Vietnam's Central Highlands and Cambodia's northern half. Hidden in The Bra was the NVA's Binh Tram 37, a major base with stockpiles defended by masses of antiaircraft guns, security battalions and counter-recon units. Encompassing targets Juliet, Hotel, India and November Nine, The Bra was the hottest area in southern Laos.

"When that target list came out every month," recalled One-Zero Lowell Stevens, "you were secretive, you were silent, you didn't want to make it too well known, but you hoped and prayed that you didn't get it." Another team leader, Lloyd O'Daniels warned, "You'd better have a full magazine with you when you went in, buddy, because you were going to need it very damned shortly."

Two weeks into the 1968 Tet Offensive, with Hue still occupied and Khe Sanh under seige, RT Maine was slated to go into Juliet Nine to learn whether the NVA were pulling back, reinforcing or resupplying their offensive in the Central Highlands. Because Zabitosky's freshly healed assistant, Doug Glover, would replace him after the mission, they reversed roles—Glover would be acting One-Zero and Zab the One-One—while Maine's newest man, Staff Sergeant Purcell Bragg, was One-Two.

The night before insert, the normally happy-go-lucky Glover went to Zab and announced he would die the next day. Zabitosky tried to make light of it, but the premonition deeply concerned him; a One-Zero needed confidence, especially in The Bra.

No recon man went into The Bra without some sense of dread, yet things didn't seem that bad the next morning when RT Maine's two Hueys came in low-level and landed with not one round of ground fire. Acting as One-Zero, Glover led them off the LZ and instinctively went for the thickest cover—he didn't realize it, but he was taking them into a box canyon whose steep walls wouldn't be apparent for a half hour.

They'd hardly entered the 300-yard-wide canyon when they made out a line of bunkers arrayed before them. When Zabitosky looked closer to assess the bunkers' age, an NVA platoon rushed in to man them—then gunfire ripped the air and RT Maine executed an IA (Immediate Action Drill) against enemy soldiers only 25 yards away, then fell back.

"Take over the team!" Glover shouted to Zabitosky; he did, just as One-Two Bragg reported Covey had radioed that two other teams were in contact and RT Maine was on its own for at least forty-five minutes. Zab told Glover to lead the team back to the LZ and set up a perimeter while he bought time. No one had been wounded.

Zabitosky watched them trot away, then hastily emplaced a claymore; SOG intelligence later determined the box canyon he was attempting to block by himself contained a regimental command post, possibly the headquarters of Binh Tram 37 itself.

Momentarily an NVA platoon arrived; Zab scattered them by blowing the claymore and tossing several grenades, then fired his CAR-15 on semi-auto to conserve ammo. The NVA kept trying to assault him, but he held them at bay by chucking a grenade and repositioning when it detonated. Moving laterally to the advancing enemy, Zab created the illusion that several men were facing them, so they couldn't quite outflank him. Outfoxing the enemy, Zab fired fifteen magazines and kept them bottled up for thirty minutes, until he heard A-1s overhead. Using his emergency radio, he called in the A-1s, which dumped their ordnance, including one 750-pound bomb that fell so close the concussion lifted him off the ground and knocked the wind out of him.

Then in one fast dash, Zab ran all the way to the LZ, where he found Doug Glover calling in more A-1s while still more fighters arrived. One bomb touched off sixty-four secondary explosions back in the box canyon—and RT Maine hadn't taken a single casualty.

But while Zab was in the canyon, other NVA had hauled in 12.7mm heavy machine guns whose tracers now arced high above the LZ. Then Covey radioed a warning: He'd spotted four companies converging on the LZ and one company was almost there.

Zabitosky hastily arrayed his men just as that company launched a wild assault with a hundred screaming NVA. Like a World War II Japanese banzai charge, the enemy stampeded right across the open space, through mass CAR-15 fire, and almost made it. No sooner did Zab's men stop one charge than another company arrived and it, too, assaulted, running a gauntlet of napalm and cannon fire. Only desperate close-range rifle and pistol fire halted them. Bodies were visibly stacking up.

RT Maine could not keep this up much longer—all that stopped the next charge was a napalm strike right across the enemy's long axis. Then Covey radioed, "Zab, you got *all* your guys there?" He looked around. "Affirmative. Why?" Covey rolled in with a marking rocket. "Then we've got another unit double-timing in from your west, about 400 meters away."

It was too dangerous to send helicopters into an LZ covered by heavy machine guns and drawing more enemy by the minute. While A-1s and gunships hit the LZ—and with Hueys just minutes away—Covey had RT Maine run 150 yards southeast along a streambed and through a woodline to a safer landing zone.

They reached the open field without contact, and no NVA had followed them. Exploiting the lull, Covey sent in the first of two Hueys to extract RT Maine—everyone held his breath. Purcell Bragg and two Yards dashed aboard the aircraft, and it lifted up, climbed over the trees and out, slick and safe!

That left Zab, Glover and four Yards for the second bird, but before it arrived a hundred NVA rose up from three sides of the new LZ and rushed them. While Glover directed A-1s, Zab and the four Yards fought fiercely and barely stopped the first wave; then came a second, and a third. By the fourth they were down to two magazines apiece and Glover was shooting like mad, too. One NVA got within arm's length before Zab dropped him.

The NVA paused to re-form, and it was now or never. Under the heavy fire of gunships and A-1s, the second Huey came in between the team and the enemy, just as the NVA rose up again—it was a race for the Huey. The door gunners and SOG men mowed down a long line of NVA. Zabitosky ran around the bird to shoot several that almost made it to the aircraft and jumped aboard, shooting one last NVA who was so close the man's blood splattered him.

Everyone fired wildly as the Huey dipped its nose and the main rotor pulled them up and away. The thought flashed in Zab's mind that Glover's premonition was wrong—he'd give him hell tonight in the club! They were 75 feet up and almost clear of the LZ when an RPG blast rocked the Huey, spinning the tail boom into the main rotor with a horrible shriek.

With one glance, Covey understood the catastrophe—the Huey, split in two, burned furiously. Not one emergency radio beacon came up; no passengers or crew climbed from the inferno. SOG policy required that downed aircraft be bombed to prevent the enemy from recovering codes, maps or radios. No one moved down there but NVA. The FAC began briefing a pair of F-4 Phantoms.

Aboard one helicopter high overhead, Special Forces medic Luke Nance, Jr., watched the blazing Huey and thought about his friend Fred Zabitosky and what a shame it was that he'd died.

"It's hot—the sun's so hot . . . hot." Fred Zabitosky forced himself to consciousness to find his clothes afire and the burning Huey 20 feet away. Zab could barely breathe; in addition to severe burns and shrapnel wounds he'd suffered several crushed vertebrae and broken ribs. He rolled clumsily on the ground to extinguish his clothes, then found his CAR-15, but the barrel had bent almost double.

The Huey had snapped in two just behind the pilots' section; they were still strapped in their seats, trapped in the flames. Lying on its side, the troop compartment was a white-hot blast furnace from which Zab heard the final cries of Doug Glover, four Yards and the two door gunners, Sergeants Melvin Dye and Robert Griffith. He couldn't have helped those poor bastards—it was an effort just to get to his knees. His crushed back and burns hurt so much he could hardly think. He forced himself to crawl toward the jungle, at least to deny the NVA his body after he died. He looked back one final time and realized the flames hadn't yet engulfed the pilots.

He would never understand how he found the strength, but Zabitosky stumbled to his feet, staggered forward and tore at the scorched door handle until it gave, then grabbed the semiconscious copilot, fell over with him and pulled him to safety. Everything was burned off the man except his leather gun belt.

The pilot still was inside, and the fire seemed too bad to go through, but Zab climbed right into the flames. He could feel his flesh burning as he undid the pilot's harness. Then the fuel cells exploded and an orange fireball swept over them, blowing both Fred and the pilot clear.

Three thousand feet overhead, Luke Nance looked down—looked again—then shouted to his aircraft commander, "Dang it, I saw somebody moving down there! Go down there, now. I'll git 'im!"

For all the chopper pilot knew, it was just NVA searching the wreckage. "We'd better get out of here," he announced.

"No," Nance insisted, "we ain't gonna get outa here, we're goin' down there to get that fella." Nance's Huey pilot took another look and confirmed, there *were* people by the aircraft. It was worth a try.

Despite 12.7mm tracers arcing above the LZ and AKs chattering from the woodlines, the Huey pilot took his bird in, door gunners straining against their tethers and spraying everywhere with M-60s. As the Huey came over the last trees, Luke Nance fired his CAR-15, then he spotted Fred Zabitosky, saw him stand and fall, stand and fall, dragging one pilot, then the other toward the sound of the Huey's whopping rotor. Ignoring the enemy, Nance leaped out and ran to Zab's side. Zab's face was so black and burned that Nance hardly recognized him. Together they carried and dragged the two aviators into the Huey, then it lifted away.

Escorting gunships and A-1s practically touched the trees, they pressed so low to fire cannons and machine guns to help get the rescue helicopter out; then the Huey pilot poured on speed to get the badly wounded men to Vietnam. All the way to the field hospital at Pleiku, Nance worked to keep them alive.

The following morning, after blanketing the LZ with tear gas, Sergeant First Class Clarence "Pappy" Webb took in a Bright Light platoon but found the burned-out Huey a molten mass. The Bright Light platoon and a FAC counted 109 enemy bodies on the first LZ and 68 on the second. RT Maine's fight had been incredible.

General Westmoreland visited the hospital to pin a Purple Heart to Zabitosky's pillow and tell him he was being submitted for the Medal of Honor; Westmoreland was almost apologetic when he told Zab his mission location and classification made it unlikely, though, that Zab would ever wear that pale blue ribbon around his neck.

Zabitosky and the two aviators were evacuated to Japan. One pilot thanked the Green Beret just before succumbing to the burns that covered 85 percent of his body. The other Huey pilot, Richard Griffith, and Zab survived.

Thankfully, Westmoreland was wrong. One year later Fred Zabitosky held his mended spine straight while President Richard Nixon fastened the Medal of Honor around his neck. The RT Maine

One-Zero could think only of his teammates. "I was presented and I wear the Medal," he said later, "but it was earned by Doug Glover and my other Special Forces team members."

It was four months after Fred Zabitosky's Medal of Honor mission that another recon One-Zero, again from Kontum FOB 2, demonstrated equally incredible valor. This time it was a twenty-three-year-old New Yorker, Specialist Five John Kedenburg, operating near Highway 110, about a dozen miles east of The Bra.

Kedenburg's team had been in a small firefight, then the enemy rushed in a battalion—five hundred NVA—to scour the jungle for them. No stranger to tough situations, Kedenburg had been present six months earlier when his first recon team leader, Sergeant First Class Dan Wagner, was killed; he managed to get Wagner's body out and inherited RT Nevada, becoming the new One-Zero.

Recon man Rich Ryan, who'd served earlier with Kedenburg, thought him smart and intense, not the kind to get drunk and do goofy things in the club. He was devoted to his team.

At one point the NVA battalion pinned and encircled RT Nevada, but the SOG team shot its way through and began running cross-country, hundreds of NVA hot on their heels. Any time RT Nevada paused, the enemy caught up and a fierce fight ensued; finally Kedenburg sent his men on and stayed behind, conducting "a gallant rear-guard fight against the pursuing enemy."

Rejoining his men, Kedenburg learned one Yard was missing, but he couldn't risk the whole team for a man who might be dead. He radioed for a string extraction and through a combination of fighting and evading finally got RT Nevada to a hole in the jungle canopy. They seemed to have shaken off their pursuers.

While a Huey came in, dropped ropes, and lifted away four men, Kedenburg called air strikes against their back trail. A second bird dropped ropes, and Kedenburg and the three remaining Nevada men climbed into the four McGuire rigs just as the NVA broke through supporting fire from gunships and A-1s. Then the team's missing Montagnard arrived, drawn by the sound of the Huey.

All John Kedenburg had to do was give a thumbs-up to the helicopter crew chief and they would have lifted away, safe and alive. Instead, he unsnapped himself, gave his rig to the newly arrived Yard and stood guard while he climbed in. Then the young Green Beret waved off the Huey and turned alone to face a horde of onrushing NVA.

Witnesses aboard the departing helicopter saw Kedenburg shoot six NVA at almost point-blank range before enemy fire struck home and he collapsed, mortally wounded. The last air strike went in right on top of the fallen One-Zero. Kedenburg's self-sacrifice surprised no one who knew him. Rich Ryan called him, "the kind of guy you'd think would do what he did." His was SOG's second posthumous Medal of Honor. A Bright Light team recovered John Kedenburg's body.

There was yet another man there at Kontum, in recon company, a contemporary and friend of both Zabitosky and Kedenburg, who would become a legend throughout SOG and the secret world of special operations, Sergeant First Class Robert Howard.

Built like a lumberjack, Howard was square-jawed handsome and rock-tough yet quiet and unassuming, with a soul and a conscience.

Growing up in Opelika, Alabama, he'd been inspired by his father and four uncles who'd all been paratroopers in World War II. Of the five, two died in combat, while three others—including his father—suffered terrible wounds to which they eventually succumbed. Poor materially but rich in family, Bob Howard and his sister picked cotton to help support their mother and maternal grandparents. The Opelika High football star was offered a scholarship, but college could wait. He enlisted at age seventeen, eager to wear silver paratrooper wings like his father and uncles.

By 1966 he was a 101st Airborne paratrooper recovering from wounds when some Green Beret wardmates befriended him. He left the hospital bound for the 5th Special Forces Group.

When he arrived at Kontum FOB 2 in early 1967, casualties had depleted recon ranks but the supply room was in equal crisis—nobody knew how to requisition supplies except the new guy, Howard, who'd once been a supply sergeant. First Sergeant Billy Greenwood tried to keep him in supply, but that didn't last: "You just couldn't keep him out of the war," Greenwood said. So Howard ran missions like anyone else, but instead of blowing off steam during stand-down, he wrote requisitions to keep supplies flowing.

Unique in U.S. military annals, Robert Howard was submitted for the Medal of Honor three times in thirteen months, and many thought he should have received all three. He remains to this day the most highly decorated American soldier, his uniform displaying the Medal of Honor, Distinguished Service Cross, Silver Star and numerous lesser awards, plus eight Purple Hearts. This is the man who one night ran alongside an enemy truck on Highway 110, holding a claymore detonator in his hand, then tossed the mine into a truck full of startled NVA and detonated it. On another occasion, he saw a VC terrorist riding the back of a motorbike toss a grenade at a GI chow line. Howard took off at a dead run, snatched an M-16 away from an amazed security guard, dropped to one knee, carefully aimed and shot the driver dead, then chased the passenger a half mile and shot him dead, too.

What's all the more impressive is that Howard thought both incidents unremarkable and received no award for either.

His first Medal of Honor submission came in November 1967, when One-Zero Johnnie Gilreath's team found a huge rice and ammunition stockpile in southeast Laos. While Gilreath kept it under surveillance, SOG assembled a Hatchet Force company to land and destroy the cache. Howard volunteered to take in a recon team to guide the company from the LZ to Gilreath's team, then scout for approaching NVA.

The element of surprise didn't last; three helicopters were badly damaged by ground fire during insert, yet Howard was able to avoid NVA ambushes and bring the Hatchet Force safely to Gilreath's team. While the Hatchet Force destroyed the cache, Howard took out a security patrol and soon encountered four NVA, all of whom he dispatched with a single magazine. But then his team became pinned down by a camouflaged machine-gun bunker.

Howard crawled toward the gun, killed an NVA sniper who tried to stop him, then rushed the machine-gun nest and killed all its occupants at point-blank range with his M-16. No sooner did he climb from the bunker than a second machine-gun position unleashed a barrage. He pulled back and called in air on it, then crawled forward to assess damage: The bombs had missed! "Pinned down directly outside the strongpoint with a blazing machine-gun barrel only six inches above his head," his award citation later said, "he threw a hand grenade into the aperture of the emplacement, killing the gunners and temporarily silencing the weapon." When more NVA took over the gun, Howard seized a LAW rocket launcher and "stood amid a hail of bullets, fired his weapon and completely demolished the position." Howard's one-man attack so demoralized the NVA that they abandoned the hill, leaving the Hatchet Force free to destroy tons of ammunition and rice.

After the operation, Chief SOG Singlaub had Howard and Gilreath flown to Saigon to brief a clearly impressed General Westmoreland. When they'd finished, Westmoreland asked if there was anything he could do for them. Gilreath said, "Sir, I'd like to go to flight school and become an aviator." The four-star U.S. commander gave Gilreath a commission on the spot, and he soon left for flight school. Howard said he only wanted back into action, and he got his wish, too, along with a Distinguished Service Cross, though he'd been recommended for the Medal of Honor.*

The Bra, that dangerous target area where Fred Zabitosky earned his Medal of Honor, figured prominently in several of Howard's most valorous deeds. One mission into The Bra began when One-Zero Joe Walker's RT California attempted to ambush a counter-recon unit along Highway 96. At the most critical second, the One-One's CAR-15 malfunctioned and instead of triggering the ambush, he compromised it. Aided by RPD machine guns and men with boards strapped to their chests, with hand grenades wired so they could pull and toss them two at a time, the NVA wounded most of Walker's men, then withdrew.

RT California spent the night hiding. In the morning a forty-man Hatchet Force platoon landed on the same LZ and while California's wounded were medevaced. Joe Walker and three RT California Yards stayed on the ground to assist the platoon, led by First Lieutenant Daniel Swain and Sergeant First Class Ratchford "Ranger" Haynes. The platoon was directed to advance along Highway 96, deeper into The Bra, and find targets for air or ground attack.

The Bra didn't seem to live up to its reputation: For two days the reinforced platoon marched northward, encountering not even a lone NVA sniper. But Walker found the inaction ominous; the longer before they made contact, he feared, the worse it would be when it came—and he had no doubt the NVA would arrive.

*A career aviator, Gilreath retired as a full colonel.

The second night they set up a perimeter and dug in between Highway 96 and a wide river, which seemed a strong position, because the NVA couldn't attack from the river side. But if the enemy mounted a mass attack from the road the platoon would be pinned against the river with no place to go.

Walker and his three Yards didn't dig in, just took shelter in a cluster of bamboo. At 3:10 A.M., Walker woke up, checked his watch and rolled over and heard truck engines. One truck stopped 200 yards away, then came a second, and a third, a fourth, a fifth—then he lost count amid the sound of dropping tailgates. A Vietnamese voice echoed through a megaphone as a large NVA force obviously formed for a quick assault.

In nearby foxholes, M-60 gunners hurriedly opened spare ammo cans while others stacked hand grenades. Walker cursed himself for not digging in and scraped what dirt he could just as enemy flashlight beams pierced the darkness.

Then every M-60 machine gun on the perimeter opened fire with such fury that Walker heard nothing above the roar. Instantly the North Vietnamese returned fire, and bullets skipped across the ground, grazing the earth, glancing off Walker's back and legs. Then mortar shells burst in the trees above them, raining down steel that killed men despite their foxholes.

Walker saw running NVA soldiers silhouetted by the flash of a blazing M-60 machine gun 15 yards away; one side of the perimeter collapsed, and NVA were everywhere. Lieutenant Swain and Ranger Haynes crawled over to Walker—then a mortar shell burst beside them, badly slashing the lieutenant's legs. Despite a gunshot wound and multiple shrapnel hits, Walker crawled away, dragging Swain. One African-American NCO made the mistake of standing up; he shook and cried out as two dozen slugs hit him, then he collapsed and slid downhill. Walker checked him but the NCO's twitching legs signaled he was near death; Walker couldn't do anything for him.

Walker kept crawling with Swain, then they rolled down the bank and into the river. With Swain holding onto his neck, Walker stumbled through the deep, cold water, carrying along an M-60 machine gun and a radio. Midstream they crossed a sandbar, then somehow made it to the other side, where several wounded Yards had sought refuge, too.

Looking back across the water, Walker could see flashlight beams, then an occasional muzzle flash as the NVA finished off the wounded.

One NVA soldier shone a flashlight in the badly wounded NCO's face and shot him again, in the head. Walker swung between rage and fear but could do nothing; he didn't have a single round for his machine gun. Then his heart stopped: In the moonlight he could see their tracks on the sandbar! Wading into the dangerous stream, he smoothed the sand and slipped back to find the lieutenant delirious, moaning. Walker had no medical supplies; all he could do was wrap Swain in a poncho and hope for the best. He finally got the radio working, raised a passing night FAC but had no means to signal in the dark. "Just shoot anywhere and you'll probably hit somebody," he whispered weakly. "I don't give a damn if you hit me or not, really." Then he passed out.

Back at Kontum, Captain Ronald Goulet got Bob Howard out of bed. "We gotta go get Walker and Swain," he announced, knowing Howard would volunteer. Sergeant First Class Lloyd "OD" O'Daniels raised his hand, too, as did several other NCOs. There were too many NVA to fight their way in, so Goulet's twelve-man Bright Light team had to land and then stealthily search the area.

Although the Bright Light team had Walker's coordinates and they moved continuously, they didn't reach the river until it was 11 P.M. and absolutely dark. Captain Goulet and one Yard spent two hours scouting for a place to ford the swift stream but failed. Yet if Walker got across, Howard reasoned, then they could, too; instead of finding a ford he took two Yards and waded into the current, bouncing off the bottom to keep his head up and holding a Yard with each hand. He finally got good footing and crawled up the washed-away bank, pulling the Yards after him.

An awful odor permeated the area, and one Yard, who had the night vision of a cat, said he could see something: It was bloated bodies. Howard went corpse to corpse, feeling the legs of each to determine if it was the lanky Joe Walker. One still figure had long legs, but to be certain Howard reached for the face where, sure enough, hung eyeglasses, with one lens blown out—then the lips moved, whispering, "You sweet motherfucker." It was Walker, playing possum. Howard almost kissed him.

Walker had multiple wounds but he insisted that Howard help Lieutenant Swain, whose pulse, he found, was strong. Just before dawn, the rest of the Bright Light team joined them; with daylight and fighters overhead and Lloyd O'Daniels on point, they recrossed the river to the overrun platoon's position. At the bank, O'Daniels passed the body of the African-American NCO, rolled in a fetal position, numerous AK wounds in his torso, arms and legs, his skull creased by a coup de grace. O'Daniels heard a gasp and looked closer and saw the man blink. He shouted, "This guy's alive!" and got a medic on him.

Everyone else was dead. While air strikes and the Bright Light team kept the enemy at bay, a chopper landed on the sandbar and lifted out Lieutenant Swain, Walker, the black NCO and several wounded Yards. All recovered. Captain Goulet's Bright Light proved a great success, snatching back lives from an area infested by NVA without taking a single casualty himself.*

Joe Walker, who'd risked his life to save Lieutenant Swain, was submitted for a Silver Star only to see it downgraded to an Army Commendation Medal, which so disgusted him that he didn't want the award.

Bob Howard did not receive any decoration.

In mid-November 1968, Howard volunteered to go back into The Bra with a Hatchet Force company, its mission to raise hell and draw NVA away from a besieged CIA/CAS force deeper in Laos. Led by a captain, the Americans included First Lieutenant James Jerson, and among the NCOs, Lloyd O'Daniels as First Platoon sergeant.

They took no fire landing, and for four days the enemy fled before them. Hour after hour they advanced among bleak, denuded trees and bomb craters, where B-52s and defoliation had laid bare the once invisible single-lane Highway 96. The enemy kept pulling back, just as they'd done before Lieutenant Swain's platoon.

Then the night of 16 November, one hundred NVA hit the SOG company but didn't penetrate the perimeter. Like ghosts, the NVA were gone by sunrise when the Hatchet Force continued along the road, unopposed but for an occasional sniper. It felt spooky.

---

*Captain Ronald Goulet was killed a few months later while leading a Hatchet Force company.

On 18 November they encountered a short but violent ambush, then again, the NVA fell back. The Green Beret NCOs saw it correctly as a delaying tactic so the enemy could prepare for them ahead; they agreed privately that tomorrow would be "the day."

The next morning, 19 November, Howard found a daring young lieutenant walking point instead of an experienced Yard. When he tried to replace him, the lieutenant complained to the captain; by then Howard was so concerned that he'd gone ahead, alone, and discovered a telephone landline. Following it into the bushes, he found a just-abandoned observation post with a field telephone and a tin bowl of still-warm soup. The attack would be bloody soon, he knew.

He slipped back to warn the lieutenant, who only wanted to argue about walking point. "Haven't you noticed how quiet it is?" Howard interjected, and, indeed, the young officer realized there was not a buzzing insect nor a bird to be heard. Howard warned him to move cautiously and went back to alert the captain, but the company commander chewed him out for going ahead on his own. Like the other NCOs, by now Howard thought it almost a waste of time even talking to this captain.

Meanwhile, the young lieutenant was still on point and wanted to lead the company across an open field—so many Yards warned him against it that he radioed the captain for guidance. The Hatchet Force commander radioed back, "Screw the Yards."

Howard rushed back to the point, where he found the lead platoon halted in the open and the lieutenant ready to cross the field. Howard could see NVA moving in the opposite woodline. "Can't you see them, Lieutenant? There's people in that far woodline." The officer shook his head.

"OK, I'm going to kill two of them, then you'll see them," Howard announced, raising his M-16. His first shot knocked down an enemy soldier—then all hell broke loose with a barrage of RPG and mortar rounds falling all over the lead platoon. One rocket impacted almost atop the lieutenant, blowing off his right foot and most of his left leg. Howard applied tourniquets and injected him with morphine, then another RPG hit and tore into Howard's back and legs, hurting him so badly it took his breath away.

OD couldn't believe what happened next: "Now the bullets are coming fast, and Howard stood up and shouted, '*Come and get me, you sons of bitches!*'" The deadliest fire was pouring from a PT-76 tank's turret-mounted 12.7mm machine gun; Howard crawled forward with a LAW (light antitank weapon), got close enough to see the tank's boat-shaped prow about 150 yards away, then crept sideways to get a flanking shot. A young lieutenant grabbed the LAW, stood beside a tree despite Howard's warning, and while he fumbled with the safety, the NVA fired an RPG that badly wounded the officer and destroyed the LAW.

Howard returned to the Hatchet Force, got two more LAWs and two Yards with M-79s for fire support. His first LAW hit the tank dead center, but the machine gun kept firing, so he fired again just below the machine gun and silenced it.

By the time he dragged back the second seriously wounded lieutenant, he and OD realized the company had to pull back into thicker cover and organize a perimeter. While the captain kept himself safely in the rear, O'Daniels got the unit repositioned and arrayed in a circular defense.

When the captain finally showed up, all he did was demand ammo status and the casualty count. Howard thought, "Is this guy serious?" Locked in battle, at that moment they needed close air support and tactical orders, not stock taking. The captain should already have known only two squads had been engaged and every man in one was wounded.

By now a medevac Huey arrived and was trying to put down inside their perimeter when a door gunner took a hit in the kneecap and let out such a scream the men heard it on the ground. Then more fire poured into the bird and it slipped sideways, then slammed down 300 yards away, in flames before the skids touched, right in the woodline where the initial NVA RPG attack had been launched. Howard saw one man jump from the chopper and collapse.

Although already wounded twice, Howard dashed 300 yards, all alone, through enemy bullets that ricocheted all around him, and reached that burning Huey. One door gunner was dead, and the aircraft commander, a feisty lieutenant, already was helping his warrant officer copilot, who'd been shot in the shoulder. Howard scooped up the other door gunner, a young specialist four with a broken back. The only weapon the crewmen had was the pilot's .38 revolver, but he assured

Howard he was motivated and ready to kill any bastard that tried to stop them. Howard told the gutsy lieutenant to follow him and stay close to the ground.

Meanwhile, Lloyd O'Daniels had pinpointed the gun that had brought down the Huey and now threatened other birds. Taking a LAW, he crawled off a ways, took careful aim and fired, silencing the gun.

With Howard in the lead, the little party ran a few yards, fell, ran a few yards and fell again, not as a tactic but because wounds and exhaustion were overcoming them. Finally, with covering fire from the SOG Yards and the Huey commander emptying his revolver, they dashed the last few yards and collapsed inside the perimeter. Howard shook his head at the pilot's guts. "You couldn't kill a grasshopper with that thirty-eight," he said. "There's plenty of dead people around, go get you a good weapon."

Three hours later, under the protective fire of gunships, another Huey lifted casualties out safely, including the lieutenant who had lost a leg, but Howard refused medevac because the fight was not over yet and, to Howard's great pleasure, the grounded Huey pilot also refused medevac. He became an acting platoon leader.

But to the disgust of all the Green Berets, the captain tried to get himself medevaced with a minor flesh wound; their disdain seemed to embarrass him, and he changed his mind. After dark, the captain called Howard over to complain about his wound, but Howard offered little sympathy; many men were more seriously wounded.

At daybreak the NVA unleashed dozens of RPGs. One rocket impacted near Howard, slicing his back and legs in fourteen places; fragments like razor blades embedded in his flesh and cut him each time he moved. It hurt so much that, like an infuriated lion, incredibly, Howard ran completely out of the perimeter, charged the enemy right through the open and surprised three NVA in an observation post. Howard shot two, then tackled the third as though he were playing football at old Opelika High School.

From the perimeter, OD hollered, "Got you covered, Bob! Come on back!" Howard crawled beneath that covering fire to deliver a healthy NVA to the captain and announce, "Captain, you want to find out what you're up against? Get an interpreter over here." The captain only looked at Howard, perforated fifty times in three days, bleeding from his arms, legs, back and face, and said nothing.

An old Yard squatted down to help Howard bind his wounds, cutting up a plastic ground cloth and taping it around his legs and waist. Howard was too disgusted to feel pain: "I'd turned over a highly prized piece of intelligence to an officer-in-charge who didn't even know how to interrogate the guy to find out what kind of activity we had around us, to try to save his company."

Finally an ARVN officer talked to the prisoner. Howard asked the old Yard what they were saying. The Yard shook his head and warned, "We must go quick." A battalion already was around them, and a whole regiment was massing 3 miles away, vowing to kill many Americans, shoot down helicopters and earn much glory.

His wounds now dressed, Howard checked the prisoner and found the NVA's hands so tightly bound they were swollen and his body contorted by plastic handcuffs around his knees and ankles; it was humiliating, an insult to him as a soldier. Howard ignored the captain's protests and untied the NVA's legs, let him get comfortably on his side, then retied his hands with wider line. He gave the NVA water and assured him he would not be harmed.

They could count on being extracted the next morning—if they lasted through the night. OD and Howard redistributed ammo from dead men's gear and stacked bodies like sandbags to protect themselves from enemy fire. They were down to a single one hundred-round belt per machine gun, less than one grenade per man and perhaps two magazines per M-16. In case the company was overrun, they organized the Yards into six-man teams to evade in the dark.

That night they held, but barely, largely because O'Daniels and the pilot lieutenant shifted men to the most endangered flank, where, like a rock, Howard held off every enemy attack. At daybreak the NVA unleashed a heavy barrage of mortars and RPGs, but before their infantry assaulted, air strikes hit them hard, pushing the NVA back. Then the first lift of choppers came in to extract the Hatchet Force, beginning with their wounded. With no warning, the captain climbed aboard the first bird, leaving Howard, the pilot lieutenant and the other NCOs to run the company.

But they had greater problems than a runaway commander—a 37mm antiaircraft gun only 600 yards away threatened to prevent any other choppers from landing. Howard took the last two M-79 grenadiers and all the remaining 40mm ammo, crept to within 100 yards of the gun and pumped a dozen rounds into it, killing the entire crew.

Ground fire downed one Huey and damaged eight others, but they got out, leaving behind not even a single body.

For the second time in twelve months, Howard was submitted for the Medal of Honor; the captain put himself in for a Distinguished Service Cross. Howard's award was downgraded to a Silver Star, but, sickeningly, the Army gave the captain his DSC. Several men tried to get Schultz court-martialed for cowardice, but since the operation was cross-border, top secret and deniable, the investigation fizzled. The captain's rationale was that he had been wounded and tried to do his best in a dangerous setting.

Everyone knew the injustice dealt Bob Howard, but he didn't let it bother him: He fought for comrades and country, not for medals.

Howard's newest wounds hadn't even healed when three weeks later he volunteered for a prisoner snatch operation, again into The Bra, this time accompanying One-Zero Larry White, his One-One, Sergeant Robert "Buckwheat" Clough, an ARVN officer and six Yards.

Enemy fire prevented them from landing on the primary LZ; more fire greeted them at the secondary LZ; they flew another mile to a backup LZ, and as the Huey flared out, bullets slammed into it from three directions. The hovering bird shook once and dropped 3 feet to the ground. White was hit and fell out, the door gunner slumped, wounded, over his M-60, the ARVN officer was killed. Almost everyone was hit except Howard and Clough.

A hundred NVA climbed from bunkers and trenches to rush the Huey, and it was a shoot-out right there at the helicopter, beneath the still-spinning rotor. "It was unbelievable," said White.

Equally unbelievable, though, was what they saw under the jungle canopy 100 yards away: Two Soviet-made Mi-4 helicopters beneath camouflage nets. There'd been claims of enemy choppers roaming Laos at night, but Saigon guffawed as if they were UFO reports. This all-out assault was intended to kill the American team quickly, before they could get off a radio message.

Some NVA got within 15 yards of the Huey. Despite throbbing pain, White fired his CAR-15 and tried to get back in the Huey. Then he was hit again and pivoted and shot three NVA at close range. Another NVA was practically at the Huey before White shot him, but the falling enemy shot White, who fell to the ground unconscious with his third gunshot wound. Meanwhile Howard and Clough fired aimed shots on semi-auto, knocking down dozens of NVA. Then in spite of a shattered windscreen and an array of flashing warning lights, the wounded pilot poured on the rpm's—Howard and Clough pulled White aboard—and that wrecked mess of a Huey lifted away. Heavy air strikes were called in to destroy the enemy helicopters.

Again, Howard received no award. He insisted that he was just doing his job.

Three weeks later Howard went into Cambodia on a Bright Light mission after a missing Green Beret. A large NVA pursuit force had caught up with a recon team in northeast Cambodia, hitting the team's rear and wounding Private First Class Robert Scherdin. One Yard saw Scherdin fall and tried to help him but then the Yard was shot and realized their team had been pushed away and he was almost surrounded. The Yard fled, rejoined the team and was extracted with them. Covey monitored an emergency radio beacon on the hill where Scherdin had disappeared—he could be lying there wounded, or it could be a trap.

The next morning a forty-man Bright Light platoon, led by Lieutenant Jim Jerson and including Howard and five other NCOs, landed under fire. The NVA fell back, too weak to hold them at the LZ. The platoon soon hit and bypassed a reinforced NVA company, made contact four times, then finally reached the hill where Scherdin's beeper was transmitting.

Howard warned Lieutenant Jerson they'd probably be ambushed, which Jerson expected, too. But they climbed uphill anyway, determined to find Scherdin, alive or dead. They were just behind the point squad when Howard noticed scrapes on the ground and lots of fresh sign. Then came a flash, a roar, and everything went black.

When Howard came to, he couldn't focus his eyes. He heard Vietnamese voices and smelled something burning. Despite his grogginess, he realized a Chinese claymore had exploded, ripping away his rifle and tearing his clothes. He ached all over, and his shredded fingers were bleeding. Then he focused his eyes and saw an NVA 10 feet away, spraying a flamethrower on Yard bodies.

Lost in his chore, the enemy soldier ignored Howard, who spotted Jerson lying facedown, 25 feet uphill. Howard grabbed a grenade and came to his knees as the NVA turned and spotted the Green Beret NCO. They looked long at each other, then Howard pulled the pin and shook the grenade, taunting him, "Go ahead, you bastard, 'cause we're both going."

The NVA turned and walked off. Howard threw the grenade but he aimed it only to chase him away. The adversary already had yielded so Howard decided he could not kill him.

Too badly wounded to stand, Howard dragged himself to Lieutenant Jerson—he was alive. When he grabbed the young officer he almost pulled two fingers off; Howard's hands were too badly torn to use. Finally he wedged Jerson's feet between his elbows and clumsily crawled backward, dragging the unconscious officer behind him.

With NVA passing them en route to the SOG platoon 100 yards downhill, Howard knew they couldn't make it undetected. He had no weapon. He whispered encouragement to Jerson, hid him in thick brush and crept downhill. He'd almost made it when one NVA sprang up and fired a burst that hit an ammo pouch, setting off an M-16 cartridge with such force that Howard was tossed the last few yards down the slope, landing beside an American NCO who was sobbing and firing an M-16.

Howard gasped, "Give me your M-16." Instead the young NCO gave him a .45 pistol and two magazines. Howard was ready to go back but he knew he couldn't make it alone. "Hey, you son of a bitch," Howard said beckoning, "it's not time to pray or cry, it's time to fight or die!" The youthful sergeant composed himself, then nodded. "OK. Let's go."

Together they fought their way back up the hill, with the young sergeant killing four NVA while Howard shot several more—one made it to within 5 feet before Howard's .45 dropped him. Then, holding the pistol in one hand, Howard grabbed Jerson with the other and they headed back down the slope; heavy fire and massed NVA forced them to abandon Jerson once, then they went back for him. Howard thought it was an eternity.

At one point they came upon a badly wounded ARVN lieutenant sitting against a tree who helped them before NVA fire killed him. Finally they got Jerson down the hill. By now Howard had been shot in the leg, he couldn't hear anymore, his hands and head hurt and he was so painfully exhausted he vomited. They'd spent almost six hours on that hill.

But Lieutenant Jerson was back in friendly hands and conscious. While others bound his wounds, Jerson urged Howard to keep the defense going and refused morphine to stay awake. Howard assured him, "Don't worry, sir, we'll get you out of here."

It was sunset as Howard assessed their position. A deep, fast stream was to their backs—they were pinned, but on the other hand the stream reduced their defensive front by half, more manageable for the twenty or so men he had left. He no longer expected to get out alive. All that remained was to fight.

As darkness set in, Howard called together his U.S. and Yard leaders. They had three strobe lights with which to direct cannon fire from Spectre C-130 gunships, he said, and held up his own. "I will be the bastard that this strobe light is on when this place falls and I want you all to know it. It will be right on top. I'll be the dead bastard with the strobe light right here on my chest. But before we give up this ground, I'll call fire right on this strobe." True to his vow, twice that night Howard called the Spectres' fire through his own position; the surrounded Hatchet Force platoon repelled assault after assault.

By 4 A.M., Howard was too exhausted and injured to think; wounded and dead Yards lay all around him. Two of the three strobe lights had been blasted to bits, and they were almost out of ammunition. "If you're going to get us out of here," he radioed Covey, "you'd better come get us now."

To his surprise, that was exactly the plan. SOG had staged a Huey unit to Dak To, and they'd just launched, while high overhead a C-130 began dropping parachute flares. The unusual night extraction caught the NVA off guard, but it was still a rush to get out before the enemy could react.

The first three Hueys carried away wounded and dead Montagnards, but one bird was overloaded and had to toss bodies out like sacks of potatoes; Howard felt terrible—it reminded him that they didn't have PFC Robert Scherdin, either.

Howard was the last man to board a chopper, just after Lieutenant Jerson was carried on; Howard was so drained that he was almost hallucinating. He lay there, silent, holding Jerson and puffing a cigarette a door gunner had given him. One pilot leaned back to give him a reassuring pat, but in his mind Howard kept seeing bodies falling, left behind, bodies of gallant Montagnards that he'd tried so hard to bring out. Almost out of his mind, Howard thought about killing the pilot though he knew that was not right and he didn't have a weapon. Then, mercifully, he passed out.

He awoke briefly in a field hospital to find his hands bandaged, his face covered with ointment, and learned Lieutenant Jim Jerson had died. But nobody could tell Jerson's family or Robert Scherdin's family that good men had not given their all for them.

The recon company commander, Captain Ed Lesesne, wrote Howard up for the Medal of Honor—for the third time. There would be no downgrading, no minimizing his role to make a superior sound braver—just the truth.

By the time Howard at last received the pale blue ribbon, American patriotism had plunged to its nadir, and in the antiwar mood of the times, the media told no one of his indomitable courage. The networks and major newspapers did not report the ceremony. It was as if it did not happen.

In 1955, every schoolkid knew Alvin York's and Audie Murphy's names. In 1970, no one had ever heard of Bob Howard's valiant deeds, though his body bore more scars and his chest more decorations than either of these acclaimed heroes.

Altogether, Howard served five tours in Vietnam, mostly in SOG, never once shrinking from the sound of guns. Whenever someone asks me today why I served three tours in SOG, I tell them, it was for the honor of having served beside such gallant men as Bob Howard.

12

THROUGH
THE LOOKING GLASS

In his historic televised address of 31 March 1968, President Johnson announced he would not seek reelection and ordered a bombing halt above the 20th Parallel in North Vietnam. Applying an expansive policy interpretation, the State Department insisted that SOG aircraft, too, cease flying above the 20th Parallel, in effect abandoning six of SOG's eight long-term agent teams.

SOG leaders argued against abandoning them, warning it would erase any doubts Hanoi harbored about America's covert sponsorship and unmask the Sacred Sword of the Patriot League as "tools of the imperialists." Observed Major Scotty Crerar, "If you're not admitting you're doing it to begin with and getting away with it, why stop it?"

Nonetheless, the cutoff of aerial resupplies and insertions took effect the day after LBJ's speech, April Fool's Day. The irony did not go unnoticed in Saigon, where Chief SOG Colonel Jack Singlaub wondered to what extent the North Vietnamese had been playing SOG's agent handlers for fools.

Unquestionably, Hanoi had captured some teams and was playing them back as doubles, but which ones? Several CIA and SOG handlers had long been suspicious. Singlaub felt an obligation to extract loyal teams, but if he was to confront the State Department, he had to know exactly which agent teams were worth the political fight and physical danger of retrieving them.

Singlaub convened an ad hoc panel of CIA and MACV J-2 experts to conduct a two-month review. The day their assessment began, SOG's map of North Vietnam displayed eight blue pins, representing the current location of eight teams, an impressive network overlooking the North's most important railroad lines, highways and ports. Up in the northwest, near China, were Teams *Remus, Easy, Tourbillon* and *Red Dragon;* in the northeast, almost on the Chinese frontier, was Team *Eagle* and nearby on the coast, Singleton Agent *Ares;* and down in the southern panhandle were Team *Hadley* and *Romeo.*

To better understand enemy control practices, the ad hoc panel studied the case of *Verse,* a captured team the North Vietnamese had played against SOG, then publicly exposed a year earlier.

Team *Verse* had parachuted in to join Team *Tourbillon* on 7 November 1965, in violation of the espionage principle of compartmenting. Of eight *Verse* agents, two were reported killed in the airdrop, which alone was cause for suspicion. Two weeks later, after supposedly teaching *Tourbillon* road-watching techniques, Team *Verse* went its own way. Over the next eighteen months, *Verse* claimed various achievements but actually accomplished very little. SOG ordered *Verse* to walk to a CIA outpost in Laos, but that never quite happened; finally in June 1967, SOG's Thailand-based 21st SOS "Pony" helicopters went into North Vietnam to exfiltrate *Verse,* but a U.S. fighter was shot down near the LZ and contact with the team was lost, supposedly as a result of nearby NVA activity.

Three weeks later, apparently realizing SOG would no longer accept *Verse*'s excuses, Radio Hanoi announced *Verse*'s capture and sucked it for propaganda effect.

Here, then, was a starting point for the review of current teams—following *Verse*'s tracks back to Team *Tourbillon* and exploring the question: When did *Verse* go bad?

Tourbillon itself had parachuted into North Vietnam on 16 May 1962 with eight agents, one killed upon landing.

During *Tourbillon*'s first reinforcement, in November 1962, all four jumpers were reported killed. In May 1964, seven more parachutists reinforced *Tourbillon,* with one killed, then in July *Tourbillon* received another eight jumpers, with two killed. All these men had graduated from SOG's rough-terrain parachuting course and wore heavy U.S. Forest Service smoke-jumper suits, yet they suffered a parachuting fatality rate one hundred times greater than jumpers at SOG's airborne school. So many men could not be dying accidentally; they must have been captured and executed to inspire their teammates to cooperate, it was reasoned.

When *Tourbillon* received four agents on 12 December 1964, two were reported killed in an ambush eight days later. Then *Verse* landed in November 1965, with two dead from parachuting injuries.

During nearly every insert, men were lost.

Twice in 1966 SOG attempted to exfiltrate *Tourbillon* agents, but both attempts were canceled because the team didn't establish radio contact at the landing zones.

On Christmas Eve 1966, *Tourbillon* received yet another two-man reinforcement team, and two weeks later the newest radio operator sent the duress code, a secret signal that he was under enemy control, an incredibly brave and probably suicidal act.

Tourbillon, it was concluded, was under enemy control when *Verse* landed; *Verse* was doomed the moment the team arrived. A review officer reached up to OPS-34's North Vietnam map, removed *Tourbillon*'s blue pin and replaced it with a red one. There were seven remaining blue pins, seven more teams to assess.

After a thorough review, the conclusion was as certain as it was horrifying: All eight agent teams were under North Vietnamese control, even Bill Colby's very first operative, *Ares.*

The panel changed the color of all eight blue pins on SOG's map of North Vietnam to red.

From its inauguration, the long-term agent program had had a troubling history. The aircraft carrying its first parachute-dropped agent, in March 1961, had been hit by antiaircraft fire and forced to land, with all aboard killed or captured. In 1963 the CIA parachuted thirteen teams into North Vietnam only to have all but one team captured by Hanoi's Ministry of Security, snatched up almost upon landing. The next year five teams were apprehended, but miraculously a single team evaded capture. This same peculiar pattern was repeated in 1965 and 1966, with just one new team landing safely each year, while the Ministry of Security seized all other teams almost upon arrival.

Yet oddly, during the same four years, reinforcement airdrops to established teams had exactly the opposite record: Every reinforcing airdrop succeeded. How could SOG be so adept at parachuting reinforcements and so inept at parachuting new teams? Clearly there *was* a pattern here, but what did it mean?

With the hindsight of the CIA/MACV J-2 review, the answer became obvious. Only one new team survived each year because that was a comfortable expansion rate for North Vietnam's double-cross program. The reinforcing agents arrived safely to join their teams because Hanoi already controlled the teams being reinforced.

But the cost was not just these eight teams evaluated in 1968. Since 1961 the CIA and SOG had trained and fielded in North Vietnam fifty-four long-term agent teams—342 men—some were self-serving dregs, but others were great Vietnamese patriots who suffered unspeakable torture and death. No less heroically than if they had thrown themselves on a hand grenade, several had given their lives by sending duress codes.

This breakdown in the long-term agent program was the greatest U.S. wartime counterintelligence failure of the past half century, yet the details went unreported.

How had North Vietnam been so successful? There could be but one compelling answer: The enemy had to have known the teams were coming. To have played the game so effectively and so long, the North Vietnamese had to have moles in Saigon, right in the bowels of SOG.

A major clue had come from an unexpected quarter. While the review panel was debating the status of Team *Remus,* an NVA prisoner captured by an American unit told interrogators a "ranger spy team" had landed near his North Vietnamese village in 1962 only to be captured immediately by Ministry of Security forces. When the prisoner pointed out his village on a map, it was near the *Remus* drop zone. Played since insert! The news rocked SOG headquarters. But how had the North Vietnamese rolled up *Remus* so quickly, in so remote an area?

Then, even more disturbing, only weeks after SOG received the NVA prisoner's disclosure, Radio Hanoi announced the capture of *Remus,* frustrating SOG's plans to play *Remus* back as a triple. The timing was most suspicious. The North Vietnamese had controlled *Remus* for seventy-two months, then mere weeks after SOG at last learned the truth, Hanoi announced the capture of the team. It now seemed certain a mole was at work, probably among the South Vietnamese officers assigned to SOG headquarters.

Agent recruiting, for instance, was entirely a South Vietnamese affair. Operating from clandestine offices in Thailand and Laos—areas rife with Communist intrigues—the South Vietnamese recruiters sought out North Vietnamese ethnic minority refugees but had no way to verify their bona fides in the North. "It was just very, very difficult to make sure that we hadn't recruited someone who had been put there for us to recruit," Colonel Singlaub later said.

Indeed, in 1968 the Bangkok recruiting operation was shut down when CIA officers discovered it was "compromised and monitored" by North Vietnamese intelligence.

Every message to or from an agent team passed through ARVN hands to be translated for the CIA and SOG handlers. A mole here could have caused incredible destruction—and the available record suggests internal sabotage. When the review panel asked to check tape recordings of team radio operators' code training "fists," or tapping patterns, to compare them to later transmissions, "we found that somehow the records had been confused and we no longer could identify the individual with a particular tape."

Despite what may seem a tremendous waste of clandestine assets, the CIA/SOG agent program had beneficial combat and intelligence effects that may well have been worth the investment. Beyond question, SOG was stinging Hanoi. In March 1968, the official Communist Party newspaper, *Nhan Dan,* announced a new security decree with the death penalty for all sorts of counterrevolutionary offenses. The article warned that although "reactionary elements and saboteurs" were few in numbers, "their plotting is very deep and their activities very dangerous." American analysts in Saigon found the new decree "an extremely significant development" and concluded nineteen of Hanoi's twenty-one new death offenses were a direct result of SOG activities.

SOG flights deep into North Vietnam and coastal raids by Nasty boats forced the enemy to activate radars, radio networks and interception procedures. All of this was monitored by U.S. radio eavesdroppers, providing valuable communications intelligence that alone saved many U.S. aviators' lives during air raids.

And the enemy's diversion of resources was real, too, and disproportionate to SOG's investment. "The impact on the war of having a guerrilla force in the North destroy a truck is not related to the loss of the matériel in the truck," Colonel Singlaub said, "so much as it is an indication that people cannot be trusted to be loyal to the Communist cause. And that forces [the North Vietnamese] to expend a great deal of extra energy, manpower and resources for internal security."

In response to SOG's Nasty boat raids, hundreds, perhaps thousands, of Communist militia patrolled the beaches each night in addition to their regular jobs, which, a SOG officer notes, "meant one hell of a lot of people were being kept awake all night, several nights of the week, week after week, on the off chance that these boats might be conducting an operation in that particular local area."

North Vietnam erected coastal security posts every 5 miles and emplaced batteries of guns to cover areas frequented by SOG boats. A SOG Naval Advisory Detachment operations officer, Lieutenant Commander W. T. "Red" Cannon, recalls the North Vietnamese even deployed special steel-hulled, armed junks to defend against Nasty boats, moored other junks as lures to draw the SOG boats into coastal gunfire traps or floated "Trojan Horse" boats packed with booby-trapped explosives to destroy Sea Commando boarding parties.

Had it not been for SOG's North Vietnam operations, more enemy manpower, firepower and logistics would have been directed toward the battlefields in South Vietnam, or the NVA infrastructure in Laos and Cambodia.

By early August 1968, the North Vietnamese surfaced the three teams most obviously under their control, so SOG kept playing the remaining five—*Red Dragon, Hadley, Eagle, Ares* and *Tourbillon*—and decided it was time for some payback.

SOG told one team to prepare for a resupply from F-4 Phantoms dropping canisters shaped like bombs. This time, instead of canisters they were real bombs, pickled right on top of the Ministry of Security troops posing as the agent team—followed by effusive SOG apologies, of course.

SOG C-123s and C-130s flew eight North Vietnam resupply drops in 1968, but now the bundles contained special "payback" packages built by SOG's "Evil Elves," under the supervision of Captain Fred

Caristo.* Blackbird navigator Lieutenant Colonel Don James found the supplies he was dropping fiendishly built: "Within that equipment would be things like radios that exploded when you keyed the mike, ammunition that exploded when you fired it, grenades that exploded as soon as the lever was released, that sort of thing." An RF-4C recon plane photographed one drop zone and found fresh truck tracks where the bundles had been gathered, and a large crater where the enemy had attempted to open a bundle packed not with supplies but TNT. After watching their troops being blown to bits one time too often, the North Vietnamese did not even pick up the bundles dropped for Teams *Hadley* and *Tourbillon*.

The paybacks came to a halt in October, after LBJ ended all North Vietnam bombing just before the 1968 presidential election. Along with the total bombing halt, SOG was instructed not even to task its agent teams anymore, though some SOG officers thought they should have kept stringing them along. "You don't just turn it off," said Major Scotty Crerar.

But the long-term agent teams were not SOG's only significant North Vietnam program. Since late 1967, SOG had been inserting other teams as deep as 150 miles north of the DMZ, under a program called STRATA (Short-Term Roadwatch and Target Acquisition). Unaffected by the 1 April bombing halt because they operated below the 20th Parallel, STRATA teams were intended to make up for long-term agent team shortcomings.

STRATA teams spent just a week or two per operation, too short a time for the enemy to capture and play them, making their intelligence more reliable and responsive.

Conceived by Captain Fred Caristo, STRATA operations focused upon the road network leading toward the Mu Gia, Ban Karai and Ban Raving passes, which all emptied into the Ho Chi Minh Trail. Nearly all STRATA teams were inserted within 10 miles of the Laotian border, in the rugged mountain country above the passes.

STRATA recruits received training similar to that of the long-term agents at SOG's secret base, Camp Long Thanh, but were segregated for

*Caristo earlier had led a Bright Light POW rescue attempt in Cambodia and was awarded the Distinguished Service Cross.

security purposes, then housed at Monkey Mountain FOB in Danang. To confuse enemy analysts, the fourteen STRATA teams were randomly numbered Team 90 through Team 122.

STRATA teams were launched clandestinely from Nakhon Phanom Air Base in Thailand. They were delivered there by SOG C-130 Blackbirds and, like the American teams secretly staged there, stayed out of sight inside panel trucks or the SOG operations building. After changing into NVA uniforms, the STRATA men climbed into 21st SOS "Pony" helicopters, then it was a half-hour flight across the 65-mile, narrow neck of Laos. The HH-3s had to climb to 10,000 feet to get out of range of antiaircraft gun concentrations, then flew on instruments through the turbulent wall clouds above the Annamite Mountains, then penetrated North Vietnam at low level to avoid SAM sites and obscure their LZ approach. It was some of the trickiest helicopter flying in Southeast Asia.

It all ended on 15 October 1968 with a "frantic call from Washington" to Colonel Cavanaugh. "Do you have any STRATA teams across the border?" a Joint Chiefs staff officer demanded.

SOG then had two teams in North Vietnam, Cavanaugh reported. "You've got to get them out. You've got a day," the JCS staffer demanded, explaining President Johnson was about to announce his total bombing halt.

"It was asinine," Cavanaugh said later. "Nobody in Washington cared about a handful of people up there." Chief SOG said it was impossible to retrieve the STRATA men in twenty-four hours, promising only, "I'll get them out as fast as I can." Due to operational inertia and weather delays, he could not make good on his promise until 23 October. The Washington bureaucracy raised not a peep.

From their first insertion until the final extraction thirteen months later, STRATA teams penetrated North Vietnam twenty-six times. Though hardly a returned man was wounded, STRATA lost twenty-six men MIA—including two entire teams—the inevitable result of bad weather that delayed even emergency extractions an average of five days and made any contact likely to be lethal. Approximately one quarter of STRATA's 102 agents were lost.

As of 1 November 1968, SOG was no longer authorized to run agent operations of any type in North Vietnam. Yet some minds at SOG headquarters began brainstorming: If SOG wasn't allowed to run a genuine agent network, perhaps it could create a false one.

It was diabolical, but SOG analysts, black propagandists and counterintelligence experts put their heads together and plotted to combine all SOG's real and imaginary assets "in an integrated effort to exploit Hanoi's almost paranoid fear of any perceived threat to their control of the population." The result was Projects Urgency, Borden and Oodles.

Project Urgency, the maritime element of SOG's diversionary program, recruited captured fishermen as pseudoagents—and to keep it all the more confusing, occasionally recruited the more reliable ones as real agents, too.

At its start, Project Urgency built upon two real agents, recruited at Paradise Island and code-named *Goldfish* and *Pergola*, who were specially trained and landed on North Vietnam's coast in late 1967. They never came on the air and failed to arrive at their rendezvous to be extracted by Nasty boat. To inaugurate the Urgency deception, SOG disseminated the myth that the presumably captured *Goldfish* and *Pergola* were just the first agents of a whole new network.

Then Urgency recruited eleven low-level agents at Paradise Island and returned them, plus two pseudoagents to convey disinformation. SOG also found ways to incriminate many other fisherman "agents" who would do little more than generate interesting debriefs.

Then came the double sting: The most zealous Communists among the fishermen brought to Paradise Island were returned to North Vietnam far away from their homes, with money and false messages hidden in their clothes that would implicate them in especially insidious ways. For instance, a returnee might swear to his debriefers that he was, in fact, wearing the same pants he had on when a SOG boat kidnapped him at sea—but he'd have no inkling his pants had been snatched at Paradise Island so a map printed on silk could be rolled tight and sewn into a seam. The map would be discovered by the North's counterspy experts, who'd examine his clothes. Other returnees were "stung" by things like secret ink pills hidden in an aspirin bottle or an encapsulated message molded in a bar of soap.

No amount of explanation could talk a suspect out of such a fix, and finally he'd have to admit that the Americans had offered him money to spy for them, but he was a good Communist and had refused—which the interrogators would never believe. Meanwhile his Communist Party friends and relatives could only wonder at the legitimacy of a regime that accused such a loyal comrade of espionage.

Project Urgency was just kicking into full swing when the November 1968 bombing halt ended most Nasty boat missions, which also curtailed the maritime deception program.

An entirely different deception wrinkle was the related but compartmented effort called Project Borden. SOG had been employing ordinary agents, double agents, triple agents, false agents and pseudoagents but it was the *unwitting* false agent under Project Borden that proved as clever a hoax as was ever perpetrated.

Unlike Urgency's pseudo- and framed agents, Project Borden recruits were NVA prisoners purposely selected because they were untrustworthy but allowed to believe they'd fooled the Americans.

Also unlike most SOG efforts, Borden was segregated from the ARVN, with American officers going to U.S. divisional POW holding areas to recruit NVA prisoners while they were still in American hands. Other Borden prospects came from prisoners brought out of Laos and Cambodia by recon teams. "Our general feeling," explained Colonel Cavanaugh, "was that these people were not loyal to us, would not be loyal to us, that they were opportunists, and that the minute they got on the ground they would immediately double on us." Borden recruits were polygraphed to check their presumed tendency to duplicity.

Each Borden "ringer" was groomed through weeks of training at Camp Long Thanh to absorb information from casual chats with his pseudoteammates—agent identities, code names, plans, secret rendezvous sites and so on. Even washouts were put to good use, being fed disinformation before being transferred to POW camps. The bottom line, according to Colonel Cavanaugh, was "to implant in their minds the idea that we had effective teams working up North, that there was a strong underground and this underground was being resupplied and that we were sending these people up there as couriers with further instructions as to what to do, and with further instructions as to impending operations."

A recurring theme was that assassination plots were afoot against senior military and government officials, with the connivance of North Vietnamese Communist Party members.

The last twist in the six-week Borden training course was so creatively original it bordered on the bizarre: As his final instruction, each Borden agent was given a tube of toothpastelike ultraviolet paste with which he was to mark fellow NVA soldiers he'd induced to defect, this secret indelible sign ensuring safe passage and great rewards from the Americans. You can almost imagine the Ministry of Defense hustle to get black lights to render the ultraviolet paste visible, then initiate endless spot checks throughout the country.

Although the declassified accounts are incomplete, SOG aircraft apparently still penetrated the North on a case-by-case basis to insert Borden agents, well after the 1968 bombing halt. The night of insertion, some Borden agents were afforded the ultimate paratrooper compliment: In honor of his training performance, he would be "man-in-the-door," the first to exit the aircraft. What he didn't know was that as quickly as he'd leaped into the blackness his "teammates" unhooked and sat down; the parachutes later found dangling in trees had been weighted with ice blocks. As quickly as he landed, the Borden agent would dash away to turn in his teammates, pour his guts out, even pass a polygraph, because he truly believed what he was reporting.

"This causes [the North Vietnamese] to alert the militia and to spend a great deal of time and energy screening the area looking for the team," a SOG report notes. "They interrogate and reinterrogate villagers, and all those who have been suspected of supporting anti-Communist activities in the past are brought in for interrogation. This merely assists in spreading distrust in the minds of the North Vietnamese officials and likewise it harasses the people and causes them to think less kindly toward the regime."

Some Borden agents inserted in Laos unknowingly carried a tiny homing transponder hidden in their equipment; of course, they'd surrender and be taken to an NVA headquarters for debriefing. But a hell of a surprise was in the offing for such an agent. "We would follow him with this beeper until he stayed in the same location for seventy-two hours," one SOG officer explained, the location presumably being a major headquarters. "Then we would Arc Light it."

Borden was a sizable effort, with forty-four agents inserted in 1968 in NVA-controlled areas of Laos, Cambodia and both North and South Vietnam. To the experts who ran it, Project Borden was thought the most successful deception program of the war.

The third element in SOG's agent deception plan was Project Oodles, which overlapped and supported the doubled and tripled agent teams and actually started in the fall of 1967, before the initial bombing halt, but kept going after the 1968 halt ended the real agent program.

In essence, Oodles was intended to convince the Ministry of Security that eighteen additional agent teams were running loose in North Vietnam, a parallel network that SOG officers believed was made "more credible by North Vietnamese knowledge of captured actual teams." Simulated messages were sent to Oodles teams identical to those sent to double-agent teams, complete with similar call signs, formats and family messages at holiday times. Oodles teams also received real aerial resupplies, at the same intervals and with the same contents as did genuine agent teams.

Like planting false clues at a crime scene, SOG fed the enemy tantalizing hints to keep the search going but, as when chasing a rumor, the Ministry of Security never quite caught up to the source. About the time a team seemed to be mythical, fresh evidence surfaced to support its existence.

One touch of genius was parachuting Borden agents as reinforcements to phantom Oodles teams; the Bordens genuinely believed they were airdropped to meet established long-term agent teams. They gave enemy debriefers exactly what counterintelligence officers most love: confirming pieces for their analytical puzzle. Eventually, SOG was playing fourteen Oodles teams, supporting them with false radio traffic, airdrops and hints delivered in myriad ways.

It was in support of Oodles, however, that SOG sustained its greatest aircraft loss over North Vietnam, the mysterious downing of a C-130 Blackbird on 29 December 1967. The SOG plane checked in just before it was to resupply Oodles phantom Team *Mikado*, in extreme northwest North Vietnam, just a dozen miles south of Yunnan Province, China. That was the last ever heard from it. Shot down, crashed, hit by a SAM—it simply vanished, the only Blackbird ever lost operationally. As in the case of the SOG recon MIAs in Laos, Hanoi to this day denies any knowledge of the Blackbird crewmen's fate.*

---

*Missing are USAF Lieutenant Colonel Donald Fisher, Major Charles Claxton, Captains Edwin Osborne, Gerald VanBuren, Frank Parker III and Gordon Wenaas, plus Sergeants Jack McCrary, Wayne Eckley, Edward Darcy, James Williams and Gean Clapper.

In early 1969, SOG created a new category of agents and called them "Earth Angels." They were recruited from among former NVA officers and NCOs who'd shown an enmity toward the Communists and a willingness to take up arms against them. After a polygraph screening and special training at Camp Long Thanh, the Earth Angels were disguised in copies of NVA uniforms and parachuted or landed by helicopter in Cambodia or Laos. Performing primarily route recons lasting about a week, the Earth Angels traveled the same roads as NVA units, posing as couriers to pass quickly and to explain their ignorance of local units and events. Usually they were inserted beyond the road network down which they had to walk to reach a pickup point. Less than a dozen Earth Angel teams existed, each with two or three former NVA.

A major challenge was keeping Earth Angels properly outfitted with current enemy passwords, recognition signs and credentials. To support them, on Okinawa CISO, the Counterinsurgency Support Office, custom-made perfect duplicates of NVA uniforms. "We copied the weave exactly," CISO civilian Ben Baker recalled. "Our problem was that we found five-digit numbers inside NVA uniform pockets, and also inside the collars." The CISO staff was perplexed, unsure what the numbers meant. "Should we duplicate the numbers? Run them in sequence? They drove me crazy," Baker confessed. "We were afraid that if we used the same number and that was a plant, we were in trouble and our agents would get picked up." CISO finally determined the numbers were just a manufacturer's stamp and came up with one of its own.

Uniform accuracy was valuable: When a recon team at Khe Sanh captured an NVA hat emblem, SOG dispatched a C-130 just to pick it up and rush it to Okinawa for duplication. "It was the first authentic hat emblem they had," said Captain Hammond Salley, SOG intelligence officer at Khe Sanh.

SOG's former NVA proved themselves surprisingly talented, especially when masquerading in Cambodian villages and demanding information from peasants about where their NVA "comrades" were and what they were up to. Cambodian civilians never doubted their genuineness. And unlike other teams, the Earth Angels stood a decent chance of talking their way out of a challenge when they encountered real NVA.

Also in 1969, SOG fielded a half dozen ethnic Cambodian teams code-named Pike Hill or Cedar Walk, according to whether they were assigned long-duration intelligence or raiding missions. Most Cambode teams operated opposite South Vietnam's III Corps.

Since the presence of any radio might betray them, SOG issued Pike Hill agents a novel but proven communication medium hardly ever employed by America since World War I—homing pigeons. During a briefing, Chief SOG Colonel Cavanaugh mystified MACV commander General Creighton Abrams by ushering him to an open window, where the colonel produced a cooing bird, and tossed it aloft with a message for SOG headquarters. "We're going back a long ways," he told Abrams, "but this *is* a secure means of communication." According to Cavanaugh, General Abrams got "quite a laugh out of it."

It could be said that all SOG's agent programs were changed decisively by President Johnson's election-eve 1968 bombing halt, which caused them to cease, shift or begin anew in different ways. As well, though, the halt signaled a decisive change in the war, leaving U.S. policy undefined until the new Nixon administration took office almost a year later and weighed its own options.

Richard Nixon had run on a promise to bring the war to an honorable end but refused to disclose the secret plan by which he'd make that happen. The new strategy—fashioned by Nixon's national security adviser, Henry Kissinger—would commence in early 1969 with the secret bombing of Cambodia.

And SOG would be in the thick of it.

13

DANIEL BOONE AGAIN

The docks at Cambodia's seaport of Sihanoukville bustled with the arrival of East European ships every few weeks in early 1969. Long lines of Hak Ly Trucking Company lorries took on the ships' cargo, then rolled two hours north on Highway 4, a modern paved road built with U.S. aid.

On Phnom Penh's outskirts the trucks turned in to an army depot, and once the vehicles were beyond public view, Vietnamese men arrived to inspect each load with considerable interest. Though seemingly operated by a Chinese businessman, the Hak Ly Company's true owner was North Vietnam's Trinh Sat secret intelligence service.

Under Trinh Sat supervision, the clandestine cargo of rockets, small-arms ammunition and mortar rounds was carried on overnight convoys northwest along Highway 7, past French-owned rubber plantations, to the heavily jungled frontier of Kampong Cham Province the Americans had nicknamed the Fishhook. Overseen by NVA Rear Transportation Unit 70, the Fishhook's vast stockpiles supported the 5th and 7th NVA Divisions, and the Viet Cong 9th Division. The Fishhook's largest base camp—a complex with hundreds of structures—was hidden less than 30 miles northeast of Tay Ninh, South Vietnam, just 3 miles inside Cambodia.

Cambodian Prince Sihanouk was well aware of these neutrality violations; indeed, his fifth wife, Monique, her mother and half-brother were peddling land rights and political protection to the NVA; other middlemen were selling them rice by the thousands of tons.

All ammunition reaching South Vietnam's III and IV Corps came through Cambodia. This ammunition contributed to the rising U.S. death toll in the so-called Mini-Tet Offensive of 1969, when NVA forces struck quickly at U.S. positions, then fled back to their sanctuaries in Cambodia. After twenty-one months of top-secret penetrations, SOG recon teams had located the major sanctuaries, which sustained 200,000 NVA and VC.*

Along with other intelligence, SOG's Daniel Boone data appeared on a top-secret map that President Nixon's new national security adviser, Henry Kissinger, studied aboard *Air Force One* at Brussels airport the morning of 24 February 1969. Sitting with Kissinger was Colonel Alexander Haig, his military assistant, and representing the president was White House Chief of Staff H. R. "Bob" Haldeman. During the new administration's transition, the president had asked Kissinger to determine how to counter Hanoi's "fight and talk" strategy and deal with the Cambodian buildup. The Johnson administration had watched passively while thousands of GIs were killed by an enemy operating from sanctuary. Not only did it do nothing about it, the LBJ administration said nothing, even denied it was happening.[†]

While the president addressed NATO's North Atlantic Council, those aboard *Air Force One* worked out details for a clandestine U.S. response: The secret bombing of Cambodia's most remote sanctuaries, which would not be acknowledged unless Prince Sihanouk protested. When *Air Force One* departed Brussels, Kissinger briefed President Nixon, who approved the plan but held back on implementing it.

---

*That spring, *Newsweek* magazine compromised the Daniel Boone code name, reporting "Americans of Oriental extraction" were infiltrating Cambodia. The Associated Press elaborated, claiming Green Berets "dye their skin and wear eye putty to look like Orientals." After a good laugh, SOG changed the Daniel Boone code name to Salem House.

[†]The heavy NVA presence was verified on 2 March, when a CCS team was detected outside a battalion base camp in the Fishhook. Hundreds of NVA took up the chase and overran them, killing Sergeant William Evans and Specialist Five Michael May. Their bodies were never recovered.

Over the coming three weeks, Nixon postponed the Arc Light raids and twice warned Hanoi, "we will not tolerate attacks which result in heavier casualties to our men at a time that we are honestly trying to seek peace at the conference table in Paris."

The day after Nixon's second warning, the NVA bombarded Saigon with 122mm rockets smuggled through Cambodia. Three days later, USAF B-52s hit the Fishhook in the first secret Cambodian raid, setting off seventy-three secondary explosions. Only the pilots and navigators knew the real target; official reports recorded the impact points as adjacent areas in South Vietnam.

Phnom Penh and Hanoi were silent. It was a fitting irony: For four years the North Vietnamese had denied their presence in Cambodia. Now, with U.S. bombs falling on them, they could say nothing. Nixon suspended further Arc Lights in hopes Hanoi's negotiators might use the hiatus for productive discussions in Paris.

A month passed with no progress, so President Nixon approved a second B-52 strike, against a target proposed by General Abrams with Ambassador Ellsworth Bunker's endorsement: COSVN, the Central Office for South Vietnam, which an NVA deserter had pinpointed fourteen miles southeast of Memot, Cambodia, just a mile inside the Cambodian border. The COSVN Arc Light was laid on for 24 April.

Apprised of the upcoming B-52 strike, it occurred to Brigadier General Phillip B. Davidson, the MACV J-2, that SOG should land a raiding force when the bombs stopped falling on COSVN. He phoned Chief SOG Colonel Cavanaugh, who agreed and ordered CCS to ready a Hatchet Force.

At CCS, the COSVN raid was assigned to its most accomplished man, a living recon legend—"Mad Dog" Shriver. At Fort Bragg no one mentioned SOG or spoke of Daniel Boone, but everyone had heard of Sergeant First Class Jerry Shriver, proclaimed a "mad dog" by Radio Hanoi.

It was Mad Dog Shriver who'd spoken the most famous rejoinder in SOG history: His team surrounded and the CCS staff concerned he might be overrun, a FAC told Shriver, "It sounds pretty bad." And Shriver replied, "No, no. I've got 'em right where I want 'em—*surrounded from the inside.*"

Shriver was blond, tall and thin, with chiseled features and piercing blue eyes. "There was no soul in the eyes, no emotion," said Captain Bill O'Rourke. "They were just eyes."

O'Rourke, who commanded the one-hundred-man Montagnard Hatchet Force company, would lead the COSVN raid, though Shriver equally would influence it, continuing an eight-month collaboration that began while running recon.

Now into his third year in SOG, Mad Dog Shriver was twenty-eight years old and, according to one SOG veteran, "the quintessential warrior-loner, antisocial, possessed by what he was doing, leading the best team, always training, constantly training."

Shriver rarely spoke and walked around camp for days wearing the same clothes. In his sleep he cradled a loaded rifle, and in the NCO club he'd buy a case of beer, open every can, then go alone to a corner and drink them all. Although he could not care less about decorations, he'd been awarded a Silver Star, five Bronze Stars and the Soldiers Medal.

Shriver was devoted to the Montagnards. He spent all his money on them and collected food, clothes, whatever people would give, to distribute in Yard villages. He taught the Yards how to play an accordion, the most sophisticated musical instrument they'd ever had. Mad Dog even built his own room in the Montagnard barracks so he could live with them. "He was almost revered by the Montagnards," O'Rourke says.

Shriver's closest companion was a German shepherd he'd brought back from Taiwan and named Klaus. One night Klaus got sick on beer some recon men fed him and crapped on the NCO club floor; the men rubbed his nose in it and threw him out. Shriver arrived, drank a beer, removed his blue velvet smoking jacket and derby hat, put his .38 revolver on a table, then dropped his pants and defecated on the floor. "If you want to rub my nose in this," he dared, "come on over." Everyone pretended not to hear him, except one man who'd fed Klaus beer and who urged the recon company commander to intervene. The captain laughed in his face, saying, "Hey, fuck you, pal."

"He had this way of looking at you with his eyes half open," Frank Burkhart remembers. "If he looked at me like that, I'd just about freeze."

Medal of Honor recipient Jim Fleming says Shriver "convinced me that for the rest of my life I would not go into a bar and cross someone I didn't know."

But no recon man was better in the woods. "He was like having a dog you could talk to," Bill O'Rourke explained. "He could hear and sense things; he was more alive in the woods than any other human being I've ever met."

Rather than stand down after an operation, Shriver would go out with another team. "He lived for the game; that's all he lived for," Dale Libby said. One time Shriver promised everyone he was going on R&R but instead sneaked up to Plei Djereng Special Forces camp to go out in the field.

Fully decked out, Mad Dog was a walking arsenal, with an imposing array of sawed-off shotgun, pistols, knives, grenades. "He looked like Rambo," First Sergeant Billy Greenwood said. Unless you were one of Mad Dog's closest friends, the image was of perfect prowess—but the truth was, Shriver confided to Sammy Hernadez, he feared death and didn't think he'd live much longer; he'd beaten bad odds too many times and could feel a terrible payback looming. By the time a recon man had accumulated twenty missions it was hard to explain why he was still alive; Shriver must have had twice that many missions.

"He wanted to quit," said Fred Zabitosky. "He really wanted to quit, Jerry did. I said, 'Why don't you just tell them, "I want off, I don't want to run anymore?"' He said he would but he never did; just kept running."

"He was wanting to get out of recon and didn't know how," agreed Recon One-Zero Sonny Franks. Shriver went halfway when he left recon to join his old team leader's Hatchet Force company. The COSVN raid would make a fitting final operation: Shriver could face his fear head-on, charge right into the mouth of COSVN and afterward at last quit.

The morning of 24 April 1969, while high-flying B-52s flew in from distant Guam, the CCS Hatchet Force company lined up beside the airfield at Quan Loi, only 20 miles southeast of COSVN's secret lair.

But just five Green Hornet Hueys were flyable that morning, enough to lift only two platoons. The big bombers could not be delayed, so Lieutenant Bob Killebrew's 3d Platoon would have to stand by at Quan Loi while the 1st Platoon, under First Lieutenant Walter Marcantel, and

2d Platoon, under First Lieutenant Greg Harrigan, landed at COSVN. Captain O'Rourke and Shriver didn't like it, but they could do nothing.

The bomber contrails were not yet visible when the Hueys began cranking and Hatchet Force men boarded; O'Rourke would be on the first bird and Shriver on the last one so they'd be at each end of the landing Hueys. As the choppers lifted off for the ten-minute flight, the B-52s were making final alignments for the run-in.

Minutes later the lead Green Hornet had to turn back because of mechanical problems; O'Rourke could do nothing but wish the others godspeed. Command passed to an operations officer in the second bird who'd come along for the raid, Captain Paul Cahill.

Momentarily the raider force could see dirt geysers hurtling skyward amid collapsing trees. As the dust settled, a violin-shaped clearing took form, and the Green Hornets descended in-trail, hovered for the men to leap off, then climbed away.

Then fire exploded from all directions—horrible fire that skimmed the ground and mowed down anyone who didn't dive into a bomb crater or roll behind a fallen tree trunk.

From the back of the LZ, Shriver radioed that a machine-gun bunker to his left-front had his men pinned and asked if anyone could fire at it to relieve the pressure. Fixed in a crater beneath murderous fire, Captain Cahill, Lieutenant Marcantel and a medic, Sergeant Ernest Jamison, replied they were pinned, too.

Then Jamison dashed out to retrieve a wounded man; heavy fire cut him down, killing him on the spot.

It was impossible for anyone else to engage the machine gun that trapped Shriver's men—it was up to Mad Dog. Skittish Yards looked to him, and his half grin restored a sense of confidence. Then they were on their feet, charging—Shriver was his old self, running to the sound of guns, a true believer Yard on either side, all of them dashing into the woodline, right into the jaws of COSVN.

And Mad Dog Shriver was never seen again.

Jamison's body lay just a few yards from the crater where Captain Cahill listened to bullets cracking and RPGs shaking the ground. When Cahill lifted his head, an AK round hit him in the mouth, deflected upward and destroyed an eye. Badly wounded, he collapsed.

In a nearby crater, young Lieutenant Harrigan directed helicopter gunships whose rockets and miniguns were the only thing holding off the incessant NVA assault. Already, Harrigan reported, more than half his platoon were killed or wounded. For forty-five minutes the Green Beret lieutenant kept the enemy at bay, then Harrigan was hit. He died within minutes.

Bill O'Rourke, aboard another helicopter, tried to land, but his bird couldn't penetrate the NVA veil of steel. Lieutenant Colonel Earl Trabue, the CCS commander, arrived and together he and O'Rourke flew overhead but they could do little.

Hours dragged by. Wounded men lay untreated, exposed in the sun. Several times the Green Hornets attempted to retrieve them, and each time heavy fire drove them off. One door gunner was badly wounded.

Finally a passing Australian twin-jet Canberra bomber from No. 2 Squadron at Phan Rang heard their predicament on the emergency radio frequency, ignored the fact that they were in Cambodia and dropped its bomb load, which "broke the stranglehold those guys were in, and it allowed us to go in," O'Rourke said. Only Lieutenant Marcantel was still directing air, and finally he had to bring ordnance so close it wounded him and his surviving nine Montagnards.

One medic ran to Harrigan's hole and attempted to lift him out but couldn't. "They were pretty well drained physically and emotionally," O'Rourke said. Finally three Hueys raced in and picked up fifteen wounded men. Lieutenant Dan Hall carried out a radio operator, then managed to drag Lieutenant Harrigan's body to the aircraft. That was it, the end of the operation.

Colonel Cavanaugh talked to survivors and learned, "The fire was so heavy and so intense that even the guys trying to evade and move out of the area were being cut down." It seemed almost an ambush. "That really shook them up at MACV, to realize anybody survived that [B-52] strike," Colonel Cavanaugh said.

The heavy losses especially affected Brigadier General Davidson, who blamed himself. "General," Chief SOG told him, "if I'd have felt we were going to lose people like that, I wouldn't have put them in there."

First Lieutenant Walter Marcantel survived his wounds only to die in a parachuting accident at Fort Devens, Massachusetts, six months later. Captain Cahill was medically retired. And Ernest Jamison's body was later recovered.

But Mad Dog Shriver's fate remains a mystery. A POW/MIA report declassified in 1993 said, "Vietnamese voices were later heard [which] stated that one American was in the process of being captured." Medal of Honor recipient Fred Zabitosky believes Shriver was taken alive, but Bill O'Rourke thinks Shriver died that day. "I felt very privileged to have been his friend," he says, "and when he died I grieved as much as for my younger brother when he was killed. Twenty-some-odd years later, it still sticks in my craw that I wasn't there. I wish I had been there."

First Sergeant Billy Greenwood didn't think the issue was so much the failed COSVN raid as just plain letting Shriver keep running and running until he met his fate. "I think maybe the commanders and the older people, maybe it was our fault," he said. "We should have stopped him and we didn't."

Alarmed by SOG's growing losses, General Abrams had MACV analyze SOG casualties for the first two months of 1969: Fifteen Americans were killed or missing in action, sixty-eight wounded and ten helicopters destroyed. But this had to be compared to SOG's accomplishments. That January and February SOG troopers demolished thirteen trucks, killed 1400 enemy soldiers and called air strikes that touched off 455 secondary explosions and 100 sustained fires. In balance, MACV found SOG "a significant economy of U.S. applied force."

The ratio was fantastic, nearly one hundred enemy killed for each SOG man lost, much higher than the conventional unit kill ratio of about 15:1. SOG records show that in 1968, 108 NVA were killed in Cambodia for each SOG Green Beret lost, which jumped to 153:1 in 1970, probably the highest combat efficiency in U.S. history.

But SOG could have done even more in Cambodia if the State Department had permitted tac air support; it was a curious logic that was so concerned about fighters leaving telltale napalm streaks or cluster-bomb fins but unconcerned about B-52s leaving house-size bomb craters from horizon to horizon. Colonel Cavanaugh found it "ridiculous" and occasionally General Abrams bent the rules a bit to save endangered recon teams. In SOG we were already bending the rules ourselves—for example, Staff Sergeant Howard "Karate" Davis, a Covey Rider, saved my whole team one afternoon by sneaking into Cambodia with a pair of Skyraiders and napalming an NVA platoon that had us cornered beside an LZ.

Nixon's third secret B-52 strike took place in early May, targeted against a number of places, including the NVA 27th Infantry Regiment's base camp. My team, RT Illinois, went in for the bomb damage assessment of the latter target. Led by Staff Sergeant Ben Thompson, with Sergeant George Bacon III as One-Two, we landed twenty minutes after the strike and had to shoot our way out, not lasting even a half day. But that meant the bombs had hit a heavily occupied spot, so the Air Force was satisfied.

Sihanouk quite likely was talking about this raid when he told reporters on 13 May, "I have not protested the bombings of Viet Cong camps because I have not heard of the bombings . . . because in certain areas of Cambodia there are no Cambodians." He declared, "Nobody was caught in those barrages—nobody, no Cambodians."*

A few months later, on 25 August, RT Florida, led by Staff Sergeant Ken Worthley, inserted in northeast Cambodia to recon an area thought to be inhabited by the 66th NVA Regiment. Sergeant Bob Garcia came along as acting One-One to help break in a new recon man, Dale Hanson, who carried the team radio. With four Vietnamese, that made a total of seven men.

Landing uneventfully at noon, they left the LZ and began climbing a steep hillside; by 2 P.M. they were sitting on the slope, taking a break, when Garcia detected two NVA trackers approaching on their back trail. The Oakland, California, native held his CAR-15 sight on one NVA and would have let him come closer but an indig got nervous and fired. Garcia shot his tracker but the other fled, then AK bursts rattled all around them, and they heard brush breaking on a wide front—apparently a company had been following the trackers and now fanned out to encircle RT Florida. Garcia spotted one NVA on their left, but his CAR-15 malfunctioned so he snatched an M-79 grenade launcher from an indig, knelt to see beneath the thick brush and fired at the enemy soldier's legs. The bursting grenade knocked

---

*A lot of NVA weren't being caught, either. Before each Arc Light, a warning was broadcast on the emergency Guard frequency (243.00 MHz), to prevent aircraft from wandering into the falling bombs. Pilots could plot the impact point within a mile—as could the NVA, too, since they'd captured hundreds of Guard-tuned radios from downed fliers and crashed planes. USAF strike planners had little respect for enemy signal intelligence capabilities.

the soldier down—then it was time to run, with One-Zero Worthley taking the lead.

As they trotted, Hanson clumsily wrapped a bandage around his hand where an AK slug had clipped off his left middle finger. Garcia relieved him of the team radio and tried to raise a FAC, but no one responded.

Then it was almost dark, and Worthley decided to hide for the night in a gully so narrow the NVA wouldn't think of searching it; just in case the NVA brought in dogs, they generously laced their back trail with tear-gas powder.

About 3 A.M., yelps awoke the recon men; then all of a sudden the tracker dogs reached the powder, cried a few minutes and went away. The rest of the night passed peacefully.

At dawn the team slipped through the jungle, quiet, cautious and alert. By 9:30 A.M. they were cresting a hill when suddenly the point man signed to freeze. Worthley crept forward and just as he reached the point he saw a trail and two NVA, who spun to shoot. Instantly Worthley and the point man fired, cutting them down. Garcia arrived to find two dead NVA and the point man bandaging his hand where a bullet had skipped across his fingers.

While the others provided security, Worthley and Garcia hurriedly stripped the bodies. By the fine cut of his uniform, they realized one was an important officer, probably a colonel, who looked Chinese and carried a new pistol. The other man was young, armed with an AK, apparently the officer's bodyguard. But most impressive was a big leather satchel the officer had. Perusing its contents, the interpreter said this was an intelligence officer, and SOG later determined RT Florida had bagged the highest-ranking intelligence officer ever killed by recon men.

The entire incident took thirty seconds, and as they turned out the dead man's last pocket, they heard NVA running down the trail. Scooping up the satchel, One-Zero Worthley led the way, and off RT Florida dashed. They were barely out of sight when the NVA found the bodies. Excited voices called out and brush crashed as enemy troops ran incautiously into the jungle, attempting to intercept the SOG men. "They were pissed," Bob Garcia said. "they were superpissed." Garcia was able to raise a FAC, and soon choppers were on the way.

RT Florida managed to evade the NVA, then they found a bamboo grove with an opening wide enough for them to be extracted by STABO rig. They hid there a half hour and kept hearing NVA voices or signal shots; then it got real quiet and Garcia grew uneasy.

When the first Huey passed low overhead dozens of nearby NVA opened fire. Garcia called in a pair of A-1s, but the fire went on unabated, then F-4 Phantoms dropped 500-pound bombs, and the concussion bounced the recon men as if on a trampoline. Then miniguns strafed danger-close, and the NVA pulled back.

Unmolested by fire, a Huey hovered at the treetops and dropped four ropes; three indigs snapped in, and Worthley should have put the wounded point man on that fourth string. Garcia turned to ask Worthley why he hadn't, and Hanson told him their One-Zero was dead. A lone bullet had hit Worthley in the neck, killing him instantly; they attached his harnessed body to the rope, and the Huey lifted away just as the NVA resumed firing.

The second chopper came in despite the fire, dropped four ropes, but a bullet cut one line and a second became snared in the trees. Garcia, Hanson and the wounded point man would have to come out on two ropes. Immediately they snapped in and the Huey began lifting. Just as Garcia reached the treetops, he could see a hundred muzzles flickering from a facing hillside but he could do nothing; he was entirely out of ammunition. He felt the rope stretch and stretch, to the point of almost snapping or dragging down the Huey. Garcia looked down and saw Hanson and the point man hacking away where their rope had snagged the bamboo. Garcia shouted in his radio, "Hold it! We're stuck! We're stuck! You're stretching the rope, we can't make it!" The crew chief probably should have cut the lines and let them fall to their fate but he didn't.

Suspended in the air, Garcia could do nothing but hope not to be shot and hope Hanson could chop the bamboo before the Huey crashed on all of them. "A warmth went over me and I just waited," Garcia recalled. "I just looked around to see where I was going to die."

A bullet creased Hanson's head, but he kept chopping; then the rope jerked free and Hanson's bloodied hand gave a thumbs-up and they rose smoothly, lifted above the jungle and floated away.

As quickly as they landed at Kontum, a SOG C-130 Blackbird was there to rush the captured documents to Saigon. Analysts could not believe the windfall: The bag contained a partial roster of enemy double agents and spies operating inside South Vietnam. The CIA and the South Vietnamese Central Intelligence Organization used the roster to apprehend a number of important enemy agents.*

Even while the documents RT Florida had captured were still being analyzed, an angry Prince Sihanouk complained publicly that northeast Cambodia's Ratanakiri Province was "practically North Vietnamese territory," its inhabitants being taxed and impressed for labor gangs. Sihanouk secretly withheld supplies from the NVA through September, when he reached a new accommodation—he thought.

To balance the growing NVA threat, Sihanouk renewed diplomatic relations with the United States in June, but true to form, ten days later he vacillated and allowed the Viet Cong to open an embassy in Phnom Penh. Then on 31 July, amid the secret bombing, Sihanouk invited President Nixon to visit Cambodia. By the end of 1969 Sihanouk's political double-dealing was wearing thin.

In one of SOG's first Cambodia penetrations of 1970, Kontum-based RT Vermont landed in heavily jungled Ratanakiri Province on 5 January to search for enemy base camps. One-Zero Staff Sergeant Franklin "Doug" Miller's point man came upon a thin cord tied across a trail and, not believing the enemy would booby-trap his own thoroughfare, he yanked on it. Instantly there was a tremendous roar and four team members collapsed, seriously wounded.

With half his men incapacitated and the enemy now alerted to their presence, Miller hastily helped bandage the wounded and told his One-One to take them to defensible terrain on a nearby hilltop. All alone, Miller would stay there to take on the NVA.

Minutes later a forty-man NVA platoon approached. Miller's quick CAR-15 bursts knocked down several, then the rest massed to assault him, but using well-aimed shots he single-handedly held them off. Miller fell back and repeated the routine, ambushing then repelling a deter-

*The documents also confirmed the identity of a South Vietnamese double agent executed by order of Colonel Robert Rheault, 5th Special Forces Group commander, in May 1969. Charged with murder and held for several months, Colonel Rheault was freed soon after Ken Worthley seized the documents, though they were never cited as contributing to his release.

mined assault by dozens of NVA, and this time his deadly fire threw them back in disorder.

Rejoining RT Vermont, Miller radioed for an extraction, then moved the team 175 yards to the only suitable LZ, a bomb crater around which he arranged a perimeter. As an evacuation Huey hovered just beyond reach, the enemy let loose with AKs and RPGs, drove off the rescue bird, then attacked RT Vermont. Miller led the team in a valiant defense that drove back the enemy, but by now every single man had been wounded, including Miller, who'd taken an AK slug in his left arm.

Despite his wound, One-Zero Miller led the team to a more protected position, then again single-handedly advanced to meet the NVA. From his forward exposed position, he twice repelled the enemy before a Bright Light team landed and helped evacuate his team.

Miller was awarded SOG's seventh Medal of Honor.

Northeast Cambodia was getting hot, very hot. On 9 January a CCS team led by Sergeant First Class Larry Bartlett, with Sergeant Richard Thomas as One-One, was moving toward an LZ about 30 miles south of where RT Vermont had been hit when a large NVA force pounced on them, killing both Americans. A Bright Light team inserted, fought its way through an NVA force, losing one Yard, and recovered their bodies.

That January, February and March of 1970, while Prince Sihanouk was on his annual sojourn at an exclusive French health spa, the NVA were openly challenging Cambodian Army units. Then the Cambodian public became incensed to learn Sihanouk's wife and relatives were making money from the North Vietnamese.

On 11 March, thousands of Cambodian nationalists sacked the North Vietnamese and Viet Cong embassies in Phnom Penh; the next day, Cambodian Deputy Prime Minister Sirik Matak, Sihanouk's cousin, announced a 10,000-man expansion of Cambodia's 35,000-man Army; one day later, Prime Minister Lon Nol kicked out the entire North Vietnamese Army, giving them forty-eight hours to vacate. The ultimatum seemed as poorly thought out as Sihanouk's earlier appeasement; it allowed no time for the NVA to withdraw and no place to go—if they crossed into South Vietnam, certainly the Americans would attack them.

Politically desperate, Sihanouk left France for Moscow and Peking "to ask them to curb the activities of the Viet Cong and Viet Minh [NVA] in my country." While he was in Moscow, the Cambodian Parliament voted unanimously to remove the absent prince from power, replacing him with Prime Minister Lon Nol.

Three days later, RT Pennsylvania, led by First Lieutenant Jerry Poole, inserted in Ratanakiri Province for an area recon. Pennsylvania's One-One was Sergeant First Class John Boronski, with Staff Sergeant Gary Harned as One-Two. They experienced three days of near contacts and evading trackers before Lloyd O'Daniels brought out helicopters to extract them. He watched their Huey go in, watched the team rush aboard, then saw it lift away and rise to 100 feet—where an RPG round blew it apart so completely that, like a plane falling into the sea, its passage left no trace in the treetops. RT Pennsylvania no longer existed; there was no attempt to retrieve the bodies.*

As intelligence was starting to show, the NVA were on the march, grabbing territory west and north of the sanctuaries; Svay Rieng Province fell within days, while other NVA forces drove southward to force Cambodian units from the Parrot's Beak. Within two weeks the NVA had doubled its occupied territory, completely controlling two of Cambodia's seventeen provinces and besieging five more. They readied their Khmer Rouge proxies to take over as soon as Phnom Penh collapsed.

Cambodia's desperate government announced its country had been invaded by North Vietnam and appealed worldwide for military aid. In response, the U.S. discreetly supplied three thousand AKs.

In central Cambodia, Sergeants Troy Gilley, Ben Lyons and Charles Chapin were sent to confirm a new way station built to accommodate VIPs, which they found along a trail exactly where SOG intel officers said it would be. They were extracted and three days later reinserted at a precise point just north of the VIP hootches, where they had been told to prepare an ambush.

Soon an NVA column arrived with an elephant, on which they'd foolishly loaded most of their combat gear. The One-Zero had his team's M-79 grenadier initiate contact with one well-placed shot in the

*The lost Huey crew were Captain Michael O'Donnell, Warrant Officer John Hosken and Specialists Four Rudy Becerra and Berman Gande, Jr.

pachyderm's leg, "and the poor old elephant just started stampeding," Lyons said. Between the team's fire and the pain-maddened elephant, the NVA put up a miserable defense.

Minutes later a flight of Green Hornet gunships arrived: Attacking the enemy in open terrain that provided almost no cover, they inflicted catastrophic casualties. The team escaped without a man wounded.

Brought to Saigon for debrief, Troy Gilley learned the NVA column was escorting two enemy generals, both of whom, SOG intelligence had independently confirmed, were dead. It was also clear that the NVA were evacuating senior officers and staffs deeper into Cambodia to escape a feared American ground attack into the sanctuaries.

President Nixon had been considering exactly such an invasion for several weeks, realizing his continuing troop withdrawals would soon make such an operation impossible. Since mid-1969 he'd withdrawn 115,000 soldiers, and had just announced another 60,000 drawdown for 1970.

On the night of Saturday, 25 April, Nixon had several friends at the White House to watch the film *Patton*. Apparently stirred by George C. Scott's Oscar-winning performance, the next day Nixon signed a presidential order authorizing the Cambodian invasion. But when Nixon addressed the nation on 30 April, his imagination fired by visions of seizing something decisive, he erred in citing COSVN—"the headquarters for the entire Communist military operation in South Vietnam," he termed it—as a major objective.

The media portrayed the headquarters complete with Hollywood-inspired images of concrete bunkers and sliding steel doors. SOG, however, had a clear picture of COSVN, described by recon man Ben Lyons as "a large area with a lot of small staffs and generals interconnected with communication lines, but it wasn't one great big target that you could take some kind of big butterfly net, drop over it and scoop it all up."

Weeks earlier, a predawn B-52 strike had impacted within a half mile of COSVN. "Around us the ground began to heave spasmodically," an enemy survivor reported, "and we were engulfed in a monstrous roar." Four days later they abandoned the camp and fled westward, carrying just cold rice balls for food. That day U.S. fighters and helicopter gunships struck their column, directed apparently by a CCS recon team.

The media gave the impression U.S. units were stumbling around blindly in Cambodia, but SOG had plotted all major sanctuaries months and even years earlier. American units did not realize they were receiving SOG intelligence because it was filtered through MACV and attributed to SOG's cover source, the "Friendly Guerrilla Unit." In a few cases, invading American units came up empty-handed, but that was exceptional.

While ARVN units swept through the open paddy land of the Parrot's Beak, the 1st Air Cavalry Division's 3d Brigade, the 11th Armored Cavalry Regiment and the ARVN 3d Airborne Brigade, attacked the heavily occupied Fishhook. MACV J-2 had estimated some seven thousand NVA in the Fishhook, but U.S. forces discovered three quarters of them had fled.

Then the 11th Armored Cavalry Regiment fought its way to a French plantation near Snuol only to learn the bulk of the 5th NVA Division had passed through three days earlier and escaped beyond the eighteen-mile invasion boundary.

U.S. 4th Infantry Division troops who'd already crated their gear for withdrawal unpacked and went back into combat, demonstrating that when given a mission, American troops are ready for action and fight well. Southwest of Pleiku they captured a hospital complex, complete with modern X-ray equipment, and seized the invasion's largest rice cache, 500 tons (200 truckloads).

Meanwhile, the 1st Air Cavalry Division's 1st Battalion, 5th Cavalry, seized the enemy's largest Cambodian base even while NVA trucks were trying to evacuate it. Nicknamed "The City," the 7th NVA Division's depot was a mile wide and 2 miles long, with hundreds of structures—classrooms, mess halls, livestock pens, even a rest area with a swimming pool. The City yielded 171 tons of ammunition, 38 tons of food and 1500 weapons.

Another major NVA depot, dubbed Rock Island East by the 1st Air Cav's 12th Cavalry troops who captured it, measured ten city blocks long and five blocks wide, and contained twenty-eight piles of palletized munitions and supplies. The haul totaled 326 tons of ordnance and more than a thousand weapons. When Army engineers detonated the cache, U.S. Army artillerymen at a firebase 30 miles away could see the resulting mushroom cloud.

A third enormous find was Shakey's Hill, beside Cambodian Highway 14, named after the 7th Cavalry private who died seizing it, nine-teen-year-old Chris "Shakey" Keffalos of Albuquerque, New Mexico. The hill yielded 203 tons of supplies and ammunition.

One major enemy sanctuary went untouched. The concentration of NVA in northeast Ratanakiri Province, known as Base Area 609, were well entrenched in terrain so rugged that an attack would have incurred heavy U.S. casualties.

Specially tasked B-52s repeatedly hit COSVN's suspected retreat route, resulting in "the most significant" Arc Light of May, which struck an encampment northwest of Mimot; afterward U.S. 25th Division soldiers found 101 enemy bodies and a velvet sack containing a stamp imprinted with the Vietnamese characters for "COSVN."

That very morning I was a dozen miles from there, leading RT California with John Yancey, Galen Musselman and Rex Jaco, when our point man halted us for an amazing discovery: A beaten trail 3 yards wide, on which all organic matter had been pulverized beneath thousands of marching feet, heading northwest. Earlier that morning we'd found a fresh campsite, 800 yards square, where a regiment had spent the night. As quickly as we reported the fresh tracks we were extracted to clear the way for an immediate Arc Light, but we never learned the results.

One enemy officer wrote after the war: "I do not know whether the Americans and Saigon government military analysts realized how close they were to annihilating or capturing the core of the southern resistance."

What saved the North Vietnamese was the 30-kilometer (18-mile) operations limit, beyond which U.S. forces were forbidden to penetrate. It was a surprise that the boundary applied to SOG, but CCS was so swamped with requirements that there weren't enough teams even for the authorized 18-mile zone. SOG shifted teams from Danang and Kontum to help in central Cambodia. My own RT California ran two CCS missions during the invasion.

By 30 June, the last American units were withdrawn from Cambodia after seizing nearly 23,000 AKs and submachine guns—seventy-four battalions' worth—plus 2500 machine guns and mortars, 62,000 hand grenades, 15 million rounds of small-arms ammo, and 143,000 rockets and mortar rounds (an amount equal to what the enemy had fired in

South Vietnam in fourteen months) plus 7000 tons of rice, enough to feed all enemy forces in South Vietnam for four months, and capturing or destroying 435 vehicles.

Allied forces had killed 11,349 Communist troops and captured 2,328 against 284 Americans killed, 13 missing and 2,339 wounded, as well as ARVN casualties of 800 killed and 3,410 wounded.

Before the invasion, U.S. fatalities in South Vietnam had climbed to four hundred per week; afterward, for the first time in four years, fewer than one hundred GIs died per week. Furthermore, the invasion preempted two enemy offensives slated for 1970 and all but ended fighting in III and IV Corps Tactical Zones for nearly two years.

President Nixon enforced covertly what he'd announced overtly: Along with those of other U.S. forces, American-led SOG missions in Cambodia ended on 30 June. The ten Ban Me Thuot U.S.-led recon teams were transferred, five to CCN at Danang and five to CCC at Kontum, leaving Cambodia entirely an ARVN responsibility.

It says much for the enemy's strategic vision that even while U.S. troops were destroying his hard-earned supplies by the thousands of tons, the NVA was attacking westward to secure new base areas and lines of communications deeper in Cambodia and southern Laos. Northern Cambodia's two largest towns, Kratie and Stung Treng, soon were in NVA hands, as was a 125-mile stretch of the Mekong River. The NVA now held one third of the country. And in adjacent southern Laos the NVA had pushed west from the Ho Chi Minh Trail corridor, seized the provincial capital of Attopeu on 28 April and secured both a major waterway, the Se Kong River, and a highway, Route 18, well beyond SOG's Laotian area of operations.

As SOG withdrew the last of its American assets from Cambodia in June, a new Chief SOG arrived in Saigon, the cigar-chewing three-war veteran, Colonel John "Skip" Sadler.

A combat paratrooper in World War II, Sadler had fought in New Guinea and the Philippines with the same 11th Airborne Division regiment as the old friend he replaced, Colonel Steve Cavanaugh. After WW II, he was a paratroop instructor at Fort Benning and one of the Army's leading parachute experts, serving on the Airborne Department tactics and techniques board. It was as a captain in the Pathfinder section that Jack Singlaub first met Skip Sadler; he was still a captain when Sadler served his first stint in the secret wars, as Singlaub's parachuting specialist in Korea on the CIA-affiliated Joint Advisory Commission, Korea (JACK).

After Korea, Sadler served with Special Forces at Fort Bragg, then did another secret-war stint with the CIA's Project White Star in Laos. He was the 8th Division chief of staff in Germany in 1970 when Colonel Cavanaugh phoned and asked if he wanted to be Chief SOG; Sadler said he'd be in Saigon twenty-four hours after he could be released from his assignment.

14

GUNS OF THE
HATCHET FORCES

Just before 10 P.M., 3 March 1969, ten PT-76 tanks and a battalion from the NVA 66th Infantry Regiment assembled in the dark jungle 700 yards west of an encircled outpost in South Vietnam's Central Highlands. For the first time since overrunning Lang Vei a year earlier, the North Vietnamese were about to send tanks into action, this time against Ben Het, a Special Forces camp three miles from the Laos border.

Behind concentric layers of barbed wire and minefields, Ben Het's dozen Green Berets and 1500 Montagnards had been reinforced with four U.S. tanks, several Special Forces–led companies of Montagnard mercenaries, "Mike Forces," plus an American artillery battery with powerful 8-inch howitzers and 175mm guns.

Arrayed against them were the NVA 28th and 66th Infantry Regiments, several artillery battalions and now a company of armor. As at Khe Sanh, enemy leaders code-named their objective Dien Bien Phu in hopes the French disaster's ghost would inspire Communist troops and intimidate the defenders. As at Dien Bien Phu and Khe Sanh, the NVA incessantly pounded Ben Het with mortars, rockets and artillery. Ambushes had cut off the only road, while massed antiaircraft guns attempted to drive off the USAF cargo planes that airdropped Ben Het's supplies.

Unlike the armor attack a year earlier on Lang Vei, though, here at Ben Het the defenders were properly armed and, thanks to SOG intelligence, well informed.

As fast as they left the dark jungle the evening of 3 March, the NVA tanks hit a minefield; then, U.S. tanks and recoilless rifles from Ben Het's westernmost hill slammed into them. Almost as fast, USAF fighters peppered them with cannon fire and cluster bombs; then a salvo from U.S. Army 8-inch guns riddled them.

Participants might forever argue about who hit what first, but not one NVA vehicle advanced 100 yards. Inept though that armor attack proved, the bomb-pocked hillsides facing Ben Het were still extremely dangerous, with the defenders badly outnumbered, cut off and more NVA pouring across the border each day.

Would the enemy launch a more effective attack the next night?

At daylight on Laotian Highway 110, a dozen miles west of Ben Het, NVA sentries patrolled truck parks and way stations piled high with ammunition ready to be moved toward the battle. Early March was the height of the dry season, Highway 110 was clear and open, and engineers were in place to repair Arc Light bomb craters or landslides in hours. The Americans could do nothing to disrupt the attack on Ben Het.

NVA sentries along Highway 110 that morning heard helicopters approaching from the east, but that wasn't unusual; they fired signal shots to alert everyone within earshot, then trotted below overhanging branches as the sound grew—and as it grew they could discern many helicopters, and that *was* unusual. Then A-1 Skyraiders flashed past, scattering cluster bombs along the road, and six Cobra gunships appeared at the treetops, spewing rockets and minigun fire.

Two large flights of choppers crossed above the trees, settled on a naked hilltop overlooking Highway 110, then lifted away. Minutes later the NVA could hear work—chain saws? Yes! And the sound of shovels and picks striking earth. What was this?

On that morning, 4 March 1969, during the Ho Chi Minh Trail's annual traffic peak, with a major battle raging a dozen miles away at Ben Het, a SOG Hatchet Force company dug in and closed Highway 110. *It was audacious.*

Commanded by Captain Bobby Evans, Operation Spindown, as the roadblock was known, employed Hatchet Force Company A from Kontum, more than a hundred men who dug frantically to get below ground before NVA mortars arrived.

The hill they occupied offered ideal terrain for a roadblock. About 300 yards high, it overlooked Highway 110 on its northern slope. The highway was completely exposed because bomb strikes had wiped the jungle away. Beyond the road lay soft ground where a stream paralleled the highway. There was no way past the choke point; trucks had to run the gauntlet of Hatchet Force guns or not roll at all.

No sooner had the Hatchet Force men finished their bunkers that afternoon than NVA mortars began pounding the hilltop. It had little effect. That night the Americans watched the road with night-vision Starlite scopes. Whenever NVA tried to sneak past, the SOG men called in USAF AC-119 and AC-130 gunships on them.

In the dark, NVA climbed the hill to toss grenades and lob RPGs; by dawn they were out of sight, licking their wounds. Daylight also brought a contest between newly arrived antiaircraft guns and SOG choppers that whisked past the hill, kicking out ammo, food and water to the entrenched Hatchet Force. No helicopters were downed.

But that afternoon an F-4 accidentally dropped napalm on the hilltop, killing six Montagnards and badly burning several more. Then NVA mortars wounded the company's only recoilless rifle crew.

On Bright Light duty 25 miles away at Dak To, the RT South Carolina One-Zero announced he was qualified with the 90mm recoilless rifle; a half hour later he landed on the hill to take over the crewless antitank weapon.

That night the NVA tried to pin the Hatchet Force with mortars and run a convoy past, but the lead truck was spotted immediately. "In order to get the right trajectory I had to stand on one of those bunkers," the South Carolina One-Zero said. "I took aim and blasted that sucker." Caught in the open, the drivers abandoned their vehicles and ran while the SOG men stitched the cabs with M-60 machine guns and blasted them with mortars.

After a few quiet hours, Hatchet Force men watching the road with Starlite scopes spotted NVA creeping forward to salvage the trucks, so they opened fire again, the RT One-Zero reports. "We fired all three M-60s until the barrels got red and two of the guns finally jammed—we really kicked ass."

The action continued for six days, the Hatchet Force blocking southern Laos's most important highway during the peak of the dry season, not permitting one truck, one bicycle, even one porter to get past. Official records credited Hatchet Force guns with destroying six trucks while dozens more stacked up behind the roadblock, creating a perfect bombing target. Tons of enemy supplies piled up, too, more than local way stations could hide from air strikes. When U.S. fighters bombed just west of Company A's hilltop, the jungle shook with secondary explosions, and sooty diesel smoke obscured the sun.

There were only four U.S. wounded, among them Captain Evans and Staff Sergeant Tom Quinn, plus about twenty Yards. The only deaths were Yards. Their overworked medic, Sergeant Verlon Cantrell, was awarded the Silver Star, as was Captain Evans.

Operation Spindown succeeded famously: It disrupted the NVA timetable, forced the enemy to divert attention to its rear, compelled the Communists to expend ammunition needed to attack Ben Het, and weakened the very units the NVA most needed to carry through the Ben Het assault. And, of course, beleaguered Ben Het held.

In addition to this first-ever roadblock, Hatchet Force platoons and companies regularly conducted raids, laid mines, destroyed caches, or just walked roads looking for trouble. They usually found it.

When the Hatchet forces were organized in 1966, the U.S. ambassador to Laos limited SOG to platoon operations, with each mission subject to his approval. Several Chief SOGs sidestepped the ambassador's rules by reporting platoons in abutting areas when actually they fought together as a company. Official records disclose not one company operation in Laos in 1967–69 though there were several each year. In 1969 the rules were revised and SOG honestly could deploy up to a Hatchet Force company with approval from CINCPAC in Hawaii. Hatchet Forces reached their peak that year, when SOG had four companies divided among Danang, Kontum and Ban Me Thuot, each company comprised of three platoons of forty-two native soldiers and three U.S. Green Berets.

But Hatchet Force operations were infrequent due to inadequate helicopter support, for a deployed company required a dozen troop-carrying Hueys or Kingbees on strip alert, committed solely to them. Unlike a recon team, a Hatchet Force could not evade or hide; if a threatened platoon or company was not extracted immediately, superior

NVA forces would surround them, pulverize them with mortars and rockets and attempt to overrun them. For that reason even a few days' unflyable weather was dangerous, limiting Hatchet Force operations to fair-weather months only. Company operations required so much support—especially aircraft—that recon missions almost came to a halt while a Hatchet Force was on the ground. Under such operational and weather constraints, there could be only about two company-size operations per year.

Still, the threat posed by these SOG companies—along with the unrelenting day-to-day pressure of recon teams—forced the NVA to devote increasing security to the Ho Chi Minh Trail. At the start of Shining Brass in 1965, 30,000 NVA operated the Trail; by 1970, there were 70,000 troops assigned there, in addition to NVA units traveling on the Trail or resting in Laos after combat in South Vietnam. Even subtracting 40,000 engineers, truck drivers, antiaircraft crewmen and supply personnel, this left three full divisions—30,000 NVA—as rear security, kept out of battle by the fifty SOG Americans who operated in Laos at any given time, a ratio of 600:1 or *more than one battalion per Green Beret,* a fantastic economy of force.

Changed, too, were the enemy's attitudes about subtlety and obscurity; with continuous Arc Lights stripping away the jungle, exposing his roads and bunker areas, the enemy devoted less effort to concealing his presence. "It really surprised me how big and how blatant they were about it," remarked Sergeant Charlie Dodge, a Huey crew chief who flew for SOG. "[After bombs exposed sections of highway] they didn't bother camouflaging it again or moving it to a more rugged area."

Expanding NVA security reflected a heightened North Vietnamese frustration with SOG platoons, companies and teams that might pop up anywhere. And it sometimes must have seemed to the NVA that whenever they dropped their guard SOG forces hit them hardest.

At almost the same time as Operation Spindown, in early 1969, a Hatchet Force platoon from Danang was prowling the Laotian jungle west of Khe Sanh. Accompanying the platoon was its company commander, Captain Jim Storter, there to help educate two young lieutenants, Peter McMurray and Vincent Sabatinelli.*

---

*Both Hatchet Force lieutenants had less than six months to live; Sabatinelli was killed 25 July and McMurray on 27 August.

Due to some gap in NVA security, the Hatchet Force platoon drew no trackers and traveled cross-country without alerting anyone to its presence. The first night, the platoon set up a defensive perimeter. Much to everyone's surprise, about 3 A.M. the platoon heard approaching truck engines that stopped and shut down nearby.

At dawn, Captain Storter hailed a FAC, explained what they'd heard and had him scramble a pair of A-1 Skyraiders from Danang. When the planes were overhead, the platoon moved quietly westward, along the azimuth they'd recorded the previous night, toward where they'd last heard the trucks.

They advanced 300 yards, climbed a ridge and peered over the reverse slope into the little valley below. "From there you could see a clearing under the canopy and see into it," Storter said. The trucks were too heavily camouflaged to make out, but the Hatchet Force men knew they were there.

Rather than spook the NVA or get locked in a firefight, Storter just called in the A-1s. After ten minutes of strafing and bombing the platoon went down to assess the damage. "There were six trucks there and the strike got all six," Storter reports. "There were some bodies but no resistance whatsoever. Once the bombs started falling whoever else was there had beat feet."

Undoubtedly the NVA shifted hundreds of troops to go after Storter's platoon, but by then the Hatchet Force men were long gone.

Hatchet Force operations were taking a toll on the NVA supply flow at the very time the enemy's growing truck fleet demanded more fuel than ever. To boost fuel flow, the NVA laid a 6-inch pipeline from Vinh in North Vietnam through the Mu Gia Pass into Laos. A SOG Covey Rider was the first to detect the pipeline west of the DMZ, in September 1969, leading to several B-52 strikes, which temporarily cut it.

Soon the pipeline reached another 25 miles to the NVA 559th Group's forward headquarters in Target Oscar Eight southwest of Khe Sanh, then began to snake eastward toward South Vietnam's Ashau Valley. A major goal for both Hatchet Forces and recon teams became searching out the heavily defended pipeline to pinpoint and interdict it.

RT Kansas, led by One-Zero Eulis "Camel" Presley and One-One Julian "J.J." Fernandez, inserted west of the Ashau Valley to hunt along Highway 922 for the elusive pipeline.

NVA were everywhere, and trackers stayed tight on the team, nearly catching up with RT Kansas the first night. "It was eerie," Presley recalled. "You had this feeling, this eerie feeling." Evasive movement kept the recon men ahead another half day, but finally they made contact, shot their way out and were extracted.

A Hatchet Force platoon inserted shortly afterward with the same mission, but numerous NVA appeared at every turn and the SOG men could not fight through to the pipeline. After taking nearly half their number in casualties the platoon was extracted.

Eventually one SOG team crept up to a heavily guarded room-size mound of earth with a pipe coming out of it. A mound of earth with a pipe coming out of it could have been a lot of things, Colonel Cavanaugh, Chief SOG, thought, and asked the team leader what else he'd seen. But so many NVA patrolled the area that they were lucky they'd seen anything. "I was never so frustrated in my life," Cavanaugh reports.

General Abrams constantly asked whether SOG had reached the pipeline. There were a few aerial photos and FAC sightings, but analysts concluded most of the pipeline must have been hidden underground and along stream bottoms.

On 9 January 1970, the USAF mounted a night AC-130 Spectre strike on two suspected pumping stations west of the DMZ, igniting intense petroleum fires. An F-4 Phantom added 500-pound bombs, which spread the flames over an area the size of a city block and consumed sixteen trucks loading fuel. Over the next two days additional strikes destroyed another fifty-five trucks, including two oil tankers. Every 100 yards, it was learned, the NVA had installed a gate valve so they could shut down and repair any break, using stockpiled pipe and valves, then keep pumping fuel.

Complementing the oil pipeline was an ingenious exploitation of nature. The North Vietnamese floated half-filled oil drums on southward-flowing Laotian rivers. Carried by the monsoon-inflated current, the drums bounced along until reaching a cable the NVA had strung over a curve so that the current pushed the barrels to shore, just like magic. This was no small-scale effort: SOG and Seventh Air Force FACs spotted an estimated 10,000 barrels floating in Laotian rivers from 1 April to 10 June 1970 alone.

SOG forces shifted their focus to more conventional kinds of inter-diction. In January 1970 two recon teams watched NVA traffic on Highway 110 at night and called in fighters and AC-130 Spectre gun-ships, which destroyed twenty-five supply-laden trucks.

With the traffic flow nearing its annual peak, on 23 February 1970 SOG launched Operation Halfback, an attempt to repeat the previous year's successful roadblock, but the Hatchet Force commander, a cap-tain, had little combat experience. Kontum's Hatchet Force Company B did not just land atop a hill above Highway 110 but atop the same hill their sister company had occupied eleven months earlier. The NVA probably didn't expect another roadblock at the same spot, but there's much to be said about never attempting the same trick twice.

Like the previous year, the 107-man Hatchet Force carried in chain saws, shovels and seventy-five sandbags apiece, and no sooner did their insert aircraft pull away then they were digging like mad. That first day the Yards complained about filling all their sandbags; by the next day they were asking for more.

Air Force fighters strafed the road and sprinkled cluster bombs on adjacent hills to buy time for the company to prepare for the heavy in-direct fire that was sure to come. Platoon Sergeant Eulis Presley's men dug in facing Highway 110, which lay just 300 yards downslope.

Enemy fire began that afternoon with an occasional 82mm mortar round or 12.7mm (51-caliber) machine-gun burst; it had little effect, be-cause the NVA were just getting the range.

Unlike the first roadblock, this one had extensive signal intercept sup-port, with EC-47 planes droning over Laos to eavesdrop on enemy ra-dios, plus new intercept gear installed on SOG's Leghorn mountaintop relay site. Called a Polaris-II, Leghorn's state-of-the-art NSA system fit in a trailer-size container and could scan hundreds of frequencies per second to snatch NVA messages from the ether. It was awesome.

Awesome, too, was Company B's continuous fire support, from A-1s, F-4s and F-100s in daytime, and AC-130s and AC-119s at night. When air wasn't overhead or ground fog made bombing impossible, U.S. 175mm guns at Ben Het filled in, firing hundreds of rounds.

That first night the NVA pounded the hilltop with 165 rounds from 60mm and 82mm mortars and 57mm recoilless rifles. At one point the NVA let loose "a hellacious volume of fire" and attempted to rush a few trucks past, but a Spectre gunship spotted them. "The Air Force had a field day," one witness said. Ground probes began that night and would continue sporadically for the following five days. From that point on, Sergeant First Class Rich Ryan recalls, "I don't think we got any sleep."

The next morning an ARVN recon team landed a mile west to scout and draw some NVA attention from the Hatchet Force.

Later that morning, Eulis Presley watched intense AK fire rise toward an A-1 from a particular clump of jungle. He fired a magazine of tracers to mark the spot, then Covey rolled in, hit it with smoke rockets and called in Skyraiders; their bombs touched off explosions and fires—the NVA had been shooting from a truck park, which the Air Force now obliterated.

All day long, the Hatchet Force called in air on the road, and the NVA lobbed RPG and mortar rounds back at them. The SOG men used loudspeakers that night to invite enemy soldiers to *chieu hoi* (defect), but the only response was intensified mortar fire.

The ARVN recon team operating a mile west along Highway 110 hit an NVA platoon just after dawn; the team leader and another man were killed, and the rest had to be extracted.

A Kingbee attempted to land supplies on the hilltop, but NVA fire shattered its windshield; the chopper flew away then raced past low-level and kicked out cases of badly needed grenades that bounced across the narrow perimeter and off the hill. Enemy small-arms fire was becoming an almost continuous hazard. To counter it, the captain had the whole company fire all their weapons for sixty seconds—a "mad minute"—but the more numerous NVA shot back in spades, and one round hit Lieutenant Billy Potter square in the chest, badly wounding him.

A medevac Huey braved NVA fire to come in for Potter, and several men hurried him aboard; Company B's panicked first sergeant snuck on the Huey. "We didn't even know it until he was gone," Rich Ryan recalled, disgusted. "That was the only helicopter to get out that day."

Soon it was night again, and the NVA launched a determined full-scale assault. Eulis Presley switched on one of SOG's newest high-tech tools, a Miniponder, a cigarette carton–size device for electronically directing an AC-130 Spectre's 20mm Vulcans and dual 40mm cannons. "They brought it right on top of us and took [the pressure] off," Presley said, striking within 10 feet of the entrenched SOG men. The assault failed.

But by now the NVA had trucked in heavy antiaircraft guns, and their concentrated flak flashed in the night sky. "It got so bad that Spectre couldn't come in anymore," Presley said.

It was apparent the NVA were digging trenches up the hill, pouring in ever more fire and tightening the noose around the company. That night a flash message arrived in Kontum from NSA's liaison at SOG headquarters: The entire NVA 27th Infantry Regiment—1500-plus NVA—was en route to overwhelm the surrounded SOG company. Major Frank Jaks, the S-3 (operations officer), went to the Kontum-CCC commander and convinced him the Hatchet Force had to be extracted or the NVA would overrun them.

That night the captain told his troops to fire their ammo to lighten their load since they were coming out the next day. Platoon Sergeant Presley disobeyed the order, conserving his platoon's ammunition; had he not, his men could not have repulsed a heavy attack that struck just after midnight.

That desperate dawn Rich Ryan cheered up Sergeant Donald Milligan, telling him, "Don't worry, we're going to get out, no problem. Just don't worry about it." Almost on cue an NVA squad rushed the perimeter a few yards away and tossed grenades in two adjoining bunkers before the Yards shot them. Then an RPG rocket sailed through a firing port and exited the open back harmlessly. See, Ryan insisted, things weren't *that* bad.

Every NVA gun for miles was zeroed in on their hilltop. With heavy air support, the plan was, Company B would march 1 kilometer to an LZ and be extracted before the NVA could react. So they wouldn't have to carry their ambulatory wounded, a Kingbee headed in with medic William Boyle, but heavy fire found it, tracers tore into its skin, then it tipped sideways and fell to the ground. "The whole thing blew up, there was nothing left," Ryan said. "The whole damned place was on fire."

Master Sergeant Boyle's body was not recovered.

Another South Vietnamese Kingbee came in but it was so badly shot up that it landed in their perimeter and shut down. A third Vietnamese helicopter tried to get in, but it crashed on the hill and set afire the disabled Kingbee. While they burned, the NVA mortared the company with tear gas to prevent any other choppers from landing: *No one is to get out,* the NVA were saying.

In his bunker, Presley was donning a gas mask when the last of his unwounded Montagnards came to tell him they were all going to die. They'd just killed four NVA in the trench line, and the weak perimeter was barely holding. "It was one of the only times that I've ever known, 'This is it,'" Presley said. He laid out his magazines and grenades and began wondering how much time they had left and where he'd be shot first.

Overhead, Sergeant First Class Lloyd O'Daniels, the supporting Covey Rider, was stacking up fighters for the most sophisticated series of air strikes he'd ever directed. First he brought in A-1s to lace the facing hillsides with CBU-19 cluster bombs containing a potent tear gas to disrupt NVA gunners' vision; then came F-4 Phantoms with time-delay cluster bombs that would explode for the next eight hours, creating a temporary minefield to cover B Company's rear; next, more Phantoms, with heavy 500-pound bombs to pound the route to the LZ and sweep it clean of any lurking NVA; then Cobra gunships with white phosphorous rockets to build a wall of smoke to mask the hill's abandonment.

While the company marched, O'Daniels would direct Phantoms to their front and any facing hillsides, while up close he'd bring in A-1s with 20mm cannons and cluster bombs. He would expend thirty-two Phantoms, carrying nearly *200 tons* of ordnance.

The march began poorly. The captain hesitated to leave the false security of the hill; it took O'Daniels' entire persuasive powers to get him moving.

The captain left the hill with the lead platoon; Presley's platoon followed with the wounded and dead; the third platoon brought up the rear. The column hadn't gone halfway to the LZ when Presley reported his slow-moving platoon was being left behind; O'Daniels radioed the captain to tell him to slow down and wait for Presley and the wounded to catch up. The captain seemed to be falling apart, afraid either to move or stop. O'Daniels shouted profanities at him, telling him all he had to do was pop smoke and all the air in Southeast Asia would dump bombs for him. He barely got the captain functioning again.

Another hour and they arrived at the LZ.

Heavy air support held back the NVA, but there was no time to lose.

To expedite loading and cram more men in each helicopter, the Hatchet Force was to abandon every piece of gear but their weapons and radios, pile it in the open, and an air strike later would destroy it.

Then the choppers came in. Sporadic fire attempted to disrupt the extraction, but it had little effect. Soon the only men left were Presley, the captain and the last of the wounded.

When the final Huey came in, the captain jumped aboard—violating the SOG ethic of a leader coming out last—while Presley struggled to carry a badly wounded Montagnard. Presley had to lay his CAR-15 and radio on the Huey's floor to lift the limp form—then ground fire forced the helicopter away but the captain stayed aboard with Presley's CAR-15, leaving the NCO alone and unarmed on the LZ with the unconscious Yard.

A Cobra gunship rolled in for a gun run, apparently thinking the LZ empty, and again that day, Presley thought it was all over; but the bird flashed by, rocked side to side and returned a moment later leading another Huey, which picked them up. The Montagnard died aboard the Huey.

Thirty minutes later, Lloyd O'Daniels landed at Dak To to greet the returning Hatchet Force and came upon the Kontum CCC commander. Instead of congratulating O'Daniels, the lieutenant colonel complained, "Sergeant O'Daniels, was it really necessary to use all that profanity?" O'Daniels put his hands in his pockets and turned away to keep from getting in trouble, thinking, "I'd just pulled off in my opinion the next thing to a miracle." A SOG colonel from Saigon shook his hand and said, "Good job, OD."

Based upon Air Force photo interpretation, the Hatchet Force was credited with killing or wounding eight hundred NVA, Presley was told. The only U.S. fatality was the medic, Bill Boyle; also lost were two South Vietnamese Kingbee crews and about ten Montagnards.

One more day, though, and all of them would have been lost.

The captain, who'd almost fallen apart, was awarded a Silver Star. "He shouldn't have been on the ground," Eulis Presley said later. "He just shouldn't have been there."

After Operation Halfback, Company B required six months of recruiting and training to rebuild, but by August 1970 they were in fighting trim and ready again for action. Their next Hatchet Force mission would prove to be SOG's most successful.

It began with a desperate request from the CIA's senior war planner in Bangkok. Atop the Bolovens Plateau in Laos he told the visiting Colonel Skip Sadler, who'd become Chief SOG in mid-1970, that a multibattalion force of Hmong mercenaries was engaged in an operation designed to recapture a strategic strongpoint and "they were getting the bejesus kicked out of them daily." With each passing day the danger grew that the entire force would be annihilated and Operation Honorable Dragon would fail, opening what remained of southern Laos to NVA domination. Could SOG insert a Hatchet Force near Chavane, 40 miles away, where the NVA had major rear-echelon facilities, and create such a ruckus that it would draw the enemy away?

It was no small request but on the other hand, here was virgin territory; no Hatchet Force had ever been within 45 miles of Chavane. But, Sadler noted, the target was 20 miles beyond SOG's authorized operations area and they'd need approval from the U.S. ambassador in Vientiane. "He's already approved it," the CIA officer announced.

Operation Tailwind, as it was code-named, was a "go." For the first time a SOG Hatchet Force would strike not where the enemy was strong—like COSVN or Oscar Eight or border sanctuaries—but raid deep where the enemy was weak and unprepared, which every Chief SOG since Donald Blackburn had advocated.

Company B at Kontum was alerted on 4 September 1970. Leading Operation Tailwind would be a powerful man with a friendly small-town demeanor, Captain Eugene McCarley. Personable and intelligent, he was well grounded in tactics, a confident former NCO with several Vietnam tours. The Yards preferred to fight for confident people.

McCarley could not tell his fifteen American subordinates where they were going but he warned it would be hot, and basically they were going to be bait. Bring lots of explosives, he ordered, because they should find lots of things to blow up.

While the Hatchet Force men readied, SOG photographer Ted Wicorek overflew the target area to snap photos along Highway 165, the Ho Chi Minh Trail's major east-west artery for supplies and troops destined for Danang and Chu Lai 100 miles to the east. Wicorek found a little valley with thatched huts, vegetable gardens and uncamouflaged roads, a mysterious Shangri-la with no sign of a military presence. His senses told him it didn't seem right.

That valley lay 60 miles northwest of the Dak To launch site, an impractical distance for Hueys, so SOG looked for heavy CH-53 Sikorskys to support Company B. The USAF 21st SOS CH-53s at Nakhon Phanom, Thailand, were already committed to CAS (Combined Area Studies); the only CH-53 squadron in South Vietnam was a USMC Sea Stallion outfit in Danang with no cross-border experience. They'd have to do.

Escorted by twelve USMC twin-engined Cobra gunships, the big Marine Sikorskys picked up Company B's 16 Americans and 110 Yards on 11 September, refueled at Dak To and, at noon, took off.

Operation Tailwind was under way.

The fifteen helicopters paralleled the remote border for 50 miles, then turned west into the high mountains of Laos. Almost right away gunners began tracking them, spraying the air with heavy machine guns. Inside the semitrailer-size cargo compartments, bullets cracked through the floors, punctuating the din of whining turbines, hit after hit after hit, sounding like someone shooting a tin can with a BB gun, but the huge choppers just kept lumbering between the jungled hills and limestone bluffs.

Inside one bird, blood sprayed on the ceiling and a Yard collapsed, badly wounded; everyone backed away while a medic treated him, then another round penetrated and another man fell, then another. Then the choppers slowed and began a wide orbit while Marine Cobras fired white phosphorous rockets to mask them from the antiaircraft guns. The Sea Stallions circled down, then the shooting almost stopped and the ramp doors dropped, disclosing bright sun and a lush green countryside.

Beneath a sky alive with fighters and gunships, the Hatchet Force men trotted to a woodline as the Sea Stallions lifted away. For the next four days, each day, all day, Cobras or A-1s or AC-130 Spectres would be overhead.

Captain McCarley wasted not a minute and immediately got his company under way, aggressively advancing to the northwest, because he knew any hesitation would allow the NVA to fix them, shell them and overrun them. So long as they kept moving, they kept the initiative.

As quickly as they left the LZ they heard telephones ringing; maneuvering toward the sound, the Hatchet Force men hit an NVA squad that fired a few rounds and fled. Then the point squad reported bunkers just a quarter mile from their LZ.

McCarley swung two platoons into a defensive perimeter while several squads swept through to see what they'd found. "It was amazing," said Specialist Five Craig Schmidt. A 500-yard-long line of earthen bunkers were crammed with 6-foot-long 122mm and 140mm rockets, *thousands of them*, intended for bombarding Danang and Chu Lai.

But that would not happen now. Hurriedly, Schmidt and Sergeant First Class Jim Brevelle laid a C-4 demolition charge in each of about twenty bunkers, linking them all together with det cord, and dual-priming it with time-delay detonators. As the company headed out they lit the thirty-minute fuses.

Company B had marched 1000 yards west when an explosion shook the ground followed by thirty secondaries, the prettiest music a Special Forces demo man can hear. Rockets would continue to cook off for twelve hours with the resounding echoes announcing a challenge: Come on down, try to stop us—*unless you come soon, we'll destroy everything within 10 miles.*

One NVA platoon took the challenge. McCarley shot it out with them for an hour, then backed off, called in several pairs of fighters on them, then swung around and continued heading west.

The fight left several Yards seriously wounded, so the Hatchet Force secured an LZ for medevac. Before a chopper could get there 150 NVA massed and assaulted. The Hatchet Force fought them off, pounded them with air and, carrying their wounded along, began moving west again.

By now it was almost dark, time to set up a perimeter for the night—at least that's what the NVA expected. Determined not to stop long enough for the enemy to mass superior forces against them, McCarley kept Company B moving.

All night the Hatchet Force bumped into NVA squads, and each time either a salvo from AC-130 gunships or a quick assault forced them aside. Nothing would stop the Hatchet Force; if they encountered NVA in strength, McCarley called air and swung right or left but kept moving. That whole night they marched west, deeper into Laos. The farther they marched, the bigger a threat they posed and the better they performed their diversionary role.

By dawn nine of the sixteen Americans and even more Montagnards had been wounded. The Hatchet Force medic, Sergeant Gary Rose, patched them up and kept them going.

Not long after sunrise they hit a small delay position manned by five NVA, then another forty NVA hit their left flank, supported by mortars and RPGs. Company B fought through the delay position and called air strikes on the others.

By midday the company was walking a ridge a half mile above Highway 165 when the jungle thinned and they could see the road where a long column of hundreds of NVA and a dozen trucks paralleled them. McCarley called in A-1s, destroying the trucks and scattering the infantry. "From the amount of men I saw on that road," Craig Schmidt said, "if they ever really knew where we were at, they could take us out."

To keep the enemy guessing, the tactically adroit McCarley kept off roads and main trails, hurrying instead along streambeds, small paths or thinly vegetated ridges. Each time the NVA blocked the Hatchet Force, he pounded them with Skyraiders or Cobras or Phantoms and bypassed them.

With over two dozen wounded, the Hatchet Force's forward movement was becoming impeded. To medevac the worst cases, a CH-53 arrived with two medics aboard, Staff Sergeant John Padgett and Sergeant John Browne. Heavy NVA fire greeted the big Sikorsky, slapping slugs through its thin aluminum skin. "You could move left and might get hit," Padgett said later, "you could move right and might get hit, so basically you stick your weapon out the window and fire and hope you don't get hit."

Lying on the CH-53's lowered ramp, Browne held Padgett by the belt while he reached for the wounded Yards the Hatchet Force medic, Gary Rose, offered up. Before the first casualty was aboard, enemy fire surged and the pilot had to climb away, banked right, and an RPG hit the Sikorsky amidships. Padgett is convinced God rode with that CH-53, for the antitank rocket punched through the bird's belly, flew through the cabin and through a gas tank, spewing high-octane fuel on everyone, but it didn't detonate. The chopper limped about 5 miles and sat down hard in the middle of an empty bunker area. Twenty minutes later another Marine CH-53 came in, and while the crews and medics climbed ladders to get aboard, enemy .51-caliber machine guns opened fire. The chopper managed to fly away but five minutes later made a forced landing, the second CH-53 lost that day. Another helicopter rescued them.

Afterward, Padgett removed his flak jacket and only then noticed a jagged tear in its protective Kevlar and a protruding shell splinter. "It was right over my heart," he said.

Back on the ground, the young Hatchet Force medic, Gary Rose, was now heavily pressed, hustling to keep men alive, helping carry the worst cases himself; several times he charged through fire to treat fallen Montagnards or Americans. "Many times he had three or four or five wounded at once," Craig Schmidt said.

Their second night they had to get some rest. Captain McCarley had them dig in on a knoll overlooking the road, the highest ground he could find. NVA probes began just after dusk, mostly RPGs lobbed from the darkness, answered by claymores and Spectre gunship fire. Few men slept.

One RPG rocket burst near Craig Schmidt, the demo man, and Gary Rose, the medic, spraying both with shrapnel; two nearby Montagnards were severely wounded. Ignoring his own injuries and the continuing fire, Rose crawled over and treated them. When others slept, Rose worked, when others ate, Rose worked. He never complained, just saved lives. "He was doing whatever it took to do the job," Schmidt said.

Sure the NVA would attack in strength at dawn, Captain McCarley had his troops up and under way by 4 A.M. Most Hatchet Force men were so tired they wanted to die; they'd fought their way 15 miles cross-country since landing, an extraordinary pace.

They'd marched west another three hours when the point took fire from a few NVA soldiers who fled into a bunker area. McCarley felt it was his to seize so he ordered an attack. After softening the NVA positions with air strikes and small-arms fire, the Hatchet Force men advanced. Craig Schmidt and another squad leader, Sergeant Manuel Orozco, got their Yards on line, and assaulted. The enemy fell back, abandoning a battalion-size base camp except for two bunkers held by cutoff NVA. While fire kept the enemy soldiers' heads down two Yards crept forward and rolled grenades inside.

The base camp was seized, but by now the friendly wounded had risen to forty-nine—nearly 50 percent casualties—and the overworked sole medic, Doc Rose, himself wounded twice, could barely keep up with the work.

While Rose performed miracles, the rest of the Hatchet Force searched the base camp's many hootches and bunkers. Fifty-four NVA bodies were discovered but none yielded significant intelligence. The camouflaged bunkers matched the terrain so perfectly they couldn't be seen 50 yards away; noticing the shrubs growing atop them, McCarley concluded the NVA had been there many months, probably several years. Along with four trucks, the most significant material finds were a 120mm mortar and 9 tons of rice.

Then one search party called Captain McCarley to a large bunker 12 feet below ground; inside were maps covering the walls and hundreds of pounds of documents stored in footlockers and pouches. Clearly this was not just a battalion base camp but a major logistical command center, probably the Binh Tram headquarters that controlled Highway 165.

Pack up all the documents, McCarley ordered, they would carry them out. Less than thirty minutes after seizing the camp, Company B was moving west again; behind them demolitions charges went off, destroying the four trucks.

Already burdened with wounded men, the Hatchet Force men were unhappy about the additional load of documents. Like any other exhausted soldier, Craig Schmidt thought, "Why in the heck do we need all this stuff, it's just going to weigh us down." Given the option of carrying three dead Montagnards or the documents, McCarley chose the documents. By now every American had been wounded, several twice.

The NVA stalked them at every turn, and now, three days into the mission, FACs overhead could see enemy units converging on Company B from two directions. It was time to get out. To expedite movement the Hatchet Force abandoned the jungle for a smooth road and poured on the speed. An NVA squad attempted to delay them, but a quick air strike and aggressive assault ended that. Then came word that the Marine CH-53s had launched and would be there in thirty minutes.

Despite his fatigue, McCarley fought smart and refused to use the first LZ they came upon, where enemy gunners on high ground too easily could fire down on the huge Sikorskys. Just before the choppers arrived, Company B encircled another LZ while a SOG Covey Rider, William "Country" Grimes, brought in A-1s with CBU-19 tear-gas bomblets to blind the antiaircraft gunners.

Then one CH-53 landed and lifted away with the worst wounded and most of the documents. NVA mortars began pounding the LZ, answered by F-4 Phantoms that pickled a dozen napalm canisters in a single pass.

Rather than get bogged down defending the threatened LZ, McCarley took the two remaining platoons to another LZ where suppressive fire and a sudden landing generated only moderate ground fire. A second platoon climbed into a CH-53 for a clean getaway. NVA by the hundreds were now streaming out of the hills and let loose a nearly constant barrage of gunfire and RPGs.

Down to his last platoon, McCarley boldly repeated his tactic of abandoning one LZ to go secure a new one. Cobras and A-1s hit ahead and behind the last forty Hatchet Force men as they moved, pounding the NVA with rockets, cannons and cluster bombs.

By the time they reached a field of elephant grass large enough to accommodate a CH-53, they learned the helicopter's station time had almost expired: Get out fast, they were told, or start evading. With NVA close behind, they trotted into the 6-foot-high grass just as that welcome bird came in for them.

Captain McCarley was the last man to climb aboard.

The extraction had been extraordinary, requiring strikes from seventy-two U.S. fighters, nearly a half-million tons of bombs, rockets and napalm. "If it wasn't for the air cover," one Company B veteran said, "there's no way we would have got out of there."

The SOG men had nothing but praise for the Marine pilots who flew repeatedly through heavy fire but never flinched. "Cool, real cool," was how one SOG man described them.

Company B's official casualties were 3 Montagnards killed and 33 wounded, along with all 16 Americans wounded. In three heavy days of fighting their guns killed 144 NVA, wounded another 50, with an estimated 288 enemy killed by air. Captain McCarley and 3 NCOs were recommended for the Silver Star, while that heroic medic, Gary Rose, who alone treated 49 wounded men, was submitted for the Distinguished Service Cross.

CIA leaders in Bangkok and Udorn, Thailand, were "most appreciative" that SOG's diversion had saved their threatened force. Not just that, but on the afternoon of 25 September, the Hmong mercenaries had assaulted all the way to the top of the NVA-held strongpoint and triumphantly swept it of Communist troops, liberating the Bolovens Plateau.

But the CIA's sentiment went unshared by senior MACV officers, who ignored the Hatchet Force's great achievement and complained that three multimillion-dollar CH-53s had been lost. From SOG headquarters, Lieutenant Colonel Galen Radke sent a staff officer to Kontum to see what could be salvaged from Tailwind to counter MACV's unreasonable criticisms.

That night the excited staff officer phoned Radke, "This will end up being something really great: I've got footlockers full of stuff up here." Those boxes of documents, Captain McCarley's horde, were rushed to the MACV J-2, who culled through them and found not nuggets but the mother lode: Four hundred pages contained what the U.S. command's most senior intelligence officer called, "the most significant collateral intelligence on the 559th Transportation Group since the beginning of the war."

Major General Potts, the MACV J-2, "was beside himself," Radke said. Potts called McCarley's footlockers "the greatest, most important intelligence find we've had in the past year." Reportedly the documents included detailed records of NVA supply shipments and codebooks. Chief SOG Colonel Sadler reported, "Potts and Abrams told me they didn't appreciate the full implications of [the 559th Group] until all those documents came back."

Tailwind's achievement was so great that rumors about it began to circulate in Saigon. Asked to comment upon hints of a dramatic ground success in Laos, a MACV spokesman told the Associated Press only, "There are no U.S. ground combat troops in Laos." The front page of the *New York Times* of 26 October 1970 carried the headline U.S. CASUALTIES REPORTED IN SECRET ACTIONS: SPECIAL FORCES SAID TO HAVE SUFFERED LOSSES THAT WERE NEVER DISCLOSED, and vaguely described Tailwind. "There are no U.S. ground combat troops in Laos," the U.S. command repeated.

Two weeks later, after press interest had declined, the Marine CH-53 and Cobra aircrews flew to Kontum to celebrate with Company B. They didn't have to buy a drink all night. "I can't say enough about those guys," said Craig Schmidt. "They were great."

Operation Tailwind proved the effectiveness of striking deep in the enemy's rear as SOG had advocated since the dawn of Shining Brass in 1965. The lesson was important, but it was too late to apply it: Operation Tailwind, SOG's most successful Hatchet Force raid, would also be its final company-size, cross-border mission. With more and more of the war transferred to the South Vietnamese, the Pentagon directed that SOG cease American-led Hatchet Force missions in Laos.

15

THE SEARCHERS

Preoccupied with agricultural matters, thirty-seven-year-old Michael Benge had scant else on his mind as he climbed into his jeep the evening of 28 January 1968, to drive from his Central Highlands home into Ban Me Thuot. A U.S. Agency for International Development (USAID) adviser bringing twentieth-century farming techniques to Vietnam, Benge had little idea the Tet Offensive was swirling his way until a band of armed men climbed from a ditch, halted his jeep and shoved him to the ground.

Benge tried to explain he was a noncombatant even as NVA soldiers bound his hands, took away his shoes and prodded him toward the jungle. When he slowed, an AK muzzle poked his back and reality hit him: He was a prisoner headed for Cambodia.

Joined by a dozen Vietnamese and Montagnard prisoners, the next day Benge arrived at a jungle camp where he watched a People's Court convict several Vietnamese captives. They were shot on the spot.

A few days later the USAID adviser was joined by two captured American missionaries, Betty Ann Olsen, thirty, a nurse from the leprosarium in Ban Me Thuot, and Henry Blood, fifty-three, who'd been translating the Bible into Montagnard dialects.

Already Betty Ann Olsen had witnessed the NVA shoot three missionaries despite their raised hands and pleas called out in Vietnamese. Blood had no idea what had become of his wife and three children, whom he'd not seen since his capture.

When the guards weren't watching, a Yard escaped; days later he was helping SOG analysts identify the jungle camp location. Under the Joint Personnel Recovery Center (JPRC), SOG dispatched five recon teams and three companies from the 173rd Airborne Brigade to search for the kidnapped American civilians. It would become SOG's longest and largest Bright Light effort.

SOG inserted the five teams on 18 February, ahead of where its planners thought the NVA party was going. Four of the teams found nothing.

The fifth team, led by Staff Sergeant Larry "Six Pack" White, with Specialist Five Grant Bollenback and four Montagnards, was sent to look for a cave at a specific grid coordinate. On their third day of searching they heard Vietnamese voices. Creeping forward, they saw about twenty-five NVA, but the enemy troops immediately spread in a tactical line—the team had been detected and the NVA were about to assault.

The recon men poured such furious fire on the more numerous NVA that they fell back. Despite enemy fire, White dashed forward to search for bodies; he hardly had time to pick up and shove a fistful of papers into his shirt when a large enemy force came crashing through the brush. With gunship support, White pulled his team back to an LZ. They were extracted an hour later.

SOG analysts translated the captured papers and found among them precise descriptions of American civilian POWs—Benge, Olsen and Blood were alive!

But alive did not mean well. Chained together and offered only a starvation diet so they'd be too weak to escape, the three prisoners continued toward Cambodia. After a month in the jungle, Benge contracted malaria, then Betty Olsen caught dengue fever. The North Vietnamese refused to treat them; they had to forage for much of their food.

SOG, though, was still on their trail. Another Montagnard captive escaped, and based upon his intelligence, SOG launched a raid one day later, on 7 April, using a CIA-affiliated Phoenix Program platoon. They found an abandoned camp and evidence the three Americans had been there only two days earlier.

In mid-May two more Yards escaped and reported Blood, Benge and Olsen were 35 miles from Ban Me Thout. SOG sent in a Phoenix Program team on 20 May that ran into an enemy company and narrowly broke free. Two more SOG teams were inserted five days later but came up empty-handed; the NVA already had moved on.

That summer of 1968, Henry Blood died of pneumonia without the NVA offering him so much as an aspirin. Benge and Olsen developed scurvy; their gums bled and unhealing skin sores covered their arms and legs. Betty Olsen's hair began falling out.

In late November, SOG inserted a fifteen-man team from Ban Me Thuot to follow up intelligence from another escapee. They encountered NVA before they reached the camp, then found it just evacuated.

During yet another forced march, Betty Ann Olsen grew weaker; when she lagged behind, the NVA would knock her down and drag her until she got back on her feet. When it became clear she was dying, Benge went to the NVA commander and requested medical help for her. The officer ignored him. It took her three days to die. Then Benge's party disappeared into Cambodia.

Forcing himself to eat bugs and roots, Mike Benge would survive his captivity. After his release in 1973, Larry White learned, Benge told debriefers he'd heard the first SOG firefight that almost rescued him.

Stationed at SOG's Saigon headquarters, Master Sergeant Sebastian "Tony" DeLuca could only shake his head at the failed nine-month effort to retrieve the kidnapped civilians. As the Joint Personnel Recovery Center's senior NCO and a SOG old hand, DeLuca understood the plight of POWs as few men ever would. A former One-Zero, he'd gone on to be recon first sergeant at CCS in Ban Me Thuot, then transferred to the JPRC.

Diplomatic concerns, DeLuca saw, often overshadowed cross-border POW rescue plans. On 5 September 1968 an agent reported two U.S. POWs near Thuong Thoi, 100 miles southwest of Saigon. SOG twice planned rescue missions but neither was authorized by Washington due to incomplete intelligence and sensitivity over adjacent Cambodia. On 21 September the POWs were moved into Cambodia's populous Parrot's Beak, scrubbing any possibility of Washington authorizing a rescue.

There were other camps, in Laos, DeLuca knew, outside SOG's area of operations, and no one was doing anything about those, either.

DeLuca knew SOG's attempts to ransom POWs at $5,000 apiece were hardly more productive. Captain Fred Caristo, a JPRC staff officer, met several times with an alleged Viet Cong POW camp commander in the Mekong Delta, offering him $25,000 cash if he brought out five Americans. Eventually Caristo determined that the "camp commander" was working a scam.

In another case, SOG negotiators offered a man who claimed to be a VC camp commander more than $100,000 for twenty-one U.S. POWs held near Tay Ninh. On 11 October 1970 JPRC officers even presented the enemy officer a personal letter from General Abrams comfirming the reward. Nothing ever came from it.

"A lot of people wanted money for information and if you checked around," JPRC Major Jim Rabdau said, "they're probably all selling it, and you're buying it from the same sources all over the place."

In July 1969, a Communist defector walked out of the jungle near Chu Lai and told debriefers he knew of a Communist hospital where a black GI was being held. SOG analysts quickly determined it was Specialist Four Larry Aiken, captured 13 May 1969. The defector agreed to lead a raiding force into the hospital, about 20 miles southwest of Chu Lai. SOG quickly obtained helicopters from the 101st Airborne Division, CIA-affiliated troops from a local Phoenix Program unit and an ARVN blocking force. On 10 July 1969, the allied force flew into a jungled valley and followed the defector into a carefully hidden enemy hospital complex. Though the rescue force advanced aggressively, the enemy already had fled, but not before hacking the young soldier's head with a machete—Larry Aiken was alive, just barely. Despite extraordinary efforts to treat him, Aiken never came out of his coma and succumbed after ten days. It was the closest DeLuca and JPRC had ever been to liberating a fellow American.

The most unfathomable impediments, Tony DeLuca thought, were political limitations that crippled POW recovery attempts in Laos and Cambodia. For instance, despite a friendly government taking power in Phnom Penh in 1970, U.S.-led SOG teams were not permitted to search Cambodia for POWs after the 30 June post-invasion pullout. The U.S. embassy in Phnom Penh and the Joint Chiefs reserved approval authority for any

Cambodian Bright Light, but not a single U.S.-led rescue mission was approved after 30 June 1970.

The situation was hardly more accommodating for POW Bright Lights into Laos. Since November 1969, the U.S. ambassador required advance coordination for POW rescues beyond SOG's 18-mile sector; records do not reflect how many requests were denied, but not a single SOG POW rescue mission was approved in Laos.

Intelligence was sometimes wrong, too. In early 1970 a SOG Bright Light team went into Cambodia to examine a pilot's survival symbol and found it was only deadfall.* "These logs just fell in that particular pattern and bleached out over the years," Ben Lyons said. But the team encountered NVA, and Master Sergeant Ralph Loff was hit badly and two other Americans sustained minor wounds.

Meanwhile MIA numbers continued to climb, especially in Laos. On 31 July 1969 a six-man SOG team led by Captain Dennis Neal and Specialist Four Mike Burns, was overrun 20 miles into Laos, near Highway 921. When last heard, one man's voice radioed, "Help, help, help, for God's sake, help!" A Bright Light team found no bodies, no sign of any kind. Then on 13 November 1969 Staff Sergeant Ronald Ray, One-Zero, and Sergeant Randy Suber, One-One, were overrun 20 miles west of the Ashau Valley near Laotian Highway 923. Dead or alive, they were in enemy hands.

Tony DeLuca recorded 104 additional Laotian MIAs in 1969 and by 1 September 1970, his wall map plotted where 59 other Americans were missing.†

"He used to come down and talk to me about this thing," Lieutenant Colonel Mike Radke said, "that he just couldn't pull anything off."

The plight of the POWs and MIAs grew and grew on DeLuca's conscience. The truth was, he concluded, the United States was going through the motions but there was no high-level emphasis; no one would ever be retrieved. In his gut, DeLuca knew something had to be done.

The catalyst came on 5 October 1970 when RT Fer De Lance was

---

*Survival symbols are modified letters and numbers memorized and displayed by downed aircrew for signaling passing aircraft.

†Of the 327 Americans missing in Laos, only ten would be released by the North Vietnamese.

overrun in Laos and its famed One-Zero, David Davidson, was lost.

An old friend of DeLuca's, Staff Sergeant David "Babysan" Davidson, was in his third year running SOG recon and was held second only to Jerry "Mad Dog" Shriver in respect and achievements at Ban Me Thuot.

"He was good in the woods," fellow One-Zero Sonny Franks said, "but he didn't mind a-scrappin' and when he got in a firefight he always got 'em out."

But Babysan didn't get them out that October afternoon of 1970, when RT Fer De Lance was on a Laotian ridge just south of Route 922, 10 miles west of the Ashau Valley. A Covey FAC arrived as Babysan reported NVA sweeping for them, but solid clouds covered the area. The FAC had to refuel, and by the time he returned, Babysan had been shot and had fallen down a slope. And now his One-One, Sergeant Fred Gassman, reported many NVA advancing from three sides. Then Gassman called, "I've been hit, and in the worst possible way." The radio went dead.

The next night one of Babysan's old recon buddies, Sergeant Frank Burkhart, former One-Zero of RTs Miter and Saw, sat alone in a Saigon bar, grieving Davidson's loss. "I was real upset," he explained, "so I was on a drunk."

A figure sat down in the booth opposite him, and he looked up to see Tony DeLuca. Burkhart said he wanted to lead a Bright Light after Babysan, but DeLuca only shook his head, insisting Davidson was dead and, instead, they should go after *living* Americans.

Burkhart's curiosity was piqued. DeLuca told him a disturbing tale. In late September an NVA lieutenant had defected to the Cambodian Army and told of a POW camp holding twelve U.S. prisoners. On 3 October SOG had inserted an Earth Angel team of former NVA that got within 500 yards of the camp before enemy patrols forced them away. Aerial photos had confirmed the camp was there. MACV J-2 even dispatched a polygrapher to Phnom Penh, and the defector passed the screening perfectly. The defector volunteered to accompany a rescue mission, but SOG was denied permission to mount an American-led operation.*

*Declassified records verify what DeLuca told Burkhart.

"He was upset that the government wouldn't do a damned thing about it," Burkhart said.

Then DeLuca confided he'd been working on something else, using his own intelligence, and this thing might actually come off. It was in Laos and—he paused, weighed whether he should say more, then grew silent, finished his drink and left.

The next morning Master Sergeant DeLuca did not arrive at SOG headquarters for duty. Instead he put on civilian clothes, took a taxi to Tan Son Nhut airport and boarded a Thai Air flight to Bangkok. Tucked away in a briefcase he carried his collection of gold chains, a small treasure worth thousands of dollars.

In Bangkok he met a mysterious Laotian woman he'd learned of through intelligence reports who claimed contacts with middlemen in Laos. With her assistance, DeLuca rode a train northeast to the Laotian frontier near Savannakhet. "And the last time anyone saw him," a SOG staff officer reports, "he was walking into Laos by himself, to go out there and try to find prisoners."

A few weeks later Major Ed Lesesne was called to the morgue at Nakhon Phanom Air Force Base in northeast Thailand to view a body. When the sheets were pulled away, he recognized it as Sebastian DeLuca. "He was shot to shit, man, shot eight or nine times," Lesesne said. "I don't know if it was execution style or not because by the time I was over to look at him he'd been cleaned up. But he was full of holes."

Burkhart heard DeLuca had run into a Royal Laotian Army patrol, got in a firefight and was killed. Then, realizing they'd mistakenly killed an American, the Laotians buried him. Equally, though, it may have been scam artists—or the North Vietnamese Trinh Sat. All DeLuca's gold, of course, had disappeared.

The identity of Tony DeLuca's killers and their motivation remain a mystery which the then-Chief SOG, Colonel Skip Sadler, could not resolve. "I don't know who did it, but I know that some of the CAS [Combined Area Studies] people reported it through CAS and they received the body."

Though Sebastian DeLuca died a selfless if misled patriot, the truth about his loss, until now, has been buried by classifying it Top Secret. He was presented no posthumous valor award since his was an unauthorized mission, conducted while AWOL.

Lieutenant Colonel Radke called DeLuca's fate "a tragic end."

"I feel so much compassion for the man because the whole idea of leaving these guys in there was so foreign to him that he just—I'm not going to say he broke—but he just decided to go in and take care of it himself," Frank Burkhart said. "I really was kind of hurt he didn't ask me to go along."

Tony DeLuca's unauthorized one-way mission was SOG's final American-led attempt to rescue POWs outside South Vietnam.

Bright Light rescues inside South Vietnam were as frustrating and difficult as those in Laos but here the problem was SOG's lack of authority to operate in-country. POW recovery inside South Vietnam was the responsibility of each corps area commander, and rarely did they place emphasis on it. "Trying to get somebody to go take a look, that was tough to do, particularly in-country because SOG wasn't dealing in-country, that was somebody else's job," JPRC Major Jim Rabdau explained.

"Because of the state of the war at the time," said SOG Lieutenant Colonel Radke, "there was no emphasis on trying to do these things. They talked about it a lot."

The major exception was a series of rescue attempts mounted by U.S. Navy SEALs assigned to SOG's Naval Advisory Detachment, and those with SEAL Teams One and Two, who put their all into POW recovery missions.

Operating in the Mekong Delta's bayou-like tangle of canals and swamps, the SEALs searched prodigiously during 1969–71, with numerous raids into suspected POW camps. Operating from small rubber boats, on 8 November 1971, SOG's SEAL-led Sea Commandos ran an especially sophisticated Mekong Delta mission in search of U.S. Army Staff Sergeant Gerasimo Arroyo-Baez.

Missing since 24 March 1969, Arroyo-Baez had been identified by six ARVN prisoners who'd escaped from a camp 50 miles from Vietnam's southernmost tip.

Disguised as Viet Cong, the Sea Commandos launched before dawn from the USS *Washtenaw County* and paddled to shore in rubber rafts. Two hundred yards from the camp they encountered a VC sentry who mistook them for fellow VC and told them six ARVN had escaped and a U.S. POW had been moved because they expected a rescue attempt.

When pressed for information on Arroyo-Baez the enemy soldier realized they were fakes, so they seized him. After a short firefight with other VC, the Sea Commandos escaped with their prisoner.

In Saigon, SOG officers made the prisoner an offer he couldn't refuse. They piled $5,000 before him: *Bring back Arroyo-Baez and this is yours,* they promised. Then they showed him a propaganda pamphlet with his photo and a caption that claimed he was working for the Americans. *Bring back Arroyo-Baez or this will be air dropped all over the Mekong Delta,* they warned. On 18 November a Sea Commando team escorted him back to the delta and fired shots in the air when the VC "escaped."

It seemed clever, but the VC was never heard from again.*

A few weeks earlier, two defectors were financially persuaded to lead a force into a Mekong Delta camp they claimed held two Americans. The raiders swarmed into the camp and found "partially cooked meals and miscellaneous equipment," a SOG report discloses. When they swept another nearby camp, "Warm rice indicated that the camp had been vacated only 2–3 hours before."

"It was very frustrating," Chief SOG Colonel Sadler said, "because it got to the point that you knew POWs had been there by writing on the wall and knots on the ropes."

SEAL Team One Master Gunners Mate Barry Enoch led several POW rescue missions. Most were originated by SOG, but one began with a Vietnamese woman who came to Enoch's SEAL platoon. Her husband was an ARVN soldier held by the VC, she reported, yet her VC contacts were strong enough that she'd just been allowed to visit him.

It was unfortunate but not a SEAL affair, it seemed.

But there were six American POWs there, too, she said, and that got their attention. Now they jotted down notes: The camp was on an island and the prisoners were held in small hootches concealed beneath overhanging tree limbs. Each hootch held six of them, had a guard, with bolt-action rifle or AK.

There was something fishy about her story, Enoch felt. "One thing about this type of operation," he said, "you're going on somebody else's

---

*Arroyo-Baez' remains were returned to the U.S. in 1985. The government of Vietnam could provide no explanation for his death.

intel, not your own, and it was always kind of spooky to us." It could be a trap designed to wipe out his whole platoon, he thought. Sensing his hesitance, the woman offered to guide them into the camp. Good enough, then, they'd go.

The next morning, before daylight, Enoch's SEAL platoon, heavily armed with Stoner 63s, M-60 machine guns and CAR-15s, was creeping toward the island camp, carefully bypassing the booby traps the woman pointed out. They'd come off boats and waded through mangrove swamp, then crept to the edge of the camp and waited for sunrise.

Organized as two six-man elements—one to rush through and eliminate the guards, the other to scramble into the hootches and secure the POWs—they began to sneak forward and had just spotted the VC around bubbling breakfast rice pots when a sentry challenged them. Instantly they rushed forward, shooting. The security team burst into each of the six hootches and found the grinning faces of 15 ARVN prisoners but not one American.

There'd been six guards, and all six lay dead.

As soon as they untied the ARVN soldiers, Enoch said, "They were all talkin' at the same time, and laughin' and grinnin' and hollerin'." Once over their initial euphoria, the liberated prisoners grabbed what booty they could carry, scooping up pigs, ducks and a sewing machine.

"But where did they take the Americans?" a SEAL asked through an interpreter. He got blank stares. "What Americans? There were never any Americans here," a liberated prisoner reported.

The SEALs looked around for the Vietnamese woman who'd guided them but already she was arm in arm with her freed husband, leading him away. Enoch realized that they'd been had.

Despite being well planned and aggressively executed, the SEAL POW rescue campaign never found a single American, although forty-nine ARVN prisoners were liberated. "After a while, after a number of POW rescue operations," Enoch said, "it got to where I didn't expect to see any Americans."

Another dramatic rescue effort began in early May 1971, when U.S. intelligence intercepted an NVA flash radio message: An American POW had escaped near Tchepone, Laos, and was fleeing cross-country. "They were just going bonkers," Colonel Roger Pezzelle, SOG's chief of ground operations, said. FACs and recon aircraft were scrambled to search the area, and 6 miles southeast of Tchepone one FAC sighted a distress symbol of stacked rocks in an open field. SOG determined the escapee was First Lieutenant Jack Butcher.

A Danang-based Covey FAC, Butcher had been shot down in his OV-10 on 24 March near Tchepone and captured upon landing. Despite suffering a broken jaw, he had been forced by his captors to talk on his survival radio, but he managed to warn away would-be rescuers. The search-and-rescue effort to bring him out was dropped.

Colonel Pezzelle and Major Charlie Beckwith, SACSA's Pacific Theater liaison, rushed a message to the Joint Chiefs. The response came in just two hours: If SOG positively located Butcher, the Joint Chiefs authorized inserting up to 365 Americans to get him out—*but first they had to find him.*

A dozen planes scoured Laos for any sight of Butcher and parachuted two SOG evasion kits, each containing food, compass, radio and weapon. Joining in the search was a SOG Blackbird flown by Colonel Bill Page, ready to employ the Fulton Recovery System to extract Butcher. "But he was never at one place long enough to get in to him," Page said.

Butcher was running for good reason. He was within 20 miles of the just-ended Lam Son 719 battle, where the NVA had massed twenty-eight regiments—nine divisions—and the enemy soon realized a SOG rescue mission was under way. To complicate SOG's job, the NVA laid out false survival symbols and inundated the area with small patrols and tracker dogs. "Here's this poor guy down there trying to survive with the whole North Vietnamese Army looking for him," Colonel Pezzelle said.

Despite the heavy enemy presence there was no shortage of SOG recon men eager to rescue Butcher. "We had guys volunteering, fighting to get on the helicopters to go," SOG's operations chief, Colonel Bobby Pinkerton, reports.

On 9 May, USAF Jolly Greens from Nakhon Phanom, Thailand, inserted an American-led Bright Light team to examine Butcher's original survival letter and confirmed it was real and fresh. Around it they found large footprints of a lone man, but forty-five minutes later they made contact and had to shoot their way out. They were flown back to Thailand.

By then a second all-volunteer team arrived at Nakhon Phanom, this one led by Sergeant Major Billy Waugh, "A real tiger, a gunslinger from the word 'go,'" Colonel Pinkerton said.

Waugh warned his men, five Americans and six Yards, they would move "brazenly and fast" and immediately began training while the aerial search continued.

The following day a FAC found another survival letter a realistic distance from the first letter for an evading man to have traveled. Major Ed Lesesne, SOG's Nakhon Phanom launch site commander, flashed that information to Saigon, and in three hours received a "go" from Washington to insert Billy Waugh.*

"Everybody was psyched," Lesesne said. In a few minutes Waugh's team was aboard a 21st SOS HH-53, escorted by a flight of A-1 Skyraiders, code-named "Sandy" when on SAR missions, en route to Tchepone. When the Jolly Green went into orbit, Waugh saw below him the evasion symbol pressed out in grass and wood between low rolling hills. Then the HH-53 hovered at 50 feet and winched Waugh and his men to the ground on a jungle penetrator.

Waugh realized they couldn't stay too long or they'd draw many NVA and make it even easier for the NVA to find Butcher, especially if he was drawn to the sound of their landing helicopter.

After checking the survival symbol, Waugh began walking wide circles. Many aircraft droned high above, including a SOG Blackbird flown by Colonel Bill Page, who'd already spent five days searching. "It was one of those things," he said, "where he'd let us know where he was and we'd go up there to get him but by that time the NVA would be so close to him that he'd have to move, then we'd lose him again." One SOG plane even used a loudspeaker to tell Butcher where to go and how to signal the planes.

Sergeant Major Waugh's team walked ever wider circles for seven hours but didn't find any sign of Butcher. "We couldn't find him and couldn't find his trail," Waugh said. Just before dark a Jolly Green extracted them.

---

*Eleven months earlier, SOG had retrieved a downed pilot, USMC First Lieutenant Larry Parsons, about 30 miles from the Butcher search scene. He had spent nineteen days behind enemy lines.

The SOG effort continued for ten days, then the NSA snatched a depressing message from the ether: The NVA had recaptured Lieutenant Butcher.*

Ed Lesesne estimates Waugh passed within 500 yards of Butcher. "We damned near got him," he said.

But SOG could not sustain an effort to find evadees and POWs, partially due to political fears in Washington after Congress imposed a ban on U.S. ground action in Laos. When a 10 May 1971 *Newsweek* article mistakenly alleged SOG teams still roamed Laos in violation of the ban on ground action there, those fears could only have been inflamed, and this helped doom further POW searches. From this point on, POWs were no longer a priority concern.

MACV twice requested Washington approval for POW-focused intelligence gathering in Laos, using American-led SOG teams, and the authority to launch rescue missions at General Abrams' discretion. "They equivocated for months," Chief SOG Colonel Sadler recalled. Finally, in June 1971, Abrams received the authority to insert American-led SOG forces into Laos for POW rescues. But the burden of proof, the justification for placing Americans on the ground, had become so great that never once would this actually happen. It was a Catch-22: Without U.S. recon teams looking for POW camps, none would ever be found, and without confirmation of such camps, there could be no rescues.

Though approval procedures and policies varied, from mid-1970 forward, every POW rescue SOG proposed for Cambodia or Laos using U.S. personnel was turned down in Washington. Meanwhile, men still were being lost and pilots downed inside South Vietnam but almost no one was left to go after them.

The last full U.S. division in Vietnam, the 1st Air Cavalry, was kept near Saigon to protect U.S. logistical centers, while elements of the 101st Airborne Division remained outside Danang, but neither unit was conducting offensive ground operations.

To handle downed pilot recoveries and POW rescues, SOG identified

---

*While both served in the Pentagon after the war, Colonel Pinkerton met Lieutenant Butcher. "He was never aware there was such a significant effort to find him," Pinkerton said. "I was struck by how appreciative he was of the effort."

a need for two special raider companies, reduced by MACV to two platoons and dubbed Combat Recon Platoons One and Two (CRP-1 and CRP-2). The concept was approved by the Joint Chiefs in May, and by General Abrams in June 1971, "to be effective only as long as MACV/SOG maintained an operational capability"—a cryptic qualifier since SOG, too, was now being cut back and its forces gradually disbanded.

CRP-2 was based at Danang, and CRP-1 at Kontum. Each platoon contained three recon teams combined as a single unit. Two of my old teams—RT California under Donald Davidson and RT Hawaii under Les Dover—constituted two thirds of CRP-1, with Larry Kramer's RT West Virginia the third, all led by Sergeant First Class Donald "Ranger" Melvin. The CRPs assumed POW rescue responsibilities throughout Southeast Asia but could do no more than U.S. policy allowed.

Inside South Vietnam, the emphasis on withdrawal impacted on POW rescues, sometimes tragically. In January 1972, SOG received photos of several NVA soldiers cultivating a field near Danang. "And lo and behold here's an American standing out there and when the plane went over this guy turned his face up in the air and they saw him, clear as a bell," a SOG officer said. "SOG analysts got these photos and said, 'Christ, there's an American.'"

As soon as he saw the evidence, General Abrams ordered, "Go!" MACV headquarters sent a message to the I Corps regional staff, ordering a battalion-size rescue mission.

"We thought it would be a one-two-three thing," the SOG officer went on. "So, nothing happens. The JPRC is going out of its mind." Abrams sent another message, offering SOG JPRC assistance to plan the operation, and again there was no response. "And finally, to my recollection, [Abrams] sent a third message and they said they had assigned a battalion to that mission and the battalion they assigned was a Marine battalion which was on ships off Danang, headed home.

"Launched quickly it would have been a great operation. But it was during that time when everybody was talking about not wanting to be the last guy killed in Vietnam," the SOG senior officer said.

On 24 February 1972, Los Angeles *Times* correspondent George McArthur warned that MACV was about to disband the SOG CRPs, "its last cloak-and-dagger outfit specifically honed to fight its way in and out of prisoner camps," which "had stirred heated words within the headquarters of U.S. General Creighton Abrams."

McArthur's exposé made no difference. In their haste to reduce U.S. personnel by twenty-five positions, MACV disbanded both CRPs, the last Bright Light elements left in Southeast Asia. Now there was no means left to react if prisoners were discovered or airmen downed behind enemy lines.

Thus, no Bright Light team was available six weeks later, on Easter Sunday 1972, four days into the largest NVA offensive of the war, when an RB-66 electronic jamming plane—call sign Bat-21—was hit by a SAM near the DMZ. Though Bat-21 had a crew of six, only one aviator got clear of the plane, USAF Lieutenant Colonel Iceal Hambleton, fifty-three, who broke a wrist and finger ejecting. In pain, Hambleton crawled away and hid himself in thick brush.

Unfortunately for Hambleton, he landed just below the DMZ, along the Mien Giang River near Cam Lo, where a multidivision NVA force was massing. Less than a mile west of Hambleton, the NVA had seized a bridge over the 150-yard-wide river. Concentrated there were SAMs, antiaircraft guns, at least a tank battalion, plus artillery and thousands of troops.

Soon, a FAC brought in A-1s around the injured navigator, and passing U.S. Army helicopters offered to go in after him. Heavy fire downed two choppers and drove the others away; one crew was retrieved but the other was lost, with the door gunner, Specialist Four José Astorga, taken prisoner and the other three crewmen killed: First Lieutenant Byron Kulland, Warrant Officer John Frink and Specialist Five Ronald Paschall.

The next morning an OV-10 FAC arrived to help Hambleton, but a SAM hit it, forcing Captain William Henderson and Lieutenant Mark Clark to eject. Henderson was captured. But Lieutenant Clark—namesake grandson of the WW II Allied commander in North Africa and Italy—evaded enemy searchers. Now there were two pilots to rescue, Hambleton and Clark.

To protect them, FACs directed up to ninety air strikes per day, everything from A-1s to B-52s, the latter with General Abrams' personal approval. Hambleton kept up his strength by eating banana stalks, green corn, roots and berries; enemy patrols passed within 5 feet of where he lay hidden.

After two days' bombing, an HH-53 Jolly Green was sent in to get Hambleton. As the chopper cleared the trees 100 yards from him, NVA guns knocked it down, killing all six aboard: Captain Peter Chapman, First Lieutenant John Call III and Sergeants Roy Prater, Allen Avery, James Alley and William Pearson.

Unable to risk another Jolly Green, the Seventh Air Force asked SOG's Blackbird squadron commander, Lieutenant Colonel Bob Pinard, to study extracting Hambleton with the Fulton Recovery System (Skyhook). Repeated Blackbird passes through SAMs and gunfire to drop then snag a Skyhook balloon, Pinard concluded, was tantamount to suicide.

The next day, 7 April, heavy gunfire near Hambleton and Clark knocked down another OV-10, carrying USAF First Lieutenant Bruce Walker and USMC First Lieutenant Larry Potts. The Marine officer reportedly died in captivity. Walker's last radio message was a warning not to come after him, that the NVA were closing in. Both men remain MIA.

Having already cost eleven airmen KIA or MIA, plus two men captured and five aircraft destroyed, the Air Force SAR effort was over. It was up to SOG now, which dispatched a JPRC staff officer, USMC Lieutenant Colonel Andrew Anderson, to the nearest ARVN outpost, a tiny position by Cam Lo, a mile east of the evading pilots on the river's south bank. Any aerial approach was impossible, Anderson could see, so he sent for a five-man SOG Naval Advisory Detachment (NAD) Sea Commando team from Danang and their adviser, SOG SEAL Lieutenant Tom Norris.

Lieutenant Clark was told to go to the river that night, inflate his survival vest and float downstream to where Norris and the Sea Commandos—disguised as VC in black pajamas and carrying AKs—would be waiting. But an NVA patrol arrived at the rendezvous, and the team had to let Clark float past. Norris's men crept around more NVA patrols and found Clark at dawn, exhausted, in shallow water.

They brought him back to Cam Lo.

Lieutenant Colonel Hambleton, too, was supposed to float downstream, but it had taken every bit of the fifty-three-year-old's stamina just to reach the river. After ten days virtually without food, he'd lost 45 pounds but still managed to creep and crawl a mile in pitch darkness.

Due to his injuries and exhaustion, however, he could not go on.

Norris and the Sea Commandos would have to go after Hambleton the next night.

By now several Sea Commandos had grown skittish, and only one volunteered to accompany Norris the second night, Petty Officer Nguyen Van Kiet. In the darkness the two of them boarded an abandoned sampan and, disguised as fishermen, paddled quietly upriver. In the foggy darkness they accidentally went all the way to the bustling Cam Lo bridge, where tanks and many troops were crossing, and they had to turn back. Finally they found Hambleton hiding under brush at the riverbank, delirious. They lifted the emaciated flyer into the sampan and hid him beneath leaves and branches and paddled away.

Several times they coasted quietly past NVA sentries, then just before dawn an enemy soldier began waving and shouting at them, ordering them to land; they pretended not to hear him. By dawn they were almost back at the ARVN outpost when a heavy machine gun opened up from the far bank; they took cover in high reeds and called in A-1s on the gun, then directed a pair of Phantoms to cover their final run-in. They landed safely.

By chance, a CBS News reporter arrived just as Hambleton was being carried away and said to Norris, "It must have been tough out there. I bet you wouldn't do that again."

The SOG SEAL's eyes flashed. "An American was down in enemy territory. *Of course I'd do it again.*" He turned and left.

His retort delighted Chief SOG Colonel Sadler, who said, "Oh, he was a tough, cocky little fucker. Fine man."

From his hospital bed in the Philippines, Hambleton told reporters, "I never lost hope." When he learned of the men lost trying to save him, he added, "It was a hell of a price to pay for one life. I'm very sorry."

Lieutenant Tom Norris received SOG's only SEAL Medal of Honor. His couragous subordinate, Nguyen Van Kiet, was awarded the Navy Cross—equal to the Army Distinguished Service Cross—the only Vietnamese to receive so high a U.S. award.

Two weeks later MACV disbanded SOG's Naval Advisory Detachment.

Why had so many SOG POW rescue missions failed? Colonel Bobby Pinkerton chalked much of it up to late intelligence. "The common problem with all the JPRC operations was late intelligence, we never got timely intelligence."

Major Ed Lesesne elaborates on the problem. "Most of the intelligence we got was very perishable," he said, "because you're taking a snapshot of a moving train, the whole enemy logistic system, the whole Ho Chi Minh Trail system, everything they did they kept on the move."

And certainly the enemy frequently moved American POWs.

But that only partly explains some troubling statistics: During the entire war, SOG-initiated raids liberated 492 ARVN but not one living American. By sheer chance there should have been, say, 10 percent—forty-nine Americans rescued—*even at 1 percent it would have been five Americans*. Why not even *one* American?

A sickening likelihood arises, reminiscent of the doubled agent teams in North Vietnam: *Compromise.*

SOG *had* been penetrated. The identities of the moles would soon come to light.

16

FIGHTING SOLDIERS
FROM THE SKY

In SOG's first Bright Light mission, in 1966, two VC battalions massacred Huckleberry Lewis and Charlie Vessels and their entire platoon. In all but one subsequent POW rescue raid, Chief SOG Jack Singlaub noted, "the evidence was that the Americans had left within an hour or just a few hours before we got there." Singlaub began to wonder.

"For a long time I thought it was operational security," he added, meaning inadvertent disclosures through radio messages, conspicuous overflights and such. Disclosure could not have happened through an enemy mole, Singlaub believed, because the only ARVN officer outside SOG he told of these missions was Chairman of the Joint Staff General Cao Van Vien, a courtesy recommended by General Westmoreland. Vien promised to tell no one; just to be safe, Singlaub disclosed nothing to Vien until twenty-four hours before an operation so the enemy wouldn't have enough time to react even if Vien leaked it.

U.S.-led recon teams had been compromised, too, thought Major Ed Rybat, the FOB 1 commander, observing that often "it looked like they knew we were coming." By 1969 the problem had grown so that Singlaub's replacement, Colonel Steve Cavananugh, too, initially thought it an operational security shortcoming.

Cavanaugh personally visited each FOB to ask the One-Zeros what could be done to keep their teams on the ground, and he brought in the Army Security Agency (ASA) to monitor SOG radios and phones. I sat through the February 1969 ASA debrief, conducted by the 101st Radio Research Company, which found "very pressing requirements for secure voice communications in all MAC/SOG systems." The Saigon staff seemed convinced this was a solution, but most recon men already were careful about encrypting and disclosing nothing on the radio—after all, they were the ones who would die.

The teams knew the NVA was monitoring their radios, verified beyond question on an occasion when an evading RT switched on an emergency radio and heard it in stereo; another emergency radio, in the hands of an NVA officer just 30 yards away, was repeating the "beep-beep-beep" of their beacon. They shut off their radio and crept away.

Cavanaugh concluded the radio security problem was serious, so in mid-1969 he directed that teams carry the KY-38 secure voice system, a 50-pound device as big as a shopping bag that connected to a team's normal PRC-25 radio. Just as certainly as Cavanaugh believed the KY-38s would help recon men, the men believed the bulky units endangered them by slowing their movement.

Unsure where the compromises originated, recon men took no chances: One-Zero Steve Keever decided "if we were going to send in a coordinate, we were going to be 200 meters north of that." The practice was widespread.

Another way to improve recon team survival, Chief SOG Cavanaugh thought, was inserting teams beyond SOG's 20-kilometer limit. "They had our LZs pretty well pegged," he said. "I finally went back to Washington and asked for authority to insert deeper, and I would have got it but for [U.S. ambassador to Laos William] Sullivan.

"We were supposed to let [the embassy in Laos] know every time we were putting a team in, which we did. Maybe that was where we were getting compromised, I don't know."

What else could be done? One possibility was night landings. There were no enemy LZ Watchers at night because Hueys and Kingbees couldn't land safely in darkness. But teams could parachute in darkness, and that would complicate NVA countermeasures considerably.

Thus, when RT Auger One-Zero Frank Oppel requested permission to parachute into Cambodia's Fishhook in December 1969, SOG head-quarters approved it immediately. The only problem was, when Oppel went to his One-One with the good news, the One-One said he wouldn't go. Oppel had to find a replacement.

That night he invited his old friend Bob Graham to play Chinese checkers and drink, their favorite avocations. While Oppel sipped his scotch and root beer, he plied his friend with liquor—and let him get ahead in the game. Then the unscrupulous Oppel described his coming airborne adventure, the first in the history of CCS, and told how his own One-One had failed him. How could the drunken Graham resist? "Well, shit, Frank, *I'll* go with you," he said. The sucker was snared!

First thing next morning, Oppel rushed to tell the S-3 that he'd found another man of steel, then he went to Graham to announce, "Well, we're on."

The previous night's liquor had wiped clean Graham's short-term memory. "What're you talking about?"

"We're making that combat jump."

"Are you crazy!?" Graham shrieked. But he vaguely recalled the fool-ish promise and the next thing he knew the two Americans and three Nungs were chuting up for their first practice jump from a USAF Green Hornet Huey.

After a week of daytime drops and one final night rehearsal jump, it became the real thing: At 4 A.M., 23 December 1969, they leaped from a Green Hornet into Cambodia.

They landed and linked up quickly, but one Nung had a broken an-kle. Later that morning a helicopter arrived to lift him out, wiping away any benefits from RT Augur's stealthy night jump, so the entire team was extracted.

A parachute insertion was a good idea, everyone agreed, but only if it went perfectly.

That same December, Colonel Cavanaugh brought in an operational security survey team from Pacific Theater Headquarters in Hawaii to study "possible sources of enemy prior knowledge and ways to deny the enemy these sources." After three weeks the survey team found SOG procedures and practices "more secure than any of the organizations and activities surveyed during the past three years." Clearly, SOG was not telegraphing its punches.

But while SOG headquarters reflected and studied, recon men had come to their own conclusions. Teams were being compromised. "Absolutely," said One-Zero Dick Gross, "they were compromised out of Saigon." How? "They had to have an agent in there." His opinion was widely shared.

Statistics supported this suspicion: During the second quarter of 1970 every team inserted west of Khe Sanh was hit; in the next quarter, teams were inserted there seventy-four times, and two out of three made "significant contact."

There was little likelihood the compromise was at Danang, Kontum or Ban Me Thuot, simply because Vietnamese had little access to operational data. SOG's top-secret documents were stamped "NOFORN," meaning No Foreign dissemination, and that included South Vietnamese.

Former Ban Me Thuot One-Zero Frank Burkhart thought that was true in Saigon, too, until he served on liaison duty there in 1970. Each morning Burkhart picked up an envelope at SOG headquarters and delivered it to an ARVN major across town; when he learned the contents he almost fainted—the previous night's U.S. team situation reports or "sitreps," which included their grid locations. "I couldn't believe it," he said. "*We gave them the locations of our teams.* There's no doubt in my mind that Charlie had it as fast as we had it, no doubt."

Burkhart learned U.S. intelligence had intercepted messages from Hanoi to NVA field units, relaying SOG target locations, and he was even polygraphed because he'd had access—but the ARVN were not polygraphed. "Every morning when we gave the sitreps to that ARVN major, bang!—it was going to the NVA just as fast as I was handing it to him." This put the NVA only a few hours behind the teams, with daily updates to fine-tune their search.

Why did ARVN have to know? "There was a big thing then," Burkhart explained, "that this wasn't our country and they were our counterparts and all that kind of bullshit."

Chief SOG could have cut off ARVN access but overnight the flap would have escalated to President Nguyen Van Thieu and drawn in the ambassador, General Abrams, perhaps the White House. But teams were vanishing: Cavanaugh had to do something. "I suddenly began to realize we were compromising them," Cavanaugh said, "no question about it."

So he started misleading the ARVN, letting them believe a team was to be inserted at one point when the real LZ was some distance away. "And then, when the mission went out to the field it was different," Cavanaugh said. Once the team was on the ground, he'd explain to the ARVN that weather or ground fire had caused a shift or someone had made a mistake.

But once a team was inserted the deception had to end because the Vietnamese could cross-check the location through Kingbee crews' or Vietnamese Air Force strike reports. It was the most Cavanaugh and his successor, Colonel John Sadler, could do. "I would say every effort consistent with basic military common sense was used to keep [the ARVN] from knowing it," Sadler said, "but sometimes you couldn't [prevent it]."

Like an evangelist, Burkhart carried his revelation to every recon man he could, warning them to report their true location only to the Covey FAC and to falsify other reports, especially the daily sitrep. "Just you and the FAC," he urged, "that's all that has to know where you really are."

Meanwhile, evidence of intelligence leaks continued to build. On 10 October 1970, a CCN team was extracted soon after landing when a shocking NVA radio message was overhead. "The team just landed," an enemy officer reported, "everybody move up." The RT was extracted, then the enemy radioed, "The team is going back, everybody stay alert." Here was undeniable proof that the enemy had lain in wait.

Down in Saigon, Chief SOG Sadler decided it was time for a completely different approach. Since the first German combat jumps in 1940, paratroopers always had gone into battle using static lines to open chutes automatically as they exited the aircraft, allowing masses of troopers to land in a predictable pattern, at a predictable rate. But there was another option.

As one of the Army's foremost parachuting experts, Sadler had served on the Airborne Board at Fort Benning and during the Korean War experimented with what civilians call skydiving and the military calls HALO (High Altitude, Low Opening) parachuting—exiting above 10,000 feet, free-falling to 1000 or 2000 feet, then gliding the rest of the way using a steerable parachute.

Though Special Forces HALO training had begun in 1957, and Sadler himself became HALO qualified a year later, no military unit—U.S. or foreign—had yet used HALO in combat.*

Although Sadler found several HALO advocates on his SOG staff—especially Colonels Bobby Pinkerton and Dan Schungel—there was still general opposition to its employment in SOG. At SOG headquarters, Billy Waugh said, "people thought [HALO] was crazy as hell because they didn't go on the ground themselves and didn't realize that if you could get in quietly without notification to the bad guys, that you could have something." A solid HALO supporter, Waugh asked to be inserted "by school bus or submarine," but "don't make me go by helicopter into the damned Ashau. Let's change it, *change it!*"

In July 1970, Colonel Sadler decided to change it and authorized Billy Waugh to select the world's first combat HALO team.

Staff Sergeant Cliff Newman and Sergeant First Class Sammy Hernandez were on a recon mission with RT Virginia, near Khe Sanh when they were told to go to the nearest LZ for extraction. They had no idea what was happening until Billy Waugh met their returning helicopter and announced he had a special mission for them, but Sammy Hernandez didn't like being volunteered before he even knew what the hell was going on. The gritty Waugh would hear none of that. "Well, you always come whinin' to me about, 'I wanna do something good, baby, you won't let me do nothin' good.'" Well, Waugh announced, *here it is.*

A HALO-school graduate with seventy-five jumps under his belt, Hernandez was a natural choice; Cliff Newman was not HALO qualified but had hundreds of sport skydives and a reputation for being "good in the air." Of equal importance, both had extensive recon experience and were accustomed to operating as a team.

To fill out the team, Waugh added Sergeant First Class Melvin Hill, who'd recently spent a month with him helping defend a cutoff Cambodian Army outpost at Ba Kev. Though Hill didn't have much recon experience, he'd been a HALO instructor at Fort Bragg, and Waugh knew him to be a reliable, dedicated NCO.

Next, they needed two Montagnards, a task entrusted to Sammy

---

*Much Special Forces interest in HALO was for the precision delivery of SADM (Special Atomic Demolition Munitions) behind enemy lines. Each Special Forces Group outside Vietnam included a HALO-SADM team to emplace these "suitcase nukes."

Hernandez, who announced to RT Virginia's indigenous soldiers, "We're going to jump out of airplanes."

"No problem, no problem," the Yards assured him.

Hernandez explained, "We're going to go real high, we're going to jump, then you fall a certain time, and you have to pull open your own parachute."

One Yard blinked, looked at him and said, "No, no. I *don't* think we're going to do that."

Still, two Montagnards volunteered, and an ARVN officer was added who, combined with the three Americans, made a six-man team, designated RT Florida. Though Cliff Newman was outranked by Hill and Hernandez, he was the most experienced man so, by SOG ethic, he was One-Zero.

A SOG Blackbird carried RT Florida to Okinawa for basic HALO training. They were kept hidden in a fenced isolation area, not just for operational security but because the Yards and ARVN officer were there without Japanese authorization.

Assisted by the 1st Special Forces Group's finest HALO instructors, Sergeants First Class Joe Markham and Ben Dennis, they began with high-altitude chamber testing to ensure all could withstand a low-oxygen, low-pressure physical environment. In the classroom they learned it takes twelve seconds for a falling body to reach terminal velocity, 125 mph, or 183 feet per second. HALO had two phases of controlled descent: First the free fall, during which a jumper had to stabilize and travel laterally to follow or group with others; and then the parachute descent, using canopy gores that could be opened and closed with toggle lines to steer the final 2500 feet to the drop zone (DZ). Thus a 12,500 foot jump meant sixty seconds in free fall, opening the chute at 2500 feet, and another two and a half minutes flying the canopy into the DZ.

Next they learned the mechanics of free fall, how to stabilize using a modified frog position, contort their bodies into a semidelta to become flying wings, to perform body turns or glide in a controlled lateral descent.

Initially the Yards had trouble stabilizing, but eventually they got the hang of it. Just in case the Yards became confused, their ripcords were equipped with an altimeter-timer to open their chutes automatically.

RT Florida made several jumps daily, sometimes two before dawn, with special emphasis on grouping in the air and following the lead or baseman as he fell toward the DZ.

After a month on Okinawa they returned to Camp Long Thanh for another fourteen days' training, especially in tactics, and made more HALO jumps. One night Sammy Hernandez drifted far from SOG's airfield and landed on the roof of a U.S. unit's orderly room. Just as he bounced to the ground, the unit first sergeant ran out. The first sergeant took one look at Sammy—parachute draped around him, goggles covering his eyes, armed to the teeth with CAR-15, sawed-off shotgun, sawed-off grenade launcher, dagger, grenades—thought it was a Communist airborne invasion and keeled over with a heart attack.

To help RT Florida, Colonel Sadler brought over Master Sergeant Frank Norbury from the HALO School at Fort Bragg, the same man who'd put him through HALO training in 1958. Until now it hadn't been realized how canned the Fort Bragg HALO training was, nor its truly experimental status. Genuine combat conditions—with heavily loaded men free-falling into an unmarked, strange DZ in almost complete darkness—had never been adequately simulated at Fort Bragg. "We didn't have any book to tell how to do it," Billy Waugh said, "we were writing the book."

Darkness caused many problems: The aircrew and jumpmaster had difficulty finding the DZ, yet the Blackbird could make just one pass; the lead jumper, or baseman, had to see the DZ so everyone could follow him to it; the parachutists had to find each other and group together midair then stay together during descent; they had to avoid injury while landing in the dark; and they had to link up in thick jungle. The slightest miscalculation in any step would quash the entire operation.

The biggest problems, they soon saw, were grouping in the air and finding each other after they landed. "There was never any doubt in my mind that they could penetrate the jungle," said Colonel Bobby Pinkerton, SOG's operations chief. "The problem was how to get them together after they landed. That's where the frustrations were."

To find each other in the jungle, Cliff Newman was issued a homing device the size of a cigarette carton, used by agent teams in North Vietnam to find resupply bundles. When he switched it on, his teammates could use ordinary Sony transistor radios tuned to his transponder's frequency and, noting the intensity of its "ping-ping-ping," track him down. It worked perfectly.

At last, in November, they made a night jump into War Zone D for a two-day final exercise, then they were ready.

During their mission briefing, RT Florida learned they'd be wiretapping a phone line in Laos beside a new road the NVA was building due west of Chu Lai, at almost the same point RT Iowa had run SOG's first Shining Brass mission in 1965. Though SOG could not plot individual NVA unit locations, approximately a division—10,000 troops—were within 10 miles of their DZ. And the closest friendlies, a U.S. 101st Airborne Division firebase, were about 50 miles away.

To support the HALO jumpers, SOG brought to bear a special window into the enemy camp unavailable to conventional units, a direct tasking to the NSA through a permanent but unacknowledged NSA liaison officer. With the highest signal intercept priority in Southeast Asia, every NSA asset—from satellites to isolated listening stations—tuned antennas for the slightest word about HALO, parachuting, the jump area or shifting NVA forces.

It saved their lives.

RT Florida was ready to go but the jump was scrubbed because, "they actually intercepted a message from Saigon to Hanoi, with the coordinates and the names of all team members," One-Zero Newman said. *The mole was back!*

A new DZ was selected and its location not circulated. Just after midnight of 28 November 1970, RT Florida's team members assembled in a shed at Camp Long Thanh to strap on their armaments: Each carried a CAR-15, while Newman added a Colt Cobra airweight snub-nose and a suppressed .22 High Standard; Hernandez couldn't go without his sawed-off shotgun; and there was a general cramming of claymores, knives, grenades and sawed-off grenade launchers. Then they donned main chutes, reserve chutes and rucksacks and waddled aboard their waiting Blackbird. The six-man team—Newman, Hernandez, Hill, two Yards and the ARVN officer—took off about 12:30 A.M.

The sky was overcast and murky, merging with the Blackbird's dull skin and even the FLIR night vision screen showed the pilots a featureless, stormy landscape. Navigation would be by Doppler radar bouncing off prominent terrain. The Blackbird navigator, Major Don James, explained, "We tried to do nothing that would seem any different from any other flight." A C-130 had even flown the route for a month. "We'd fly a straight, level flight over the drop zone," as if it was a milk run to Thailand.

Though they wouldn't jump with oxygen bottles, the HALO men still breathed oxygen from a portable console during their final thirty minutes of flight. Bathed in red light to preserve their night vision, they sprayed temporary luminous paint on their parachute packs to help find each other during descent. Then the jumpmaster, Frank Norbury, signaled five minutes out.

At 2 A.M., the red lights went out and the tail ramp opened, dropping the temperature 20 degrees. The Blackbird was cruising at 18,000 feet, which meant the HALO team would free-fall seventy-one seconds, then open at 1500 feet.

Lying on the lowered ramp, Norbury looked hard for landmarks, but it was utterly dark with not even glints off streams visible. It was raining steadily. They'd have to jump using radar.

Watching the dark clouds flash past, Sammy Hernandez thought, "I've done a lot of crazy things but this is the main one here. If I'm going to lose my life, it will probably be on this one."

Then it was time to leave the oxygen console and assemble at the ramp in three groups, each with one American, his hand on the shoulder of an indig standing in front of him.

Colonel Pinkerton watched them. "They just looked like a black blob, and they'd grin at you and give you a thumbs-up."

When Norbury signaled "Go," they fell gracefully away and instantly plunged from sight. Pinkerton recalls that he thought, "What courage it takes to do this, to step out into darkness, two miles above the jungle, [and] you don't know what's down there."

To any NVA within earshot, it was only a high, passing hum in the dead of night, then the C-130 was gone.

For the jumpers, though, it was anything but graceful or quiet. The wind rushing across him and pressing his face, Cliff Newman looked for landmarks but saw only layer after layer of dark clouds and drifting rain. Above him, Sammy Hernandez scanned desperately for any sign of Newman; despite the luminous paint, he hadn't seen his One-Zero since he went into the clouds five seconds after exiting the aircraft.

With hundred-mile-per-hour raindrops stinging his face, Mel Hill looked around but in the darkness and clouds couldn't see anyone, not another soul.

Newman opened his chute at 1500 feet, still in the clouds; he had two orange panels in his parachute suspension line to help the others follow him, but that was pointless now.

Hernandez couldn't see a single landmark, nor another jumper. When his altimeter indicated 1500 feet, he pulled his ripcord, deploying the chute. He didn't see the ground coming until he felt himself slide between trees. Then came a wild crashing and snapping of branches, amplified by the quiet of monotonous falling drizzle. For five minutes he hung motionless in his harness, then scrambled down, gathered his canopy and hid it under heavy vegetation.

Meanwhile Newman had landed in a small stream and learned the hard way his homing beacon wasn't waterproof; it wouldn't work, making an electronic linkup impossible. He climbed to high ground and fortuitously came upon a Yard teammate.

They assembled as four elements: Newman and one Yard; one Yard and the ARVN; then Sammy Hernandez and Mel Hill, each alone. None was injured. When Covey arrived after daylight, the FAC determined the Doppler radar had put them 6 miles from their intended DZ, completely off their maps. But that would not stop their mission.

As four units they would perform three separate recons while Hernandez looked for the landline to wiretap. But they'd have to move cautiously, because the low overcast precluded extraction, and even if it cleared and one unit got in trouble, that unit could not safely call in tac air without endangering the other team members.

Carrying his wiretap device, Hernandez carefully picked his way downhill, heavy rain masking his movement, toward where he heard voices and, later, bulldozers on the road. Then he heard shots to his right and left—signal shots? Were the NVA onto him?

No, he discovered, it was only soldiers hunting for fresh meat.

On the third day Hernandez saw an NVA squad walking along a trail, chattering, weapons on their shoulders—and he smiled. For the first time he knew the NVA had no idea they were there.

It wasn't until the fourth day that the rain ended, and by then every unit had seen NVA or heard considerable shooting, later thought by analysts to have been marksmanship practice or a tactical exercise.

By the fifth morning Hernandez still hadn't found the large communications wire, and SOG headquarters decided it was time to pull all of them. Thailand-based Jolly Green Giants plucked RT Florida from four different LZs, dropping a jungle penetrator to Sammy Hernandez for the final extract.

The penetrator lifted him above the treetops, and he saw Phantoms shriek past to drop bombs, a pair of A-1s duel with antiaircraft guns, and more bomb-laden planes circling overhead. Then he was aboard, back with his teammates and safely en route to Nakhon Phanom.

In the movies there'd have been a celebration, but at Nakhon Phanom it was one beer, a warm meal and then the exhausted men slept.

A SOG report concluded HALO had been "proven as a means of entering [Laos] undetected since an active enemy search was not made to locate the team." Of course, there was no public disclosure that the world's first combat HALO jump had been performed.

Afterward, Cliff Newman was reassigned to Camp Long Thanh as a HALO instructor, and SOG instituted a three-week HALO course and a one-week HALO refresher to continue the program.

As for that telling signal intercept that had caused the mission to be shifted, no serious mole hunt was conducted, though word of the mole spread among recon ranks. One-Zero Richard Gross was told, "They had all [the team members'] names, the drop zone, the time of the drop." He wasn't a counterintelligence expert but Gross had little doubt of the source. "Where could that come from?" he asked. *"Saigon."*

A month later Chief SOG Colonel Sadler brought in a Counterintelligence Technical Survey Team to look for enemy wiretaps and to listen for loose talk on unsecure phone lines. The team found some compromising conversations, but these disclosed nothing about specific operations or specific locations.

Security problems, however, continued. As Colonel Roger Pezzelle, chief of SOG cross-border operations, observed, "I'm sure there was a lot of [Trinh Sat] effort against SOG because we were a prime intelligence target." One surprising indicator that the Trinh Sat (North Vietnam's secret intelligence service) was sharing SOG data with its Bloc comrades came when an NCO received a letter from his wife's East German sister, who'd been denied permission to marry a Communist soldier. "The East German security police paid a visit to the sister-in-law," a SOG document notes, "and informed her that her brother-in-law is now serving with MACV/SOG in Vietnam."

By April 1971, SOG's mole problem even reached the ears of syndicated columnist Jack Anderson, who cited SOG by name and wrote in the *Washington Post*, "It became evident in the fall of 1970 . . . that [SOG's] surprise raids, planned under the secret code name, 'Prairie Fire,' were no longer surprising anyone. Someone began tipping off the enemy exactly where and when to expect the raids, with disastrous results for the raiders."

The Anderson column compelled SOG to change its Laos code name from Prairie Fire to *Phu Dung* (literally, "Opium Smoke"), which also reflected the growing impact of Vietnamization. Still, no concerted mole search began.

But the HALO program continued. In early 1971 a second HALO team was selected, this one led by Captain Larry Manes, a respected two-tour SOG recon veteran and former NCO, and now the CCN Recon Company commander.

To simplify grouping in the air and raise the jumpers' skill levels, this second HALO mission would be entirely American, with only four men. Manes selected three CCN recon men with HALO experience, Specialist Six Noel Gast, Staff Sergeant Robert Castillo and Sergeant John "Spider" Trantanella, for his team.

Freed of the complications of using Montagnard or ARVN novices, their training went quickly.

In the predawn of 7 May 1971, their team flew by Blackbird toward a drop zone inside South Vietnam, midway between the Ashau Valley and Khe Sanh, where the North Vietnamese were extending Laotian Highway 921 into South Vietnam. It would be an area recon mission.

En route to the DZ they ran into weather so stormy that it seemed the jump would be postponed. When the C-130 tailgate opened at 18,500 feet, the jumpmaster, Frank Norbury, gazed out, then shouted in Manes' ear, "Weather's cleared, it's a go."

Looking at the rain and dark clouds, Manes thought Norbury was kidding and kept shaking his head, even as the team unsnapped from the oxygen console and shuffled toward the open door. But Norbury kept nodding yes.

Using a technique they'd practiced at Camp Long Thanh, Manes and Gast grabbed each other's harnesses, and Castillo and Trantanella linked up, to free-fall as pairs. Then they were off.

In the pitch black all they could see were silhouettes of each other, yet when they opened, "I saw all the canopies," Manes reported. "We were all together." His toggle lines twisted and unresponsive, Castillo drifted away, but that wasn't their worst problem.

A toe popper mine in Gast's rucksack activated because of the sudden change in atmospheric pressure and exploded, when he landed, seriously injuring his back. Trantanella had a bad landing, too. Not long after daylight a helicopter extracted both of them.

Because Castillo was almost a mile away, Manes didn't even try to rendezvous with him. Going their separate ways, they slipped toward the road. They heard a lot of shooting and explosions, and like the first HALO mission, it was thought to be an NVA unit conducting training. They went four days without water.

On the fifth day Manes and Castillo were extracted.

Their team's insert was "apparently undetected," SOG concluded.

But the jury was still undecided on HALO: In the first two HALO jumps only Noel Gast was seriously injured, and that was from a mine, not the jump. The problem remained grouping in the air and landing together. Another HALO team was in training, this one led by that SOG old hand who'd been everywhere and done everything *except* a HALO jump, Sergeant Major Billy Waugh. "He was hard to keep down," Major Ed Rybat said of the tough old sergeant major who refused to sit behind a desk.

Joining him would be Staff Sergeant James "J.D." Bath and Sergeants Jesse Campbell and Madison Strohlein. Four years earlier Bath had been Medal of Honor recipient George Sisler's One-One, gone home and now was back for another SOG tour; he'd already made a static-line jump into Laos and, with nearly three hundred military free falls, was the team's strongest jumper. He would be Waugh's baseman and One-One. Strohlein, the youngest at twenty-three, had headed his own recon team and had been wounded twice in the past six months. Campbell, too, was a seasoned recon man, with twenty-four HALO free falls, approximately the same number as Strohlein.*

After refresher training on Okinawa, they practiced one month at Long Thanh, including ten jumps from Hueys and C-130s, four night HALO jumps and a final exercise in War Zone D.

The target SOG selected for them was 60 miles southwest of Danang, far beyond any ARVN outpost, practically on the Laotian frontier. Two CCN teams recently had attempted to insert there by chopper: One lasted only forty-five minutes, the other had had its Huey shot up on the LZ. USAF infrared photos disclosed numerous NVA cooking fires, while daytime photos showed fresh row crops.

In addition to a CAR-15, each jumper would carry a sawed-off shotgun or sawed-off grenade launcher, a suppressed pistol, twenty minigrenades, and miniclaymore mines fashioned from soap dishes. As a joke, Jesse Campbell wore captain's bars and Billy Waugh pinned on a general's star. If the NVA captured them, Waugh told the others, "they'll think they've really got something."

And if they became separated? Waugh didn't want to hear about it. "You've got to have a pair of balls and be able to do it on your own," he told them.

From a drop altitude of 19,000 feet, they'd free-fall 14,000 feet— over 2 miles—then open at 5000 feet, just above the area's highest peak, and glide that final mile. Learning from the previous HALO missions, Frank Norbury installed a dull green light on Bath's parachute container so the others could follow him during free fall, with another light atop his parachute canopy for the last phase.

Their first insert was canceled due to weather; the second time they were within ten seconds of exiting the Blackbird when the mission was scrubbed. "It was an eternity," Bath said. "Our adrenaline started to mix with anxiety and a whole hell of a lot of fear."

On 22 June 1971, they chuted up a third time, climbed into a Blackbird and flew two hours toward their DZ. As they neared the release point, the tailgate opened and J.D. Bath lay there beside Larry Manes,

---

*Bath replaced Staff Sergeant Andre Smith, who'd injured his back in a HALO practice jump at Camp Long Thanh.

their jumpmaster, to try to make out any landmarks. There was supposed to be 8 percent illumination but it was solid black, so solid it lacked definition but for a passing cloud. But it wasn't too stormy this night; they'd jump using Doppler radar.

Moments later the four HALO men stood on the edge of the ramp, looked back once to Manes, and on his signal, off they went. Bath, the baseman, saw two jumpers following him, then turned and flipped the toggle switch that controlled his backpack light. He could see the drop zone in the distance and realized the radar had proven inaccurate yet again.

As Bath reached 5000 feet, he flipped the light on and off to signal the others he was at opening altitude. At 4500 feet he shut it off and deployed his chute, but it responded sluggishly; he looked up and saw that the opening shock had blown out the canopy center, tearing away the light. He was descending dangerously fast, with almost no canopy control.

Unable to see Bath's light, Strohlein, Campbell and Waugh drifted away in heavy rain, and though unable to see the others, Waugh made out an NVA truck convoy on a road about 5 miles north, boldly driving with lights on.

Though he could feel the temperature rising, Bath couldn't see the ground; then his chute collapsed on a tree branch, plunging him the last dozen yards, and he hit the ground hard, wrenching his knee and back, and knocking him unconscious.

Across the ridge where Bath landed, Strohlein crashed through the trees and was jerked to a halt. Waugh landed in a tree and used his descender to lower himself to the ground in a maddening rain. Campbell, too, went in the trees, but he was safe.

When Bath awoke it was still dark. His back, feet and legs throbbed painfully, his mouth bled and his pants were torn. He had a silenced .22 High Standard on a cord around his neck that had swung down so that the barrel touched his head; in his confused, groggy state, he thought an NVA soldier had crept up and put a gun to his head. When he saw the truth, he almost laughed.

He tried to radio Waugh and Campbell with no response, but he did reach Strohlein, and the news wasn't good. Like Bath, Strohlein had crashed through the trees but he'd broken his right arm and could not operate his descender; he was stuck in his harness, high above the jungle floor. With a ridgeline between them, Bath could barely read Strohlein's transmissions. And Bath's left ankle was so swollen he couldn't walk, so he put out his claymore, readied grenades and stacked magazines.

Covey arrived after daylight. Hearing the pilot's half of a conversation with Campbell, Bath could tell Campbell was moving and had NVA in pursuit. Meanwhile, Waugh had crept up to a cliff and peeked down to where five NVA chattered while hunting monkeys.

Soon choppers with a Bright Light team in rappeling gear on board crisscrossed above the treetops and offered to come in for Bath, but he told them to get Strohlein first since he was injured worse. Then Bath saw a couple men walking toward him; thinking they were Waugh and Campbell he almost waved—but they were NVA! He lay low and they passed, never seeing him.

Meanwhile, Strohlein tried to vector the rescue Hueys toward him by radio, using the sound of their rotors, but there were several birds and he'd hear one but talk to another, and everyone became confused. By the time this approach was abandoned, heavy clouds began to build and, desperate, Strohlein threw a smoke grenade but the aircrews still couldn't pinpoint his location. But the NVA saw that smoke; Strohlein warned he could see enemy soldiers.

With the weather closing and fuel nearly exhausted, the Hueys extracted Campbell and Waugh and left. They came back early that afternoon but were unable to raise Strohlein on his emergency radio. Two men rappeled down to Bath and helped him into a STABO rig; then the Huey lifted away under light ground fire. Strohlein's ridge was covered by ground fog.

The next day, in his hospital bed in Danang, one leg in a cast, J.D. Bath looked up to see Billy Waugh and asked which room Strohlein was in, explaining he'd been unable to leave his bed to look for him.

"We didn't get him," Waugh reported. "Charlie got him."

That morning a Hatchet Force platoon had inserted and found the tree where Strohlein had been. Strohlein and his parachute were gone, and there were piles of expended AK and CAR-15 brass. "Strohlein did not go without kicking some NVA ass," Waugh reported. The Hatchet Force found Strohlein's map and CAR-15 at the bottom of the tree; one AK slug had ricocheted off the CAR-15 stock. There was no blood, no bandages.

It was the NVA, not Strohlein, who had removed the chute, the platoon realized, because a tree limb had been shot off by AKs to free the canopy. The platoon believed they heard movement as they neared the tree, which they took to be NVA pulling away.

To recon men, the evidence left one inescapable conclusion: The NVA had captured Strohlein since no SOG man *ever* would abandon a functional CAR-15. The bullet that hit his CAR-15 had knocked it from Strohlein's one good hand, most men thought, disarming him. Waugh and Bath are absolutely convinced the NVA got Strohlein, but Hanoi denied knowing anything about him.

That summer of 1971, after months of troubled consideration, Colonel Sadler decided, "Too many things were happening, too many hot LZs had been chosen at random and away from any known activity. Well, accidents happen but the repetitious [nature of the] situation just meant something was wrong." He, too, decided there must be a mole and he had to track it down.

The footprints had been there for years, begging to be followed: Three of SOG's most critical Hatchet Force operations had been death-traps on the insert LZ: Crimson Tide, with a whole platoon wiped out; the 1967 Oscar Eight raid against the Ho Chi Minh Trail headquarters in Laos, when Charles Wilklow was captured; and the 1969 COSVN raid, where Jerry Shriver vanished.

Only one major raid, 1970's Operation Tailwind, had been a success. Yet many recon missions succeeded, which meant the mole's access was limited in scope or only intermittent. What a clue! A shrewd investigator could compare dates and access, and quickly narrow down the suspects.

But SOG had no authority to investigate its ARVN counterparts, nor could it even vet them for security clearances. "At one point," a declassified SOG report discloses, "the U.S. capability to conduct a counter-espionage operation against [SOG's ARVN counterpart] STD was researched. The conclusion reached was that such was not within the capability of the military or CAS-Saigon, in terms of quality of assets available . . . to have some assurance that the effort would not be blown. If the South Vietnamese became aware that the U.S. was conducting such an investigation, irreparable harm would be done to counterpart relationships."

Behind all enemy moles in South Vietnamese and U.S. agencies was an especially shadowy Trinh Sat entity called Unit B-36. In 1967 the CIA Saigon station uncovered a B-36 mole in their counterpart South Vietnamese Central Intelligence Organization; from that point, the CIA refused to share agent identities and operational details with their counterparts. Another B-36 operative was a mole that penetrated the 5th Special Forces Group's Project Gamma in 1969.

The most highly placed moles could thank ARVN Colonel Pham Ngoc Thao for their achievements. Himself a mole, Thao had headed security for the entire South Vietnamese Armed Forces prior to his death, in 1965, giving him an incredible opportunity to insinuate enemy operatives and purge security files of information. Thao's true allegiance did not become known until after Saigon's fall.

In the realpolitik of 1971, Colonel Sadler knew he could not deny ARVN counterparts access to SOG data, and even the mildest accusation of treachery would be politically explosive. The moles—and there was no longer any doubt at all they were there—were certain to raise all sorts of manipulative delays and objections, exploiting bias, pride, nationalism, whatever it took to thwart their exposure.

Sadler decided upon an indirect approach and told the ARVN commander he was setting up a polygraph screening of Americans on SOG's staff, that this was good, state-of-the-art security, and he was going to take the first polygraph himself. The Vietnamese colonel could see Sadler was waiting for some reciprocation but did not offer to participate. Instead, he announced, his staff would arrange its own polygraph screening.

Within months every American had been "boxed," but the ARVN was still planning its program. Heels were dragging, but the ARVN polygraphs plodded slowly along; at least, Colonel Sadler thought, that would put pressure on the moles and perhaps inspire a degree of caution to reduce their effectiveness.

But not all the suspects were Vietnamese.

One young American, a non-Special Forces clerk working at SOG headquarters, had become involved with a questionable Vietnamese woman. One day he was transporting classified SOG documents in a jeep but arrived at headquarters empty-handed. "He claimed somebody drove up on a motorcycle and stole them," Frank Burkhart said. There was many a thief in Saigon ready to steal watches or cameras or wallets, but there was little larcenous interest in document satchels. Though the clerk was interrogated, nothing came of it.

There were repeated rumors, too, of an American sergeant at SOG headquarters suspected of selling data to the enemy, particularly advance information of B-52 strikes, but the rumors were not substantiated.

That summer of 1971, while Sadler was polygraphing the SOG staff, South Vietnamese President Thieu's government was rocked by the exposure of the most important mole ever unearthed in Saigon, Huynh Van Trong.

It was an especially embarrassing revelation to General Cao Van Vien, South Vietnam's chairman of the Joint General Staff, the equivalent of the U.S. JCS. Back in 1966–68, when Chief SOG Colonel Singlaub would tell him about upcoming Bright Lights, Vien assured him he would tell no one. Actually, General Vien had gone to the president's office to brief Thieu's most trusted political assistant—who shared the information with his aide Huynh Van Trong, the newly exposed mole.

No ordinary spy could possibly have relayed word in time to disrupt a Bright Light, but Trong was so critical an operative that he was believed to have an assigned radio clerk who could transmit messages to Hanoi and certain NVA commands instantly.

Despite the security problems in Saigon, operations continued in the field.

SOG had yet to completely succeed with a HALO operation, a subject raised by General Abrams, who asked Chief SOG, "When are you ever going to run one that accomplishes the mission?" The CCC commander, Lieutenant Colonel Galen "Mike" Radke, was in that briefing and Abrams' words were still fresh in his mind when he sat in the club one night with Captain Jim Storter, the CCC recon company commander, talking about HALO.

Inspired by the challenge, Storter insisted that Radke phone Chief SOG and get authority for him to lead another HALO jump.

The next morning Radke called Storter into his office and announced, "I just phoned Chief SOG and we've got permission to run the next HALO operation."

Storter was perplexed. "*What* HALO operation?"

"The one you talked me into last night, dammit."

Storter, who'd had too much to drink, thought, "God Almighty, what have I done?" But it was too late: He would lead SOG's fourth HALO jump.

He recruited Sergeant First Class Newman Ruff, Staff Sergeamt Miller Moye and Sergeant Jim Bentley, and took them to Long Thanh, where he made an embarrassing confession. "Boys, I've got to tell you," Storter said, "I ain't never made a damned free fall in my life." Storter's was undoubtedly SOG's most intense HALO "refresher" course ever conducted.*

Fortunately his NCOs were experienced: Ruff already had a combat static-line jump and twenty-five HALO free falls; Moye, an accomplished civilian skydiver, would be their baseman; and though Bentley had only a few HALO jumps, he could carry his own weight.

When they finished training, SOG targeted them for the Plei Trap Valley, northwest of Pleiku, where the NVA was dramatically expanding its presence. Overnight, new roads were being cut into the Plei Trap from Cambodia, just 5 miles away, and rapidly it was becoming another Ashau Valley. Several thousand NVA were within 5 miles of the HALO team's planned drop zone.

Unlike the previous HALO teams, Storter's men had state-of-the-art civilian Para-Commander chutes, and each man carried a compact Uzi submachine gun. Bentley, who would walk point, took along a suppressor for his Uzi.

One night in early September the team chuted up at Camp Long Thanh, "and here came a jeep racing out," Storter recalled. "Mission's off," the driver shouted but offered no explanation.

The next morning Storter learned why. The previous day he'd sent a teletype to Saigon that included his team's names, individual serial numbers, weapon serial numbers and their drop zone. The previous evening the NSA had intercepted an enemy radio message with exactly those details, alerting a major NVA headquarters to prepare for their jump.

As in the previous HALO compromise, their insertion was resched-

---

*Sergeant First Class Ronnie Knight volunteered, too, but had to drop out after an injury during a practice jump.

uled and the DZ shifted without transmitting the changes to SOG head-quarters. Two nights later they jumped from 16,000 feet into the Plei Trap Valley. Were they uptight? "You could've taken a team of mules and not pulled a greasy string out of any of our asses," Storter said.

Their baseman, Miller Moye, spotted the DZ and tracked toward it; the other three saw Moye and followed him.

Then Ruff's rucksack came loose and he went into a flat spin, whipping with such force that the capillaries in his eyes burst, making his eyes turn pink, though this did not impair his vision. Dizzy, he could concentrate on just one thing so he watched his altimeter to ensure he opened his chute at the correct altitude. He knew he was still over Moye, so it would be OK.

All of them landed within 30 yards of Moye, exactly in their appointed DZ. "We were 100 percent assembled within ten minutes of landing, and moving," Storter said.

They reconned the Plei Trap for four days, and there was never a hint the NVA knew they were there. "It was picture perfect," Storter said. For the first time in military history, a unit had skydived behind enemy lines at night, landed without injury, assembled and conducted an entire area recon mission, Chief SOG was able to report to General Abrams.

Riding that success, SOG launched another HALO insertion a month later, again using a CCC team against an objective on the Cambodian border, this time 25 miles southwest of Pleiku, in the Ia Drang Valley.

Led by Sergeant First Class Dick Gross, it included Sergeants First Class Mark Gentry and Bob McNair, Staff Sergeant Howard Sugar, and Master Sergeant Charles Behler.

Jumping from 17,000 feet, the team became separated during descent. Gentry's rucksack came loose, spinning him wildly, then he had canopy problems and landed away from the rest.

Gross and Sugar found each other beside the Ia Drang River, then reached Gentry by radio. He said he'd meet them. It was still dark when Gross heard voices and NVA walking through the thin brush around them. "Apparently the NVA already had started looking," he said.

I was extremely concerned for the HALO team, because, flying above them in an O-2 FAC plane, I could see the weather precluded bringing in fighters or gunships. Besides, until we knew where everyone was, fire support for one man could endanger another.

Just after daylight, Mark Gentry walked into a squad of NVA eating breakfast; they went for their guns, but he was faster, shot several, then ran and found a bomb crater to hide in.

Two hours later the overcast broke, we brought in Cobras and Hueys and extracted the whole team, without casualties.

It was SOG's last American HALO jump.*

Though SOG parachutists landed amid enemy troops, fought, died, broke limbs, became MIA—faced dangers as great as any faced by American paratroopers—their jumps did not meet the U.S. Army's official criteria for a combat parachute landing, so they were not awarded gold stars for their jump wings. Instead, SOG presented each man a "Jump Certificate," which had only ceremonial value.

"But it doesn't matter," said Cliff Newman, the world's first combat HALO team leader. "That isn't why we do these things."

And the mole problem was never fully resolved. The ARVN STD polygraphs were still under way when Colonel Sadler rotated home in 1972, though he learned that eventually they uncovered one agent, a young corporal with access to target data.

Undoubtedly a "throwaway," a low-level operative given up to protect a higher, more important source, the corporal could not possibly have been SOG's only source of compromise for six years.

"Where else they were," Colonel Sadler said, "I don't know."

*Two ARVN-led SOG HALO teams jumped near Kratie, Cambodia, in October and December 1971 to look for a POW camp. The first team was scattered, the second was discovered on their DZ. Both had to be extracted.

17

SOG STANDS ALONE

After the Cambodian Invasion, American troop withdrawals accelerated while the remaining U.S. units ceased offensive operations and
moved to enclaves near major cities, air bases and the coast. Except for
a few artillery firebases, no American ground forces remained in South
Vietnam's interior.

As U.S. units pulled out of the DMZ, Central Highlands and remote
frontiers, ARVN forces—lacking firepower, airpower and sometimes
willpower—could not fill the void. So the NVA stepped in, extending
their Laotian highways into South Vietnam creating strategic bastions
all along the border. There were more NVA troops than ever, better situated, better armed and ready to fight, but nobody to oppose them.

Nobody except SOG.

"I maintained that everybody had gone home and there was nobody
in the war but SOG, which is true," said Colonel Roger Pezzelle, SOG's
ground operations chief. "There was nobody in this goddang war but
SOG!"*

---

*One of Special Forces' earliest officers, Pezzelle, in 1952, first adopted the green
beret, patterned after the berets worn by OSS operatives serving with the French Resistance.

One-Zeros "continued to take risks," Pezzelle said, "because the unit felt like it was our responsibility to protect through the gathering of intelligence and giving people advance warning, all the rest of these people in the command who were getting ready to leave, and the [South] Vietnamese Army."

It was also a matter of pride. FOB 2 recon First Sergeant Billy Greenwood noted, "We still ran missions just as aggressively, just as regular with the same amount of enthusiasm as we always did."

It wasn't easy. One afternoon Lloyd O'Daniels watched a helicopter bring in the body of Sergeant First Class David "Baby Huey" Hayes. "The day they brought him in on strings, his helicopter flew in very slowly and it took forever to lower his body to the ground. And this is a guy who had a wife and three kids. God Almighty, is it worth it?" he remembered wondering.

Worth it or not, alone or not, SOG fought on, continuing to penetrate the enemy's most heavily defended bastions in Laos, the DMZ and inside Vietnam. Half the missions went smoothly, half did not, with RT Washington experiencing it both ways during two recons into Laotian Target Charlie Three that fall of 1970.

Inserting in southern Laos on 5 November, Washington's One-Zero, Captain Steve Wallace, took four days of careful movement before he, One-One Jeff Mauceri and One-Two Curt Green and three Yards reached a just-vacated battalion bivouac site. Alert but quiet, they soon crossed a wide trail and discovered a heavy coaxial communications cable; beyond there the jungle opened into an enormous rice field being worked by uniformed NVA. Now the NVA seemed everywhere.

In an adjacent little valley they found an empty field hospital and hundreds of graves, likely casualties from the siege of Dak Seang and Dak Pek Special Forces Camps five months earlier.

By the next afternoon RT Washington heard constant movement, so One-Zero Wallace found a spot to hide overnight. Hardly had they stopped when Mauceri shot an NVA tracker—the race was on!

The team ran a half mile, waded across a creek, then lay in ambush; approaching NVA flashlight beams cut the darkness, but the tracker dogs lost the scent. All night the team sat back to back until Covey arrived at dawn and directed them to an LZ.

En route they bumped into two NVA on a trail, one carrying a thick

ledger, and shot them dead. Mauceri grabbed the book just as more
NVA arrived, then they dashed the final 100 yards to the LZ. Minutes
later the NVA attacked. RT Washington repelled the attack with
grenades and CAR-15 fire, then Covey's OV-10 made gun runs. Momentarily Cobras arrived to add still more fire, then a Huey swooped in,
they leaped aboard and lifted away.

Looking back, Mauceri could see dozens more NVA converging on
the now vacant LZ. It had been a hell of a close shave.

Later they learned the ledger contained rice-growing reports; its
bearer, a citation said, was a recipient of the coveted "American-Killer
Award." He'd never see an oak leaf cluster.

Saigon congratulated RT Washington for uncovering the NVA 28th
Regiment's new base area, then tasked them to go back and wiretap that
coaxial cable they'd found. Having just escaped by the skin of their
teeth, they'd have rather gone anywhere else.

On 1 December back they went, stalking cross-country for three days
to reach the hill where they'd found the cable. That night they slept near
the wire and planned to tap it the next morning.

By 8 A.M. they were searching for the cable when the point man
opened fire on an NVA sentry—just beyond him an entire company was
eating breakfast. Captain Wallace fired two quick shots, which dropped
a Chinese adviser, then an AK slug hit Curt Green's CAR-15, disabling
it and injuring his hand.

They flashed through an IA (Immediate Action) Drill, then ran for all
they were worth. They crossed a ridge and took fire from more NVA,
dashed away and began evasive turns. Mauceri gave Green a .38 revolver so he'd have a working weapon.

Then Covey arrived and shot up their back trail while steering RT
Washington toward an LZ atop a steep knoll. In a few minutes they
were there, apparently having shaken off the NVA. When Covey announced the helicopters were ten minutes away, One-Zero Wallace had
Mauceri knock down five small trees with claymore mines and begin
chopping bamboo in preparation. Meanwhile, One-Two Green called
in A-1 Skyraiders against their back trail just in case any NVA were approaching. They were.

Intense fire erupted suddenly, near Green; then Wallace shouted,
"He's dead." Mauceri saw his teammate lying still, three gaping exit

wounds in his back, and NVA massing just beyond him. He could do nothing for Green. But they needed the radio.

The One-One rushed down, shooting and throwing grenades, squatted behind a tree and covered while a Yard grabbed Green's rucksack; a round hit the Yard in the pelvis and he slumped over. Mauceri fired madly and somehow dragged the Yard to safety while another Yard recovered the team radio.

By now a Huey was landing, just as an NVA platoon assaulted; Mauceri, Wallace and two unwounded Yards fired as NVA bullets smacked the helicopter, forcing it to pull out. Four RPGs shook the ground, and Wallace grabbed his face and groaned, "Oh, God, I'm hit." Then a Cobra, flying so low Mauceri felt it over his shoulder, let loose a minigun burst that churned the ground 5 yards away. "He just cooked them," Mauceri said, "and that broke the attack."

Temporarily blind, Wallace also had difficulty breathing, so Mauceri laid him beside a tree and lied, saying that they'd get out just fine. "By that time," he said, "I thought we were toast."

Then Covey Rider Larry White's voice crackled on the radio, "They're sneaking around your right flank." With White directing from above, Mauceri crawled to the edge of the knoll and rolled three grenades over a rise. White reported, "You got 'em."

Momentarily another Huey came in low above the treetops, just as the NVA rushed the LZ. Only two Yards and Mauceri still fired, and by now the One-One's overheated CAR-15 scorched his hand and melted off the nylon sling; he poured water on it, grabbed magazines off teammates' bodies and kept shooting. Then A-1s dropped cluster bombs right across the NVA, buying barely enough time to get the Huey in. Somehow Mauceri got RT Washington's wounded Yards and his blinded team leader aboard, but there was no chance to retrieve Curt Green's body.

Medevaced Stateside, Captain Wallace lost an eye; though he died, Curt Green was carried MIA; and having shown the right stuff, Jeff Mauceri was appointed RT Washington's new One-Zero.

It was combat such as this—close-quarters, all-out gunfights against masses of NVA—that characterized SOG recon's final year, a time when its men could no longer even operate as Green Berets of the 5th Special Forces Group.

The 5th Group turned over its last A Camp to the ARVN on 21 January 1971, shortly before its withdrawal—a withdrawal accelerated by General Abrams despite its catastrophic effects on the border camps and Mike Force Montagnard units.

The Green Berets' official departure created a cover problem for SOG's Special Forces troops, solved by changing CCN to Task Force 1, Advisory Element, while CCC was redubbed Task Force 2, Advisory Element. Recon men swapped green berets for black baseball caps and switched to the U.S. Army, Vietnam patch.

But more momentous changes were in the wind.

On 29 January I was flying Covey with USAF Captain Jim Cryer over southern Laos when RT Hawaii, led by One-Zero Les Dover, declared an emergency after a heavy firefight. While Hawaii was being extracted, RT Colorado, 8 miles away, also declared an emergency.

I turned over Hawaii's extraction to Cobra lead, then raced south to help Colorado.

RT Colorado One-One David "Lurch" Mixter was well liked, an adventurer offspring of a prominent New England family. A solid athlete, Mixter stood 6 feet 6 inches, making him a foot taller than his One-Zero, Pat Mitchell, and probably 50 pounds heavier than their One-Two, John St. Laurent.

An RPG had killed Lurch and wounded St. Laurent, and though they'd killed ten NVA, their Yards had panicked and fled, and more NVA were massing. Unable to carry Lurch, Mitchell and St. Laurent were about to fight to the death for his body. While my pilot, Jim Cryer, set up for a gun run, I spoke to Mitchell, assuring him, "It's OK, Lurch would understand. We have to think about the living right now, partner. Now get moving." It hurt immensely to leave Lurch behind, but we managed to extract Mitchell and St. Laurent, cheating the NVA of two more lives.

Though we wouldn't realize it for another week, David Mixter would be SOG's final recon man MIA in Laos.

On 6 February the Joint Chiefs ordered SOG to cease U.S.-led Laotian missions, a complete surprise to Chief SOG Sadler, who at that moment was overseeing an elaborate deception campaign to support Lam Son 719, the imminent ARVN invasion of Laos.

Sensitive to media and congressional charges of "illegal" Laotian activities, the previous April President Nixon had danced the edge of a lie, telling the *New York Times,* "No American stationed in Laos has ever been killed in ground combat operations." Although later conceding a few CIA officers had been lost, the White House still didn't mention SOG's ground casualties, and with good reason: After the Cambodian incursion, Congress had passed the Cooper-Church Amendment, which prohibited the introduction of U.S. ground forces into Laos. Fearing an embarrassing incident during the upcoming ARVN invasion scheduled for 8 February, the White House ordered SOG to stop using Americans in cross-border operations.

Yet U.S.-led recon missions hardly ended: The Joint Chiefs gave SOG a 10-kilometer-deep strip along the DMZ and Laotian border, with orders to penetrate these heavily occupied NVA base areas, now linked by roads to Laos and North Vietnam.

As for Lam Son 719, this was to be a three-division spoiling attack to destroy enemy stockpiles and disrupt truck traffic at the height of the dry season, buying time for South Vietnam as had the Cambodian invasion. Launching from Khe Sanh, ARVN forces would roll west along Highway 9, destroy NVA facilities around Tchepone, turn south on Highway 92, sweep through NVA 559th Group Forward headquarters and return to South Vietnam along Highway 922 into the Ashau Valley. It looked fabulous on paper.

Three times, Chief SOG said, he gave General Abrams, the MACV J-2 and the U.S. XXIV Corps commander a blunt recommendation: *"Stay out of there."* Sadler knew that over the past four months only 40 percent of SOG teams had remained in Laos over twenty-four hours, so strong had the NVA become, and warned, "They're in position, they know you're coming, and that's a recipe for deadly results."

"When we briefed XXIV Corps staff," recalled Colonel Pinkerton, SOG's operations chief, "General [James] Sutherland said his biggest worry was being able to get in there, and we told him, 'Your biggest worry ought to be how in the hell you're going to get out.'"

An official U.S. after-action report never cites SOG's repeated warnings, instead claiming, "United States intelligence felt that the operation would be lightly opposed. . . ." The same report said, "the [NVA] reinforcement capability was listed as fourteen days for two divisions from north of the DMZ," but disingenuously did not note that fourteen days before the operation there was intelligence that the NVA already knew the ARVN were coming.

SOG laid on an elaborate campaign to support Lam Son, beginning in mid-January with SOG Blackbirds dropping dummy parachutists with firecrackers (Nightingale Devices) on seven DZs west of Khe Sanh, while U.S. teams faked inserts at another four points.*

Meanwhile, atop Co Roc, just west of Khe Sanh, SOG inserted three U.S. recon teams and two ARVN-led Hatchet Force platoons; after the Pentagon message of 6 February the U.S. teams had to be extracted.

On 8 February the ARVN finally launched its much-anticipated invasion, rolling west from Khe Sanh along Highway 9 while several battalions of ARVN rangers and paratroopers were helilifted to hilltops on the right and left flanks. Vehicle columns advanced at a reasonable pace on the mostly single-lane Highway 9, which could be blocked by a single disabled vehicle: Cut that lifeline and the ARVN were trapped.

For four days the ARVN had it easy.

While the ARVN advanced into Laos, SOG's Naval Advisory Detachment staged its first Nasty-class boat raids above the DMZ in twenty-seven months, in hopes Hanoi might fear its vulnerable homeland was about to be invaded. In December 1970, SOG's top Navy officer, Commander Tom Millen, had studied enemy coastal defenses and bet Chief SOG, "I could drive two [Nastys] up the coast as far as Haiphong and back and not take more than three rounds of gunfire, all in my wake."

With White House restrictions on SOG raids above the DMZ temporarily rescinded, that's exactly what Sadler wanted to do, raid Haiphong Harbor, which CINCPAC approved subject to a hydrographic study, but sure enough, the Nastys required 8 feet 3 inches minimum draft, and at low tide their safe passage through the Red River Delta could not be assured.

Instead, the Joint Chiefs authorized surface combat against North Vietnamese ships. One of the first Nasty forays had to pass up a nice fat 380-foot Chinese freighter, but shortly afterward, on the night of 11

---

*SOG also was diverting NVA attention from Operation Silver Buckle, a CIA-advised, four-battalion Laotian attack from southwest of Tchepone that had begun on 5 January. Two NVA regiments quickly routed the CIA-SGU force.

February, three Nastys patrolling 60 miles north of the DMZ sank a junk, a trawler and a 100-ton coastal steamer, and damaged two Soviet-made submarine chasers.

On 19 February came the most successful Nasty surface action of the war, when four PTFs on night patrol sank a 60-foot patrol boat and heavily damaged a 130-foot Shanghai II fast attack craft and a Swatow-class gunboat. When the North Vietnamese Navy attempted to intercept the escaping SOG boats with a P-4 patrol boat and another Shanghai II, again the SOG crews got the better of them, disabling the P-4 and sinking the Shanghai II.

Only one SOG Vietnamese crewman was killed.

One day earlier, on 18 February, the first of six SOG recon teams inserted into the Ashau Valley in support of Lam Son 719, to tie down NVA forces and gather intelligence for when the ARVN returned along Highway 922, coming out of Laos.

Initially the Ashau diversion had been assigned to the 1st Brigade, 101st Airborne Division, which was to storm the valley with four battalions; the specter of heavy American casualties apparently scotched that. Instead, a handful of recon men were given a job originally planned for a two-thousand-man paratroop unit.

The Ashau Valley had never been hotter.

Captured documents revealed the NVA had moved eleven counter-recon companies there to reinforce LZ Watchers, trackers, dogs, rear security units and infantry battalions. Two antiaircraft battalions defended the valley, one at each end. Billy Waugh used Nightingale firefight simulators and false landings on six LZs to land a single team, and ten minutes later the team made contact. The NVA were everywhere. "That's what made me realize finally that the war's lost," he said, "because if they can be in every goddamn kilometer in this son of a bitch, just think of how they are in War Zone D [near Saigon]."

When Sammy Hernandez told Rich Gross he was going into the Ashau for a roadblock mission, Gross advised him not to go, thinking that the operation had no chance.

But Hernandez, a recent veteran of the world's first HALO parachute insert, went anyhow, accompanying RT Intruder to advise and evaluate a new One-Zero, Captain Ronald "Doc" Watson, and his One-One, Sergeant Allen "Little Jesus" Lloyd. Watson, who had a doctorate in history from Berkeley, had been assigned to SOG to write a book and ran missions to get a feel for the subject.

Inserting on a steep ridge along the Ashau's west wall, RT Intruder had not been on the ground thirty minutes when they came upon a heavily camouflaged road.

Hernandez had them pull back to wait and listen, and not two minutes later a Yard on their left flank signaled people coming—a six-man NVA porter party, which Intruder engaged. Two of the enemy were shot dead and the others fled, abandoning their loads.

Quickly the recon men gathered their booty and beat feet to an LZ. Covey was still within earshot and got a Huey to them in minutes, but half of RT Intruder's men would have to wait for the helicopter to fly to Phu Bai, refuel and return.

Concerned that too many NVA were converging on the area, Sammy Hernandez told the Covey FAC not to bring back a Huey that afternoon, but to wait until morning. Until then, he, Watson and Lloyd—the last three on the ground—would hide, letting the NVA conclude the entire team had left. That was much safer, Hernandez believed.

But thirty minutes later the FAC radioed that another Huey was on its way in. Watson, Lloyd and Hernandez had gone only 200 yards from the old LZ and only about 700 yards from the ambush site. Hernandez thought the extraction a bad idea and warned, "I don't want to do this."

The USAF FAC, flying without a SOG Covey Rider, disregarded Sammy's warning and sent in the Huey.

The bird hovered at the treetops and dropped strings, which the three Americans snapped into, then gave a thumbs-up to the Huey crew chief. As they lifted up and away, light ground fire erupted, returned by the Huey door gunners, then Hernandez heard fire right underneath him; he was high enough almost to run across the treetops, "and the next thing I knew, I'd come back crashing through the trees." The Huey flew away, beyond where the ridge dropped off.

Numb after impact and the wind knocked out of him, his face bleeding, Hernandez thought his rope had snagged and snapped but found it was cut clean, apparently by the door gunner, to save Sammy from being dragged through the trees.

But Hernandez was mistaken. The door gunner's last act was slicing

Sammy's line when the Huey, fatally hit, tipped upside down. Dragged behind it, Watson and Lloyd followed the falling Huey right over the cliff and died along with the whole Huey crew.

In the ebbing light, Hernandez heard movement and voices, so he crawled and slid downhill; he was on his own again, like on the HALO mission. Enemy flashlights scanned the brush for him for about an hour and a half, but his repeated buttonhooks finally lost them. He found a place to hide and tried to sleep.

The next morning he heard a Huey, crawled into a small clearing and waved a panel; an hour later he was back at Phu Bai, safe and secure and surprised by all the bear hugs from his recon buddies. "It was only twenty-four hours," he kept saying.

Finally Billy Waugh put an arm around his shoulder and told him about Doc Watson and Allen Lloyd.

But Sammy's rescue didn't end the story of RT Intruder. RT Habu, led by Cliff Newman, along with Billy Waugh, went after the bodies of Watson and Allen and the Huey crew, and had to rappel down a cliff to reach the crash site.

While the Bright Light was under way, a Covey aircraft was shot down, killing both the pilot, USAF Captain Larry Hull, and his Covey Rider, Sergeant First Class William Fernandez.

Although RT Habu found Watson's and Lloyd's bodies, the loss of the FAC plane so complicated everything that the bodies could not be extracted that day. That night a reinforced NVA company pinned RT Habu against a sheer drop and likely would have overrun them at dawn except the team, with half its men wounded, left behind the bodies and escaped by jumping off the cliff.

For months the NVA left Watson's and Lloyd's body bags in the open, hoping a SOG team or helicopter might come for them. They were never recovered.

While the RT Intruder Bright Light was under way, another team, RT Python, on the Ashau's east wall, was hit by an NVA battalion.

Led by Captain Jim Butler, with Staff Sergeant Leslie Chapman as One-One, RT Python's fourteen men had occupied Firebase Thor, a small abandoned hilltop strongpoint, to block the NVA-controlled highway below them. The audacious Butler had even erected a flagpole and run up Old Glory for all the world to see.

RT Python had gone in heavily armed, with a 60mm mortar, four M-60 machine guns with five thousand rounds per gun and whole cases of M-79 grenade rounds. They ringed their little fortress with fifty-seven claymore mines.

The first night they were only probed and took occasional mortar rounds. All night they watched flashlights and vehicle headlights on the valley floor. They suffered two wounded, but the RT Intruder Bright Light precluded a medevac.

Just after dark the next night, the NVA began shelling their hilltop with mortars and recoilless rifles, then launched a heavy assault at 11:30 P.M., making it within hand-grenade range before a C-130 Spectre's 40mm and 20mm guns pushed them back.

At 4 A.M. the NVA launched another attack, beaten back by 60mm mortar fire and CAR-15s, and another Spectre. But the NVA would not quit: At 8:30 A.M., in broad daylight, with aircraft circling above, the NVA launched an all-out, battalion-strength assault that should have swept right over the team.

Concentrated A-1 strafing runs and napalm, along with heavy fire from Butler's men, barely held the enemy back. Then a Yard was shot and rolled down the slope. Despite heavy enemy fire, One-One Chapman scrambled after the wounded Montagnard, killing four NVA and throwing the Yard over his shoulder, then running back to safety.

Their supporting Covey pilot, Captain Tom Yarborough, hailed two passing Hueys, which narrowly snatched away RT Python before NVA swarmed over the top—then it was realized one Yard had been left behind. His ordnance expended, Captain Yarborough held off the NVA by "bombing" them with empty rocket pods and his auxiliary gas tank while a Huey retrieved the Yard.

Butler's men were credited with killing forty-two enemy and directing air that killed an additional three hundred NVA. Les Chapman was awarded the Distinguished Service Cross.

Although SOG's Ashau Valley diversions killed a considerable number of NVA and diverted enemy attention, the SOG teams did not support the ARVN's return from Laos because the ARVN invasion force never got anywhere near the Ashau.

Lam Son 719, as Chief SOG had warned, had bogged down and become a bloody debacle, with the ARVN's Laotian hilltop strongholds cut off and annihilated piecemeal. American TV viewers witnessed the sickening sight of ARVN deserters mobbing Hueys and hanging from skids, the result of the NVA rushing in ten infantry regiments from five divisions, plus tank and artillery regiments. Heavily supported by U.S. helicopters, most of Lam Son 719's American killed and missing—219 and 38, respectively—were aircrew.

The ARVN incurred severe losses in their 1st Division, South Vietnam's finest infantry unit, plus the 1st Airborne Division, the Marine Division and the 1st Ranger Group. Chief SOG called the invasion "the biggest fiasco I saw in my whole time over there," because it "broke the back of the South Vietnamese Army." Particularly irreplaceable were the dead ARVN paratroop officers, he said, since "That's the Gavins, the West-morelands if you will, the future leaders. They were all dead."

After Lam Son, the ARVN all but abandoned western I Corps and the DMZ, yielding immense areas to the NVA, and it became SOG's job to find these new redoubts and document what the enemy was doing in them.

Ominously, in April CCN teams discovered a new road coming out of Laos just north of the Ashau, pointed dangerously toward the popu-lous coastal plain north of Hue. Heavy NVA forces made penetrations all but impossible; it was as if a curtain were being lowered to conceal enemy activities.

Sent to penetrate that veil, on 3 May RT Asp, consisting of Staff Sergeants Klaus Bingham, James Luttrell, Lewis Walton and three Yards, landed without ground fire in the Ashau Valley. It seemed RT Asp had slipped safely past the NVA. Ten minutes after landing they ra-dioed a "Team OK" and went on their way.

That was the last transmission from RT Asp.

"There were indications they may have been captured," a SOG re-port noted.

Then on 17 May, another team in the Ashau Valley, RT Alaska, was overrun by hordes of NVA. Although the bodies of Specialist Four Gary Hollingsworth and Staff Sergeant Dale Denhke were recovered, their One-Zero, First Lieutenant Danny Entrican, was MIA, with strong intelligence he'd been taken alive. The body retrieval proved so perilous that the Bright Light team leader, Sergeant Richard

Hendrick, was awarded a Distinguished Service Cross.

Another SOG team in the Ashau, however, paid back the NVA in spades. Occupying a small peak, the SOG team used a mortar and recoilless rifle to pin NVA trucks and troops along Highway 548, then brought in USAF AC-119 gunships night after night. Along with two other teams, they interdicted the road for twenty-one days, destroying fifteen NVA trucks and inflicting numerous enemy casualties at a cost of two Americans and four Yards slightly wounded.

Despite occasional SOG successes, though, the NVA continued to expand and extend their security curtain. From the Ashau Valley north to the DMZ, a distance of 75 miles, the North Vietnamese reigned nearly supreme by June 1971, with Khe Sanh again empty and Lang Vei Special Forces Camp a ghost town. In Vietnam's entire northwest region, the last burr under the NVA's saddle was a CCN radio relay site, Outpost Hickory, situated on a peak 2½ miles north of Khe Sanh. The closest friendlies were at Firebases Fuller and Carroll, 20 miles east of there.

Although ostensibly only a radio relay site, Hickory's greatest utility was as a secret NSA radio monitoring post, using state-of-the-art automated equipment to intercept enemy radio traffic.

Just 29 yards wide and 73 yards long, Hickory was held by twenty-seven U.S. and sixty-seven indigenous soldiers, including SOG men, sensor readers and a squad from L Company, 75th Rangers. The site was commanded by CCN Staff Sergeant Jon Cavaiani, who, despite being outranked by several Americans, led the Montagnard security platoon, assisted by Sergeant John Jones.

That Hickory was threatened came as no surprise. For weeks Saigon analysts electronically tracked units closing in on the little base so closely that Lieutenant Colonel Mike Radke finally announced an assault was imminent. "I said seventy-two hours and it was hit within twenty-four," he recalled. Due to its valuable radio intercept role, SOG planned to hold Hickory until it became untenable.

At dawn on 4 June a security man pointed to something odd in Hickory's concertina wire. Looking closer, Cavaiani realized it was a Chinese claymore mine and noticed ten more all along the perimeter, planted the previous night during a blinding downpour. Cavaiani grabbed an M-60 machine gun and began knocking down the mines with gunfire, disabling six, then—KABOOM!—one mine detonated, wounding several men, then—KABOOM!—another mine exploded, wounding more men, including John Jones, slightly.

The NVA's intended effect fizzled, and a simultaneous ground assault never materialized, though 60 yards downhill, several dug-in enemy fired sporadically. Scrambling to a .50-caliber machine gun, Cavaiani let loose a furious fusillade, matched by fire from other defenders just as the NVA launched a mortar and RPG barrage. A few more defenders suffered shrapnel wounds.

While a pair of F-4 Phantoms bombed the entrenched NVA, a young American sensor reader named Walton climbed into the .50 caliber's bunker with Cavaiani, who took one look at his pudgy frame and thick glasses and asked what he wanted. "I came up here to take over the .50 cal.," he said. "There are a lot of guys roaming around like they don't know what to do." He was right—Cavaiani had to lead the defense, not fight it all alone.

Cavaiani put a Yard with Walton and took off to reposition men, re-distribute ammo and secure the wounded, which by now numbered more than a dozen. When an RPG rocked the .50 caliber's position, Cavaiani looked up to see the wounded Walton drag the gun back. For a moment the sensor reader thought he was blind but then learned the RPG only had damaged his glasses. He resumed firing.

Another RPG hit a U.S. captain. With Walton's supporting fire, Cav-aiani carried the officer across the helipad to an ARVN medic. Then an-other mortar barrage shook Hickory, and a sniper in a spider hole opened fire only to be shot dead by Cavaiani. More Americans, Yards and Vietnamese were hit by shrapnel.

The situation seemed to have become untenable, so Cavaiani called for an evacuation, which began early that afternoon.

Cavaiani carried the wounded captain to a Huey and told him Wal-ton had knocked out five NVA machine guns and exposed himself to a lot of fire, so Cavaiani had hastily written him up for the Medal of Honor; he wanted the captain to carry the recommendation back to Danang. Cavaiani then hustled Walton and as many others as he could squeeze aboard onto another helicopter. After it lifted away, there stood Walton, grinning, claiming he'd fallen out.

With Walton's and Jones' help, Cavaiani began scuttling gear so they all could leave in the next helicopter lift. He was careful to destroy the NSA van and its top-secret radio intercept gear.

Except for an occasional mortar round, the action had ebbed by 4:30 P.M. when Cavaiani heard a Huey coming in and received a shocking radio message: "This is the last ship. Get on it." The Huey had room for seven passengers, he protested, he had four times that many men! Never before had a SOG American abandoned his indigenous soldiers, and Cavaiani was not about to be the first. He put Walton aboard the Huey along with six Yards and waved them off.

With that last load he'd evacuated sixty-nine men—fifteen of them wounded—leaving nineteen Yards, four Vietnamese, the slightly wounded John Jones and himself. Cavaiani couldn't understand what was happening: It wasn't even 5 P.M., the sky was clear and SOG couldn't get helicopters? It didn't make sense.

But all was not lost. A Thailand-based USAF Jolly Green was en route to Hickory to extract Cavaiani and his men. But when the big Sikorsky was 7 miles away the pilot radioed, "I just got told I will get court-martialed if I don't turn this bird around."

It was a bureaucratic pissing contest, instigated by a senior officer of the U.S. division then providing helicopter support to SOG. Not only had he terminated Huey support at 5 P.M., but when he learned SOG had gone through its own channels to get the Jolly Green, he'd contacted MACV headquarters and had Seventh Air Force turn the Thailand-based aircraft around.

The contest had begun two weeks earlier, when the senior officer suddenly demanded that his division's helicopters supporting CCN be returned—impossible because recon men were that moment locked in a firefight, their lives on the line. Colonel Pezzelle said the officer "apparently didn't think much of unconventional warfare."

Although General Abrams formally ordered the U.S. division to provide SOG with helicopter support, the officer found ways around it, Pezzelle explained. "Without just refusing the order they could say, 'Well, the helicopters aren't available,' 'Christ, we've got maintenance problems, etc., etc.,' or 'We had too many shot up or this and that and the other thing.' And then they would show up with fewer than necessary and they'd come late. That was their way of fighting the requirement."

Colonel Pezzelle and Chief SOG went to Abrams several times, "but there was a reluctance, apparently," to enforce compliance, and Abrams expected SOG to solve its own problems.

It was an arrangement courting disaster, which came on 4 June 1971, at Outpost Hickory, where Cavaiani and Jones kept looking to the sky for evacuation birds, but none appeared. Realizing they were on their own with night fast approaching, Cavaiani had Jones take the radio, while he stood atop a bunker, surveying what could be done to improve defenses.

Shaped like an hourglass, with the helipad in its narrow neck, Hickory straddled a slightly rising ridgeline with steep dropoffs on the sides. Cavaiani decided to abandon the lower half, concentrating his men on the higher, north half so they could shoot downhill as the enemy came across the open helipad. To slow the NVA, he placed on the helipad a booby-trapped 4.2-inch mortar shell that would explode when touched.

From the outhouse he dragged the washtub-size honey bucket and cut a shooting port, then hid a Yard machine-gunner there behind sandbags. Next he positioned two more machine guns to provide cross fire on the helipad, then he built a little firing position for himself atop a bunker so he could see over the pad.

About 7 P.M. the sun sank below Co Roc Mountain, and as it got dark a thick fog rolled over Hickory, just as a USAF AC-119 Stinger gunship arrived. An hour later came the first probes—the booby-trapped mortar shell exploded and several NVA cried out and fell back. The fog was so dense that the Stinger couldn't fire.

It was quiet for an hour and a half.

Then fifteen NVA rushed onto the helipad, right into the intersecting fire of the three machine guns; by the time they saw the muzzle flashes, they were dead. Ten minutes later came another fifteen NVA, with the same result—then another fifteen. Eight times they stormed the helipad, and each time the SOG defenders mowed them down, until just after midnight the enemy pulled back to reconsider.

Cavaiani discerned the NVA were about to launch a mass assault, so he shifted his men into Hickory's heaviest bunkers—but the NVA struck while the Yards were pulling back, and in the confusion dozens of enemy stormed over the helipad and across Hickory. Standing atop a bunker, Cavaiani fired a few rounds, then realized he was exposed and bent over to get down. An AK slug hit the small of his back, tearing flesh almost to his shoulder, knocking him to the ground. He rolled into a bunker with John Jones and radioed the Stinger, "I've got eighty to a hundred people in the open. My people are all under cover, come in from the northeast to the southwest." Fearing friendly casualties, the pilot refused. Cavaiani again called for a gun run, this time giving his initials. "If you don't know what my initials mean, it means I accept full responsiblity for this fire mission—*Fire!*" But the gunship pilot would not fire.

By now NVA could be heard going bunker to bunker, shooting and tossing grenades. Any second they'd find the two Americans.

Cavaiani pulled his Gerber Mk II fighting knife and announced, "Anybody comes through the door, I'll take him." As quickly, two NVA climbed in, one with a flashlight and his rifle slung over his back, the second, his rifle at the ready; Cavaiani seized the second NVA's hair and jammed his dagger up through his chin, killing him, then Jones shot the other NVA, who rolled out the door, screamed and collapsed.

Momentarily a hand grenade bounced in, which wounded Jones seriously and all but deafened Cavaiani. Too badly injured to resist further, Jones announced, "Jon, I'm going to surrender," and climbed out. An NVA soldier yelled, an AK fired and Jones tumbled back in, dead.

Then another grenade fell into the bunker and exploded and knocked Cavaiani unconscious, also destroying his radio.

When he groped back to consciousness it was still dark but he could feel a fresh leg wound and blood flowing from his ears. At the sight of flickering flashlights, he played dead, leaving his eyes wide open and unblinking while an NVA prodded his chest with an AK. Satisfied, the NVA pulled a cigarette lighter and set the bunker's tar paper ceiling afire, then went outside with other NVA to watch the flames.

Hot tar dripped on Cavaiani's face and his pants caught fire, but he dared not move; the torture was excruciating. Finally he decided, "I'm gonna John Wayne these bastards," and tried to jump to his feet, but rubble had collapsed on him, and he had to squeeze and heave to free himself. The NVA soldiers had walked away.

Exhausted, he stumbled out the door just as a slug cooked off from a burning machine gun. The round grazed his head and knocked him out. When he awoke the bunker was burned out, it was pitch black and he could hear the enemy looting Hickory. Gooey, burned skin hung from his fingers.

When a rummaging NVA almost stepped on him, Cavaiani pulled his final weapon, the Gerber knife, and slammed it so hard into the man's chest that he couldn't extract it, only pulled burned skin from his hand. Just before dawn he crawled through the wire, slid down a cliff face and evaded toward Firebase Fuller.*

For ten days Cavaiani stumbled, crawled and dragged himself eastward before reaching Firebase Fuller one morning at 3 A.M. He decided to sleep and wait until dawn to approach the wire. At sunrise he stood and an old man stuck a bolt-action rifle in his back; momentarily five more Communists appeared, and Cavaiani was on his way to Laos, a POW.

The NVA beat Cavaiani severely, trying to learn what he knew of the NSA van; he maintained he was only an NCO and not privy to whatever secrets the mysterious van possessed.

Eventually the NVA trucked him, two surviving Yards and his Vietnamese intepreter to Vinh, where they boarded a train for Hanoi. When they arrived, Cavaiani's interpreter dropped all pretense of being a fellow prisoner and proudly donned the uniform of an NVA intelligence officer—he was an enemy mole!

The North Vietnamese did not admit capturing Cavaiani for a year. Then, in March 1973, he was released with other U.S. POWs. For his determined, selfless defense of Hickory, Cavaiani was awarded the Medal of Honor in 1974.

After the Hickory helicopter fiasco, SOG reassigned its own 20th SOS Green Hornet Hueys to CCN. Never again would a SOG man be abandoned due to institutional or personal vanities.

In early August, CCN RT Kansas was assigned the job of penetrating the NVA curtain near Khe Sanh, no small task since there were as many NVA there in 1971 as during the 1968 siege.

For several months, U.S. intelligence had monitored a major concentration of NVA gradually moving across the DMZ then down South

*After Hickory fell, a U.S. spokesman told the Associated Press there was "no report of any such base."

Vietnam's Cam Lo River valley, about a dozen miles east of Khe Sanh. What they were up to seemed a mystery best solved by interrogating a fresh NVA prisoner.

Studying his mission, the RT Kansas One-Zero, First Lieutenant Loren "Festus" Hagen, brainstormed with his One-One, Sergeant Tony "Fast Eddie" Andersen, and One-Two, Sergeant Bruce Berg.

In recent months there'd been a flurry of heavily armed teams landing on old firebases, shooting hell out of the enemy and extracting; why not try that—except, only extract about half the team, leaving the other half hidden on the hill. When the NVA sent a squad up there to see if the Americans had left anything behind—as the NVA always did—the stay-behind element would ambush them, seize a prisoner and come out.

It was perfect, and it would take only twenty-four hours.

Lieutenant Hagen decided to take fourteen men, reinforcing his team with three straphangers—Staff Sergeant Oran Bingham and Sergeants Bill Queen and William Rimondi—for eight Yards and six U.S.

Everyone was confident and upbeat under Hagen's leadership. Easygoing and smart, the Fargo, North Dakota, native was one of those rare junior officers who thrived on Special Forces' informality yet didn't become "one of the boys." He was both liked and respected.

RT Kansas inserted at last light on 6 August 1971, landing on the old hilltop firebase, just 50 yards wide. Hagen's men went to work immediately, restoring its two dilapidated bunkers and shallow trenches and digging in their heaviest weapon, a 60mm mortar. Surveying the scrub brush and bomb craters below them, Hagen split his defense into three sectors to fit three slopes, grouping together Berg and Rimondi on the south, One-One Andersen and several Yards to the northwest, with himself, Bingham, Queen and the rest of the Yards covering the west.

Hagen could see that several approaches afforded decent cover and concealment, especially to the south. Still, with a C-130 Spectre above them, they could throw back any force the NVA could muster at short notice, and besides, they only had to hold the hilltop one night. Just to be safe, he positioned Tony Andersen, his most experienced NCO—who had both an M-60 machine gun and a CAR-15—to cover the most vulnerable slope. Certainly the NVA had seen them land, and Hagen reckoned to be ready for them.

Indeed the North Vietnamese had seen RT Kansas' two Hueys

hover above the old firebase, instigating a phone call to the nearby 304th NVA Division Headquarters, which found the recon team's presence intolerable.

From their little hilltop, RT Kansas' first inkling of an NVA presence came at 9 P.M., well after dark, when they saw campfires on the ridge-lines north and west of them, unusual because the enemy normally masked himself. At midnight the NVA fired shots below the hill from north, south, east and west—the SOG men had never seen such wide-scale probing and, of course, didn't return fire.

At 1 A.M., Spectre arrived and the team invisibly marked their perimeter with infrared strobe lights. The big C-130 gunship fired for them all night, walking 40mm and 20mm rounds within 10 yards of them. Not once did RT Kansas fire, staying blanketed protectively in darkness. Then at 3 A.M. they heard trucks arrive and tailgates dropping—it was odd, very odd.

Beneath the hill, dismounting NVA soldiers formed up into platoons and companies, which their leaders marched in careful order to their as-signed attack positions, to wait for dawn.

Just before sunrise the enemy ceased probing fire and it became fore-bodingly quiet. Then the SOG men heard more trucks.

At Phu Bai, Covey and a flight of helicopters was lifting away for the planned false extract; they would be above RT Kansas in thirty minutes. Already, Lieutenant Hagen had radioed Covey, telling him something was developing, that the NVA were moving through the heavy ground fog.

As darkness gave way to light, Hagen detected glimpses of enemy on one slope, which his men could certainly handle; then on another slope NVA pith helmets were seen bobbing in the fog, and he grew concerned, especially since he didn't know anything about the third slope. When his men reported NVA there, too, Hagen realized the entire hill was ringed by NVA, a force spread so wide that it would have to be more than a thousand men, a whole regiment!

The NVA regimental commander understood he had to dispatch the Americans, and do it quickly. RT Kansas had inadvertently landed al-most within sight of the Hanoi High Command's most critical new ven-ture, the first 6-inch fuel pipeline laid across the DMZ and down the Cam Lo River valley, absolutely essential in a few months when entire tank battalions would roll through here for the war's largest offensive. Already the NVA 304th Division, plus a regiment of the 308th Division, were massing nearby, preparing for the offensive.

A fourth NVA battalion commander radioed that his men were in place and prepared to assault. Ground fog concealed them from American air strikes, so the regimental commander waited for yet a fifth battalion to get into position, by which time he'd have committed nearly two thousand infantrymen to crush RT Kansas.

Later, Chief SOG Sadler would learn an entire regiment had stormed the hill, supported by a second regiment, the most one-sided fight of the war. A regiment was all it took to overrun Kham Duc Special Forces Camp in 1968; one third that many NVA swallowed up Lang Vei Special Forces Camp in one night. Here on this remote, scrub-covered hill, RT Kansas' fourteen men with CAR-15s, grenade launchers and a single M-60 machine gun, were outnumbered 107 to 1, a mismatch seven times greater than that at the Alamo.

As the truth became evident, Lieutenant Hagen saw there was no time for gestures or inspiring words, just serious soldier work; he spent those final moments repositioning men and weapons, readying grenades and stacking magazines. One-One Andersen crawled out and checked their claymores to ensure they hadn't been turned around or disabled. The Catholic Montagnards made the sign of the cross.

Then the NVA came.

A single, well-aimed RPG round smashed into Bruce Berg's bunker, collapsing it and signaling the attack. As if a dam had burst, NVA fire went from nothing to all out in two seconds. Ten thousand rounds per second were striking a space the size of a tennis court!

Hagen looked to Berg's bunker and shouted to Andersen, "We're getting hit on that side, we're being assaulted!" At the same time, Andersen could see dozens of NVA rushing in lines up his slope and was meeting them with his M-60 machine gun. Hagen hollered that he was going to check Berg; Andersen nodded to one Yard, "Tsao, go with him."

Tremendous AK fire was cutting the air from all directions—terrible fire, equal to fifty miniguns sweeping back and forth—but Berg could be bleeding to death, so Hagen ran directly into that maelstrom, toward the collapsed bunker, bullets ricocheting and slamming the earth in front of, behind, and beneath his dashing feet. Momentarily, Tsao trotted

back to Andersen and shouted, "The *trung ui* (lieutenant) is dead." Hagen had hardly gone a dozen yards when fire from NVA rushing up another slope cut him down.

Then Klaus Bingham left a bunker to reposition a claymore and
didn't get 6 feet before a bullet struck him in the head, apparently killing
him. The Yard with Bingham could not even risk checking him, the fire
was so furious.

One Yard in a trench below Andersen fired several bursts, then
jumped up to pull back. He attracted intense fire and fell into Andersen's lap, dead. The bullet that struck him would have hit Andersen had
the Yard not taken it instead. Four men had died in less than four minutes.

It was up to Andersen now, the senior man.

Small-arms fire rattled closer on all sides, and grenades lobbed up
from below the hillcrest, beyond the defenders' vision. The danger
wasn't just the NVA they saw, but the more numerous enemy crawling
and scurrying nearer behind small rises and from bomb crater to bomb
crater.

Andersen dashed across the hill to look for Hagen but couldn't see
him anywhere—just one hundred khaki-clad NVA almost at the top! He
ran back for his M-60, fired one belt at NVA coming up his own slope,
then sped to the other approach and ran belt after belt on the one hundred assaulting enemy. By then grenades started coming from behind
him as NVA closed in from his rear.

Now within a dozen yards, just beyond the curvature of the hill,
NVA popped up their heads, cracked a few shots at Andersen, then
dropped back down.

Covey arrived, took one look at that hillside alive with NVA,
scrubbed the snatch mission and called for fighters. But it would be
more precious minutes before they were overhead.

Fighting a westerly headwind, the helicopters were still a dozen minutes away. The Cobra gunships went to full throttle, leaving the slower
Hueys behind.

Meanwhile RT Kansas was pulling hand grenade pins, counting to
three then heaving the grenades to airburst above the NVA—then they
were out of grenades. A North Vietnamese grenade exploded beside Andersen's M-60, rendering it useless—he spun his CAR-15 off his back

and kept shooting, then he tossed back one enemy grenade that went off in front of him, leaving bright spots in his vision, but he kept shooting. More shrapnel tore into him, then an AK round slammed through his web gear and lodged in his elbow, knocking him down. He stumbled back to his knees and kept shooting.

The perimeter was pinched almost in half when Andersen grabbed his two remaining Yards, circled below and around the nearest NVA and somehow managed to reach the survivors on the opposite side. He found Bingham, started to lift him, and saw he, too, was dead, from a head wound. All around him he heard *zzzsss, zzssss, zzssss* as bullets flashed past his ears.

Andersen dragged Bingham's body back to where Bill Queen lay, wounded. Only Rimondi wasn't yet hit and still fired furiously. Andersen put them in a back-to-back circle just off the hilltop where they would make their last stand. An AK slug already had destroyed their team radio, another had shot Andersen's little survival radio out of his hand, so Rimondi tossed the One-One another survival radio, their last.

Now the NVA were *streaming,* rolling over the hillcrest like a tidal wave, their rattling AKs blending together into one never-ending burst. Andersen's men were shooting not at NVA but at hands wielding AKs over parapets and around bunkers. There was no place left to fall back and they could no longer spare five seconds to talk to Covey—Andersen was shooting NVA not much farther away than the end of his CAR-15's muzzle. The time it took to speed-change a CAR-15 magazine meant life or death.

From the air it looked like an ant mound, with moving figures everywhere. Cobra lead rolled in and sparkled 20mm cannon shells around the surviving RT Kansas men while Covey's OV-10 slipped sideways to strafe with machine guns and rockets. Then at last fighters arrived, adding splashing napalm and groaning Vulcan cannons to the melee.

Precise Cobra gunship fire stacked NVA in front of RT Kansas' final holdouts, then at last the assault ebbed, turned, and the surviving NVA fled for cover, just as the Hueys arrived.

The smoke-shrouded hill was an unforgettable sight: Beneath wisps of napalm flames lay khaki-clad bodies all the way up the slopes, then heaps of dead NVA radiated outward from a handful of dark green figures.

Though wounded repeatedly, Andersen crawled out to fire his CAR-

15 to cover the landing Hueys as they came in, machine guns blazing, while their escorting Cobra gunships sprayed cannon and minigun fire all around them. With Rimondi's help, Andersen got as many team-mates' bodies as he could find aboard the first Huey, then helped the wounded Queen and others aboard the second.

Under intense fighter and Cobra attack, few NVA fired at the Hueys as they lifted away.

Despite his wounds, three hours later Andersen accompanied the Bright Light mission, commanded by Noel Gast, which included RTs Cobra and Indiana. Along with Jimmy Reeves and Sam "Injun" Adams, and even the CCN commander, Lieutenant Colonel Donnie Bellfi, they searched the hilltop, recovered Lieutenant Hagen's body and those of several Montagnards but never found Bruce Berg.

Already the NVA had recovered their own bodies and withdrawn.

The Bright Light team withdrew under light ground fire.

Lieutenant Hagen had died, along with Bingham, Berg was presumed dead, three Yards had died, Rimondi and Queen both suffered multiple frag wounds, Andersen had been struck by both small-arms fire and shrapnel, and their other Yards, too, had all been wounded.

Against this, Tony Andersen learned, the USAF had confirmed that 185 NVA lay dead on that hill. Little RT Kansas had wiped out half a battalion. But compared to the loss of his best friends, that gave Andersen sparse satisfaction.

The RT Kansas debriefing resulted in one of SOG's most dramatic documents, and a quote from Andersen so inspired Colonel Pezzelle that he had it engraved on a plaque: *"I looked up at the bunker in front of me and saw a khaki-uniformed NVA with pith helmet, chest web gear, green Bata boots and an AK, Type 56, and no other identifying insignia. Then I shot him."*

"It's just perfect," Pezzelle said. "It epitomized the SOG soldier who knew what his job was, which was gathering intelligence, then he turns around and fights when he has to."

First Lieutenant Loren Hagen's family was presented the U.S. Army's final Vietnam War Medal of Honor; Tony Andersen, his One-One who held together what remained of RT Kansas through those final mass assaults, received the Distinguished Service Cross, while Queen, Rimondi, Berg and Bingham were awarded Silver Stars.

A few days after coming off the hill, Tony Andersen took the bodies of his three Montagnard teammates to their little village, a place where they'd feasted and drunk rice wine together. As his truck rolled in, fearful women looked up from their work, knowing unannounced visitors meant bad news, and sobbing started as soon as the truck halted.

The entire village gathered at the headman's longhouse, where in their tribe's tradition, Andersen told of the fallen men's bravery and the many NVA they'd killed. It gave comfort to mothers and sisters to know their men had fought honorably, and to the brothers and fathers, great pride that they'd killed so many of the detested North Vietnamese. The Montagnard boys' dark eyes watched, as they hung on Andersen's every detail as the interpreter related the battle.

Despite the tragedy there was pride in the village.

When Andersen returned to his truck he found a cluster of nervous Montagnard boys, one of whom explained they wanted to return with him, learn how to fight and go kill the NVA. Most of the eager faces belonged to thirteen- and fourteen-year-olds, standing erect and swelling their chests to look older. Andersen nodded to the two oldest, who grinned and scrambled happily aboard the truck.

SOG's secret war continued into the fall of 1971, as teams documented the continuing NVA buildup. By October, seven of every nine missions had teams fighting for survival, yet they were always ready to go back, as if it were still 1965 and America was fighting to win.

In early October, USAF Captain Jim Cryer and I spotted an NVA regiment walking a Laotian road in broad daylight, which led to three days' incessant bombing—directed as well by Covey Riders Lowell Stevens and Larry White—which practically wiped out the entire unit, quite likely one of the most effective air attacks of the war.

That same month, NVA tanks were spotted in southern Laos, their first significant appearance there in over two years. When CCC commander Lieutenant Colonel Mike Radke reported this, the civilian II Corps adviser, John Paul Vann, shouted, "That's a lot of horseshit!" Vann's humility returned as evidence mounted.

In Saigon there was a hesitance to accept SOG's warnings by minimizing and nitpicking intelligence reports, which came to a head during a briefing for General Abrams. Chief SOG had just presented recon team reports of tanks and tank trails coming out of Laos, when a MACV staff officer began demanding arcane details before the intelligence could be accepted. Abrams suddenly grew furious, slammed his fist on the table and barked, "I don't know what you want these soldiers to do! Do you want them to personally bring back the battalion flag so you can see what the hell his unit is before you believe? Because goddamn it, I send these guys out there, they have the worst job in this command and do it brilliantly, and they bring back intelligence and they risk their lives and you guys sit on your hands and say, 'We don't believe this shit.'" There were no further credibility problems.

Each evening that fall, SOG data was consolidated and rushed to a courier plane, which carried the intelligence to Paris, allowing American negotiators to follow the NVA buildup and refer to it in their deliberations. When North Vietnamese negotiator Le Duc Tho walked out on Henry Kissinger's secret talks that November, Kissinger fully understood a major new offensive was in the offing.

While on a recon mission on 11 October, Sergeant First Class Audley Mills was killed, SOG's final ground fatality. He was on his third Vietnam combat tour.

During November, eight of eleven recon teams spent less than two hours on the ground before large numbers of NVA forced them out.

Then in December, one last recon team dared to penetrate the Ashau Valley, found tracked vehicles, called air strikes on NVA trucks and made it out unscathed.

SOG's combat role came to a quiet, unacknowledged close. SOG's men had acquitted themselves bravely, to the very end.

AFTERWORD

It was several more months before SOG disbanded officially, an event as unheralded as its creation had been eight years earlier. But during those secretive years, SOG had logged a combat record unequaled in U.S. history.

The Vietnam War's most highly decorated unit, with five Medals of Honor, was SOG's understrength, sixty-man recon company at Kontum. Surely no unit that size had been so decorated since the Civil War. And in that final perilous year when SOG fought alone, Danang-based CCN, with only about seventy combat operatives, earned two Medals of Honor and three Distinguished Service Crosses. Among SOG's recon units, Purple Hearts were earned at a pace unparalleled in American wars of this century, with casualties at times exceeding 100 percent.

Although steep relative to the numbers of men involved, of course, SOG's losses were small compared to the war's overall American casualties. SOG's precise losses, however, remain difficult to pin down because the U.S. government falsely attributed those killed or missing in North Vietnam, Laos and Cambodia to combat in South Vietnam. In July 1973, the Defense Department attempted to make a clean breast of it, admitting to the *New York Times* that "81 American servicemen, most of them members of the Special Forces, had been killed in Laos and Cambodia since 1965 while on secret missions." But the double-bookkeeping system proved so confounding that the Pentagon had understated casualties, a fact that became evident when families of MIAs demanded more information. Today, although the records remain imperfect, it is apparent that more than three hundred SOG Americans were lost, fifty-seven of them MIA. As recently as 1991, for example, SOG's first MIA in Laos, Larry Thorne, was incorrectly listed as missing in South Vietnam.

Most SOG MIAs were bodies left behind when teams were about to be overrun. But a sizable portion of those missing—perhaps fifteen or more— were likely captured, their disappearance a grim testament to the vindictiveness with which those who dared to trespass in the NVA's backyard were treated. Not only does Hanoi continue to deny any knowledge of these men, it still insists it never had troops in Laos, and its postwar maps depict the Ho Chi Minh Trail as having been inside South Vietnam.

SOG recon and Hatchet Force operations were the most successful economy of force in U.S. history, pulling away tens of thousands of NVA from the battlefields of South Vietnam for rear security duty in Laos and Cambodia. At one point each American Green Beret operating in Laos was tying down six hundred NVA defenders, or about one NVA battalion per SOG recon man in the field.

U.S. Marine and Army units benefited from SOG's destruction or capture of thousands of tons of munitions and supplies, which thereby could not be used against them. No small contribution, either: Thousands of enemy soldiers killed by SOG men would never fight in South Vietnam. SOG recon men consistently killed more than one hundred NVA for each lost Green Beret, a ratio that climbed as high as 150:1, which MACV documented in 1969. This was the highest documented kill ratio of any American unit in the war, exceeding the average by a factor of ten, and quite likely is the highest such ratio in U.S. history.

Still more lives were saved when SOG's intelligence enabled U.S. forces to counter or pinpoint the NVA, especially after American troops invaded Cambodia in 1970.

To these many GIs saved indirectly must be added the lives saved directly when SOG Bright Light teams rescued downed pilots from deep behind NVA lines.

Another legacy of SOG is the impact it had within the special operations community. The ever-dynamic Chief SOG Jack Singlaub, after retiring as a major general, influenced the congressional creation of Special

Operations Command, lifting special ops to a career field for Special Forces officers and NCOs while bringing together all services' special ops units under a single headquarters. Special Forces received its own air arm, the 160th Aviation Regiment, to ensure today's Green Berets don't have to beg, borrow and steal helicopters, as was the case with SOG.

Just as the OSS helped define the path for the CIA and Special Forces, SOG's improvisations helped forge today's special ops doctrine for units such as Delta Force. Indeed, Delta Force's founding sergeant major was Walter Shumate, while its primary trainer was Dick Meadows, both distinguished SOG veterans.

By no casual coincidence, the U.S. Green Beret teams that landed deep behind Iraqi lines to rescue downed pilots during the Persian Gulf War were on "Bright Light" duty, their concept and operational procedures having evolved from SOG.

Likewise, the Green Beret strategic reconnaissance teams that HALO parachuted into Iraq's Tigris and Euphrates River Valley were executing missions quite familiar to the SOG old hands who secretly had developed such techniques twenty-five years ago.

Visitors at Fort Bragg, North Carolina, today can see hints of SOG's once secret existence. The Special Warfare Museum is housed in Simons Hall, named for SOG's Shining Brass chief, the burly Colonel Arthur "Bull" Simons, who also led the 1970 attempt to rescue POWs from North Vietnam's Son Tay Prison.

Then there's the vertical wind tower where Special Forces HALO parachutists perfect their skills, Strohlein Hall, named for SOG HALO jumper Madison Strohlein, MIA and believed captured.

Scattered here and there across the country are other, small memorials. A highway rest stop near Rockford, Illinois, bears the name of MIA Lieutenant Jerry Poole, the One-Zero of RT Pennsylvania. The family and friends of David Mixter, SOG's final MIA in Laos, donated a sailing sloop in his name to Maine's Hurricane Island Outward Bound, where today's young people might discover a love of the sea and sailing such as he had known.

Perhaps the most unique memorial is one to Walter Shumate, the focus of Special Forces' longest-running practical joke. When Shumate died two years ago, Cliff Newman—One-Zero of SOG's first HALO team—skydived above Delta Force's top secret compound at Fort Bragg to scatter Shumate's ashes. In accordance with Walter's other last request, visitors to Delta's headquarters will find displayed under glass his handlebar mustache.

Though they never cared much about awards, in 1995 Cliff Newman and other SOG HALO jumpers finally were authorized to receive special HALO wings with a combat star attachment, a quarter century after the fact.

However, Charles Wilklow, the only SOG man to escape enemy captivity in Laos, was denied a POW Service Medal when that medal was created four years ago. The problem, his family was told, was a lack of records to document his capture because SOG's top-secret files had not been declassified. Wilklow passed away in 1992.

It is men like Charles Wilklow, "tremendous unsung heroes," that Chief SOG Steve Cavanaugh had in mind when he explained his greatest disappointment was the lack of public recognition for SOG men's secret missions.

"They were the greatest troops our army ever had," said Colonel Roger Pezzelle, "and I'd put 'em up against anybody's." His opinion is shared by SOG's former adversaries, the North Vietnamese. Nguyen Tuong Lai, an NVA officer who'd served on the Ho Chi Minh Trail, said SOG's Green Berets "effectively attacked and weakened our forces and hurt our morale because we could not stop these attacks. We understood that these American soldiers were very skillful and very brave in their tactics to disrupt infiltration from the North." Another former NVA told write Al Santoli that SOG recon men were unquestionably America's finest fighters in the war.

Despite the war's outcome, SOG veterans carry an intense pride at having performed dangerous missions among brave men, and their good memories outweigh the bad ones. "It was the best assignment I had," said Blackbird crewman Don James, a sentiment almost universal among SOG veterans.

"If you had to sell parts of your life," explained One-Zero Will Curry, "the last piece I'd sell is the eighteen months I spent running recon at Kontum."

SOG fades into the past, its secret initials taking their place among distinguished ranks—OSS, SOE, JACK, CIA. Old recon men still gather to toast departed comrades and sing "Hey, Blue," reciting name after name. The war may be forgotten, but those names are not.

GLOSSARY

A Camps: Border surveillance camps manned by U.S. Special Forces–led mercenaries, to detect infiltrating NVA units. SOG sometimes launched cross-border operations from A Camps.

A-1 Skyraider: Korean War vintage, propeller-driven fighter-bomber, a SOG favorite because of its heavy payload, long loiter time and precision ordnance delivery.

Arc Light: Code name for a B-52 strike. Arc Lights were planned in multiples of cells of three planes each.

ARVN (Army of the Republic of Vietnam): South Vietnamese Army. *See* STD

ASA (Army Security Agency): Agency responsible for U.S. Army signal and code security.

BDA (Bomb Damage Assessment): Post-strike ground reconnaissance of a B-52 target, conducted by SOG recon teams.

Benson Silk: Code name for counterfeit North Vietnamese currency.

Binh Tram: Literally, a "commo-liaison site." North Vietnamese complexes along the Ho Chi Minh Trail, with autonomous engineer, transport, antiaircraft, supply and security units. More than a dozen such complexes operated the Trail in Laos.

Black propaganda: Purposeful lies and deceptions, intended to confuse the enemy or cast him in the worst possible light. The originator of an item of black propaganda is obscured or misidentified.

Blackbirds: Unofficial term for the black USAF C-130s in SOG's 90th Special Operations Squadron.

Bra: Especially dangerous NVA base area in southern Laos, called The Bra because Highway 96 crossed a double-curved river there.

Bright Light: SOG code name for POW and evadee rescue attempts behind enemy lines.

C&C (Command and Control): Danang field headquarters for SOG's U.S.-led cross-border operations. Also a generic term for these operations.

CAR-15: Submachine gun version of M-16 rifle, with folding stock and shortened barrel. A SOG recon man's favorite weapon.

CAS (Combined Area Studies): Cover name for CIA elements and programs in South Vietnam.

CCC (Command and Control Central): SOG base at Kontum, South Vietnam, for U.S.-led SOG missions into northern Cambodia and southern Laos. Also called FOB-2. *See* Project Omega

CCN (Command and Control North): SOG base at Danang near Marble Mountain, with outlying FOBs [see] at Khe Sanh, Phu Bai, Kham Duc and Kontum. CCN men operated mostly in Laos and the DMZ.

CCS (Command and Control South): SOG base at Ban Me Thuot, for U.S.-led missions into central Cambodia.

Chief SOG: Official title for the SOG commander.

CISO (Counterinsurgency Support Office): Okinawa-based office that handled covert logistic duties after the CIA transferred its covert programs to SOG.

COSVN (Central Office for South Vietnam): Field headquarters for the Viet Cong's political wing, the National Liberation Front (NLF), located 2 miles inside Cambodia, northwest of Saigon.

Covey: Call sign for USAF Forward Air Control (FAC) units at Danang and Pleiku that directly supported SOG cross-border missions.

Covey Rider: Longtime Special Forces recon man who flew with USAF FACs to help direct air strikes, insert and extract SOG teams and monitor the Ho Chi Minh Trail corridor.

Daniel Boone: SOG code name for its Cambodian operations area. *See* Salem House

DMZ (Demilitarized Zone): A 14-mile-strip straddling the 17th Parallel in which neither North nor South Vietnam was to place military forces. Grossly violated by the NVA. *See* Nickel Steel

DSC (Distinguished Service Cross): U.S. Army award immediately lower in precedence to the Medal of Honor, equivalent to the Navy Cross and Air Force Cross.

FAC (Forward Air Controller): USAF pilot flying a small airplane such as the Cessna O-1 Bird Dog, and tasked to find and mark bombing targets and to control air strikes.

FGU (Friendly Guerrilla Unit): SOG-created cover, designed to conceal the fact that intelligence was gathered by Special Forces teams.

5th Special Forces Group: Official headquarters for all Green Berets in South Vietnam, although SOG's Green Berets actually took their orders from Saigon and the Pentagon.

1st Flight Detachment: Ostensibly a USAF unit, the First Flight's SOG C-123 transports often were flown by Chinese Nationalist pilots so, if they were downed over North Vietnam and captured, U.S. involvement could be plausibly denied.

1st Special Forces Group: The Okinawa-based 1st Group provided support and personnel to SOG; the 1st Shining Brass recon men were 1st Group volunteers.

Fishhook: Major NVA base area in southeast Cambodia, that typically housed two or three enemy divisions. One of SOG's most dangerous cross-border targets.

559th Transportation Group: Secret North Vietnamese unit that operated the Ho Chi Minh Trail. Based in Vinh, North Vietnam, the 559th had its forward headquarters in SOG Target Oscar Eight, 25 miles southwest of Khe Sanh.

FOB (Forward Operating Base): Permanent SOG camp where Special Forces and mercenary troops were housed and trained.

Fulton Recovery System: A clandestine extraction system using a gas-filled balloon to suspend a cable, that the yoke installed on a C-130 Blackbird's nose could snare, snatching a man from the ground and then winching him inside. Nicknamed "Skyhook."

Green Hornets: Code name for a USAF Huey unit, the 20th Special Operations Squadron, which flew SOG missions in Cambodia.

HALO (High Altitude, Low Opening): Military skydiving.

Hatchet Force: Code name for SOG platoons and companies.

Hmongs: Laotian tribesmen who were the backbone of CIA mercenary forces. Fighting almost exclusively around the Plain of Jars, they had no impact on the Ho Chi Minh Trail.

Ho Chi Minh Trail: A camouflaged highway network, in the jungled southeastern Laos corridor occupied by the NVA after 1959, across which flowed supplies and soldiers for the war in South Vietnam.

Immediate Action Drill (IA Drill): A series of planned, practiced actions a recon team executed to break contact with numerically superior enemy forces.

JACK (Joint Advisory Commission, Korea): The CIA-affiliated Korean War unit that conducted covert special operations.

Jolly Green Giant: Originally the Sikorsky HH-3 helicopter. When the larger but similar-looking HH-53 was introduced, it was dubbed the Super Jolly Green Giant. Both were flown by the Ponies. *See* Ponies

JPRC (Joint Personnel Recovery Center): Cover organization for SOG's OPS-80, which supervised Bright Light rescue attempts of American POWs and evadees behind enemy lines.

Kingbee: Code name for South Vietnamese Air Force (VNAF) H-34 helicopters that supported SOG cross-border operations.

Leghorn: SOG radio relay and NSA signal intercept site atop a pinnacle in southern Laos.

Long-Term Agent Teams: CIA- and SOG-recruited North Vietnamese refugees, trained then infiltrated back into the North, for long-term intelligence missions.

McGuire rig: A large swing seat attached to a rope, lowered from a helicopter hovering above the treetops, for emergency extraction of SOG recon men. Also called "strings." *See* STABO rig

Mike Force: Highly regarded companies and battalions of mercenaries, usually Montagnards, led by Green Berets of the 5th Special Forces Group, for combat inside South Vietnam.

Montagnards: South Vietnamese hill tribesmen related ethnically to Polynesians. Heavily recruited as mercenaries for SOG and other Special Forces units. Called "Yards" by Americans.

NAD (Naval Advisory Detachment): SOG element based in Danang, where Navy SEALs and USMC Force Recon men oversaw the training and operations of Vietnamese-led teams that carried out clandestine naval missions along North Vietnam's coastline. NAD's U.S. personnel were not allowed to accompany their indigenous operatives above the DMZ.

Nasty-class PTF: CIA-acquired, Norwegian-built gunboats SOG used for hit-and-run raids against North Vietnam's coastline.

Nickel Steel: Code name for SOG operations area that straddled the western DMZ.

Nightingale Device: A CIA-developed diversionary device whose continuing explosions sounded like a firefight.

NKP (Nakhon Phanom Royal Thai Air Force Base): SOG launch site for operations into Laos and North Vietnam, beginning in 1967.

NSA (National Security Agency): U.S. organization responsible for intercepting enemy signals and code breaking.

Nungs: South Vietnamese tribesmen of Chinese origin, renowned for their fighting qualities. Employed as mercenaries by SOG.

NVA: North Vietnamese Army.

One-One: Code name for a U.S. Special Forces SOG recon team assistant team leader.

One-Two: Code name for a U.S. Special Forces SOG recon team radio operator.

One-Zero: Code name for a U.S. Special Forces SOG recon team leader.

Operation Switchback: Designation for CIA's December 1963 transfer of Southeast Asian covert activities to military control and, in January 1964, to the newly created SOG.

OPS-33: Numerical designation for SOG's Psychological Studies Branch, which supervised black propaganda activities.

OPS-34: Designation for Airborne Studies Branch, which oversaw agent team operations in North Vietnam and, later, in Laos and Cambodia.

OPS-35: SOG's Ground Studies Branch, headquarters to the U.S.-led cross-border recon and Hatchet Force operations.

OPS-80: SOG's Recovery Studies Branch, responsible for Bright Light missions. *See* JPRC

OSS (Office of Strategic Services): America's World War II precursor to the CIA, responsible for espionage, sabotage and covert operations. The OSS was the model for SOG.

Outpost Hickory: SOG radio relay and NSA signal intercept site, located on a precipice northeast of abandoned Khe Sanh base.

Parrot's Beak: A Cambodian salient just northwest of Saigon, across which the NVA sometimes infiltrated units, especially during the 1968 Tet Offensive.

Ponies: Call sign for NKP-based USAF 21st Special Operations Squadron helicopters, that supported SOG and the CIA in Laos and North Vietnam.

Prairie Fire: SOG code name for Laotian operations area. Replaced Shining Brass in 1967.

Prairie Fire Emergency: A One-Zero's declaration that his team was about to be overrun, which conferred on his team priority for all U.S. strike aircraft over Laos.

Project Delta: Special Forces recon unit that operated inside South Vietnam, assigned to 5th Special Forces Group.

Project Eldest Son: A SOG black propaganda project that inserted booby-trapped Chinese ammunition into NVA stockpiles.

Project Omega: Initial code name for Special Forces–led recon unit that penetrated northern Cambodia. Later combined with CCC. *See* CCC

Project Sigma: Initial code name for Special Forces–led recon unit that penetrated southern Cambodia. Later became CCS. *See* CCS

Project White Star: CIA clandestine project that brought U.S. Special Forces advisers to western and northern Laos, 1960–61.

Psychological Studies Branch: See OPS-33

PTF (Patrol Type, Fast): See Nasty-class PTF

Recon team: A SOG recon team typically consisted of three U.S. Special Forces men and nine Nungs or Montagnards. To minimize detection, however, most One-Zeros took only six or eight men on each operation.

Sacred Sword of the Patriot League: False North Vietnamese resistance organization created by SOG to divert and confuse enemy counterintelligence.

SACSA (Special Assistant for Counterinsurgency and Special Activities): Pentagon element in the Office of the Joint Chiefs that oversaw and coordinated SOG activities with the White House, State Department and CIA. Headed by a general officer.

Salem House: SOG code name for its Cambodian operations area; replaced Daniel Boone in 1969.

SCU (Special Commando Unit): The ostensible unit to which SOG's Nung and Montagnard mercenaries supposedly belonged.

Sea Commandos: South Vietnamese counterparts to U.S. Navy SEALs.

Shining Brass: SOG code name for Laotian operations area. *See* Prairie Fire

Sihanoukville: Cambodia's major seaport, through which entire shiploads of military supplies were smuggled for the NVA.

Skyhook: See Fulton Recovery System

SOE (Special Operations Executive): Clandestine British WW II unit that conducted sabotage, espionage and special operations in Occupied Europe.

SOG (Studies and Observations Group): The Vietnam War's covert special warfare unit, essentially the OSS of Southeast Asia.

Spectre: Heavily armed gunship version of USAF C-130 transport plane.

STABO rig: An emergency extraction rig using special web gear that converts to a harness for attaching to a rope lowered through the treetops from a hovering helicopter. Also called "strings." *See* McGuire rig

STD (Strategic Technical Directorate): SOG's South Vietnamese counterpart organization.

Sterile: Unmarked or untraceable, usually referring to weapons or aircraft employed in covert operations.

Sterilize: Remove any sign of a team's passage, to throw off enemy trackers. Normally the responsibility of a team's One-One.

STRATA (Short-Term Roadwatch and Target Acquisition Teams): Vietnamese-led recon teams that SOG inserted in the panhandle of North Vietnam to monitor supply routes, usually for ten to twenty days per mission. No U.S. personnel accompanied these teams.

Strings: SOG slang for McGuire and STABO rigs. *See* McGuire rig; STABO rig

Swedish K submachine gun: A popular CIA and SOG weapon, the Swedish K was easily controlled and untraceable, but its 9mm round proved a bit underpowered. *See* CAR-15

Toe popper: U.S. M-14 antipersonnel mine. Small and fast to conceal, the M-14 was used by SOG recon men to defeat enemy trackers.

Trinh Sat: North Vietnam's secret intelligence service.

Viet Cong: Military units of indigenous South Vietnamese Communists. Almost ceased to exist after the 1968 Tet offensive.

Viet Minh: Communist military forces in the French-Indochina War, 1946–54. Some Indochinese, such as Cambodian Prince Sihanouk, also referred to the NVA as "Viet Minh."

Yard: American slang for Montagnard tribesman.

BIBLIOGRAPHY

Books

Anderson, William. *Bat-21.* New York: Bantam Books, 1980.

Benavidez, Roy, with Oscar Griffin. *The Three Wars of Roy Benavidez.* New York: Pocket Books, 1986.

Berry, John Stevens. *Those Gallant Men: On Trial in Vietnam.* Novato, CA: Presidio Press, 1984.

Blaufarb, Douglas. *Organizing and Managing Unconventional War in Laos, 1962–70.* RAND Study Reprint. Christiansburg, VA: Dalley Book Service, 1972.

Center for Air Force History. *USAF in Southeast Asia: Search and Rescue.* Washington, DC: Government Printing Office, 1992.

Chanoff, David, and Doan Van Toai. *Portrait of the Enemy.* New York: Random House, 1986.

Colby, William, and Peter Forbath. *Honorable Men: My Life in the CIA.* New York: Simon and Schuster, 1978.

Colby, William, with James McCargar. *Lost Victory.* Chicago: Contemporary Books, 1989.

Conboy, Kenneth, and James Morrison. *Shadow War: The CIA's Secret War in Laos.* Boulder, CO: Paladin Press, 1995.

DeForest, Orrin, and David Chanoff. *Slow Burn.* New York: Pocket Books, 1990.

Department of Defense, Joint Chiefs of Staff. *MACSOG Documentation Study.* Washington, DC: Joint Chiefs, 1970. (Note: This study includes dozens of appendices and annexes,many interviews and other reports. With a length of 2551 pages, it is the largest declassified source of SOG data.)

Department of the Air Force. USAF Southeast Asia Monograph Series. Vol. III, Monographs 4 & 5: *The Vietnamese Air Force, 1951–75.* Washington, DC: Government Printing Office, 1975.

———.USAF Southeast Asia Monograph Series. Vol. VII, Monograph 9: *Air Force Heroes in Vietnam.* Washington, DC: Government Printing Office, 1979.

———.*The U.S. Air Force in Southeast Asia: Development and Employment of Fixed-Wing Gunships, 1962–1972.* Washington, DC: Government Printing Office, 1982.

Department of the Army. Ethnographic Study Series. *Minority Groups in the Republic of Vietnam.* Washington, DC: Government Printing Office, 1966.

———. *Vietnam Studies: The Role of Military Intelligence.* Washington, DC: Government Printing Office, 1974.

———. *Vietnam Studies: U.S. Army Special Forces, 1961–71.* Washington, DC: Government Printing Office, 1973.

———. *Vietnam Studies: The War in the Northern Provinces, 1966–68.* Washington, DC: Government Printing Office, 1975.

Diem, Bui, with David Chanoff. *In the Jaws of History.* Boston: Houghton Mifflin Company, 1987.

Dorr, Robert. *Air War Hanoi.* London: Blandford Press, 1988.

———.*Douglas A-1 Skyraider.* London: Osprey, 1989.

Ellsberg, Daniel. *Papers on the War.* New York: Simon and Schuster, 1972.

Fall, Bernard. *Hell in a Very Small Place.* New York: Vintage Books, 1966.

———. *Street Without Joy.* Harrisburg, PA: The Stackpole Company, 1961.

———. *The Two Vietnams,* 2d rev. ed. New York: Praeger, 1966.

Fifth Special Forces Group. *The Green Beret, 1965–70.* Reprints. Vols. 1–5. Houston, TX: Radix Press, 1990.

Generous, Kevin. *Vietnam: The Secret War.* New York: Gallery Books, 1985.

Giap, Vo Nguyen. *How We Won the War.* Philadelphia: RECON Publications, 1976.

Grimes, Keith. *Special Operations Weatherman: An Oral Autobiography.* Scott AFB, IL: Military Airlift Command, 1978.

Gunston, Bill. *Aircraft of the Vietnam War.* Wellingborough, UK: Patrick Stephens, 1987.

Halpern, Joel, and William Turley, eds. *The Training of Vietnamese Communist Cadres in Laos.* Christiansburg, VA: Dalley Book Service, 1990.

Hammel, Eric. *Khe Sanh: Siege in the Clouds.* New York: Crown Books, 1989.

Harrison, Marshall. *A Lonely Kind of War.* Novato, CA: Presidio Press, 1989.

Hinh, Nguyen Duy. *Lam Son 719.* Washington, DC: U.S. Army Center of Military History, 1979.

Hubbell, John. *P.O.W.* New York: Reader's Digest Press, 1976.

Kissinger, Henry. *White House Years.* Boston: Little, Brown & Co., 1979.

Ky, Nguyen Cao. *Twenty Years and Twenty Days.* New York: Stein and Day, 1976.

Lanning, Michael, and Dan Cragg. *Inside the VC and the NVA.* New York: Fawcett/Columbine, 1992.

Le Gro, William. *Vietnam from Cease-Fire to Capitulation.* Washington, DC: U.S. Army Center of Military History, 1985.

McCoy, J. W. *Secrets of the Viet Cong.* New York: Hippocrene Books, 1992.

Miller, Franklin, with Elwood Kureth. *Reflections of a Warrior.* Novato, CA: Presidio Press, 1991.

Nixon, Richard. *No More Vietnams.* New York: Avon Books, 1985.

———. *The Real War.* New York: Warner Books, 1980.

Nolan, Keith. *Into Cambodia.* Novato, CA: Presidio Press, 1990.

————. *Into Laos.* New York: Dell Publishing, 1986.

Pike, Douglas. *PAVN: People's Army of Vietnam.* Novato, CA: Presidio Press, 1986.

————. *Viet Cong.* Cambridge, MA: MIT Press, 1966.

Pugh, Harry. *U.S. Special Forces Shoulder & Pocket Insignia.* Arlington, VA: C&D Enterprises, 1993.

Schemmer, Benjamin. *The Raid.* New York: Harper & Row, 1976

Sheehan, Neil, and Hedrick Smith, E. W. Kenworthy, Fox Butterfield. *The Pentagon Papers.* New York: Bantam Books, 1971.

Simpson, Charles. *Inside the Green Berets: The First Thirty Years.* Novato, CA: Presidio Press, 1983.

Singlaub, John, with Malcolm McConnell. *Hazardous Duty.* New York: Summit Books, 1991.

Snepp, Frank. *A Decent Interval.* New York: Vintage Books, 1978.

Sylvester, John. *Orders & Decorations of Communist Governments of Southeast Asia.* Raleigh, NC: privately printed, 1987.

Stanton, Shelby. *Green Berets at War.* Novato, CA: Presidio Press, 1985.

Stein, Jeff. *A Murder in Wartime.* New York: St. Martin's Press, 1992.

Tang, Truong Nhu. *A Vietcong Memoir.* San Diego, CA: Harcourt Brace Jovanovich, 1985.

Tho, Tran Dinh. *The Cambodian Incursion.* Washington, DC: U.S. Army Center of Military History, 1979.

Tragos, John. *The President's Secret Wars: CIA & Pentagon Covert Operations Since WWII.* New York: William Morrow, 1986.

U.S. Air Force. *The Air War in Vietnam, 1968–69.* Honolulu: HQ, Pacific Air Force, 1970.

————. *Air War Vietnam.* Reprint. New York: Arno Press, 1978.

————. *Ashau Valley Campaign, December 1968–May 1969.* Honolulu: HQ, Pacific Air Force, 1970.

————. *The Bolovens Campaign, 28 July–28 December 1971.* Honolulu: HQ, Pacific Air Force, 1974.

————. *The Cambodian Campaign, 29 April–30 June 1970.* Honolulu: HQ, Pacific Air Force, 1971.

————. *Khe Sanh (Operation Niagara), 22 January–31 March 1968.* Honolulu: HQ, Pacific Air Force, 1969.

U.S. Army. *Changing an Army: An Oral History of General William DePuy, USA Retired.* Washington: U.S. Army Center of Military History, 1979.

————. *Special Forces Reconnaissance Handbook.* Ft. Bragg, NC: Institute for Military Assistance, 1970.

U.S. Army Military History Institute. Senior Officer Oral History Program. *Interview with Col. J. H. Crerar.* Carlisle Barracks, PA: U.S. Army War College, 1983.

————. Senior Officer Oral History Program. *Interview with Maj. Gen. John Singlaub.* Carlisle Barracks, PA: U.S. Army War College, n.d.

U.S. Military Assistance Command, Vietnam, Strategic Technical Directorate

Assistance Team 158. *1973 Command History.* Saigon: STDA Team 158, 1973.

U.S. Military Assistance Command, Vietnam, Studies and Observation Group. *Annex A, Command History, 1964.* Saigon: MACV-SOG, 1965.

————. *Annex N, Command History, 1965.* Saigon: MACV-SOG, 1966.

————. *Annex M, Command History, 1966.* Saigon: MACV-SOG, 1967.

————. *Annex G, Command History, 1967.* Saigon: MACV-SOG, 1968.

————. *Annex F, Command History, 1968.* Saigon: MACV-SOG, 1969.

————. *Annex F, Command History, 1969.* Saigon: MACV-SOG, 1970.

————. *Annex B, Command History, 1970.* Saigon: MACV-SOG, 1971.

————. *Annex B, Command History, 1971–72.* Saigon: MACV-SOG, 1972.

Vongsavanh, Southchay. *Indochina Monographs: RLG Military Operations and Activities in the Laotian Panhandle.* Washington, DC: U.S. Army Center of Military History, 1981.

Westmoreland, William. *A Soldier Reports.* Garden City, NY: Doubleday, 1976.

Yarborough, Tom. *Danang Diary.* New York: St. Martin's Press, 1990.

Zaffiri, Samuel. *Hamburger Hill.* Novato, CA: Presidio Press, 1988.

Articles

"Americans Are Barred from Spy Raids in Laos," *New York Times,* 12 June 1971.

Graves, Jim. "SOG's Secret War." *Soldier of Fortune,* June 1981, 39.

Horn, Arthur. "The PT Fleet That Never Was." *Sea Classics,* vol. 19, no. 2 (Mar-Apr 1988).

"Pentagon Admits GIs Went Along on Laos Raids," Associated Press, 11 September 1973.

"Reconnaissance Operations." Handout. Special Forces School, U.S. Army JFK Special Warfare Center, October 1984.

Staats, Issac. "Heroes in a Hornet's Nest." *Soldier of Fortune,* April 1993, 44.

INDEX

rice cache incident and, 75–77, 83
Target Oscar Eight raid and,
90–92, 94
Wilklow's ordeal and, 92–94
see also Shining Brass operations
Prater, Roy, 287
Predmore, Larry, 140
Presley, Eulis "Camel," 68, 256–62
prisoner snatches, 154–74
Ashtray Operation and, 166–67
Ashtray II Operation and, 167–74
bicycle incident and, 164–65
demo ambushes and, 161–62
tactics and weapons for, 155–59,
160
Psychological Studies Branch, *see*
OPS-33
Pulliam, Lonnie, 136
Pyles, Harley, 36–37
Python, RT, 322–23

Quamo, George, 178, 179, 180
Queen, Bill, 331, 335–36
Quinn, Tom, 254
Quiroz, Joe, 47
Quy, Lieutenant, 178–79

Rabdau, Jim, 275, 279
Radike, Don, 25
Radio Hanoi, 122, 123, 219, 221,
234
Radke, Galen "Mike," 137, 270,
276, 279, 309–10, 325, 337
Ray, Ronald, 276
Raye, Martha, 78*n*
Reagan, Ronald, 182
Rear Transportation Unit 70, North
Vietnamese, 232
recon teams, 34
armament of, 144–46
camouflage by, 139–40
compromised security of, 290–93,
301–2
countertactics of, 141–44
dangers of, 137–38

defined, 347
equipment carried by, 135
IA Drills and, 138–39
insertion techniques of, 146–47
McGuire rig developed for,
148–49
mission planning and, 134, 139
night attacks and, 150–51
STABO rig of, 149–50
stand-down and, 152–53
tactical air strikes and, 151–52
unspoken code of, 135–36
see also individual teams
Red Dragon, Team, 219, 223, 224
Reeves, Jimmy, 336
Remus, Team, 25, 69, 221–22
Reno, Ralph, 51, 57
Rest-Over-Night (RON) position, 150
Rheault, Robert, 243*n*
Rimondi, William, 331, 335–36
Ripanti, Jim, 136–37
Roberts, Clifford, 149
Robertson, John, 190
Rodd, Ralph, 165
Romeo, Team, 69, 219
Ropka, Larry, 21
Rose, Bill, 24–25, 75
Rose, Gary, 266–69
Rose, Harold, 90
Ross, Dan, 140
Ruff, Newman, 81, 156, 310–11
Russell, Clyde, 23–24
Ryan, Rich, 202–3, 259, 260
Rybat, Ed, 131, 177, 290, 303

Saal, Harvey, 152, 177
Sabatinelli, Vincent, 255
Sacred Sword of the Patriot League
(SSPL), 116–18, 119, 218, 347
Sadler, John "Skip," 249–50, 263,
270, 278, 280, 284, 288, 294,
295, 297, 301, 307–9, 311,
317, 318, 333
SADM (Special Atomic Demolition
Munitions), 295*n*